# 100 YEARS OF STATE PENSION

CW00740516

## Learning
## from the past

*By Tony Salter, Andrew Bryans,*
*Colin Redman & Martin Hewitt*

ISBN 978-19-03965-16-0

Design and origination by Blenheim Colour Ltd.  www.blencolour.com
Printed by Information Press Ltd, Eynsham, Oxford

# CONTENTS

# ACKNOWLEDGEMENTS

This book has been sponsored by the Actuarial Profession to celebrate 100 years of state pension provision. The Profession is particularly indebted to Tony Salter who carried out the initial research and wrote the text on which the book is based. The authors would like to extend their profound thanks to both the Faculty and the Institute of Actuaries for making this book possible. The authors would also like to thank the many people who have assisted in the publication of this book, in particular, Pat Thane, Leverhulme Professor of Contemporary British History at the Institute of Historical Research, University of London, and Barbara Waine, Honorary Senior Research Fellow, Institute of Applied Social Studies, University of Birmingham, for reviewing the work and making thoughtful suggestions to improve its contents. Further the authors would like to thank Gloria Tucker and Val Bryans for producing the many versions of the document and inserting the corrections.

Governments and commissions have increasingly used public consultation to gain responses to reviews, green papers and white papers. This has resulted in an increasing abundance of submissions by organisations and individuals together with the holding of conferences to discuss the issues. In this document reference is made to some of these submissions and conferences to indicate some of the views being expressed at the time without in any way indicating that these were necessarily either the views of the majority or the extremes of the range of views.

Although the Profession has sponsored the book, the views expressed are those of the authors, except where credited to others.

TS, AB, CR, MH
1 September 2008

# FOREWORD

2008 – the centenary year of the Old Age Pensions Act 1908 which provided the first state pension in the UK – was preceded by 10 years of pensions debate which paved the way for new pensions provision for the 21st century. After 18 years of Conservative governments, New Labour won the 1997 general election. The following year they published their first pensions Green Paper *A New Contract for Pensions*, passed a series of pensions acts in the early 2000s, and set up the Pensions Commission in 2002. They in turn published a series of reports recommending major changes to be brought into effect over the next half century. The government has implemented many of the Commission's proposals in the Pensions Act 2007 with others being contained in the Pensions Bill 2008 which parliament is currently debating. This legislation is to have major long term implications for the future course of pensions.

Undoubtedly these developments have provided important opportunities for rethinking pensions at this historic juncture. Although this major review has been aided by the unprecedented amount of pensions data amassed by the Commission, less consideration has been given to the central question of the purpose of the state pension. After 100 years, current reform has been dominated by managerial, technical and actuarial considerations. It has paid less attention to questions such as what the aims of the state pension should be, what range of value choices are faced, and what implications these choices have for the management of pensions provision. Given the breadth of the many debates on the state pension over the last 100 years, this may represent a missed opportunity. Where the question of what the state pension should aim to achieve has been addressed, it was in the context of the narrower policy aspirations and shortfalls of the last two or three decades. Although the new policies represent an improvement in pension provision and may provide greater certainty for increasing numbers of retired people, questions remain about how effectively the policies will resolve some of the most insurmountable problems of the last 100 years, namely sustaining the basic state pension relative to average earnings; overcoming growing reliance on means testing; lessening inequalities in work that lead to inequalities in retirement and reaching agreement on the core question of how best to reward remuneration in work with an adequate pension in retirement.

The anniversary of the Old Age Pensions Act 1908 provides provides an opportune moment to re-examine the achievements and shortfalls of the last 100 years. With this in mind the Actuarial Profession has published this history of *100 Years of State Pension* with the following objectives:

- to provide a 100 year history of the development of state pension provision from the 1908 Act to the present;
- to rediscover what past governments sought to achieve through state pensions provision and the thinking that led to the changes in pensions policy;
- to identify the key players including the role of actuaries in this history; and
- to draw lessons from the past for the future.

*'Those who cannot remember the past are condemned to repeat it'.* GEORGE SANTAYANA

# CHAPTER ONE
# Before 1908

## The failure of the new poor law

A critical factor in the advent of state pension provision in Britain was the rise of pauperism in the 19th and early 20th centuries resulting from the failure of the new poor law (introduced by the Poor Law Amendment Act 1834) to relieve old age poverty outside the workhouses – 'the pitiless bastilles'.[1] Old people constituted the largest single group of paupers. Pat Thane, the social policy historian, in *Old Age in English History* mentions that, according to one source, immediately following the Poor Law Amendment Act the majority of all elderly persons were maintained by the poor law. Poor relief was a strictly residual safety net for those unable to survive on other resources with the able-bodied in old age having to continue to work. Families were expected to support older relatives and poor law officials were prepared to enforce this when it was not willingly undertaken. Enforcement was rarely through the courts as the threat of the alternative of the workhouse was often sufficient. Payments under the poor law were of the order of 2 shillings 6 pence (12½p) to 3s (15p) per week.[2] Thane then quotes another source which suggests that these payments of 2s 6d to 3s per week were then generally reduced to 1s to 2s and that increasing numbers of old people were forced into workhouses.[3]

The poor law was the system for the relief of the poor from the 16th century. It originated in a series of measures enacted by the parliaments of Elizabeth I, most notably in 1563, 1572, 1576 and 1598.[4] The 'Acte for the Releife of the Poore' of 1598, which facilitated the founding of almshouses and hospitals, consolidated the poor relief laws enacted earlier in the century (including those of 1536 in the reign of Henry VIII).[5] With minor variations, the 16th century legislation was re-enacted in 1601 and, in Thane's view, from that time 'a national poor relief system was permanently in place'.[6] Writing his report in 1942, Beveridge saw the Poor Relief Act 1601 as 'the starting point of State provision for social security' despite the fact that it was 'not the first statute to deal with the relief of destitution'.[7] Over the next 200 years, the 1601 Act was amended a number of times with the introduction of workhouses at the end of the 17th century and in 1782 the establishment of poor houses solely for the aged and infirm and the introduction of a system of outdoor relief for the able-bodied.

From the 18th century onwards, some leading thinkers and social reformers began to put forward ideas for the introduction of a state pension. This included the inspirational radical Thomas Paine (1737–1809) who argued for a national fund to pay '£10 per annum during life to every person now living of the age of 50 years and to all others when they shall arrive at that age to enable them to live in old age without wretchedness and go decently out of the world'.[8]

By the beginning of the 19th century, it was felt that the poor law system was too costly and was widely perceived as encouraging the underlying problem – pushing more people into poverty even while it helped those who were already in poverty. This resulted in the reform of the

1

poor law with the Poor Law Amendment Act 1834. The Act established a Poor Law Commission to oversee the national operation of the system. This included the building of workhouses for the giving of poor relief with every area of the country being covered by a workhouse. Social historians conventionally divide the poor law into the old poor law, which was codified in 1598 and 1601 legislation, and the new poor law of 1834.[9] The former mainly differed from the latter by having different types of provision for different categories of poor; e.g. poorhouses for the aged and disabled, houses of correction for 'persistent idlers' and workhouses providing pay for labour on a residential or non-residential basis.[10]

The failure of the new poor law to relieve old age poverty outside the workhouses was aggravated by a campaign led by the Charity Organisation Society (COS) (it was founded in 1869 and opposed to state intervention except through workhouse relief) and the Local Government Board against out-relief,[11] which had left poor law recipients free to live in a community rather than be incarcerated in an institution. The aim was to concentrate poor relief on fewer people by targeting resources on the genuinely needy at levels adequate for survival. The numbers of old people receiving out-relief declined after 1871, and, as intended by the policy of targeting out-relief on those in greatest need, the number of indoor paupers aged over 65 increased significantly, from 38,500 in 1871 to 76,100 in 1901.[12]

## Concern about the friendly societies

As Thane has pointed out, although the failure of the new poor law to relieve the more severe poverty among older persons underlay the campaign which emerged for old age pensions, there was also another factor. This was the growing concern about the financial problems afflicting the friendly societies to which better off working people entrusted their savings for protection against poverty in old age.[13] Lower paid men and most women were not members of friendly societies because they could not afford to pay the contributions. Macnicol, the social policy historian, mentions that public concern over the growing insolvency of friendly societies has been held as a major reason for their support for state pensions at the end of the 19th century. He quoted Bentley Gilbert's argument that changing patterns of morbidity and mortality over the course of the 19th century were creating serious financial problems for the societies.[14]

The friendly societies offered mutual insurance to their members against sickness and death. Sickness benefit, contingent on the inability to follow one's usual employment, tended to become permanent with the onset of old age infirmity, becoming in effect a pension. 'Old age' was defined in the Friendly Societies Act 1875 as any age after 50 and despite the ruling by the Court of Queen's Bench that 'natural decay' was not sickness most of the societies were averse to following the ruling.[15] Provision for old age was, however, uncommon and the superannuation schemes offered by the larger societies – notably the Ancient Order of Foresters and the Manchester Unity of Oddfellows – were not largely subscribed.[16]

Towards the end of the 19th century, consulting actuaries were advising the societies to terminate sickness benefit at age 65 and to introduce deferred annuities for members who wished to provide for old age. Reuben Watson, the actuary to the Manchester Unity of Oddfellows, was advocating this in 1878 and Macnicol quotes Brabrook, the Chief Registrar, as commenting, when referring to the need to separate sickness from superannuation benefits, 'this is the moral every actuary is preaching'.[17] Macnicol also cautions that comments about 'insolvency' should be viewed with some scepticism because it is an actuarial construct. An actuarial deficiency, concerned as it is with payments to meet liabilities for future benefits, should not be confused with a commercial deficit where finances are insufficient to cover current claims and bankruptcy ensues.[18]

## Canon Blackley's proposal

Among the critics of the financial management of the friendly societies was Canon William Blackley, vicar of King's Somborne in Hampshire and an Honorary Canon of Westminster. Blackley was much concerned with what he saw as national improvidence. He considered that the root of this was idleness, self-indulgence and poverty, and a manifestation of it was the dependence of some 700,000 persons on the poor law which was paid for by the forced taxation of the provident of all classes. His proposed solution was a compulsory scheme of national provident insurance for sickness and old age which would instil into the working man a sense of responsibility for his own financial security and distance him from the 'new pauper class'.[19]

The scheme, which would be sponsored by the state but not subsidised by it, would be based on individual capital accumulation of workers' contributions. The state would assume the role of the administering agency because he believed that most of the friendly societies were insolvent (a view shared by some but not by all). For all young wage earners between the ages of 18 and 21 it would be compulsory to contribute during these ages a sufficient amount to be entitled to a weekly payment of 8s per week, if and when sick, together with a pension of 4s per week from age 70.[20] In setting out his proposals, Blackley had assessed the required total contribution at £10 based on the report given by an actuarial committee appointed by the Committee on the Friendly Societies Act that reported in 1875.[21]

Blackley's proposals were published in the *Nineteenth Century* review in an article *National Insurance: a Cheap, Practical and Popular Means of Abolishing Poor Rates*. The timing of the article's publication, November 1878, and his tireless advocacy of the scheme (including his submission of the scheme to a Select Committee of the Commons in 1885–7) gave Blackley's scheme its place in history.[22] In the 1880s the notion of a state old age pension scheme became the subject of public debate. Later Blackley acknowledged that with the fall in interest rates it would be necessary for the contribution to be higher but he did not produce a revised figure.[23] It was likely that even a £10 contribution would have been beyond the capacity of young labourers to make. As Macnicol remarked, as Blackley devised his scheme in his vicarage, young agricultural workers in the fields nearby were earning an average of just over 13s 0d per week (10s 4d in Dorset) whereas the income from the living at King's Somborne was nearly £700 per annum.[24]

## German social insurance scheme

Interest in the idea of a contributory national scheme of social insurance, which had been first aroused in Britain by Blackley's proposals, increased as a result of the introduction in Germany by Chancellor Bismarck between 1883 and 1885 of a compulsory national insurance scheme for sickness and accident at work. It was the first such scheme in the world. Because of public interest in Britain a Parliamentary Select Committee on National Provident Insurance was appointed. Its conclusion was that any such scheme, including Blackley's, would be unable to relieve poverty in sickness and old age because low paid workers could not pay the contributions required. Such workers were excluded from Bismarck's scheme.[25] Those British workers able to pay social insurance contributions, it was argued, were already satisfactorily covered by friendly society schemes.

In 1889 Bismarck added 'a few drops of social oil' with the introduction of a state old age and invalidity pensions scheme. Like the sickness and accident scheme, the German state pension scheme was the first of its kind in the world. Contributions and benefits were graduated according to income. As Thane comments, the scheme was targeted at better paid male workers rather than low paid male workers or women. Old age pensions were originally payable at age 70 (later at age 65). Invalidity pensions, however, became payable at any age in case of permanent incapacity to work, subject to the claimant having an insurance record of at least five years' contributions.[26]

The German state pension scheme, based on contributory social insurance, was designed to encourage productive effort among better paid workers and to promote social stability by integrating them into the existing political and economic order. The Bismarck schemes gave the skilled workers who were their members a 'stake' in the society of the day.[27] In contrast, the public debate which was developing in Britain was primarily focused on the alleviation of poverty. As Thane points out, the British reformers were striving for an extension of traditional poor law principles, and the state old age pension which was eventually introduced in 1908 had a higher real value than the Bismarck scheme pension.[28]

## The British reformers

Work was begun by the philanthropist, Charles Booth, on his survey *The Life and Labour of the People in London* in 1886. The research showed that in East London 39% of people over 65 were paupers, i.e. those receiving poor law relief.[29] There had been a curious blindness by the Local Government Board and COS officials to 'the desperate poverty that would do anything rather than enter the house'.[30] Booth encouraged by Canon Samuel Barnett (founder of Toynbee Hall, a charity still in existence today) and an advocate of universal non-contributory state old age pensions since 1883) argued that the only solution to widespread pauperism was a pension to be paid entirely by the Exchequer to all above a specified age.[31] Booth's proposal was a pension of 5s a week for all age 70 and over (although his initial preference had been for 65 as the qualifying age). He estimated the initial annual cost at £20m. However his critics, such as the Royal Statistical Society, estimated it at £26m (more than one-sixth of UK public revenue in 1899[32]) and saw the proposal as inadequate, impracticable and ruinously expensive.[33]

The late 19th century social reformers, Booth, Barnett and Rowntree*, agreed that the only solution to widespread pauperism was a pension paid entirely by the Exchequer to all above a certain age. The same thinking is evident in the paper *Old Age Pensioning* by Ralph Price

---

* Benjamin Seebohm Rowntree (1871–1954) was the third son of Joseph Rowntree and continued his father's work of trying to alleviate poverty in Britain.

Hardy, an actuary with expert knowledge of friendly societies and an advocate of state old age pensions. He read the paper before the County of London Poor Law Officers' Association on 30 October 1891 in which he said:

> You must have welcomed the suggestions of a system of public pensioning which, if carried, will have the effect of relieving you from the distressing duty of pauperising a deserving class of citizens, whose chief fault would appear to be that, wages being cut down by competition to the lowest point, they had not achieved the impossible task of saving enough for their independent support in helpless old age.[34]

He saw public pensioning as a measure which would transform this class of citizens into one 'not shrouded in workhouses, not bearing the badge and mark of what is stigmatised as pauperism, but living open and independent lives, still in the midst of their families, still bound to life by all the ties that endear existence and distinguish humanity'.[35] All this would be made possible because these citizens would be able to rest 'upon means assigned to them by Society as the reward and recognition of indispensable services rendered by them to the cause of our common civilisation'.[36] Hardy concludes by reminding his audience that:

> It has been estimated that over 40% of the aged persons in this country become chargeable to the poor rates – a proportion most distressing to contemplate, and constituting a grim commentary upon our social system.[37]

It is instructive that Hardy sees public pensioning as a service rendered by society to citizens as the reward for and recognition of the services rendered by them. Hardy does not refer, even by implication, to any group of citizens somehow less eligible for reward because the services they have rendered, or the lives they had led, are deemed to have been less useful to society. He, unlike the first Phillips committee which was set up to consider the Beveridge Report in 1943 resulting in it criticising the proposals, does not conceive of an 'irreducible helpless and feckless class, whose existence meant that a deterrent poor law could never be abolished'.[38] Hardy makes no distinction between the *deserving* and *undeserving* poor unlike some of our contemporary politicians, including ministers of the Crown, whose statements are reminiscent of the views of the COS at the end of the 19th century.[39] He was too concerned with what may deaden 'our sense of what is due to the human creature'[40] to have thought in those terms.

## Joseph Chamberlain and the encouragement of voluntary thrift

Joseph Chamberlain, the first senior national politician to engage publicly in the debate on old age pensions, had a different conception of the purpose of social pension provision from the other reformers. He had been impressed by the 1889 Bismarck scheme although he was personally averse to its element of compulsion.[41] The scheme's features broadly accorded to his individualistic notion of what constituted the desirable elements of social reform. The aim should be to infuse working class culture with the values of ethical capitalism, conceived as thrift and self-reliance, combined with a sense of obligation to help others. He also believed in selective state intervention to reduce the grosser inequalities created by the economic market and to foster the health and productivity of workers.[42]

Chamberlain's background in business had been highly successful and he had a record of practical benevolence towards the poor based on personal philanthropy. His work in local government, for example, had been instrumental in bringing about improvement in social conditions, including the conditions of paupers receiving poor relief solely for medical needs. In national politics he made speeches in which old age pensions were a major issue, and he did much to enliven and sustain the public debate on the subject.[43]

In contemplating the design of a state pension scheme, which he undertook with the help of a voluntary parliamentary committee, he recognised that a scheme on the Bismarck model, or indeed any contributory social insurance scheme, could not include the low paid or provide pensions for the elderly poor. He dismissed the idea of a universal tax funded scheme, as proposed by Booth, which would be redistributive and socialistic to a degree he found ideologically unacceptable.[44] He also rejected the widely discussed proposal for more generous outdoor relief for the elderly poor.

His own proposal for an old age pension, which emerged in 1891, was based on the encouragement of voluntary thrift through an arrangement entailing payment of a state subsidy to the Post Office voluntary annuities scheme (established in 1864 by William Gladstone, then the Chancellor of Exchequer). With adequate contributions, this would enable contributors to receive an annuity of 5s per week payable from age 65. As Thane points out, this scheme would also have been inaccessible to the very poor.[45] Macnicol takes the view that Chamberlain's reasoning on old age pensions was built upon a set of contradictions that reflected the limitations of his own ideological preferences (in this case radical liberalism) and class loyalties.[46]

The case of Chamberlain as an architect of proposals for social pension provision may be instructive. For it would seem that so often in the history of British state pensions policy, earnest attempts at reform have been preceded by a painstaking and disinterested analysis of the problems that have to be solved in order to improve the quality and scope of pension provision, only for the reform to founder on proposals trammelled by the need to accommodate ideological preferences and prevailing economic interests. What principles of social pension provision, one may wonder, would reasonable people adopt if they were not biased in some way (perhaps quite unwittingly) by the special interests attaching to their own positions in society?

## The Royal Commission on the Aged Poor

The Royal Commission on the Aged Poor was established in 1893 with the brief to consider whether any alterations in the system of poor law relief were desirable, in the case of persons whose destitution is occasioned by incapacity for work, resulting from old age, or whether assistance could otherwise be afforded in those cases.[47] There were 19 Commissioners including Booth, Chamberlain and the then Prince of Wales, later to become King Edward VII.

The Prince took an active interest attending meetings as frequently as possible. However he did not attach his signature to the report indicating that he felt it was not appropriate to do so as the subject had to a considerable extent become one of party controversy, both inside and outside of Parliament and so it had assumed a phase inconsistent with his position of political neutrality.[48]

Under the chairmanship of Lord Aberdare, the Commission took evidence over some 48 days from a considerable number of organisations and individuals resulting in some 900 pages of published minutes together with 100 pages of appendices. These included Canon Blackley, Hardy and Reuben Watson. In his evidence, Hardy expressed the following view, which was shared by many giving evidence:

> Thrift is quite a relative term, and the mere saving of money, to the neglect of other duties, is not to be held up as the sole virtue of a citizen. To stint the education of children, to continue to overburden a woman with domestic duties, to stand churlishly aside from support of all great humanitarian movements, with the object of saving something for personal old age, would deteriorate the nation far more than even the present pauperism does. The true citizen first performs such duties as will keep his family together, by providing sick and burial allowances, and then, last of all, thinks of himself. This elevation of character exists amongst the poor to a much larger extent than is commonly believed, and this is one of the grounds upon which they object to a diversion of their income to merely pension purposes.[49]

Aberdare drafted the report and chaired the initial discussion meetings on it until the adjournment at the end of July 1894. The Commission reassembled on 11 December 1894 but because of ill health Aberdare took no further active part. He died on 25 February 1895, the day before the report was signed.

Lord Playfair succeeded Lord Aberdare as chairman. In his explanatory memorandum on the report, he stated that in the prolonged consideration of the report, numerous alterations were made in the original draft; and, as there was a strong desire to obtain a unanimous report, various paragraphs and sentences were accepted by the Commission from members whose signatures are not attached to the main report, some of which are expressed in language not altogether in harmony with the general spirit of the report.[50]

The report included a number of tables indicating the level of poverty in the population in the 19th century. The Commissioners could not agree on what these statistics showed. Some considered that the percentage of the population affected by pauperism was reducing and, that with greater thrift by the working population, would be eradicated over time while others thought quite the reverse.

The Commission's inquiry was wide ranging including examination of the state schemes proposed by Canon Blackley, Booth and Chamberlain and others, including those proposed by Hardy and Lansbury, requiring state funding on a means tested basis.

The main report indicated that they deplored the fact that so large a proportion of the working classes were in old age in receipt of poor law relief. However the often held view, that the aged labourer had in general only the workhouse before him in which to end his days, had been shown to be erroneous.[51] As a consequence they considered that no fundamental alterations were needed in the existing system of poor law relief as it affected the aged.[52]

Their recommendations were therefore confined to administrative aspects on the system, none of which were radical.

On the various schemes for state assistance that the Commission considered, the main report concluded that none could be recommended in view of the financial and economic difficulties involved.[53] However the report's summary went on to indicate:

> Having regard to the widespread expectation, in and out of Parliament, some provision other than that by the poor law should be devised for the assistance in old age of those among the poor who have led respectable and industrious lives, we do not desire that our inquiry should preclude the future consideration of any plan which may hereafter be proposed and be free from the objections which had prevented the adoption of the schemes submitted to us.[54]

The main report was signed by Playfair and nine other Commissioners with these other nine issuing seven memoranda qualifying their support to the main report. These memoranda showed that some were vehemently against any form of state assistance while others considered that the recommendations did not go far enough.[55]

Five Commissioners who did not sign the main report, including Booth and Chamberlain, issued a report indicating again that the 'recommendations are inadequate and do not go far enough as the evidence warrants'.[56] They considered that the main report had not addressed the second part of the Commission's brief, namely whether alternative assistance could be afforded to the aged. As a consequence they proposed that a further commission be appointed to address this. The two remaining Commissioners signed none of the other reports but instead issued their own separate reports indicating again that the recommendations had been inadequate with one of them, Henry Broadhurst MP, considering that the time had come for a 'great and fundamental changes in the provision for the aged poor'.[57]

## The public debate on old age pensions

The discussion now tended to become channelled into a debate which continued well into the 20th century.[58] This debate was broadly between two groups of protagonists. The first group favoured a universal non-contributory tax funded pension scheme which they believed was the only means to eliminate or alleviate old age poverty. The second group advocated either a contributory social insurance scheme with benefits related to contributions in order to stimulate productivity and foster social cohesion, or a voluntary national pension savings scheme, administered by the post office or building societies, as envisaged by Joseph Chamberlain to encourage individual responsibility and thrift.

It was evident to the reformers such as Booth, Barnett, Rowntree and the friendly society actuary, Hardy, who were in the first group of protagonists, that a contributory social insurance scheme, or a pensions savings scheme, would not help the current generation of poorest old people. Nor would it relieve the future old age poverty of the current generation of low paid men workers and most women because they would be unable to afford the contributions. Most women either were not paid for their work or were paid very little. As Booth wrote in 1892 'women … have often spent lives of the most active and invaluable citizenship without ever having the smallest opportunity for saving'.[59] Women generally outlived men and comprised the majority of poor old people, which is still the case in 2008.

Booth and the other reformers were joined in their support for a universal wholly tax funded old age pension by socialists such as Beatrice and Sidney Webb and Keir Hardie. Support for the measure from socialists increased after the formation of the Independent Labour Party in 1893 and, as Macnicol records, by 1896 the party was explicitly demanding 'state pensions for every person at 50 years of age, and adequate provision for all widows, orphans, sick and disabled workers'.[60] Other socialist groups were making similar demands for a tax funded state pension scheme. Also the Social Democratic Foundation* was calling for old age pensions, payable from age 50, with no qualifying conditions.[61] Together with demands for the abolition of indirect taxation, and the substitution of graduated income tax, old age pensions were part of a wider social programme for the redistribution of income and wealth through welfare policies.[62]

The protagonists of the second group represented a broad coalition of people with fairly divergent views but united on the assumption, strongly argued by the COS, that the 'knowledge that a free state pension awaited one at the end of a working life would fatally erode working-class thrift, self-reliance and prudence'.[63] Some of these, such as the neo-Malthusian Thomas Mackay, Albert Pell and Charles Stewart Loch† and, perhaps less dogmatically, Octavia Hill who had helped to form the COS philosophy were of the view that state intervention to relieve poverty should be strictly limited.[64]

To the COS ideologues, as to many of the more pragmatic members of the group who were not opposed to state intervention including even some redistribution, social problems often had an ethical origin. It was essential to distinguish between poverty and pauperism. Poverty was the inevitable consequence of social and economic inequalities which provided a stimulus to self improvement and benefited the whole society. Pauperism, by contrast was often the result of fecklessness.[65] Among the pragmatic opponents of universal tax funded old age pensions who supported, or came to support, social insurance pensions as the most efficient means to eliminate old age poverty, were Joseph Chamberlain, another friendly society actuary, Sir Alfred Watson, and later, the young William Beveridge and Neville Chamberlain (son of Joseph) both of whom strongly criticised the tax funded scheme which eventually emerged in 1908.[66]

## Campaign for universal state old age pensions

Following discussions between Trade Union representatives and Booth, a series of meetings took place throughout the country during late 1898 and early 1899 resulting in the establishment of the National Committee of Organised Labour (NCOL) to promote universal old age pensions with trade unions, trade councils, Co-operative Societies and friendly societies supporting the movement.[67] In the view of Macnicol, NCOL was 'the principal pressure group that brought about the Old Age Pensions Act 1908'.[68] Its campaign was accompanied by interventions in Parliament from the Liberal opposition. In March 1899 a petition was delivered by 100 Conservative and

---

* The first socialist political party formed by Hyndman in 1891 although many socialists refused to join it because they were suspicious of Hyndman, a wealthy man, funding a radical political party.

† Pell and Loch were on the Royal Commission for the Aged Poor 1895 with Octavia Hill giving evidence to it.

Unionist MPs to the government to 'fulfil the pledges on pensions given by so many of them'.[69] This led to the appointment of the Select Committee on the Aged Deserving Poor known as the Chaplin Committee (after its Chairman Henry Chaplin of the Local Government Board). The Committee received a resolution from the Association of Poor Law Unions of England and Wales that it was desirable that a system of old age pensions should be established.[70] The Committee's report unequivocally recommended a scheme of state pensions. Arthur Balfour* put to the Cabinet a modified proposal for a scheme based on the Chaplin recommendations. The Chancellor of the Exchequer, Sir Michael Hicks-Beach, responded by rejecting all pension proposals as socialistic and too costly to be borne by taxpayers.[71] In that year, 1899, no fewer than eight private members' bills with pensions proposals were presented to Parliament.

Towards the end of 1899 the growing seriousness of the South African War overshadowed the pension issue. In Balfour's words, referring to Joseph Chamberlain, 'Joe's war stopped Joe's pensions'.[72] Encouraged by Booth, Rowntree in 1899 carried out his famous investigation into poverty in York *Poverty: A Study of Town Life*. Published in 1901 it largely confirmed Booth's conclusions about widespread poverty of the aged and suggested that because their own survival was so hard-earned, so many younger people could neither save for their old age nor support their elderly parents.[73] In the general election of 1906, the Liberal Party obtained a clear majority with the Labour Representation Committee† (later in the year it changed its name to the Labour Party) winning 29 seats. The majority of MPs now supported the introduction of state old age pensions.[74]

---

* Robert Gascoyne-Cecil, Marquess of Salisbury, became the Prime Minister for the third time when the Conservatives won the general election in July 1895. He was effectively the last peer to serve as Prime Minister. Instead of the traditional role of First Lord of the Treasury, Salisbury unusually combined the role of the Prime Minister with that of Foreign Secretary. Arthur Balfour, Salisbury's nephew, was reappointed the First Lord of the Treasury and Leader of the Commons, holding these positions until July 1902 when Salisbury resigned and Balfour became Prime Minster.

† The Social Democratic Federation (SDF), the Independent Labour Party (ILP), the Fabian Society and trade union leaders met on 27 February 1900 at the Memorial Hall in Farringdon Street, London. The meeting passed the motion proposed by Hardie to establish a distinct Labour group in Parliament, to have their own whips and to agree upon their policy, which must embrace a readiness to cooperate with any party which for the time being may be engaged in promoting legislation in the direct interests of labour. To make this possible, the meeting established the Labour Representation Committee (LRC). Its committee included two from both the SDF and ILP, one from the Fabian Society and seven trade unionists. The LRC became the Labour Party in 1906.

## CHAPTER TWO

# Introduction of state old age pensions

In November 1907 a Cabinet committee was set up by the Liberal government to prepare a bill for state pensions. The pensions had to be provided within the Treasury limit of £7m per annum. Accordingly the universal tax funded pension scheme which Booth had advocated was deemed to be unaffordable. The principal saving was achieved by raising the initially proposed pension age of 65 to 70 and by granting the pension subject to a stringent test of means.[1] All who received poor relief after 1 January 1908 were to be excluded. Criminals, lunatics and aliens (i.e. those without British nationality) were also excluded, the largest group being Jewish immigrants.[2] When Campbell-Bannerman resigned as Prime Minister in April 1908, Asquith took his place and appointed Lloyd George to succeed him as Chancellor. Asquith presented the budget which he had prepared and outlined the forthcoming pensions bill. The response was mixed. The Trade Union Congress (TUC) and the NCOL argued for a pension age of 65 and a higher means limit.[3] Beveridge was highly critical of the Liberal government's *ad hoc* approach to social reform and argued that a system of social insurance would be more cost effective in the long term because it would be self-financing. He believed that a non-contributory scheme sets up the state in the eyes of the individual as a source of free gifts, whereas social insurance facilitates social integration.[4]

## Old Age Pensions Act 1908

It fell to Lloyd George, the Chancellor, to pilot Asquith's bill through Parliament. The Old Age Pensions Act 1908* consists of 12 easy to read clauses and a schedule that set out the framework of the whole scheme. It awarded a non-contributory pension of 5s a week to those aged 70 or over provided their incomes did not exceed £21 a year. The pension was reduced by weekly units of 1s for those with incomes between £21 and £31 10s a year, subject to a minimum pension of 1s per week. Additionally, pension claimants were subject to the tests of having worked for the support of themselves and their families, and not been convicted for drunkenness, or any other misdemeanour, during a specified period immediately prior to their claim.[5] Such tests appear to have been devised to disqualify claimants who were not judged to fall within the category of the deserving poor. From both sides of the Commons, the proposed pension rates were criticised as inadequate. However Lloyd George made it clear that the 5s per

---

* It is interesting to note that, like the Old Age Pensions Act 1908, the Married Women's Property Act 1908 received the Royal Assent on 1 August 1908 and came into effect on 1 January 1909. Its sole principal clause as stated in the Act was that 'a married woman having separate property shall be subject to all such liability for the maintenance of her parent or parents as a *feme sole* is now by law subject to for the maintenance of such parent or parents'. Subsequently it was repealed.

week pension was not intended to be an income sufficient to live on. The intention was that it should supplement modest retirement savings and financial assistance from relatives, and be set at a level where it would provide an incentive for people to save during their working years, and for their relatives to continue to provide some financial support after their retirement.[6] In the Lords, however, opposition to the principle of a state old age pension continued unabated until the Parliament Act 1911* came into force. There were warnings from the peers that the consequences of a pension provided by the state would be 'profoundly demoralising', with the scheme being compared with the 'policy of doles which had been fatal to Rome'.[7]

It is interesting that, in July 1908, Austen Chamberlain (son of Joseph and elder brother of Neville) recorded in his diary that senior Conservatives were of the opinion that they should accept the Old Age Pensions Bill as a temporary bridge to a complete scheme on a contributory basis.[8] Asquith also believed that a more permanent arrangement for the 1908 pension scheme should wait upon a radical overhaul of the poor law. A Royal Commission on the poor law had been established in 1905 and was expected to report in 1909. Consequently paupers were provisionally excluded from the 1908 scheme. Lloyd George in the meantime had become converted to the contributory insurance principle.[9]

Thane maintains, however, that Lloyd George had not been converted to contributory social insurance as a means of financing old age pensions which were designed to alleviate poverty among the elderly poor. The social insurance schemes which he established in 1911 (his 9d for 4d schemes) were designed to provide national health and unemployment benefits. These benefits were intended to assist skilled and generally better paid workers, to help them recover from sickness, or survive unemployment and, in either event, to return to work as soon as possible. When the costs of the 1908 scheme started to exceed their estimates, the Treasury which, for a long time, was sceptical of social insurance because of its objection to assigned revenues, became more supportive of social insurance pensions.[10]

The passing into law of the Old Age Pensions Act on 1 August 1908 is viewed as a watershed in British social policy. State pensions represented an entirely new principle in social provision being the first welfare measure wholly funded by the Exchequer. Before the introduction of the state pension all relief payments were made to persons in need from local funds and were subject to a test of destitution. State pension payments, however, were made to persons as a right from national funds, subject only to a test of age and means, but not destitution, as certain classes (e.g. those in poor law relief) were disqualified.[11] Moreover, acceptance of a state pension did not entail loss of voting rights, as did receipt of poor law relief.[12]

As the bill passed through Parliament, various estimates were given with the numbers expected to receive pensions increasing from 500,000 to well over 600,000 and the cost similarly increasing from £6m to £7.5m in the first year.[13]

---

* The preamble to the Parliament Act 1911 states that 'it is intended to substitute for the House of Lords as it at present exists a Second Chamber constituted on a popular instead of hereditary basis, but such substitution cannot be immediately brought into operation'. As a consequence, the provisions of the Act regulated the relationship between the two Houses of Parliament so limiting the Lords' power to block legislation approved by the Commons and reduced the maximum duration of Parliament from 7 to 5 years. The Act received the Royal Assent on 18 August 1911.

No social security offices then existed to administer the pensions. This was carried out by local committees set up through local government authorities and assisted in their enquiries by the Board of Customs and Excise[14] with the pension being paid through the Post Office. By 5 December 1908 some 690,000 people had submitted their claim for pension with 490,000 cases being approved, 51,000 rejected and a further 146,000 still to be finalised.[15]

The first state old age pensions were paid in January 1909 with pension payments being made to 490,000 people, the great majority of payments at the maximum rate. Approximately 37% of pensioners were men, with this proportion remaining constant for some years. The number of pensioners increased to 650,000 by March 1909[16] with some 190,000 having their claims turned down. By 30 September 1909 some £6m of pension payments had been paid to 680,000 pensioners.[17]

*The Times* of 2 January 1909 indicated that in many cases claimants were waiting to receive their pensions when the Post Office opened. Others were less eager with four Post Offices in London having only 25 out of 500 possible people coming to collect their pensions by 10 30am. There was also the sad incident of a man of 75 from Bishop's Stortford who died after signing his pension paper in the Post Office.

In G. M. Trevelyan's memorable phrase, 'the old age pension helped to empty the workhouses and give happiness to the old'[18] The images conveyed by Trevelyan's words perhaps gain depth and poignancy from the reminiscences of Flora Thompson, who was a Post Office clerk at the time. In *Lark Rise* she recounts that in the village there were one or two poorer couples, just holding on to their homes, but in daily fear of the workhouse. When the old age pensions began, life was transformed for such aged cottagers. They were relieved of anxiety when they went to the Post Office to draw it, tears of gratitude would run down the cheeks of some, and they would say 'God bless you, miss' and there were flowers from their gardens and apples from their trees for the girl who merely handed them the money.[19]

Nevertheless, as Thane points out, the workhouses were not emptied of the elderly poor by the 1908 Act. The number of those aged 70 or above in workhouses fell only from 61,400 in 1906 to 57,700 in 1910 and to 49,300 in 1912. This was because the pension alone was not sufficient to live on, and regardless of their income, many older people were in need of residential care which at the time was generally only available to the poor in workhouses. Thane mentions that about 40% of the population aged 70 and over qualified for the pension in 1908, compared with 25% in this age group in 1906 who qualified for poor relief. This is an indication of the measure of severe unmet need before the 1908 old age pension scheme was introduced.[20]

The Royal Commission established in 1905 to consider reforming the administration of the poor law and relief of distress submitted in 1909 a majority and a minority report. On the basis of the evidence presented, both reports rejected the principles of the new poor law. This included the principle of less eligibility under which poor law relief was granted only on terms that ensured that the economic position of recipients remained below that of the poorest independent worker.[21]

The reports accepted that poverty was mainly an involuntary condition for which the existing social and economic arrangements of society were in large measure responsible. The main point of difference between the two reports in Thane's view lay in the practical aspects of reform. The majority, among whom the views of the COS were influential, preferred voluntary action whereas the minority, led by Beatrice Webb and including George Lansbury, argued for 'publicly funded social services'.[22] Beatrice Webb believed that the resources of the community should be mobilised to prevent anyone, of any age, falling into destitution; there should be a recognised 'national minimum' below which no-one should be allowed to fall.[23]

Appended to both reports were criticisms of the 1908 Act. The majority recommended the provision of compulsory invalidity insurance as part of a more general scheme of health insurance. The minority recommended a means tested non-contributory old age pension, payable at age 60 at rates linked to the local cost of living. Both reports advocated removal of the pauper disqualification from the 1908 scheme, and objected that the age limit of 70 years was too high.[24] With effect from 1 January 1911 the pauper disqualification was removed with the number of pensioners increasing so that by March 1911 there were 1,070,000 in receipt of pension.[25]

Between 1909 and the start of the First World War in 1914, the weekly basic pension of 5s had fallen in real terms by less than 10% but by 1918, when the war ended, this had altered to about 50%.[26] During the war years, for those over age 70 able to work, there were improved job opportunities and with the effective fall in the means tested income limits many initially in receipt of pensions became ineligible. By 1915 the number in receipt of pensions had fallen to 987,000 and then to 920,000 by 1919, with women remaining roughly two thirds of the pensioners.[27]

For those pensioners who could not work, the effect of wartime inflation was serious and there was considerable public pressure for the government to do something. As Macnicol mentions, in August 1916 the government introduced a supplementary allowance of 2s 6d per week to those pensioners on the maximum pension suffering from special hardship owing to rising food prices. The special hardship condition was removed in August 1917 together with the means test being relaxed. It was expected that once the war ended these supplementary payments could be terminated but like many welfare innovations they became permanent. By March 1919, these supplementary allowances totalling just under £6m were paid to 912,000 pensioners out of a total number of 920,000 in receipt of the old age pension.[28]

## CHAPTER THREE

# Interwar years

## Occupational pensions

In Britain, the origins of private sector occupational pensions can be traced back to labour market conditions in the last half of the 19th century. In 1859 the civil service pension scheme, an unfunded scheme with a standard retirement age of 60, replaced earlier schemes for civil servants and became an influential model for occupational pension schemes for clerical and managerial staff in other economic sectors. The civil service pension scheme provided retirement benefits calculated by reference to service and pay at or near retirement age and was the prototype of the final salary pension scheme which was subsequently adopted as the model for the schemes of most of the larger employer organisations. Its benefits became an acceptable standard for the Inland Revenue in assessing the reasonableness of the provision of occupational schemes for granting tax reliefs.[1]

The practice of ex gratia pensioning was widespread in the 19th century[2] and in some cases it is difficult to distinguish such arrangements from formal retirement benefit schemes. The historical evidence shows that it was the larger employers in all the industrialising countries who became the sponsors of the first occupational pension schemes. The development of these schemes, whilst reflecting the drive for economic efficiency and productivity in the workforce, represented a fundamental change in the employment relationship. It can be seen as an attempt to create a long term identity of interest between capital and labour in industrial and commercial organisations.[3]

Also during the 19th century, friendly societies and some trade associations (such as the well-paid London Compositors) had developed schemes for the accumulation of retirement savings. According to Leslie Hannah, the economic historian, trade unions sometimes paid to their older workers unemployment or sickness benefits which became in effect an old age pension. In Britain, one working man's society, the Northumberland and Durham Miners' Permanent Relief Society, developed, with the support of the employers, one of the largest occupational pension schemes in the country in terms of the number of contributing members. At the beginning of the 20th century the scheme had about 140,000 members and nearly 4,000 pensions in payment. The noteworthy point is that it was the employers, and not the labour unions, who were the prime movers in the development of occupational pensions. Hannah has described how old age savings vested in the employment relationship, and how collective provision for old age by workers was confined to relatively affluent groups of employees such as miners and railwaymen.[4]

By 1920 few of the smaller and medium sized private sector organisations had occupational pension schemes for their employees, although some had established the practice of paying pensions out of current income to retired employees.[5] Section 32 of the Finance Act of 1921 gave favourable tax treatment to properly established pension funds, that is, those set up under irrevocable trusts. The important tax reliefs accorded by the 1921 Act became increasingly attractive as levels of company and personal taxation increased. During the period between the two world wars many private companies established occupational pension schemes for approval under the 1921 Act or for recognition as a bona fide pension scheme under the earlier Income Tax Act of 1918, although it was the usual practice to limit membership of these schemes to non-manual employees.[6]

## Persistence of pensioner poverty: The Ryland Adkins Committee

The increasing number of pensioners in poverty, and the militancy of their supporters in calling for pension reform, compelled the post-war coalition government of Lloyd George to re-examine the issue of old age pensions in 1919.[7] The government, as Thane points out, was also aware that should it seek to withdraw the wartime temporary increase in the pension it would probably have to face a public furore. In 1919 a committee was accordingly appointed, under the chairmanship of Sir Ryland Adkins KC (a leading Liberal MP), to 'consider and report what alterations, if any, as regards rate of pension and qualification should be made in the existing statutory scheme of old age pensions'.[8] Among the Committee's members were MPs of all political parties, Miss M Cecile Matheson, who was an eminent voluntary social worker, and representatives of government departments, trade unions, friendly societies and the National Conference on Old Age Pensions (NCOAP), a pensioners' organisation grounded in organised labour.[9] The Committee received such overwhelming evidence of 'the abject poverty of pensioners' that it issued a radical majority report.[10] Matheson was largely responsible for arranging the appearance before the Committee of two women pensioners aged in their early 70s whose evidence was a devastating revelation of old age poverty.[11]

Sir John Bradbury, the Permanent Secretary at the Treasury, nevertheless insisted that the underlying principle of the Old Age Pension Acts was not to provide for the entire maintenance of the pensioner, but to supplement such provision as might otherwise be available to the point necessary to receive decent subsistence.[12] The Treasury view was represented by Sir Alfred Watson who had been appointed the first Government Actuary in 1917 and who, according to Macnicol, was arguably to play the most important part in the early development of state pensions policy in Britain. Watson argued that, in view of the nation's post-war economic difficulties, any increase in pension rates should be minimal.[13] Thane mentions that an official from the newly established Ministry of Health sought to undermine claims that pensioners starved to death by referring to annually compiled national statistics of deaths from starvation. These showed, for example, that the number of recorded deaths of people aged over 70 due to starvation were 119 in 1909 and 26 in 1918. Of these deaths, only three and two respectively were pensioners.[14]

The most critical issue confronting the Committee, however, was the effect of means testing in rendering so many claimants ineligible for the pension. In 1919 some 62% of the population aged 70 or over were receiving the pension. The statistical evidence showed clearly that the majority of unsuccessful pension claimants had been disqualified on account of their means, i.e. savings, employment income, occupational pensions and gifts from family or friends. Even furniture over a certain value was deemed to have an imputed investment income for the purposes of assessment, and the income from home-grown vegetables was also included.[15] Watson who was always formidable in his examination of witnesses in government enquiries was a resolute opponent of tax funded non-contributory universal pensions. He was probably, as Macnicol suggests, unimpressed by the call of the representatives of NCOAP to remove the penalty on thrift. He believed that means testing was a morally neutral instrument: no more than 'a Treasury device to keep down costs and target the really needy'.[16] Watson saw insurance as a solution to the penalty on thrift problem for 'the class in whose case a means limit really does amount to a thrift disqualification'.[17]

The Committee considered state pension provision in a number of different countries. These included Australia and New Zealand[18] whose state pension schemes (along with that of Denmark established in 1891) had been carefully studied by the 1903–04 Select Committee for their eligibility clauses. It is not surprising therefore that the British 1908 scheme had provisions broadly similar to these schemes, particularly in terms of the 'good character' clauses employed to legitimise them as pension schemes quite distinct from the poor law.[19] In fact, as Thane points out, it became quite evident to the Ryland Adkins Committee that the poorest pensioners would have been better off on poor law relief. Such relief would generally have not been less than 10s per week and may have been as much as 15s per week, but would often have been supplemented by services in kind. Despite this, however, resistance of old people to the poor law scarcely diminished. It would appear that, for many of them, recourse to the poor law was a desperate final option. They preferred to try to subsist on an inadequate pension, even at the risk of becoming destitute.[20]

The Committee gave unhampered public exposure to the economic and social circumstances of pensioners and other aged persons, and engendered a widespread sympathy for the pensioners' cause, possibly without historical precedent. According to Macnicol the Committee's proceedings engendered sympathy for the pensioners' cause among almost all the MPs on the Committee,[21] even if this was not reflected in the Commons which seemed 'intent upon stringent economy in public expenditure'. For this, the Commons was characterised as a 'selfish malign lot'.[22] In Thane's view, however, sympathy for the pensioners' cause was not particularly widespread among the general public, and such support as there was certainly bore no comparison to the general concern for the elderly poor which had been generated in the years just before 1908.

The Committee's majority report recommended a doubling of the universal pension to 10s per week without a means test for all citizens aged 70 or over.[23] It was accepted that the sum of 10s per week barely compensated for price rises since 1914, but hope was expressed that prices would fall in the near future. The universal pension would be largely paid by the better off through the tax system. Should the estimated annual cost of the universal scheme (£41m) be unaffordable, the majority report recommended retention of means testing as a temporary measure, but subject to a doubling of the income (i.e. means) limit.[24]

A minority report, signed by the economic conservatives including Watson, agreed that the pension should be doubled but that the means test should be retained with the limits doubled. Although recommending the retention of means testing, the minority group admitted that it caused resentment, suggesting that the only solution to the problem of financing state pension provision was contributory social insurance.[25]

The Committee's recommendations led to the Old Age Pensions Act 1919 which increased the old age pension to 10s per week (the supplementary allowance that was introduced in 1916 ceased). It also raised the income limits for means testing (£21 increased to £26 5s per annum and £31 10s to £49 17s 6d per annum) which were well short of the doubling which the minority report recommended.[26]

## Anderson Committee and contributory social insurance

The hope expressed in the Commons by Andrew Bonor Law (then Leader of the House) that the 1919 pensions legislation would have 'a quieting effect on the general unrest which exists in the country'[27] was to be disappointed with NCOAP continuing with its campaign for better state pensions. The social historian, Andrew Blaikie, recounts how representatives of the NCOAP addressed a crowd of 40,000 people at a football match between Newcastle United and Bradford City in January 1921 and obtained from them a unanimous resolution demanding the abolition of the means limit applying to old age pensions.[28]

In Thane's view, the public debate on state pensions which then ensued was an important preliminary to the Beveridge proposals of 1942. In 1921 there were more than a million pensioners in Britain and 70% of them were women. It was a time of severe economic recession and the search for public expenditure cuts continued unabated.[29] To explore ways in which government spending could be reduced, a Select Committee on National Expenditure was appointed in June 1921. The Committee's chairman was Sir Eric Geddes, a businessman turned politician, and its proposals for expenditure cuts came to be known as the Geddes axe.[30] It was discovered that there was no real scope for reducing public spending on pensions. It was hardly possible for the government to claw back any saving from the state pension so soon after its amount had been increased and the qualifying income limit been raised.

Watson, the Government Actuary, however, in a reasoned statement, appended to the December 1921 interim report of the Committee, was able to suggest that a potential source of saving might lie in combining the social insurance schemes, which had been established in 1911, to provide state health and unemployment insurance. These were Lloyd George's 9d for 4d schemes under which the insured person paid 4d, his employer 3d and the government 2d.[31]

Watson's ideas were seminal for the future development of social security policy in Britain. They provided a stimulus for public debate which culminated in the campaign for all-in insurance, i.e. 'integration of all aspects of social security administration including pensions'. The idea gained the support not only of those seeking reductions in social policy expenditure but also those, such as the NCOAP, who were campaigning for improved state pension provision and recognised that all-in insurance provided a real opportunity for reform.[32]

Economic conditions deteriorated towards the end of 1923 as the general election approached. The increase in the level of unemployment was accompanied by a rise in state spending on unemployment relief and interest in all-in insurance grew. Many who may initially have been sceptical of the idea began to see it as a means to increasing social provision, including public pension provision, whilst simultaneously reducing state social expenditure. Before the election the Conservative government established an inter-departmental committee to examine and report on all-in insurance. Sir John Anderson,* Permanent Secretary at the Home Office, was appointed as its chairman.[33]

The Anderson Committee delivered an interim report, dealing only with pensions, to the Conservative government in January 1924, at the very end of its period in office. The Committee rejected proposals that the old age pension should be made contributory, arguing in its report that a contributory pension was impractical because insurance depends upon employment and the pension is related to need. If entitlement to the pension was to be contingent upon a person's employment history, many old people would fail to qualify for a pension, especially women. At the time about 63% of the female population aged over 70 were receiving an old age pension, whilst only about 7% of those between the ages of 60 and 70 were contributing to the national insurance scheme.[34]

The Committee, however, was nevertheless forced to draw the same conclusion as the Ryland Adkins Committee that any extension or improvement of the existing non-contributory scheme would result in an unacceptable increase in cost. Because of this they undertook to examine the possibility of introducing a contributory pension for the 65 to 70 age group.[35]

As expected, the second report of the Anderson Committee, issued in July 1924, firmly rejected any extension of the existing non-contributory pension scheme. It also rejected the idea of introducing a contributory supplement to pensions for the over 70s, but unsurprisingly recommended the provision of a contributory supplementary pension for old people aged between 65 and 70 which would be provided through the national health insurance system in return for a single contribution.[36]

## Beveridge's proposal for Insurance for All and Everything

The deliberations of the Anderson Committee continued and this encouraged new contributions to the all-in insurance debate. Growing support for a unified system of social insurance founded on a desire for administrative rationalisation and an abhorrence of means tests seemed a logical development of the views Beveridge had expressed in 1907, some 17 years earlier as a leader writer for the *Morning Post*. The movement had also received an added impetus from the economy drive that swept through Whitehall during the depression of 1921–2.[37]

This served as an encouragement to Beveridge, who since 1919 had been Director of the London School of Economics, to make a further contribution to the debate. In 1924 he published his pamphlet *Insurance for All and Everything* envisaging the introduction in Britain of 'a system of social insurance coverage even wider in scope than the system invented by Bismarck'.[38] Jose Harris, Beveridge's biographer, points out that the proposals in the pamphlet have frequently been recognised as the germ of Beveridge's later contribution to the structure of the welfare state.[39]

Social insurance, financed by flat rate contributions, would be extended to include, in addition to sickness and unemployment insurance, old age pensions, income support for

---

* Sir John Anderson (1st Viscount Waverley) was a distinguished administrator and politician being both the Home Secretary (1939–40) and Chancellor of the Exchequer (1943–5). The Second World War Anderson air raid shelter was named after him and he introduced the pay-as-you earn (PAYE) system for income tax payment.

orphans and elderly widows and benefits in the case of industrial accidents. The aim was not to provide full subsistence but to reduce to a minimum the need for discretionary poor law relief as a safety net. The existing old age pension scheme, which Beveridge in 1908 had denounced so strongly for penalizing thrift, would gradually shift to a contributory basis entitling all new social insurance contributors to pensions.[40]

Economies would be obtained through a simplification of the system entailing the division of social security administration into two contributory sectors – health and unemployment – with contributions for both sectors being collected through a single weekly stamp. Benefits, such as those payable for sickness, disability and maternity, which were subject to enquiries into eligibility, would be administered under the national health insurance system. Benefits such as old age and widow's pensions which, as the scheme became progressively contributory, would not require any investigation of eligibility, apart from an examination of an insurance record, and would be administered under the unemployment insurance system.[41]

## Contributory state pensions

The all-in insurance planning, undertaken by the Anderson Committee, was aimed at combining health and unemployment insurance into a single scheme, reforming workmen's compensation, expanding old age pension provision and including widows' and orphans' benefits in a new contributory scheme.[42] This was at a time of falling birth rates following the First World War, when support for a contributory pension scheme may have increased because of the 'disquieting spectre' of an ageing population requiring support from the 'thinned ranks' of the young.[43] In the event, possibly because of mass unemployment, the all-in insurance plans were never implemented, apart from the proposals for social insurance based pensions.[44]

The labour movement generally, but particularly the left, opposed the principle of contributory social insurance, which was perceived to be fraudulent. It imposed a double burden of cost on workers. The contribution they paid out of their wage packets was deemed a regressive poll tax. As contributions were flat rate, there was no re-distribution from rich to poor as with tax funded pensions. Moreover, in addition to their own contributions, workers would have to pay their employer's contributions as well, either out of future wage increases or through higher prices. Nobody believed that employers really paid their own social insurance contributions.[45] The last hope of the introduction of a completely tax funded universal pension scheme without means testing, providing a pension as 'a civic right and not a compassionate grant' faded with the demise in November 1924 of the nine-month minority Labour government.[46] The opportunity having been lost, the way was clear for the Conservatives to introduce contributory state pensions through the Widows', Orphans' and Old Age Contributory Pensions Act 1925.[47]

The contributory state pension scheme introduced in 1925 by the government of Stanley Baldwin was based upon the existing system of National Health Insurance (NHI). Supported by Churchill, the Chancellor, its principal architect was Neville Chamberlain, the Minister of Health. As a young man, Chamberlain had dismissed the 1908 scheme as 'radically rotten in principle' and a 'discouragement to thrift'.[48]

By 1924 he had come to see a contributory pension scheme as a foundation for his party's social policy. He presided over a party committee on social insurance which received advice from Duncan C Fraser (then the actuary to the Royal Insurance Company) at the same time as the Anderson Committee was preparing its second report on all-in insurance planning. There was some degree of discreet cross-fertilization of ideas between the two committees, if not covert collaboration, as evidenced by a note recorded on 7 July 1924 by Fraser that he had seen Watson a month ago to discuss some actuarial calculations.[49] The resulting 1925 Act was, according to Macnicol, an amalgamation of the recommendations of both the Anderson and Chamberlain Committees.[50] The actuaries, Watson and Fraser, had both contributed to the formulation of those recommendations.

## Taxation, class conflict and state pensions reform

A cogent reason for adopting the contributory social insurance model of state pension provision in the years between the two world wars was the low tax base which also continued to exist for some time after the Second World War and which was a serious obstacle to tax funded social policy. On account of tax allowances, as Macnicol points out, a married man supporting a wife and three children on earnings of £350 per annum in 1925 would not have paid income tax. With earnings of £500 per annum, he would have had an effective tax rate of 2%, and with £1,000 per annum an effective tax rate of 8.1%.[51] To ease the financial burden of pension provision on the Exchequer, it was necessary to raise contributions through social insurance.

Social insurance was also favoured by the occupational pension interests as an alternative to the means tested pension introduced by the 1908 Act. This was because the pensions accumulated through members' savings in occupational schemes were taken into account in assessing entitlement to the state pension. Accordingly, for many members with occupational pensions, eligibility for the non-contributory state pension was either reduced or eliminated.[52]

Macnicol notes that in relation to the development of state pensions in Britain, events between 1919 and 1925 represented an intricate interplay of political, economic, social and administrative factors. The need for state pensions was at no time in dispute. Impoverishment of the elderly could no longer, as in the 1890s, be attributed to fecklessness. The advent of mass political democracy, and the growing power of the labour movement through the Labour Party and the trades unions, rendered such a view politically unacceptable.[53] As already observed, there was still a demand from the left in the Labour Party and other socialist groups for redistribution through tax funded welfare, including a universal non-contributory pension scheme without test of means. At the time a particular edge had been lent to this demand by the Bolshevik revolution in Russia in 1917. The 'revolutionary potential' of ex-servicemen was taken very seriously in Whitehall.[54]

Although the small tax base in Britain in the 1920s constituted a serious obstacle to tax funded social policy, there was a strong feeling at the time that there was massive wealth that could be taxed and redistributed through welfare. According to estimates quoted by Macnicol, the top 5% of wealth holders in Britain at that time owned 91% of all marketable wealth. Moreover, estimates of income distribution in 1928 revealed that nearly a half of national income (£1.7 billion out of a total of £3.7 billion) was received by the top 10% of income earners (2,080,000 earners) who earned more than £250 per annum (the NHI income limit). The remaining 90% of income earners (18,065,000) earning less than £250 per annum shared what was left. Not surprisingly it was said in the Commons that the aim of the 1925 scheme, by being contributory, was to make the working classes pay for their own poor.[55]

## Widows', Orphans' and Old Age Contributory Pensions Act 1925

For Macnicol, the Widow's, Orphans' and Old Age Contributory Pensions Act 1925 stands as a crucial mid-point between the 1908 and 1946 Act. The 1925 Act drew state pensions into the existing social insurance framework, a convenient device for establishing eligibility to the new benefits by reference to a record of past contributions. All employed persons with earnings of less than the NHI upper income limit of £250 per annum and a record of at least five years continuous insurance contributions, including contributions made prior to the commencement of the new scheme, qualified for pensions under it. The flat rate contributions for pensions were 9d per week for men (4½d for women) which were added to the contributions for health insurance using the same card. The flat rate contributions for pensions were shared equally between employee and employer in the case of men. In the case of women, the employee paid 2d and the employer 2½d.[56]

A substantial Exchequer contribution was paid into a Treasury pensions account to extinguish the large capital liability for past years' pension accrual. This Exchequer subsidy was in addition to a Treasury supplement under a tripartite insurance system which was later continued by Beveridge.[57]

The 1925 Act provided for the new contributory social insurance pension scheme to operate alongside the means tested non-contributory pension system established in 1908. The pension under both schemes continued to be paid at the rate of 10s per week. Insured workers qualified for pension under the new scheme at age 65. However, for technical reasons, payment of their pension from age 70 was provided under the old 1908 scheme although, in their case, without means test because of their social insurance entitlement accrued under the 1925 Act.[58] Thane has explained that it was planned that the entire state system would gradually be changed to a social insurance basis although this was not expected to be completed until the 1950s. The 1925 Act, however, can be seen as representing the first steps towards the creation of a universalist state pension scheme (eventually achieved by the legislation of 1946) because it provided for the accrual of pensions as of right, upon the insurance principle, and was therefore not subject to any means test. It also increased the proportion of people aged over 70 who were entitled to the state pension to 79%.[59]

On 1 January 1926, 15.1 million workers (10,445,000 men and 4,645,000 women) entered the state pension insurance system. On the same day, 166,132 people aged 70 and over not previously eligible for a state pension became entitled, irrespective of their means, to the full state pension rate on the basis of their previous national insurance record. As Thane points out, however, although wives of insured men qualified, as a result of the legislation, for the social insurance pension on the basis of their husband's contribution record, a great number of older people, mostly women, did not qualify for pensions under the system. In 1928 the first social insurance pensions were paid to 360,000 men and 177,000 women in the age group 65 to 70 with the number some 10 years later, in 1938, being 524,493 men and 316,909 women. The numerical preponderance of male pension recipients arising from the social insurance basis of the new pension system was in direct contrast to the female majority of pensioners there had always been in the non-contributory scheme of 1908.[60]

Thane records that the number of the uninsured pensioners still subject to a means test or other disqualifications declined steadily after 1925. She indicates that the non-contributory pension took on second class status, and the problem of severe poverty among these pensioners was unresolved.[61]

For Churchill, as for Neville Chamberlain, the contributory principle was 'a way of instilling capitalist values'.[62] As in the case of Joseph Chamberlain, however, the values that Churchill and Neville Chamberlain were concerned to infuse into working class culture were most probably those of ethical capitalism, conceived as thrift and self reliance and a sense of obligation to help others. There was an intention to extend as soon as practicable the 1925 scheme on a voluntary basis to those people on small incomes who were outside the scope of national insurance. This extension of coverage did not in fact take place until 1937 when voluntary contributions were brought under the scheme by means of a measure which came to be known as the Black-coated Workers Act.[63]

As already noted, the 1925 scheme represented the first step towards 'universalism' in public pension provision in Britain. The scheme itself was not a universal scheme on account of the upper income limit of £250 which disqualified those with earnings above the limit from membership of national insurance. Although the scheme in its initial stages was only intended to provide pensions for workers on low incomes, the Black-coated Workers Act enabled persons with small incomes, whether working on their own account or not, who were not in insurable employment to become voluntary insured persons under the 1925 Act. These were mainly people such as ministers of religion, shopkeepers, farmers, clerks, dressmakers and music teachers.[64] The annual upper income limit under the Black-coated Workers Act was £400 for men (£250 for women). This sex discrimination occasioned a good deal of controversy. Thane points out, however, that the voluntary section of the scheme was primarily intended to appeal to married men whose income provided for at least two adult persons and possibly children in addition. A woman, it was thought, only needed to insure herself for a single person's old age pension.[65] However, as Beveridge was later to note in his report on Social Insurance and Allied Services in 1942, the Black-coated Workers Act broke the interlocking of health and pensions insurance, so far as voluntary contributors were concerned, allowing such persons to select the insurance most suited to their needs. In so doing, the Act for the first time enabled married women to become voluntary contributors for pensions'.[66] By December 1938, 759,683 applicants to join the voluntary section of the scheme had been recorded.[67] However higher income earners were excluded from membership of national insurance until after the Second World War when the 1948 Scheme came into existence.

## Old Age and Widows' Pensions Act 1940

Thane's research into the relation of age to paid employment among women in the 1920s and 1930s sheds light on the social background. During these two decades an increasing number of women had entered full-time paid employment. At that time, however, working women were very much more likely to be dismissed from employment at an earlier age than working men.

A source, cited by Thane, estimated that of all single women in the age group 45–54 who were in full-time work in 1921, some 18% had left their employment within 10 years for reasons other than marriage or death. The corresponding figure for men in the same age group was 8%.[68] Dismissal from employment on account of age affected women 'most notoriously' in the retail trades and in domestic service.[69] It also seems to have affected women textile workers.

The incidence of unemployment among women after age 45 and the virtual impossibility of regaining employment for older women who had lost their jobs, led to the formation in 1935 of the National Spinsters' Pensions Association (NSPA). This was founded in Bradford by Florence White who had a small confectionary business. It immediately instituted a campaign for an earlier state pension age for women than for men.[70]

NSPA chose to centre its demands on a pensionable age for women some 10 years lower than the current state pension age, namely 55 instead of 65. In this they were supported by the textile trade unions, although not by the TUC which gave priority to a demand for higher state pensions for all workers, whether men or women. Nor was the campaign supported by the professional women's organisations whose members doubtless perceived their interests to differ from those of NSPA's membership comprising of some 150,000 largely working and lower middle class women. Professional women tended to be concerned that any reduction in the women's state pension age would aggravate discrimination against women in employment opportunities, particularly in promotion.[71]

The claims of the campaign for a reduction in women's state pension age were nevertheless taken seriously by government which set up a Parliamentary Committee on Pensions for Unmarried Women to investigate them.[72] The Committee reported in 1939 that it was generally more difficult for widows and married women to regain employment than it was for spinsters. They also argued that there was a case for greater social concern over the plight of women left pensionless and often in poverty by virtue of devoting much of their lives to caring for elderly parents or other infirm relatives.[73] The Committee was influenced by statistics provided by the Government Actuary which, whilst showing that all women tended to experience deterioration in health from age 55, also revealed that age specific death rates of women in the age groups 45 to 65 were slightly lower for unmarried than for married or widowed women. The Committee decided that, on the whole, the spinsters had not proved their case for special treatment and pointed out that a possible consequence of a state pension age of 55 would be that employers would force more women of working age into retirement.[74]

There was also pressure building up in all political circles concerning the plight of the male worker made redundant at age 65 with a younger wife not working. In such a circumstance the couple were forced to live on the man's pension of 10s a week. This provided an inadequate income for subsistence living. Consequently there was considerable pressure to lower the eligibility age for a pensioner's wife to 60 – it was estimated at that time that on average the wife was four years younger than her husband. However there was concern that if the age was reduced to 60 for only married women then this would cause inequalities between women, in particular a married woman who had never contributed in her own right would receive her pension from age 60 while a single woman could have contributed all her working life and yet have to wait until age 65.[75]

After much deliberation, it was decided to lower the pension age to 60 for all women who were insured in their own right or were the wives of insured male pensioners.[76] It has also been said that the reduction of the state pension age to 60 for women was an incentive designed to encourage more women (particularly housewives) to volunteer for war work.

As a result the 1940 Act provided that, as from 1 July 1940, the old age pension was payable as from age 60, instead of 65, to an insured woman and to the wife of an insured man who has himself attained the age of 65. Part I amended the 1925 Act so that insured women and wives of pensioners aged 60 and over could qualify for the contributory pension.[77]

Although the 1925 scheme was the first step towards a universalist pension scheme, providing pension rights on the basis of a record of at least five years continuous contributions, poverty among pensioners was still widespread. Part II of the 1940 Act provided for contributory pensioners and widows to be permitted to apply to the Assistance Board for supplementary allowances if they could prove they were in need. This was to assist poorer pensioners by allowing them access to means tested supplementary allowances without losing their pension. In the Treasury's view, supplementation of assistance was seen as 'an easier and cheaper alternative to an overall rise in pensions'.[78]

The National Federation of Old Age Pensions Associations (NFOAPA) had been campaigning for an increase in the pension to £1 per week, presenting a petition with five million signatures to Parliament in 1939. They criticised MPs for having just awarded themselves a salary of £12 per week and a pension of £4 per week when a pensioner had to survive on 10s per week.[79] NFOAPA was suspicious of the concession in the 1940 Act but maintained nevertheless that, by permitting pensioners to claim means tested supplements, the 1940 Act was evidence of public recognition of their case.[80]

## CHAPTER FOUR

# Beveridge Report and the National Insurance Scheme of 1948

## Committee on Social Insurance and Allied Services

In July 1940 Ernest Bevin, the Minister of Labour in the war time coalition government, asked Beveridge, now Master of University College, Oxford, to carry out a brief survey of the government's wartime manpower requirements. Soon afterwards, Beveridge became the chairman of the Manpower Requirements Committee of the Production Council. By the end of the year, Beveridge was again a full-time civil servant becoming an Under-Secretary in the Ministry of Labour.[1]

However the working relationship between Bevin and Beveridge became increasingly strained so much so that by June 1941 Beveridge had lost most of his responsibilities. At that time he was offered and accepted the job of chairman of an inter-departmental inquiry that was about to be established to consider the co-ordination of social insurance (Committee on Social Insurance and Allied Services). Harris, in her book *William Beveridge: A Biography*, recounts that, some 21 years later, Beveridge recalled that Bevin 'pushed me as Chairman of the Committee by way of parting with me'.[2]

On 10 June 1941, at perhaps the lowest point for Britain in the Second World War, Arthur Greenwood, the Minister without Portfolio, announced to the Commons the setting up of this committee (Committee on Social Insurance and Allied Services) to report back to the Committee on Reconstruction Problems of which Greenwood was chairman. The terms of reference of the Beveridge Committee were:

> To undertake, with special reference to the inter-relation of the schemes, a survey of the existing national schemes of social insurance and allied services, including workmen's compensation, and to make recommendations.[3]

The other 11 members of the Beveridge Committee, including the Government Actuary, Sir George Epps, and two women, were all civil servants from the relevant Departments. When the nature of the issues to be raised before the Committee became apparent, it was realised that a potential conflict of interest could arise as many of the matters under consideration were questions of policy. It would have been inappropriate for any civil servant to express an opinion except on behalf of the Minister to whom he was responsible. This matter was brought to the government's attention and, in an exchange of letters between Greenwood and Beveridge in January 1942, Greenwood indicated:

> In view of the issues of high policy which will arise, we think that the departmental representatives should henceforward be regarded as your advisers and assessors on the various technical and administrative matters with which they are severally concerned. This means that the report, when made, will be your own report; it will be signed by you alone.[4]

Beveridge replied saying that he accepted the decision and thought that the change would be beneficial.[5]

The government also announced in the Commons on 27 January 1942 that 'it will be within the power of the Committee to consider developments of the National Insurance Schemes in the way of adding death benefits with any other risks which are at present not covered by such schemes'.[6]

On submitting his report dated 20 November 1942 to Sir William Jowitt, Paymaster-General, Beveridge stated that:

> The departmental representatives have given their views within the Committee and have placed at the disposal of Beveridge their expert knowledge of the problems with which the Committee was concerned. In discussion and in examination of witnesses the Committee has functioned as a Committee. Through their representatives and otherwise the various Departments have been able to express views on questions arising in the course of the enquiry, but they have done so, if at all, without associating themselves or any Minister or the Government in any way whatever with anything that is written here. For every recommendation and every word in the report ... Beveridge alone is responsible. The report stands or falls on its merits and its argument, with no authority behind it except that of a sincere attempt, with expert guidance from the departments and after consideration of views presented by interested bodies, to understand the innumerable problems of social security, to balance arguments and equities, to compare desires and resources, and to devise methods of making all the immense good that has been accomplished into something better still.[7]

The Beveridge Report is arguably the most important document with regard to pensions over the past 100 years. However Harris' biography of Beveridge reveals that the tensions within the Committee and the concerns within the government during the Committee's deliberations and preparation of the report were considerable.[8]

A major task of the Committee was to bring together the 1908 non-contributory scheme and the 1925 contributory scheme into a single administrative system with the 1908 scheme continuing for retired persons who had never contributed to the 1925 scheme.[9] Beveridge's next objective was to create the framework for a universal contributory state pension which would provide a sufficient livable income.[10] The proposal eventually embodied in the report was entirely unequivocal on this point. The pension should provide 'enough for subsistence even though the pensioner has no other resources whatever'.[11]

As a result of reading Rowntree's second study, *Poverty and Progress: a Second Social Survey of York*, published in 1941, Beveridge had become convinced that his universal insurance scheme could serve as 'a vehicle for achieving a national minimum',[12] an idea originally conceived in the 1890s by the social reformers Sidney and Beatrice Webb.[13] Rowntree's findings in the study also convinced him that such a scheme, if it covered periods of unemployment and provided benefits set at the threshold of need, could eliminate poverty entirely.[14] The scheme eventually presented in the report was accordingly designed to abolish want, but without recourse to radical measures, and to accord to all a 'national minimum standard of life'. It was based on the insurance principle and would provide, in return for flat rate contributions paid by employees, employers and the state, flat rate benefits up to subsistence level to meet basic needs as of right and without means test.[15]

By providing a minimum income needed for subsistence (payable from age 65 for men and 60 for women) the state retirement pension would leave individuals free without disincentive to build upon their basic entitlement pensions from employment and personal savings.[16] In calculating his minimum pension for subsistence Beveridge used what is known as household budget standards i.e. specified baskets of goods and services which when priced represent particular living standards.

The idea was pioneered by Rowntree in his first study of poverty in York, *Poverty: A Study of Town Life*, published in 1901.[17] Rates of pension adequate for subsistence were based on the calculations of an advisory sub-committee comprising Rowntree and Arthur Bowley, another veteran of poverty research as well as a doctor and a nutritionist from the British Medical Association.[18] Unlike Rowntree, Beveridge took the view that the subsistence needs of retired persons differed from those of working age. For example, food and clothing needs are less and fuel and lighting needs are greater. Nevertheless the overall recommendations for determining pension rates in the Beveridge Report reflected the stringent calculations of needs as used by Rowntree in his second study of poverty in York[19] and according to one commentator approximated closely to Rowntree's 'statistical measure of primary poverty'.[20]

Rowntree, however, had always contended that an income sufficient to meet human needs had to be higher than one which equated to a statistically determined primary poverty threshold below which people are considered to be poor, because human beings needed some degree of personal autonomy in their lives and cannot reasonably be expected to spend their income with total efficiency or to be entirely free from domestic or personal emergencies.[21] In his second York study, he used not merely a primary poverty scale covering nutritional necessities and other essential items, but also a human needs scale which took cognizance of changing views of what constituted a minimum standard of civilised life.[22] There is documentary evidence that in principle Beveridge had as early as January 1942 rejected the idea of basing his subsistence definition on the more stringent primary poverty scale as being unacceptable to current public opinion. He clearly envisaged the broader concept of human needs as representing the proper basis of calculation for all social insurance benefits.[23]

A serious disagreement between Beveridge and Rowntree arose, however, in relation to the treatment of rent. Beveridge's plan was that there should be a benefit, set at the same level for the whole country, which would nevertheless be 'enough for subsistence even though the pensioner has no other resources whatever'.[24] The problem is that liability for rent is a basic cost which varies so much from household to household, locally and regionally, that it is not feasible to try to bring it within a uniform subsistence definition.[25] Rowntree argued that if Beveridge tried to do so it would 'go far to defeat the purpose he had in view',[26] and urged him to exclude any allowance for rent from his subsistence level, leaving provision for household costs to be made separately. Beveridge believed, however, that a variable allowance for rent would 'infect social insurance with the taint of a means test', and accordingly proceeded with his original idea of a flat rate benefit which included a uniform notional sum for weekly rent.[27] It was an inescapable dilemma of the Beveridge pension design – a problem insoluble in its own terms – which his friends would generally regret and his enemies criticise.

Social insurance embodying the contributory principle stemmed from Beveridge's fundamental belief that social security should be achieved by co-operation between the state and the individual citizen. The Beveridge Report was explicit:

> The state should offer security in return for service and contribution.[28]

The proposal was not about giving something for nothing or for freeing recipients from personal responsibilities. The benefit was strictly conditional on the citizen accepting responsibility to give service (through labour) and to pay contributions.[29] The contributory principle received a great deal of criticism at the time, as it had when first introduced many years earlier and which has continued. Critics have called into question the need for two different systems of revenue. Why does the state need National Insurance (NI) contributions when it has income tax? However in the 1940s, the majority of employed persons did not pay income tax, a situation that did not significantly change until the 1960s and 1970s.[30] Beveridge believed that citizens had claims upon the community for social welfare not because of need alone but as a reward for service to that community by way of performance of work and civic duties. For him contributory insurance was tangible evidence of the performance of civic duty.[31] In the 1940s, the Treasury reverted to its opposition to the contributory principle because it 'did not favour assigned revenues and [they] felt it was objectionable to give a first charge on any source of revenue'.[32] If such a fund showed a surplus it would lead to demand for increased benefits; if a deficit, the Treasury would be expected to provide a subsidy.[33] It is worth reflecting on these words of warning when considering what happened to occupational pension schemes in the last quarter of the 20th century, which went from enjoying surpluses to combating deficits.

## Women and social insurance

Beveridge was an active sponsor of equal rights for women[34] and was well aware that, because most women had different work histories from those of men, it would be difficult to integrate women's entitlements into his social insurance scheme.[35] The Committee discussed how the different social and economic categories of women should be treated under the scheme: i.e. 'employed women, housewives, widows, divorcees, deserted and unmarried mothers, domestic spinsters, and unmarried wives or cohabitees'.[36] Existing provisions for women showed clearly the 'tangle of contradictory principle and inadequate coverage' resulting from a half century of piecemeal social welfare reforms.[37] Under the 1908 scheme women of pension age without means received equality of treatment with men. Under the 1925 scheme, employed single women paid lower contributions and at retirement received less benefits than men, on the often incorrect assumption, that they had fewer family responsibilities than most men. From 1940, they could draw their pensions at age 60 whilst men had to work until 65. Widows, on the basis of their husband's insurance record, were entitled to pensions on their husband's death. Divorcees, deserted mothers and domestic spinsters without means were entirely dependent on means tested public welfare.[38]

Beveridge wanted to introduce equity and rationality into social security for women. However, because he tried to reconcile the aims of those seeking to enhance 'women's equal but different' roles with the aims of those who sought greater 'sexual and functional equality' for women,[39] he found his task beset by almost insuperable difficulties. Thane has succinctly summarised how, early in the deliberations over his report, Beveridge proposed that the social security needs of women should be met in a number of different ways.[40] These included: –

1. Men and women in employment would contribute for social insurance.

2. A housewife's policy for married women based on their husband's contributions providing lower benefits than for men in the expectation that housing would be provided by their husbands. The benefits included (i) a furnishing grant (or 'marriage grant' in the final report); (ii) maternity benefits; (iii) dependants' benefits when their husbands were sick, disabled or unemployed; (iv) funeral benefit, widowhood allowance and benefit and separation allowance on breakdown of marriage; and (v) domestic help when ill.

3. An option for married women in employment not to contribute for benefits in their own right and instead to rely on the housewife's policy.

4. Pensions for widows with dependent children, followed by a training benefit for work.

5. A housewife's policy for unmarried wives i.e. cohabitants, which would have entitled them to the same benefits (except for the furnishing grant and the widow's pension) as those under the married women's housewife's policy assuming that they had been married.

6. An option for domestic spinsters and other categories of women (including men) not in employment to make voluntary contributions in order to safeguard their full entitlement to state benefits.

7. Means tested public assistance for all other categories.[41]

In Thane's view, these proposals, which were not implemented by the resulting legislation, would have provided a framework with a greater capacity for adaptation to long term social change than the provisions which were actually embodied in the National Insurance Act 1946. Feminist critics have tended to overlook Beveridge's proposal for a housewife's policy as indicated above.

The proposals in the report drew strong criticism from feminists and women's organisations who were seeking full equal treatment with men. Many of these objected to Beveridge's assumptions about the structure of the family and relations between the sexes. Beveridge was always very responsive and sympathetic to the claims of women. However, in seeking solutions to the problem of pensions for women with work histories so different from those of men, he was nevertheless constrained by the principle of social insurance.[42] His compromise solution bore the marks of a trade off between social protection and public acknowledgement of women's uniquely different values as mothers, partners and carers on the one hand, and equal treatment with men on the other,[43] with adequacy of provision for some categories of women suffering as a result. For Beveridge the role of the family was the 'pivotal focus of human life,[44] a view which has received much criticism. He did, however, believe that marriage was 'a companionship of different but equal partners',[45] and he wanted to improve the social security status of the housewife and mother who, by virtue of her work in the home, should 'be regarded as a contributor in kind if not in cash'.[46]

## Retirement and old age

It is noteworthy that Beveridge never regarded old age as a problem in itself. His primary aim was to meet the needs of citizens in old age (particularly the needs of the aged poor) to protect them from want.[47] His advocacy of a retirement test as a precondition for pension payment is consistent with this. He had confronted the demographic issues as far as he was able and, as his report made clear, was concerned about the conjunction of declining fertility and increasing longevity.[48] The proposals in the report were scrutinised in detail by the Government Actuary in a 38 page appendix to the report,[49] although the calculations relating to the financing of Beveridge's social security proposals did not include any allowance for improvements in life expectancy.[50] Beveridge had been advised by Sir George Epps, the Government Actuary, to refrain from attempting to anticipate the financial effects of declining mortality on the grounds that specific estimates of future populations of pensioners would be unreliable in the context of 'prolonged economic crisis and global war'.[51] It is clear that this view was supported, if not actually influenced, by John Maynard Keynes, the eminent economist, who, after reading an early draft of the report had commented to Beveridge: The future can well be left to look after itself… It will have far more resources for doing so than the immediate present.[52]

Consistent with his view that old age was not a problem, Beveridge always stressed the advantages of a flexible retirement age. It is arguable that his report laid the foundations of at least upward flexibility in retirement age. The state pension age is not a mark of the onset of old age. It is the earliest age at which a state pension becomes payable on the basis of a record of insurance contributions.

The report refers to provision for old age retirement as 'the most important and, in some ways the most difficult, of all the problems of social security'.[53] On account of the cost of full subsistence pensions to the immediate post-war economy, Beveridge reluctantly was persuaded by Keynes (who was at the Treasury during the war) that pensions should be phased in over 20 years. Also to contain state pension costs during post-war reconstruction, Beveridge recommended on the advice of Keynes[54] that through additions to the basic pension rate the active elderly should be encouraged to defer retirement and pension for as long as possible. The pension should be regarded as an income for retirement, rather than as an income payable for old age as commonly understood. When this principle was applied in 1948 about two thirds of men and one half of women who reached state pension age elected to stay at work.[55] With this change implemented, Britain moved from a fixed state pension age to a minimum state pension age. Thane makes the point that Beveridge would have built in stronger incentives in the form of a higher uplift than the government actually implemented.

## The Beveridge Report: reception and aftermath

The publication of the Beveridge Report in December 1942, shortly after the victory of El Alamein, was greeted with widespread popular enthusiasm. It is still viewed as a significant document of social history. Its proposals for a universal scheme of social insurance under which 'as recipients of benefit the poorer man and the richer man are treated alike'[56] seemed to be imbued with the vision of an economically fairer and more socially just post-war society. Social insurance, the report argues 'may provide income security; it is an attack upon Want. But Want is one only of five giants on the road of reconstruction and in some ways the easiest to attack. The others are Disease, Ignorance, Squalor and Idleness'.[57]

On the night before its publication queues formed to buy the report outside the Stationery Office in London. All initial copies of the report, 60,000 in number, were almost immediately sold out.[58] The BBC broadcast details of the report in 22 languages. Abridged copies were circulated among the Armed Forces and Civil Defence and parachuted to the resistance movements throughout occupied Europe. The government was concerned with social planning for post-war European society as well as military action.[59]

A public opinion survey, carried out soon after the report's publication, revealed that 86% were in favour compared with 6% against. Among employers, 73% supported adoption of its proposals.[60] However, despite the very positive reaction of press and public, the report was not without its critics. Chancellor of the Exchequer, Sir Kingsley Wood, a few days before publication minuted Churchill, the Prime Minister in the wartime coalition government, that the proposals represented an impracticable financial commitment.[61] Beveridge was the sole signatory of the report and some have suggested that the coalition government may have considered that this would enable it to detract from the report's importance and preserve a degree of distance from its proposals.[62] The Treasury sought to delay publication and, after that failed, attempted to remove some of the more 'radical evidence' from the companion volume of committee evidence.[63] Churchill wanted to delay government approval for fear that it would hinder the delicate negotiations with the US over the extension of Lend Lease (the system of American wartime aid).[64]

Early in 1943, shortly after its publication, the report was submitted for scrutiny to a committee chaired by Sir Thomas Phillips (a senior civil servant) who, it was said, was 'never an enthusiast for anything suggested by Beveridge'.[65] This committee was highly critical of several aspects of Beveridge's proposals. Whilst they accepted the principle of universalism, they rejected the concept of subsistence on the basis that universal flat rate benefits could never meet subsistence requirements because of widespread variation in rent: the very weakness in Beveridge's subsistence definition against which Rowntree had warned. The committee argued that there was an irreducible helpless and feckless class, whose existence meant that a deterrent poor law could never be abolished.[66]

In February 1943 parliamentary pressure forced a debate on the Beveridge Report. Sir John Anderson who led for the government declared that there could at present be no binding commitment and Sir Kingsley Wood the Chancellor expressed concern 'over the financial perils of the plan'.[67] The war time government's lack of commitment to Beveridge's proposals is thought to stem largely from the hostility to the report which leading Conservative members of the government shared with the majority of Conservative MPs and the party rank and file.[68] Although a number of progressive Conservatives, who were influenced by Harold Macmillan's middle way concept of a mixed economy combining elements of socialism and laissez-faire capitalism, argued for compromise,[69] there was strong and consistent Conservative opposition to universal social insurance during the war and after. The party tended to favour targeting benefits on those in need and not wasting them on those who were not.[70]

The lack of government commitment to the report led to one of the largest anti-government votes of the war. This was led by Arthur Greenwood and Lloyd George* with 121 MPs from the Labour, Liberal and Communist parties and 11 independents voting against the government[71]. In April 1943 a group of civil servants, led by Thomas Sheepshanks, was appointed to consider the practicalities of implementing Beveridge's proposals and they went on to prepare a white paper on social security in 1944. Sheepshanks had privately expressed the view that 'the Beveridge proposals could be called a fraud'[72]. This committee abandoned the subsistence principle using different arguments for rejecting it for different benefits; whereas the Treasury argued that subsistence could not be afforded.[73]

The exclusion of Beveridge from these deliberations has never been fully explained, although Harris considers the reasons are not difficult to find. In her book she cites Beveridge's lack of skill in handling relationships with ministers and senior officials, his imperious and unrealistic demands in implementing proposals, his attitude of constantly shifting the discussion of matter of fact questions onto a wider strategic and philosophic plane and his behaviour in courting massive advance publicity for his report.[74] This last one was seen by many people inside government as a flagrant breach of Whitehall conventions and an attempt to usurp the powers and functions of the regular policy making machine. However as Harris suggests it is far from certain whether the report would have made the impact that it did without the publicity.[75]

The white paper was debated in Parliament in November 1944. During the debate, Sir William Jowitt, Minister for Reconstruction, acknowledged that the government had received criticism for its 'refusal to adopt what is called the subsistence level'. However, he went on to argue that the proposal was for a social insurance scheme, 'which involves premiums which we hope all should be able to pay, in return for which benefits are to be received which we hope will at least take the edge off the mishaps of life. It is not and does not pretend to be a scheme of social security'.[76]

## Post-war social solidarity

Public support has generally been ascribed to the 'widespread sense of social solidarity' which had developed during the war. Competitive pluralism and, in the view of some, excessive individualism had characterised much of British life in the pre-war years. This was largely replaced by social cohesion founded on the need to co-operate for survival in conditions of total war in which no man, woman or child of whatever class was free from becoming a casualty of indiscriminate enemy action. The old tension between classes had lessened: 'bombs respected neither class nor income'.[77]

---

* This was the last ever Commons' vote by David Lloyd George.

By the end of the war, social planning in relation to goods and services, which had been necessary to deliver a just and reasonable distribution of scarce resources, received a wide measure of public acceptance. People had become accustomed to food rationing. The Board of Trade's slogan 'Fair Shares for All',[78] when clothes rationing was introduced, encapsulated the principle that had made rationing a popular policy.[79] Beveridge's scheme of universal social insurance was entirely consonant with the wartime ethic of 'bread for everyone before cake for anyone'.[80]

The Liberals had endorsed the Beveridge Report[81] with enthusiasm from the beginning, but after the 1945 election the Liberal representation in the Commons was reduced to a mere 12 seats. Beveridge himself lost his Berwick-upon-Tweed seat which he had only gained in October 1944. The report had also been endorsed by the National Council of Labour, which represented both the Labour Party and the trade unions. This had been followed by the endorsement of the British Council of Churches.[82] A national conference of free churchmen had described the report as the embodiment of practical Christianity.[83]

The election of a Labour government in July 1945 has been attributed in part to the largely negative response of the Conservatives to the Beveridge Report, ranging from qualified acceptance to outright hostility.[84] According to Thane, the Conservatives were bewildered by the overwhelming public support for Beveridge's proposals.[85]

## Labour's pension reforms

The Labour government of 1945 was determined that social security reform should be one of its top priorities.[86] One month after Labour's election victory, however, Britain was facing what Keynes called a 'Financial Dunkirk'.[87] On 21 August 1945, Lend Lease was abruptly cancelled. Economic ruin was only averted by a US loan, negotiated by Keynes, which had to be repaid with interest over 50 years beginning in 1951 (the period was extended with the loan finally being discharged on 31 December 2006). The loan was granted subject to sterling becoming freely convertible into US dollars after a period of only 12 months. Although this might put an intolerable strain on the British economy, it was accepted as the price to be paid if Labour was to introduce its programme of social reform.[88]

The National Insurance Act 1946 gave effect to the core proposals in the Beveridge Report – state administered social insurance financed by employees, employers and the general taxpayer[89] (the Exchequer contribution to the NI Fund). The basic weekly rate of benefit was 26s. A married man drawing a pension with a dependent wife under age 60 received an additional 16s a week. If the wife was over 60 and not at work this sum was paid as a pension to her. If the wife was herself insured the wife received 26s a week on her retirement at state pension age (i.e. 60).

The government decided that old age pensions would be paid in full from the 'Appointed Day', 5 July 1948, although special provisions applied to persons who first became insured at the outset of the scheme (see Appendix 1). To Ernest Bevin and the other members of the Cabinet Committee on Reconstruction Priorities, which was responsible for implementing the Beveridge Report, the 20 years phasing in period for full pensions rights (the golden staircase) seemed impractical. They felt that a more generous settlement was essential in view of the sacrifices made by those of working age during the 1930s depression and the Second World War[90]. Economic restraints, however, dictated lower full rates of benefit. When the scheme came into force in 1948, benefit rates were nearly a third below what Beveridge had recommended for subsistence.[91]

However, James Griffiths, Minister of National Insurance, maintained that Labour's benefit levels were in line with Beveridge's calculations, modified by cost of living adjustments. In the Commons debate on the bill, having touched upon the problem of subsistence, he said, 'I believe that we have in this way, endeavoured to give a broad subsistence basis to the leading rates, within the framework of a contributory insurance scheme'.[92] However, the Treasury rejected Griffith's proposal to link the pension rate to an index of prices or earnings and instead there was a promise to review benefits on a quinquennial basis.[93]

## Benefit levels and transition to the new scheme

Beveridge's main objectives of rationalizing the administration of the 1908 and the 1925 state pension schemes to create the framework for a new universal contributory social insurance scheme had been achieved. However, his aim of a pension payable as of right and sufficient to live on, and so eliminating the need for means tested social assistance, was not.[94] The new social insurance pension was inadequate for subsistence from the beginning. This was aggravated by the fact that recipients of means tested social assistance benefits were eligible for housing allowance, whereas recipients of non-means tested social insurance benefits were not elibible.[95]

Beveridge's caution, in 1942, in recommending transitional arrangements seemed well founded at the time. Churchill was concerned that full endorsement of the Beveridge Report, even after Keynes' economies, could undermine the negotiations being conducted for the extension of Land Lease.[96] The irony was that at a meeting of the Cabinet Committee on Reconstruction Priorities in February 1943, a few months later, Bevin, a veteran campaigner for better state pensions, insisted on immediate payment of full pension rates at the scheme's commencement. As Macnicol describes it 'at a stroke he [Bevin] squashed Beveridge's miserable golden staircase to full pension rights'.[97] In the Commons debate on the report, a few days later, the phasing in period was abandoned, but so also was the commitment to the subsistence principle.[98] Macnicol sums up the situation that emerged in 1948 as a dual state pension scheme – the two tiers comprising a flat rate social insurance pension and, underpinning it, a system of means tested social assistance – which reflected the Treasury's preference for a low level universal pension, supplemented by means tested benefits for the poorest pensioners.[99] This can be seen as perhaps the cause of many of the future problems in social pension provision. It was, in effect, 'the cheapest combination of the 1925 and 1908 principles'.[100]

NFOAPA felt that their evidence had had no influence on the proposals published in the Beveridge Report. In contrast, the Fabian Society found themselves in substantial agreement with Beveridge on the pension amount, but warned about the risks of inequitable treatment of the young having to make excessive provision for the old. It 'would be a fundamental error in social policy unduly to divert resources to the aged at the expense of the young'. Later the Fabians acquiesced in the use of 'crude demographic determinism … to justify the abandonment of the subsistence principle for old people'.[101] While never departing from his insistence upon the subsistence principle, Beveridge had nevertheless sounded a note of caution in his report about the dangers of being 'in any way lavish to old age, until adequate provision had been assured for all other vital needs, such as the prevention of disease and the adequate nutrition of the young'.[102]

Accordingly the 1946 Act was only of limited benefit to the then current generation of pensioners. Those retirees who were already within the NI Scheme in 1946 received the full pension rate immediately. The scheme also provided an accelerated rate of accrual for late age entrants previously excluded because their earnings were in excess of the scheme income limit which was abolished in 1946 as part of the move to full universality.

## National insurance day and replacement of the poor law

5 July 1948 was the Appointed Day for both NI and the National Health Service (NHS). It was also the day that the new service provided under the National Assistance Act 1948 came into operation with the aim to terminate the existing poor law. It superseded the Assistance Board and the public assistance responsibilities of the local authorities originating in the Elizabethan poor law.[103] The local authorities, however, retained residual responsibilities for welfare services for the elderly or infirm or others in need, including old people's homes which had started to replace the workhouses.[104] The National Assistance Board (NAB) assumed responsibility for some 800,000 recipients of assistance benefits in 1948, a figure which by the end of that year exceeded one million. The figure increased steadily to about 1.8 million in 1954 and to 2 million in 1962, remaining at about that level until 1966 when the NAB was integrated into the new Ministry of Social Security (now the Department for Work and Pensions).[105]

It has been argued that a factor in the ultimate dependence of many married women and widows on means tested income support benefits in retirement was their election, whilst in employment, to pay lower contributions (married women's reduced contribution rate). This option to pay a lower rate of NI contributions, which only provided cover for industrial injuries benefits, was offered to married women when the post-war NI system was introduced in 1948. It was offered on the grounds that married women in employment would rely on their husband's insurance record for pension provision when they retired. The married women's reduced contribution rate was abolished in 1977 although women already paying the lower rate at that time could continue to do so but would lose the right if they did not have paid work for two tax years or became divorced.[106]

## Beveridge and tax-based welfare

Beveridge had envisaged that his contributory social insurance scheme would largely replace tax-based welfare, which would remain as a safety net for a small residual number of persons whose subsistence needs were not met by the insurance system. It would be a contributory scheme as Beveridge had always insisted that benefits should be in return for contributions and should not be 'something for nothing'.[107] Further such contributions would have to be separate from general taxation as liability for income tax in the 1940s commenced at a much higher income threshold than at the beginning of the 21st century (e.g. the starting rate for tax for a single person in the late 1940s was around 40% of average earnings compared with less than 25% in the early 1990s[108] and around 20% for the tax year 2008–09).

The contributions would be paid into a NI fund where, together with the contribution from employers and the Exchequer (the latter representing the modest redistributive component), they would be used to provide benefits. Beveridge proposed that the National Exchequer would provide one third of the total cost of unemployment benefit and one sixth of the costs of pensions with the balance of cost being met through the flat rate contributions.[109] It was intended that the overall contribution would be set at the level actuarially required to be paid over the working lifetime of an entrant from the minimum age of 16 to fund the value of future benefits. However for the membership at the introduction of the scheme, their actuarial contribution would be higher and Beveridge proposed that the Exchequer would meet also this shortfall in contributions.[110] Appendix A of the Beveridge Report contained the Government Actuary's memorandum examining the financial aspects. He estimated that if Beveridge's proposed plan was implemented then the shortfall of contributions to be met by the Exchequer would be 50% of the income initially rising to 55% and then 61% in 10 and 20 years time respectively.[111]

The actual plan implemented was somewhat different to that proposed by Beveridge. The contribution basis still included the specific Exchequer contribution. In addition the Exchequer was to make further contributions to meet the transitional cost of implementing the scheme. In his January 1946 report, the Government Actuary estimated that these additional payments would be 26% of the income in 1948 increasing in 10 years periods to 35%, 47% and then 55% by 1978.[112]

## National Insurance Fund

As Pemberton and others have pointed out, Beveridge's concept of social insurance implied a funded scheme.[113] The Labour government's decision, however, to abandon the 20 year transition period for entitlement to the full pension rate and pay full, if reduced, rates of benefit from the outset, meant that there would be no build-up of contributions. The financial basis of the scheme would accordingly be weakened as it would be an unfunded system,[114] financed on the pay as you go principle which entails the use of current contributions to provide current benefits. This arrangement was described in a Treasury note some years later as a 'regressive poll tax' with the rate determined by an 'arbitrary guess' of the Government Actuary.[115] Some have argued that this rendered NI a fiction.[116] A more general view, however, is that the NI Scheme is nevertheless a properly constituted social insurance scheme because it embodies a contract between the state and the citizen under which the former undertakes to provide specified benefits in return for the latter's contributions. The manner and timing of contributions to provide benefits, and the relationship of income to outgo in the NI fund, are simply administrative matters not affecting the nature of the underlying social insurance contract.

## National Insurance versus National Assistance

The Labour government's decision to pay NI pensions at a rate significantly lower than subsistence resulted in greater numbers of pensioners becoming dependent on means tested social assistance than originally intended. The situation was compounded by two factors. First, under the social security legislation of 1946–48, means tested benefits were subject to regular uprating to allow for inflation, whilst NI benefits were subject to quinquennial reviews.[117] Second, recipients of means tested benefits usually received a rental allowance which covered the claimant's actual housing costs, whilst those receiving NI benefits did not.[118] Accordingly, the national assistance system (which replaced the poor law in 1948) did not wither away as Beveridge had predicted but continued to have a vital role in supplementing social insurance benefits as well as providing for those not covered by social insurance.[119]

Beveridge always criticised the anomaly of means tested social assistance benefits being greater than non means tested social insurance benefits, and continued to argue, as he had at the beginning of the 20th century, that targeting the poor increased poverty in society by penalising work and thrift and failed to help significant numbers of people who through pride or ignorance failed to claim means tested benefits.[120]

The disadvantage of social assistance as a major element of social security is that it entails a means test and so is a disincentive to voluntary insurance or personal savings. By contrast, social insurance providing a national minimum benefit at subsistence level as of right leaves 'room and encouragement for voluntary action by each individual to provide more than that minimum for himself and his family'.[121] Perhaps, however, the most serious disadvantage of means tested income support benefits is the persistent problem of the lack of take up by those entitled to claim. This is generally attributed to the complexity of the claiming process and the stigma attached to being dependent on social security benefits.

## Citizenship and the contributory principle: Beveridge's social philosophy

Beveridge's belief in the contributory principle stemmed from his social philosophy. He viewed social assistance or poor law relief as servile and not compatible with full and equal citizenship. Contributory social insurance, however, entailed the exercise of duty as a prior condition of a right to benefit which arose from 'the solidarity of free and equal citizens'. He argued that the citizen's claim on the community for social welfare, to use Ruskin's term, rested not on need alone, but on a reward for service to that community by way of performance, as far as the citizen was able, of work and civic duties.[122] This is reminiscent of the view of public pensioning expressed by the actuary Hardy in 1891.

The contributory principle was an indispensable element in Beveridge's pensions framework, as was subsistence. The benefit was to be 'a minimum income for subsistence with equality of contributions', to ensure that 'as recipients of benefit the poorer man and the richer man are treated alike'.[123] Harris commented that Beveridge's vision of the good society – and hence of the provision of social welfare – was a republican rather than a democratic vision, in the classical sense of Plato, that different economic and political interests were balanced against those of the state as a whole.[124] The vision was certainly not a mass democratic consumerist one. By incorporating the contributory principle into his scheme, he sought, unlike Churchill or Neville Chamberlain, not to instil capitalist values, but promote the ideals of citizenship.

As the underlying principles of Labour's 1946 social security legislation were those embodied in the principles of his report, Beveridge has come to be seen as the founding father of the welfare state. However he thought that the term welfare state signified a paternalist Santa Claus state with its connotation of something for nothing. He preferred the term social service state which seemed to place the prior emphasis on 'duties rather than rights'.[125]

The idea of a social service state as an enabling polity, founded on solidarity and reciprocal rights and duties, received at that time a wide measure of support across the political spectrum, as is shown by the following declaration in the 1950 Conservative election manifesto:

> The Social Services are no longer even in theory a form of poor relief. They are a co-operative system of mutual aid and self-help provided by the whole nation and designed to give all [citizens] the basic minimum of security, of housing, of opportunity, of employment and of living standards below which our duty to one another forbids us to permit anyone to fall.

It would arguably be difficult to find a clearer statement of the values which Beveridge sought for his social service state than that contained in this manifesto declaration.

# CHAPTER FIVE
# Post-war Conservative social policy

## Occupational pensions

Up to 1947 it had been possible for approved occupational schemes to pay retirement benefits entirely as a cash lump sum, apart from trust funds approved under the Finance Act 1921 which were not in general permitted to provide cash retirement benefits. This was brought to an end by the Finance Act 1947, which limited the proportion of retirement benefits receivable as a lump sum and restricted the amount of the approvable pension benefit. The Act radically altered the basis of approval of pension schemes. Although its immediate aim was to strengthen control of the fiscal aspects of occupational pensions, the Finance Act 1947 has to be seen in the wider context of the new social policy introduced by the 1946 Act. It provided a state pension based on social insurance contributions on which individuals could build by means of occupational and/or personal pension arrangements.[1] The Income Tax Act 1952 consolidated the tax legislation governing pensions which had been embodied in the 1947 Act and in the two earlier Acts of 1918 and 1921.[2]

James Millard Tucker KC, the eminent tax lawyer, was in the midst of chairing a committee on the taxation of trading profits (report issued in 1951) when in August 1950 Sir Stafford Cripps, the Chancellor, appointed him also to chair a committee to address the issue of 'inequitable anomalies in the tax treatment of occupational pension schemes'.[3] The Committee which included the actuary, Reginald Simmonds, did not report until 1954, after the Conservative government came to power in 1951. The report advocated removal of the anomalies through a framework which provided more consistent tax treatment of both insured and uninsured schemes. This entailed extending to insured schemes tax relief on employee contributions and scheme investment income as under the 1921 Act trust funds, and extending to the uninsured schemes the tax free lump sum benefit concessions available under insured schemes and public sector schemes. The report also recommended that the tax exemptions of the 1921 Act, and the proposed lump sum benefit concessions, should be made available to the self-employed. The cost to the Exchequer of the recommendations, however, caused concern at the Treasury with the result that no action was taken by the Conservative government until 1956.[4]

The Committee considered the tax treatment of the lump sum on retirement and concluded that they had 'not been able to find any satisfactory explanation why this lump sum ever came to be treated as non-taxable. If we were dealing with the matter without any reference to existing practice we should have found it very difficult to recommend that any part of the benefit should be in tax-free form, but since the practice is now so firmly established and seems to have been tacitly approved in the 1947 legislation and in the 1950 legislation relating to judges, we find it impossible to say that in future it should not apply. We therefore recommend that it should be permissible for an approved scheme to pay up to one quarter of the capital value of the total benefit payable to an employee on his retirement in lump sum form, or in a form capable of conversion into a lump sum [with] an absolute upper limit of £10,000.[5] Increasing this upper limit in line with price inflation, it would now be roughly £200,000, while the normal limit under the current pensions tax regime is £412,500 for 2008/09.

The Finance Act 1956 only implemented some of the Millard Tucker proposals. Nevertheless the Act had an important influence on methods of financing pension schemes. It exempted from tax the investment income of insurance companies insofar as this was attributable to premiums paid under certain types of pension fund contracts, and accordingly gave an impetus to the growth of insured pension schemes.[6] Following the Second World War there had been a substantial increase in the number and membership of occupational schemes and by the late 1950s these schemes, as a result of the funds they were making available for industrial investment, were becoming an important source of influence on the national economy.[7]

## Conservatives and Beveridge

The Conservatives under Churchill formed their first post-war administration after winning the general election of 1951 with an overall majority of 17 seats. The party has always been a broad coalition of groups with different interests and views of society, reflecting different conceptions of the role of the state and hence of social policy. These range from the more traditional Conservatives who have an organic view of society and a belief in a relatively substantial role for the state in governing the body politic, to the economic liberals with their more 'atomistic' view of society and emphasis on individualism and a minimal role for the state. Also in the party, and not without influence, were those smaller groups such as the middle way Conservatives who had formed themselves into the Tory Reform group, and the One Nation group of backbench MPs, both of which pragmatically accepted a role for social policy.[8] The One Nation group (formed in 1950) explicitly endorsed the provision through social security of a guaranteed minimum income as it would enlarge both freedom and security.[9]

The Conservative Party as a whole never accepted the universalist principle of the Beveridge proposals and generally maintained a preference for targeted benefits.[10] Even the One Nation group admitted failure in 'fully squaring the circle of market economics and state welfare'.[11] This was manifest in the proposals of two of its original members, Ian Macleod and Enoch Powell, to reduce and target social expenditure by replacing universal benefits with selectivity.[12] Macleod wrote in 1949 that the social services were increasingly 'being used not for the relief of destitution or misfortune or ill-health but as a means to redistribute wealth'.[13]

A study group established to develop a post-war Conservative approach to social policy had criticised the proposals of the Beveridge Report on the basis that they were excessively costly and did not concentrate spending on the really poor.[14] There was hostility to the report on financial, moral and distributive grounds.[15] There was pressure on the Conservative government from the party in Parliament and the country to reduce public expenditure and 'to reorient social policy around accepted Conservative goals'.[16] As Thane points out, the Conservative parliamentary majority was small and the government was anxious not to alienate lower middle class voters who had benefited from the Beveridge pension reform. There were also significant numbers of Conservative voters on low fixed incomes who were reluctant to apply for means tested national assistance.[17] Because the Conservative government's decision, in its first budget, to reduce food subsidies would inevitably raise the retail price of food, it was also decided to increase NI pensions and contributions.[18]

## Phillips Committee 1953–1954

In 1953 the Conservatives resolved to challenge the viability of the Beveridge social insurance pension, which had fallen below the level of means tested national assistance benefits. It was decided to establish a committee to review the 'Economic and Financial Problems of the Provision for Old Age'[19] under Sir Thomas Phillips. Phillips was one of the foremost critics of the Beveridge Report[20] and, at the instigation of the Churchill National Government, he had headed the scrutineers of the report early in 1943, shortly after its publication.

In 1954 the Committee, which was composed mainly of conservatives, produced a report which recommended raising the retirement age.[21] It was highly critical of the Beveridge principle of a social insurance pension sufficient to live on. This principle was characterised as 'an extravagant use of the community's resources'.[22]

The future burden of ageing was a serious concern when the NI contribution rates were settled in 1946. Rates were calculated on a pessimistic basis assuming significant falls in mortality at older ages, increased sickness rates for men (20%) and women (25%) and a trend towards earlier retirement. It was also assumed that proportionately fewer widows would work and that unemployment would be as high as 10%. This continuing concern about future population ageing and increasing public expenditure resulting from the growth of old age dependency, anticipated by the 1949 Royal Commission on Population,[23] greatly influenced the Phillips Committee. This became a principal pensions policy preoccupation of the first and second Conservative administrations.

Although the Phillips Committee used lower estimates of the future population than used in 1946, it still predicted a pensionable population of 9,500,000* in 1979 (18.2% of the total population). It estimated that, if the employment rates of older people did not increase, the proportion of dependent older people would rise from the current 12% to almost one third by 1979.[24]

The reaction of the Phillips Committee to their own estimated trends in the growth of the pensionable population was to recommend an increase of three years in the pension age from 65 to 68 for men and from 60 to 63 for women. The Phillips Committee also expressed grave concern at what they saw as the mounting burden of cost on the Exchequer resulting from the increasing expenditure on NI pensions and recommended that a higher proportion of the cost of the scheme should be borne by the contributors.[25]

Although the recommendation of the Phillips Committee to raise the pension age was supported by the Treasury, it was rejected by the government because of fears that it would be an electoral liability.[26]

---

*The 1981 census shows that the pensionable population (i.e. men 65 and over and women 60 and over) was 9,691,000 being 17.9% of the total population.

The Committee also considered whether to restore parity between the pension ages of men and women. They recognised that there were strong reasons for doing so including sex equality but were persuaded not to recommend equalising the pension age to that of men because in effect increasing the age would apply only to single women and it would not achieve any considerable saving.[27]

## Conservative government's pensions policy

Before the 1955 general election, the government again raised the state pension and the flat rate contributions 'above the level actuarially required'. The process of transferring more of pension cost away from the Exchequer to contributors was continued in successive Conservative budgets.[28] This not only undermined the redistributive mechanism implicit in Beveridge's tripartite system of NI contributions (i.e. contributions from the insured persons and the employers and payments by the Exchequer), but because of the flat rate nature of the contributions, it disproportionately penalised contributors on lower incomes. Such a situation was in stark contrast to the existing income tax system, constructed on the basis of values of fairness and progression which were widely accepted in the community as a whole.[29]

When Churchill resigned in April 1955, Sir Anthony Eden took over as Prime Minister. On 25 May 1955 he led the Conservatives into a general election from which they emerged with an overall majority of some 60 seats.[30]

Despite concerns about rising public expenditure, the Conservatives' first term had been a period in which the Exchequer had greatly benefited from the unprecedented high levels of post-war employment, which were even reflected among those of state pension age who had been encouraged to defer their retirement.[31] This resulted in a rising accumulation of the yearly contributions in excess of benefit payments in the NI Fund.[32]

## Problem of adequacy

The numbers of claimants on means tested national assistance benefits had risen from 0.8 million in 1948 to 1.8 million in 1954.[33] This growth can be explained by the reluctance of successive governments since 1946 to uprate insurance benefits to a level which would provide a sufficient livable income. This led to a situation where a high proportion of claimants for such payments were people who needed to supplement NI benefits.[34]

In an attempt to resolve this anomalous situation, and to float large numbers off the means test, the Conservative government increased insurance benefits by 22% just before the 1955 general election.[35] As Nicholas Timmins points out, between 1948, when the Beveridge scheme commenced, and 1964 when the Conservatives left office at the end of their third successive term, NI benefits were increased six times and means tested national assistance benefits ten times, so the two were continually out of step, reflecting a confusion over objectives.[36]

The uprating of NI benefits imposed a strain on the resources of the NI Fund. According to Rodney Lowe, the social policy historian, by 1955 the real cost of retirement pensions was nearly 50% more than Beveridge had predicted.[37] The difficulty of raising the NI pension has been attributed by some to the system of flat rate contributions which, in effect, restricted the rate of the contributions to what the government of the day estimated that the lowest paid insured employee could afford to pay. This is what Helen Fawcett has referred to as the Beveridge straightjacket.[38] This straightjacket, in the view of Pemberton and others, exerted a constraining influence on pensions policy from 1945 until 1959 when a limited modification of the flat rate principle was introduced.[39]

The Conservatives in their second term, however, were faced with the prospect of a large and inescapable increase in social security expenditure occurring in 1958 with the end of the transitional arrangements that applied to those people previously excluded from the NI Schemes including employees with earnings exceeding £420 per annum and certain of the less well paid self-employed who had opted not to pay voluntary contributions.[40] It meant that a 55 year old man who commenced contributions in 1948 and who retired in 1958 could expect to receive a pension 'worth ten times the contributions he had paid' to the NI Fund.[41]

In the autumn of 1955 the Conservative government was faced with more general economic problems. Rab Butler, the Chancellor, was forced to introduce a supplementary budget in October which took back from the electorate the additional spending power only conferred on them in the previous April. There had been rumours of deflation and speculative pressure on sterling.[42] Butler was replaced by Macmillan in December, and the latter introduced a whole series of deflationary measures in April 1956. The disastrous Suez crisis erupted in October and was followed in November by a run on the pound which could only be halted by a loan from the International Monetary Fund (IMF) supported by the US. On 10 January 1957 Eden resigned from the premiership and was succeeded by Macmillan.[43]

As noted earlier, following the Second World War there was a substantial increase in the number and membership of occupational pension schemes. The 1954 Phillips report recorded that occupational schemes were becoming major providers of pensions. Indeed Richard Titmuss of the London School of Economics commented in 1955 that, although these schemes had through tax relief subsidies become more costly to the Exchequer than NI pensions, the Phillips Committee had advanced 'the curious argument' that their continued development might, in the long run, give substantial relief to the Exchequer.[44] By 1956 the proportion of workers in membership of occupational schemes had increased to 33%, but that meant that two thirds of workers were entirely dependent on a flat rate NI pension, the value of which was not keeping pace with the general increase in earnings.[45]

## Titmuss and the social division of welfare

In December 1955, nearly half way through the period of 100 years since the Old Age Pensions Act 1908, Titmuss delivered his Eleanor Rathbone Memorial Lecture on the subject *Social division of welfare*.[46] The contribution of Titmuss's lecture (which was subtitled *Some reflections on the search for equity*) helped to clarify the central issues in the debate on pensions policy being conducted at that time.

Looking back, Titmuss wrote:

> It is this period of roughly 50 years … that has witnessed the emergence and growth of those forms of state intervention which … have come to be called the social services.[47]

He went on to argue that the whole apparatus of state provided welfare including pensions reflected a lack of clear thinking about what is, and what is not, a social service.

The definition of what is a social service, he said, 'should take its stand on aims; not on the administrative methods and institutional devices employed to achieve them'.[48] Titmuss noted that by failing to address the aims of policy certain anomalies arose. For example, social security pension payments were treated as social service expenditure, whereas allowances and reliefs from income tax associated with occupational pensions were not, despite the fact that they provided similar benefits, and achieved a similar social purpose, in the recognition of dependent needs.[49] Any tax saving that accrued to the individual was in effect a transfer payment. The cost to the Exchequer of tax reliefs given to occupational pension schemes in 1955–56 amounted to £100 million per year compared with the cost to the Exchequer for NI retirement pensions of £45 million.[50]

Titmuss argued that Treasury classifications relating to social service expenditure provided some indication of the area of confusion concealed by the assumptions of the critics of social policy, some of whom maintained that the burden of redistribution from rich to poor had been pushed too far, and others that sections of society had been impoverished partly as a consequence of providing benefits for those workers who did not really need them.[51]

In this debate, Macleod and Powell were still arguing, as they had in their *One Nation* pamphlet in 1952, that the question to be asked of welfare provision was not 'should a means test be applied to a social service?', but rather 'why should any social service be provided without a test of need?'.[52]

In drawing attention to the different ways public and private social services are treated as public expenditure, Titmuss unearthed the structural features characterising the social division of welfare. Far from the welfare state producing greater social equality, as commentators like Macleod and Powell claimed, the divisions between public and private welfare maintained and in some cases deepened inequalities between rich and poor. Further, Titmuss argued that the process of social change in the 20th century required new provisions of welfare which in turn demanded a new understanding of their purpose – hence his insistence on analysing policy aims. This can be seen when we apply the threefold division of welfare he describes – between social, occupational and fiscal (ie tax-based) welfare – to the social consequences of pensions developments during the 1908–2008 pensions century.

Titmuss' notion of the social division of welfare has provided a major conceptual resource for analysing social policy in the last 50 years of the 20th century. Indeed key developments of pensions policy during this period, as described at greater length in the following chapters, can be briefly analysed in these terms. First, whilst universal NI state pensions have existed since 1925, their value relative to earnings has never risen higher than 26% in 1979 and has fallen steadily since – making a quarter of pensioners in 2008 reliant on means tested benefits to lift them out of poverty. Secondly, occupational welfare has benefited an increasing proportion of working men throughout the first half of the century, only to hit a ceiling of around 50% in the second half (a ceiling that is substantially lower for women workers). Thirdly, fiscal welfare has benefited working people contributing to occupational and personal pensions more than people contributing only to NI provision. Among private pensions contributors, higher earners paying higher rates of income tax benefit more from higher tax exemptions than standard rate tax payers. Overall the benefits of state and private pensions and fiscal welfare throughout the century have been distributed unevenly and reinforced social divisions: in the different groups benefiting, in the differential levels of benefit received, and in the combined impact of pensions provision on social structure.

Titmuss always emphasised that there is no escape from value choices in social policy. As an aid to understanding the complexity of the value choices that are open to us in social policy in general, and pensions in particular, Titmuss developed three contrasting models.[53]

A. The residual welfare or public burden model is based on the premise that an individual's needs should be met by the private market and family. Only when these break down should social welfare institutions come into play and then only temporarily. This is the philosophy of the poor law, means tested benefits and free market economics. The public burden model views social service expenditure – particularly that of a redistributive kind – as a burden; as a waste of resources in the provision of benefits for those who, it is said, do not need them.[54]

B. The industrial achievement performance model incorporates a significant role for welfare institutions that provide for social needs on the basis of merit, work performance and productivity. It is the philosophy of self-help and is concerned with incentives, efforts and rewards. A flat rate state pension scheme where benefits are directly linked to an individual's flat rate contribution record and where thrift and savings are rewarded is a good example of this model.

C. The institutional redistributive model sees social welfare as a major integrated institution in society providing universalist services outside the market. This model is based on the principle of social equality and incorporates systems of redistribution. An example of this approach is where a flat rate pension, sufficient to live on, is paid to everyone in retirement funded out of general taxation or paid for by contributions related to income so that the well off pay a much higher proportion of the costs.

Elements of all three models are found in most pensions policy proposals. What has generally emerged in practice has been a blend of principle and pragmatism. All systems try and resolve the conflict between what it is socially just and what is economically and politically viable.

## Moves towards state pension reform

By the mid-1950s, the future looked bleak for the NI pension because the Treasury was opposed to the principle of an increasing contribution to the NI Fund from general taxation which was essential to sustain the financing of the scheme.[55] The opposition Labour Party had been exploring the concept of a state sponsored superannuation scheme to supplement the flat rate benefits of the NI Scheme by providing earnings related benefits in return for earnings related contributions. This concept was similar to the model of state pension arrangements developing in Germany and Sweden.[56]

There is little doubt that the aim of extending earnings related pension provision to the high proportion of workers excluded from occupational schemes was the prime mover for state pension reform in the late 1950s and throughout the 1960s. In 1957 Labour launched their national superannuation plan – a comprehensive system designed to extend earnings related pension benefit to all workers.[57] Macmillan, who succeeded Eden as Prime Minister in 1957, responded by asking for an immediate review of pensions policy.[58]

The Labour Party's proposals for a state earnings related pension were published in 1957 in the paper *National Superannuation*, the official statement of party policy. Under the proposals, the average wage earner would be provided, when the scheme matured after 20 years, with a retirement pension approximately equal to 50% of pay at or near pension age. This would be achieved by adding an earnings related pension, as a second tier, to the flat rate NI pension.[59]

The second tier pension would be financed by earnings related contributions from employees and their employers, supplemented by an Exchequer contribution equal to 18% of the combined contributions payable by and in respect of the insured persons. It was envisaged in the proposals that the earnings related contributions would be invested by the state in stocks and shares to build up a fund from which the second tier pensions would be paid.[60]

The proposals were welcomed by the trades unions which tended to prefer pension entitlements arising under a state run scheme as occupational pensions then were commonly not transferable.[61] It was also quite widely acknowledged, even among opponents of the scheme, that Labour's national superannuation plan represented a highly sophisticated and coherent solution to the problem of adequacy in social pension provision. As a concept for a state pension scheme, it was considered to be 'as advanced as any under discussion in the social democratic parties of Europe'.[62]

## Conservative response to reform

One of the first steps taken by Macmillan's government in 1957 to curb public expenditure on pensions had been to cap the Exchequer's contribution to the NI Fund.[63] This meant that if the resources of the Fund were not to be seriously depleted, additional revenue would have to be raised by increasing NI contributions. The only way in which this could be done without increasing financial pressure on the lower-paid would be to introduce NI contributions which were earnings related.

A further problem for the government was that the growing number of pensioners on means tested benefits served to confirm Labour accusations that the old were slipping further into poverty,[64] and that Labour's national superannuation plan, providing benefits related to insured persons' earnings, was likely to be electorally popular.[65]

In the Cabinet's NI Committee, John Boyd-Carpenter, the Minister for Pensions and National Insurance, having publicly dismissed the architects of Labour's plan as 'a skiffle group of professors', argued strongly for an expansion of private occupational pension schemes to extend cover to as many workers as possible.[66] The Life Offices' Association (LOA), keen that the state should not provide more than the flat rate basic retirement pension and convinced that occupational schemes, with improved transferability terms, could meet the need for retirement income security above the basic level, suggested privately to Ministers and MPs that it would welcome legislation to compel employees to join an occupational scheme. This, however, was considered by Boyd-Carpenter as an interventionary measure too far.[67] It was admitted by the life offices that the provision of universal coverage for all workers under an occupational pension scheme was not really practicable because there were many small firms which could not afford to operate such schemes.[68]

The support of Boyd-Carpenter and others in the Cabinet for the expansion of occupational schemes reflected, in Pemberton's view, a powerful commitment to private sector solutions among many Conservatives (and among many officials).[69] The logic of the limitations of occupational schemes to provide retirement income security for all workers, however, provided a justification for pragmatically minded Conservatives to extend state pension provision, at least for those without an occupational pension, or for those not adequately provided for by an occupational scheme.

Macleod, the Minister of Labour, with the support of Macmillan, developed preliminary proposals for a radical revision of the Beveridge scheme which would entail the addition of a supplementary earnings related tier to the flat rate pension. This would be combined with compulsion for employers either to offer their workers an occupational pension of comparable value to the benefits of the new state pension system or to enrol them in that system.[70]

Macleod's proposals were inimical to most strands of Conservative social philosophy. They were opposed by Boyd-Carpenter and Chancellor Thorneycroft, as well as by others in the Cabinet on the right of the party, including Powell, who were hostile to the notion of a greater role for the state in the provision of pensions. The debate about a radical reorganisation of the 1946 state scheme continued into 1958 and after a Cabinet deadlock Macleod's proposals were quietly dropped.[71]

The proposals for state pension reform which eventually emerged were very much less ambitious in character than Macleod's. They were based on an alternative put forward by the Treasury[72] and supported by Boyd-Carpenter. Although they represented a distinctly limited step towards reform, they would nevertheless achieve for the government two critical objectives: namely to raise additional revenue for the NI Fund and to divert public attention away from Labour's promised reform of national superannuation.

The new scheme, which would be superimposed on the Beveridge flat rate scheme, would entail the addition of an income related contribution, based on a band of earnings above a low threshold. The income related contribution would, in time, earn contributors an additional (graduated) pension of a modest amount on top of their flat rate NI pension. The advantage for the government would be that the revenue from the income related contributions would be available 'long before any [graduated] pension had to be paid'.[73] The graduated pensions accrued in units of 6d a week for each specified amount of income related contribution, and there was to be no provision for uprating the units of pension to keep pace with inflation.

Against strong opposition from the Treasury, occupational pension schemes would be allowed to contract out of the graduated component of the state scheme. To Boyd-Carpenter this was an indispensable element in the state scheme reform, if occupational pension schemes were to grow both in their number and membership. To the Treasury the contracting out option represented a pointless loss of revenue and the 'principle of contracting out was conceded only after an unusually intense Cabinet battle'.[74]

In January 1958, while the debate on the graduated scheme continued, the government granted an increase of 25% in the flat rate NI pension, significantly higher than was required to compensate for price inflation since the last uprating. Later that year Boyd-Carpenter announced that the government intended to introduce his graduated pension scheme to supplement the flat rate NI pension.[75]

In October 1958 the government published its White Paper *Provision for Old Age: The Future Development of the NI Scheme*[76] detailing the graduated scheme. It explicitly stated that the scheme's first objective was to place the NI Scheme on a sound financial basis.[77] The enabling legislation was embodied in the National Insurance Act 1959, which was enacted just before the general election. In the cross-party argument at the 1959 election, Labour referred to the scheme 'as a swindle' and Boyd-Carpenter called it 'a good bargain'.[78] Speaking about the scheme in the Commons in January 1959, Macleod commented 'too small and far too timid a step forward... a little mouse of a scheme.'[79]

## The Conservatives' third term 1959–1964

In the run-up to the general election on 8 October 1959, the polls suggested that nearly 40% of the voters thought it made no difference which party was in power.[80] Hugh Gaitskell, who had been elected leader of the Labour Party after Attlee's retirement in December 1955, promised 'a 10s rise in pensions as well as more hospitals' without a rise in income tax.[81] A series of astute budgetary moves, including the above inflation state pension increase by the government before the election, had served, however, to vindicate in the public mind the Conservatives' record in office.[82] Moreover, in less than three years as Prime Minister, Macmillan had done much to restore public faith in his party after the Suez crisis. He was also reassuringly the champion of middle-way conservatism, with a reputation for social awareness and concern for the material condition of the nation.[83] At the election the Conservatives secured a large increase in the popular vote and emerged with an overall majority of 100 seats.[84]

The graduated scheme, which applied only to the employed, came into operation in April 1961. The declared aims of the 1959 Act were to:

1. place the NI Scheme on a sound financial basis;
2. make provision for employed persons, who cannot be covered by an appropriate occupational scheme, to obtain some pension benefits related to their earnings; and
3. preserve and encourage the best development of occupational pension schemes.[85]

The graduated scheme, as the Act made clear, was designed primarily to raise additional Class 1 NI revenue by income related contributions initially on the band of earnings between £9 and £15 per week. The rate of contribution was 4¼% on earnings between these two limits by the employee and 4¼% by the employer. The system of graduated benefits and contributions introduced by the Act was superimposed on the basic pension scheme with lower paid workers (i.e. those with earnings less than £9 a week) being excluded from the graduated part. The graduated pension which was added to the basic state pension accrued at the rate of 6d per week for each £7 10s for men (£9 for women) of graduated contributions paid by the contributor only (i.e. the employer's contributions were ignored).[86]

Employers operating occupational pension schemes which satisfied certain conditions could apply for a contracting out certificate in respect of all or certain categories of members over age 18. This allowed provision to be made in the occupational scheme instead of the graduated scheme. However, although by contracting out the employee and employer ceased to pay the graduated contribution, the weekly flat rate contribution was higher.

The National Insurance Act 1963 raised the upper limit of band earnings from £15 to £18 per week with the contracting out arrangements being extended correspondingly. Although subsequent legislation increased the upper limit over stages to £62 per week and also increased the graduated contribution rate, they did not extend the contracting out arrangement beyond the band earnings of £9 to £18 per week.

A large number of occupational schemes were set up just before the graduated scheme came into existence in 1961, but many of these schemes provided only the bare minimum benefits sufficient for contracting out. Initially about 4.5 million employees[87] were contracted out, with this being a minority of the employees in occupational schemes. This was presumably because employers generally did not believe that graduated scheme benefits or contributions were sufficiently significant to have any bearing on their employee benefits strategy.[88] The take up did not increase until after the Social Security Act 1973 had confirmed that state graduated pension benefits would not be up-rated to keep pace with the cost of living. This decision was reversed by the 1974 Labour government.

It has been suggested that the persistence of pensioner poverty and the increasing affluence of the rest of society, combined with other factors such as the growth of earnings related pension provision in other European countries and the publicity given to Labour's plans for radical pension reform (i.e. National Superannuation), all stimulated the establishment of the graduated pension scheme by the Conservative government.[89]

## Genesis of contracting out

What is particularly noteworthy about the graduated scheme from an historical perspective is the facility for the contracting out of employees from a part of the NI Scheme. Prior to 1961 there was no precedent for contracting out of any state pension arrangements apart from the provisions in the 1925 Act permitting contracting out of the basic state pension for employees of the Crown, local authorities and statutory companies such as the railways and public utilities.[90]

In January 1946 the Association of Superannuation and Pension Funds and other pensions interests* had requested the Labour government to grant contracting out from the Beveridge flat rate NI pension to occupational pension schemes which provided adequate benefits. However this was rejected outright by the government.[91]

Boyd-Carpenter saw contracting out as vital to the development of occupational pensions, which he believed should, in conjunction with the basic pension, be the prime source of retirement income security for most people in a free society.

In the event, the contracting out terms for members of occupational schemes were not very stringent, which is probably the main reason why they were never extended beyond the

---

* The term pensions interests covers those involved directly in occupational pensions, namely employers, trade unions, actuaries, pension consultants and representatives of organisations concerned with the management and the investment of the assets of the schemes.

earnings band of £9 to £18 per week as provided for under the 1963 Act. In return for providing a minimum occupational pension equal to the maximum graduated pension, the occupational scheme received a contracting out certificate entitling the members and their employers to pay reduced income related NI contributions. For lower paid employees, however, the graduated contributions saved by contracting out were not attractive as higher flat rate NI contributions became payable, which more than offset the savings.[92] There was also the illogical feature that contracted out schemes were not required to offer a widow's pension equal to half the graduated pension, which was an entitlement under the graduated scheme.[93]

## CHAPTER SIX

# Labour and National Superannuation

## Roots of National Superannuation as an idea

The roots of Labour's National Superannuation can be traced back to the party's years in opposition in the 1950s. The situation that had led the Conservative government to appoint the Phillips Committee in 1953, namely the increasing marginalisation of the below subsistence flat rate Beveridge pension and the steadily rising number of claimants of means tested benefits, prompted the Labour leadership to reassess the principles of the social insurance settlement of 1946. Moreover, there was a growing aspiration among workers generally to have earnings related benefits like American, German and Swedish workers, and, with critical labour shortages in the 1950s (and the 1960s), many employers (often abetted by trades unions keen to recruit members) offered occupational pension scheme membership to attract and retain employees.[1]

As a result of the widening base of occupational scheme membership, the state pension was becoming of marginal interest to an increasing number of voters.[2] Nevertheless there was little prospect of occupational pensions being available to the great majority of workers. There were also problems of the lack of the full value transferability of accrued pension rights between schemes on change of employment and of the lack of commitment to protecting the purchasing power of deferred pension rights retained in a former employer's scheme. Titmuss was among the most vocal of the critics of employers' control over pension rights and other constraints on industrial mobility at that time, which he saw as potentially contributing to the 'gradual hardening in the economic arteries of the nation'.[3]

Titmuss had also commented that in Britain it was already 'possible to see two nations in old age'.[4] US workers by contrast had very much better prospects of security in retirement. In 1935 the Federal Government had started to develop, as part of the New Deal, an income related state social security scheme for all gainfully employed persons including self-employed. The scheme was compulsory for all workers, except casual agricultural and domestic employees and those covered by special systems for federal, state and local government employees and railroad workers. The scheme had a redistributive element where part of the revenue from higher earners was used to provide minimum benefits for lower paid workers.[5] (This minimum benefit was eliminated by legislation in 1981 during Reagan's presidency.[6]) Retirement benefits from the scheme were considered an important component of the average worker's retirement income and collective bargaining agreements were established on top of it. The policy of National Superannuation was partly based on this US model of social security.[7]

## A post Beveridge basis for social insurance

When in the Labour Party Research Department, Howard Glennerster, the social policy academic, recounts how Peter Shore persuaded Richard Crossman, the pension spokesman in Labour's National Executive Committee, to use the services of Titmuss (regarded at the time as the foremost academic expert on social security), and his LSE colleagues Brian Abel-Smith, Peter Townsend and Tony Lynes, to put forward proposals for a new post Beveridge approach to social insurance.[8]

Richard Crossman was appointed Chairman of a Labour Party committee on social security pensions policy, a study group which had been approved at the 1955 Labour Party conference and Titmuss and his LSE colleagues – Boyd-Carpenter's so called 'skiffle group of professors' – were co-opted as advisers. As already noted, Titmuss believed that the Beveridge flat rate principle was an impediment to the development of an adequate state pension system.[9] It seemed indefensible that the state should place increased reliance on a regressive flat rate social insurance contribution for financing its pension system at a time when the income tax system was based on publicly shared values of fairness and progression.[10] For Titmuss, the notion of a flat rate social insurance contribution conflicts with *social justice* because it is 'a poll tax which hurts the poorest most and it also directly restricts the size of the old age pension'.[11]

Hannah has argued that it would have been better if the social security and tax systems had been integrated as recommended by the two actuaries Messrs Haynes and Kirton[12] – an idea which in a rudimentary form appeared in the Labour Party's manifesto for the 1964 general election.

## National superannuation – Genesis of a new concept of adequacy

Titmuss was highly critical of the Conservative government for complaining about the high annual cost to the Exchequer of the flat rate NI pension, which he estimated at £45m, while accepting as reasonable the £100m a year foregone by the Exchequer in tax allowances granted to occupational pension schemes.[13] He argued that, if the Treasury was opposed in principle to financing the state pension through general taxation, the alternative would be a system of earnings related social insurance contributions with a redistributive element, like the US social security scheme, to provide an adequate state pension without increasing the contribution burden on the lower paid.[14] He believed that adequacy should be measured by reference to average incomes, not according to need. This adequate pension would be achieved by those on higher incomes paying higher contributions than were actuarially required. The aim was to guarantee to the average wage earner an inflation proof state pension equivalent to half pay at pension age through the addition of an income related benefit to the flat rate pension.[15] In this way a single national superannuation scheme would be created which extended to state pensioners benefits comparable to those provided for higher paid employees under occupational schemes.[16] Such provision, however, would be accomplished without the insecurity of the effect on pension rights of a change of employment.[17]

Titmuss and his colleagues' proposals were embodied in the paper *National Superannuation* which was published by the Labour Party in 1957.[18] The paper is noteworthy for its consistent emphasis that pension issues could not be viewed in isolation from the economy as a whole. It unequivocally warned:

> The much more generous provision for old age … will demand both self-restraint and hard work. If the old are to spend more, the rest of us will have that much less to spend – unless we make up the loss by increased production …

> Collectively we must be ready to see national consumption held back and the necessary savings built up in our new National Pensions Fund.[19]

The savings were to be 'used wisely for capital investment.'[20] According to Thane, Titmuss was concerned about the increasing investment power of private pension funds and, in the interests of balance, wanted equivalent power to be acquired by the state to promote economic growth and enable society to pay the constantly increasing bill for old age pensions over the next 25 years.[21] The paper also proposed that the retirement condition (the rule requiring retirement from paid employment as a precondition for payment of pension) should be abolished because 'the interest of the national economy requires old people to postpone their retirement for as long as possible'. In the context of improving healthy life expectancy which Britain was experiencing in the late 1950s, the retirement condition did not seem as sensible as in 1942.[22] Finally, to reduce the gross social inequalities, under national superannuation there would be a ceiling for benefits and contributions and a benefit floor beneath which no pensioner would fall.[23]

Labour's national superannuation plan was ardently supported by Crossman on the left of the party and by the leader, Gaitskell, on the right. It did not, however, have unequivocal support within the party.[24] The TUC and many on the left of the party including Aneurin Bevan were opposed to earnings related benefits from the outset. They believed that flat rate benefits represented an egalitarian principle that should be maintained and that the basic state pension should be increased sufficiently to provide a livable income.[25]

The Titmuss group responded that, as the Treasury would not countenance increasing the Exchequer subsidy to flat rate contributions, the pension would have to be raised with the burden falling unequally on poorer workers. Without some form of national superannuation there could be no higher contributions from workers on higher incomes to provide revenue to improve benefits for workers on lower incomes, with the result that real inequality, namely that between those wholly dependent on the state pension and those with occupational pensions, would grow, so offending the egalitarian principle.[26] National Superannuation was adopted as official Labour Party policy at the annual conference in 1957.

## Labour government 1964 – 1966

In January 1963 Gaitskell, who died unexpectedly after a short illness, was succeeded by Harold Wilson as the leader of the Labour Party. With a general election expected in 1964, the Conservative government increased the state pension in May 1963 as part of their bid to stay in power.[27] In June, however, the government was engulfed in controversy following the Profumo inquiry. In a division following a Commons debate on the Profumo affair and national security,

27 Conservative back benchers refrained from voting against an opposition censure motion and although the vote was not lost the government sustained a moral defeat.[28]

This was followed by a Labour onslaught on the Conservatives' Rent Act 1957, claiming it had encouraged the exploitation of private tenants by slum landlords, a practice which came to be known as 'Rachmanism' after Peter Rachman the notorious slum landlord. In reality, it was argued only a privileged minority had 'never had it so good' – as Macmillan claimed.[29]

Although Macmillan had been determined to lead the Conservatives at the 1964 election, his health began to fail. Because he was expected to be incapacitated for several weeks after a major operation, he resigned in Autumn 1963 and was succeeded by Sir Alec Douglas-Home as the Conservatives leader and Prime Minister. The latter, having renounced his peerage on 23 October, won a by-election in a safe Scottish seat and entered the Commons early in November.[30]

The Labour manifesto *The New Britain* for the October 1964 election gave prominence to policies on internal, rather than external, affairs. This was in spite of the worsening conflict in Vietnam and the uncertainties in the Soviet Union with Khrushchev's removal from power the day after polling day. A new ministry for the development of technology was to be established, as well as a Ministry for Economic Affairs to plan the longer term economic future, with the Treasury remaining responsible for financial affairs day-to-day. The gains produced by technological change were to be made available to improve the welfare of all citizens.[31]

Responding to pressure from its National Executive, Labour promised a large immediate increase in the flat rate pension if it should win the 1964 election, despite the Conservative government's pension increase of 17.4% in May 1963.[32] The result of the general election was very close. Based on a total poll of 77.1% of eligible voters, Labour secured 44.1% against the Conservatives 43.4%. The swing to Labour since the last election was only 0.3%, but it nevertheless provided them with an overall parliamentary majority of 4 seats.[33]

The Conservative government has been criticised for its lack of achievement in social policy between 1951 and 1964. Not a single new hospital nor prison was built. There was a lag in subsidised housing and inadequate provision for old age pensioners.[34] The improvement in the real standard of living of ordinary workers was only 50% in 13 years. It was argued that this did not compare favourably with the rise of 183% (in real terms) in the value of equity shares (225% with net dividends added) which benefited the owners of capital.

The 1964 Labour Party manifesto stated: Social security benefits – retirement and widows' pension, sickness and unemployment pay – have been allowed to fall below minimum levels of human need … one in four of NI pensioners today are depending upon means tested national assistance benefits.[35] Labour promised to reconstruct social security, but cautioned in its manifesto that the pace at which new and higher levels of benefit can be introduced will be the 'rate at which the … economy can advance'.[36]

Michael Hill, the social policy academic, pointed out that the condition required for economic advance rendered problematic the comprehensive character of Labour's aspirations for reforming social security. The government's aim was to reduce the number of pensioners compelled to claim income assistance by increasing the NI benefits at a faster rate than that to the minimum under the national assistance arrangement. However, with subsequent increases to both, the government was unable to achieve this and so the proportion of pensioners with income below the national assistance minimum maintained its status quo.[37]

## The attempt to integrate taxes and benefits

Labour's manifesto contained a specific undertaking that national assistance would be reformed by the introduction of an income guarantee which would provide a new national minimum benefit. This would ensure that any person whose income fell below a specified minimum would receive as of right an income supplement without recourse to national assistance.[38] No person in this category would need to apply for income supplementation because they would receive it automatically through the tax system.[39]

A number of influential members of the party, including Douglas Houghton, a leading sceptic of Crossman's national superannuation plan, believed that taxes and benefits should be integrated to achieve the most effective reform of social security and specifically to determine and deliver a basic income guarantee for old people.

Once in power, however, Labour discovered that the integration of taxes and benefits was neither administratively nor financially feasible[40] as the PAYE tax system did not cover the majority of old people. Moreover, the definition of household income for social security purposes and taxable income for Inland Revenue purposes were different.[41] Furthermore, pensioners' needs for housing and other services were more complex than could be covered by an affordable unmeans tested sum.[42]

It was Houghton however, not Crossman, who was appointed as the Cabinet Minister to co-ordinate social services policy and to oversee the two newly appointed Ministers of Health and Social Security. Persistence in the attempt to integrate taxes and benefits, in the view of Glennerster, delayed action on pension reform for a long period. A unified pension book for those on means tested additions to the basic pension so they were not easily identifiable as assistance claimants, appeared to be the only tangible result.[43]

The pledge of the income guarantee was eventually abandoned. Yet it was evident to Glennerster and other commentators at the time that it would not be possible to increase the flat rate pension to a level which eliminated the need for means tested supplementation and the plans for national superannuation would take many years to come to fruition. They suggested that attention should be directed to making the system of income testing more humane and less stigmatic.[44] With the income guarantee, this would have been achieved because administering the guarantee would have been 'a more or less automatic process … very much like income tax in reverse' or negative income tax.[45]

During the 1964 election campaign Labour had criticised the Conservative government for allowing the build-up of one of the largest balance of payments deficits in Britain's peacetime history.[46] The full dimensions of the problem became apparent to Wilson and his Cabinet shortly after the election. They rejected devaluation and opted for a 15% surcharge on imports to curtail the deficit. The economic problem, according to historians Sked and Cook, was exacerbated by Labour's commitment to increase NI pensions.[47]

By early November there were rumblings of discontent on the Labour benches at the government's refusal to speed up the payments of increased old age pensions which had been announced in Callaghan's autumn budget,[48] to redeem Labour's election promises on pensions and prescription charges and to encourage the trade unions to co-operate on incomes policy.[49] In contrast Callaghan's budget was seen by observers in the City and abroad as evidence that the Labour government was giving social policy priority over the strength of sterling. Following heavy sales of sterling from Europe and North America, the government decided to raise $3 billion of overseas rescue credit to bolster sterling.

By the end of the year, the government had established a prices and incomes policy as a first step to restore Britain's balance of payments.[50] The deteriorating economic situation finally convinced the government that any policy entailing a major uprating of universal NI benefits was unaffordable and consequently there was no alternative but to extend the system of means tested benefits.[51]

## Redeeming the pledge to increase pensions

Despite the economic situation, however, Labour's pledge to increase old age pensions, sickness and unemployment benefits was redeemed in March 1965[52] and the earnings rule for widows abolished. NI contributions were raised despite the additional burden this put on the incomes of low paid workers.

Against the difficult economic background, there was a continual need for government to reassure the foreign holders of sterling that it was not embarking on extravagant social policies. In July 1965 to avoid devaluation the government introduced its third deflationary budget in its first year in office.[53] The large increase of 18.5% in the flat rate pension from £3 7s 6d to £4 per week was seen by some in government, including Crossman, as pre-empting resources which could have been used for a deeper review of social security. According to Glennerster, Crossman was appalled at what was happening in pensions policy, his former area of responsibility. At the first annual public spending review in July 1965, Crossman noted that 'the whole strategy of our pensioneering, worked out for years before the election, had been jettisoned … under the diktat of Douglas Houghton'.[54]

In Crossman's view, Margaret Herbison, the Minister of Social Security (who was not in the Cabinet) aided and abetted by Houghton (who was in the Cabinet), had upset the pensions reform strategy by conceding 'an enormously increased flat rate pension financed by increased flat rate contributions' thus 'imposing an intolerable burden on the lower paid worker'.[55] As Crossman pointed out in his diary entry for 17 July 1965, this meant a rejection of the original idea which had been to switch as soon as possible from flat rate to earnings related contributions to increase the NI Fund so as to be able to dynamise the existing flat rate pension.[56]

Houghton's recollection of the events was somewhat different. What was 'salvaged from the wreck' of social security policy in the period of trade deficit and pressure on sterling in July 1965 was the supplementary benefits scheme.[57] To minimise stigma for benefit claimants and improve administration, the NAB became the Supplementary Benefits Commission. This was then partly merged with the Ministry of Pensions and National Insurance to form a new Ministry of Social Security.[58] In this way the administration of national assistance and NI was finally, as Beveridge had recommended in his 1942 report, brought together in a single Ministry of Social Security.[59]

National assistance was given the new name of supplementary benefit, and rules for claimants were upgraded into rights on the principle that receipt of benefit, once the test of means had been satisfied, would be an entitlement and not a payment dependent on state charity. The test of need which had been applied by the NAB was now called a test of requirements. Houghton subsequently reflected that the reform was publicised with all the presentational subtleties one could imagine.[60] Crossman commented from the sidelines that it was no doubt brilliantly worked out but a cheap substitute for the income guarantee.[61]

In reality the reform, which ostensibly had been aimed at relieving the predicament of the estimated 700,000 pensioners entitled to but not claiming means tested benefits, made very little impression on the problem of stigma. In practice its questionable granting of rights increased disputes over decision making about claims. It nevertheless rendered it impossible to reduce benefits to pensioners below a statutorily guaranteed minimum.[62]

## Reflections on the manifesto at the end of term

Most of the 1964 manifesto promises relating to benefits, other than pensions, had been fulfilled by 1966. These included abolition of the earnings rule for widows, and the addition of earnings related supplements to the basic NI benefits for sickness, industrial injury, unemployment and widowhood. These supplements amounted to a third of previous earnings up to a specified limit, but were payable only for a period of six months. There was, however, no provision for contracting out of these earnings related benefits.[63] They were, of course, funded from the increases in NI contributions.

The minimum income guarantee, the social policy centre-piece of the 1964 Labour government's reform programme, was finally abandoned as impractical and unaffordable. The promise to uprate all NI benefits in line with increases in earnings was not kept. The reform of national assistance, however flawed, may well have been due to 'the desire to get something onto the statute book ready for the 1966 election, something, that is, relating to pensions'.[64] During the years 1965 to 1970 the number of claimants of means tested supplementary benefit and their dependents had increased from 2,840,000 (5.4% of the population) to 4,167,000 (7.7% of the population).[65] Prime Minister Harold Wilson, however, had at least been able to proclaim that hundreds of thousands of the less well off now claimed their rights.[66]

## Labour government 1966–1970

Labour's small majority in the 1964 election and the political and economic difficulties which followed made an early general election highly probable and precluded any immediate change to the Conservative leadership. This altered when Wilson categorically announced in June 1965 that there would be no election that year and so created enough time for the Conservatives to hold a leadership election. Hume resigned and, after winning on the first ballot against Maudling and Powell, Edward Heath became leader of the Conservatives. Both Macleod and Powell, who had declined to serve under Hume, returned to the Shadow Cabinet.[67]

A by-election win in January 1966, with a swing of 4.5% to Labour and an eleven point lead over the Conservatives in a Gallup Poll in March, was a good omen for Labour. On 28 February 1966 Wilson ended speculation about the date of the general election by announcing that

31 March would be polling day.[68] For Labour the 1966 election was the second round of a bout begun in 1964. The campaign reflected the significance of the 1964–66 period with its record of social achievement[69] including an increase in old age pensions and the Rent Act 1965.

In the general election Labour were returned to office with an overall parliamentary majority of 97 seats. They polled 48% of the vote against the Conservatives 42%. The swing to Labour was 3.5%.[70]

One month after Labour was returned to power, it faced a major economic crisis and severe industrial problems. A strike by the National Union of Seamen paralysed the London docks and exports fell to a critically low level. The London Labour Party supported the strikers who ignored the government's call to return to work. On the foreign exchange markets the pound began to slide. The government had to choose between devaluation and deflation and opted for the latter. The £599 million deflation package assembled by the government included tighter currency restrictions, increases in purchase tax and a six months freeze on wages and prices.[71] There was no uprating of the flat rate NI pension in 1966. As Thane has recorded serious financial problems persisted and pensions did not appear to be regarded with particular seriousness.[72]

The six months' wages and prices freeze was succeeded by a period of severe restraint. When this ended on 1 July 1967, the government decided to retain a reserve power to delay wage increases for a further twelve months from August 1967. It was disclosed on 4 July that Britain's gold and dollar reserves had fallen by £36 million and the June trade figures showed a deficit of £39 million. Wilson assumed direct control of economic management and personally took charge of the Department of Economic Affairs.[73]

In October 1967 the flat rate pension was uprated by 12.5% from £4.00 to £4.50 per week.[74] The economic storm, which in the words of Sked and Cook would shake the Labour government to its foundations, grew steadily worse. The trade deficit for October spiralled to £162 million partly as a consequence of the dock strikes. As hopes of a large overseas loan finally faded, devaluation apparently seemed the only course open to the government to stabilise the situation. On Saturday evening 18 November 1967, the Treasury announced a 14.3% devaluation of sterling from $2.80 to $2.40.[75]

Devaluation had been anticipated by foreign speculators and the extensive selling of sterling the day before was said to be greater than at any time in the past. Britain obtained credits from overseas central bankers of up to $3 billion, including a reserve credit of $1.4 billion from the IMF to protect the country's reserves against speculators. Repayment was to be a first charge on trade surpluses arising during the ensuing years. There followed large scale reductions in public expenditure which seriously affected the deployment of the armed forces overseas and entailed the withdrawal of forces from the Far East and the Persian Gulf.

Many social policy changes were initiated to reduce public expenditure. These included reimposing prescription charges, increases in dental charges, abolition of free milk in secondary schools, deferment to 1973 (from 1971) of raising the school leaving age, and reductions in the social housing programme.[76]

Pensions were not affected. Pension reform had not been on the agenda as national superannuation had been shelved for some years, because it was recognised that the plan would take many years to come to fruition. As a result of pressure from the TUC and Labour back benchers the priority was ostensibly to improve benefits for existing pensioners who would not gain from national superannuation.[77] Wilson was concerned that if the government did not give priority to existing pensioners over future pensioners in resource allocation it could risk alienating its own supporters.[78] Nevertheless the political climate was beginning to change.

In the spring of 1968 the government experienced yet another economic reverse with the eruption of a major international monetary crisis. This resulted from an increasing flight from the dollar into gold and silver. In the previous three months US gold reserves had fallen by $1000 million and Washington asked the British government to close the London Gold Market. This necessitated raising further stand-by-credits (this time $4,000 million) to protect sterling against foreign speculators.[79]

In the deflationary budget which followed, the government announced a taxation increase of £923 million, almost all from indirect taxes. Despite devaluation there was little sign of economic recovery, with no improvement in the balance of payments and, due to a series of strikes undermining incomes policy, the trade gap widened. Towards the end of 1968 sterling again came under pressure on the foreign exchange markets due to pressure on the French franc and the corresponding strength of the German mark. The gravity of the financial crisis was made clear in December when it was disclosed that the gold and dollar reserves for November had fallen by £82 million.[80]

## The selectivist versus universalist debate

During the period immediately before the 1966 election, the Conservatives had re-opened the old debate about the efficacy of selectivist versus universalist provision in social welfare, ostensibly because of the widespread failure of universal NI benefits to provide a livable income. A high proportion of insured benefit recipients had to claim means tested, i.e. selective, supplementary benefit. The proposition of the Conservative One Nation group, widely enunciated in the 1950s that less money might be better spent if it was concentrated on those who really needed it, re-entered the political debate.[81] The argument that greater selectivity in the distribution of social services was more effective than universality in meeting need was widely mooted in the campaign and reflected in the Conservative election manifeso.[82]

Even within the Labour Party of the 1960s there were some, like Brian Waldon and Patrick Gordon-Walker who were vocal supporters of selectivist provision in social welfare. Douglas Houghton, after leaving the Cabinet in 1967, where he was responsible for social services, argued in an Institute of Economic Affairs paper that there had been a shift in public opinion away from universalism towards selectivity in meeting need.[83] (This was not inconsistent with his support for integration of taxes and benefits.) It was certainly the case that in the late 1960s the large growth in public expenditure had already brought about a significant lowering of income tax thresholds compared with the late 1940s, so that low paid workers, even those with incomes below half average earnings, had a significantly increased tax burden.[84] Crossman records in his diary for 5 January 1968: 'The trade unionists want to see us spending less on social services so there will be more for wage packets'.[85] According to one opinion poll, public support for spending on social services had declined from 77% in 1964 when Labour returned to government to 43% by 1969.[86]

The Conservative 1966 election manifesto had proclaimed it as an aspiration to see social services recognise the overriding claims of those in most need. This led to accusations that Heath and his colleagues were planning to dismantle the welfare state.[87] However, as Timmins points out, Heath believed that greater selectivity was required to modernise state welfare, not abolish it, and that Conservatives' demand for more selectivity was prompted above all by their opposition to Crossman's grand pension plan.[88]

## Planning for National Superannuation

During these years of Labour government there had been clear and consistent warnings from several groups in the party that there was no intention to abandon the party's commitment to the more ambitious earnings related state pension plan embodied in the National Superannuation proposals. Hannah's study of the period shows that the pensions interests were well aware that the limited earnings related scope of the Boyd-Carpenter scheme had given them only a brief respite in the process of reform.[89]

In 1968 Crossman was appointed Secretary of State for Health and Social Security and in his new role he turned to executing his plans for National Superannuation. He invited back Titmuss and his colleagues from the London School of Economics. Civil service work on National Superannuation was immediately resumed. Following so soon after a series of financial crises and the devaluation of the pound, it was a difficult time to embark on a major reform of the state pensions system.[90] The new scheme was going to be expensive and introducing large increases in NI contributions would be problematical at a time when the government was striving to hold back pay rises.[91]

In discussions with government colleagues, Crossman argued that the scheme would increase overall pension benefits only gradually over many years.[92] The new scheme pensions would be paid from a fund accumulated from earnings related contributions. This last proposal attracted criticism. In his diary, Crossman noted that:

> I am fighting both the Ministry and the Treasury in support of a properly funded scheme. Alas, the unanswerable Treasury argument is that if we piled up millions in the fund it would only be appropriated for the existing pensioners. We must therefore really accept pay as you go.[93]

After it was decided that the scheme would be financed on a pay as you go principle, the proposed 40 year period for maturity (whereby future benefits would be funded over 40 years) was reduced to a period of 20 years.[94]

## Crossman and the occupational pensions interests

Crossman consulted both the Confederation of British Industry (CBI) and the TUC on virtually every detail and eventually gained their support. He had certain moments of difficulty with the TUC. He recounts in his diary how one delegate argued that the proposed scheme's disregard of current pensioners was a fatal defect to which he replied that this was simply unavoidable.[95]

He realised that the successful implementation of the scheme would depend on detailed discussions with the occupational pensions interests. Such a step would in any event be necessary to maintain the support of the TUC, particularly its white-collar unions. He accordingly entered into discussions with experts in the industry. It has been suggested that Crossman's initiation of these discussions concerned the Titmuss group who feared too much would be given away to interest groups.[96]

During the ten years following Boyd-Carpenter's 1958 announcement of the graduated scheme, the proportion of the workforce covered by occupational pensions had increased from around a third to almost a half.[97] Because of the value attached by so many workers and trade unions to occupational schemes, Crossman knew that he would have to adapt his proposals to ensure that they were acceptable to occupational pensions interests. At the same time he believed he would need to encourage those interests to improve the quality of their schemes to meet standards compatible with the new state scheme.[98]

Perhaps the majority of the people who ran occupational pensions schemes, including the members of the National Association of Pension Funds (NAPF), maintained the view that in pension provisions the state should confine itself to flat rate pensions. The provision of earnings related pensions should be solely a voluntary initiative.[99] This was close to the classical Beveridge view, still broadly supported by the Liberal Party at that time. When Crossman's initial plan for National Superannuation was discussed in Parliament in 1957, its feature of higher (because earnings related) contributions was criticised by Beveridge, speaking in the Lords, as inflationary because higher contributions from employers would mean higher prices.[100]

There were, however, others in the pensions institutions who took a broader view of the social and economic implications of Crossman's National Superannuation scheme, particularly in relation to those groups in society less advantaged in pension provision than were most members of occupational pension schemes. State earnings related pensions in Germany and Sweden, and even in the US, had achieved more in providing retirement income security for low paid workers than had occupational pension schemes in Britain.[101] Moreover, a state pension system of the kind proposed would be able to cover efficiently those workers who were in casual or part-time employment, who changed jobs often, or were employed by small firms, something that occupational schemes at that time had not covered.[102]

These considerations lent support to the Crossman scheme, even by some who formerly did not favour an extension of state pension provision. An example of such qualified support was the actuary Stewart Lyon at Legal & General (a leading company in the insured pensions market) who was well known among professionals in the pensions institutions for his quiet and persuasive reasoning manner and his openness to new ideas.[103] There was widespread agreement, however, throughout the institutions that it was in the public interest that a consensus should be formed on the structure of the new state scheme and the relationship of occupational pension schemes to it. Without a consensus there would be a serious risk that pension provision in Britain would be destabilised.[104]

During his discussions with the pensions institutions, Crossman realised the difficulties occupational schemes faced in matching his scheme. Contracting out by occupational schemes would be permitted on condition they provided equivalent benefits. This condition – which was the key to the true costs and benefits of contracting out for any scheme – was the subject of protracted and difficult discussions. The pensions institutions realised that they would be strained to meet the contracting out standards. A pressure group known as STOP, an acronym for 'Save the Occupational Pension', was set up to oppose the Crossman scheme. In practice, however, its lobbying activity was largely confined to negotiating more favourable terms for contracting out than those actually offered by the government to occupational schemes.[105]

Glennerster recounts that the plan for National Superannuation was steered through the Cabinet Social Services Committee with little opposition.[106] In his diary, however, Crossman adds an illuminating gloss:

> My complete pensions plan went through without any serious questioning except from James Callaghan, who after being Chancellor knew a great deal about it. The rest ... spent nearly all their time asking about the effect of the scheme on the pensions of the civil service. It's mainly because Ministers get so ministerial that we have such appallingly ineffective discussion of great social issues. No one looked at the main economic impact or its effect on women or ... trade unions.[107]

The scheme unveiled in two white papers published in 1969, although differing in certain points of detail from the 1957 Labour Party publication *National Superannuation*, was still recognisably derived from those blueprints.[108] The absence of any provisions in the new scheme which would improve the pensions of existing pensioners was a question that was never ultimately addressed. There was, however, a somewhat low key statement in the associated DHSS explanatory booklet which referred to the position of current pensioners.

> The new pensions will not be paid to those who are pensioners already or who go on to pension before the scheme starts ... They will however continue to share in the nation's rising living standards. This will be done through a new system for periodical increases in their pensions.[109]

## National Superannuation and Social Insurance

In January 1969 the Labour government issued the White Paper *National Superannuation and Social Insurance: Proposals for Earnings Related Social Security* describing proposals to introduce a new earnings related state pension scheme in April 1972. The White Paper stated that there was no question of the new state provision replacing occupational schemes. The second White Paper *National Superannuation Terms for Partial Contracting-out of the National Superannuation Scheme* described the terms upon which government proposed to allow occupational schemes to contract out of a portion of the provision.[110] As implied by the name, the Crossman proposals represented the first attempt to create a full national scheme of superannuation.

The new scheme, in effecting a transition to income related benefits and contributions, would, after the phase in period of 20 years, be able to cater for a considerable range of individual needs and differing standards of life. Further, its redistributive scope would ensure that the living standards of pensioners would be more closely related to a wider standard of living. The proposal was to replace the one fund which existed for all NI contributions and benefits by two separate funds: a National Superannuation Fund for pensions, widowhood benefits and death grant; and a Social Insurance Fund for all other benefits. Both employer and employee contributions to each fund would be specified so that contributors knew what proportion of their contributions were for National Superannuation and what for other social benefits. The two funds would operate like the existing fund on the pay as you go principle. The benefits would continue to be essentially transfer payments financed from current contribution income.[111]

Employees were to contribute 6¾% of their earnings up to the scheme's ceiling (about 1½ times average earnings) – 4¾% being allocated to superannuation benefits, and 2% to the provision of other social security benefits. Employers were to contribute 6¾% of their total pay-roll, without any ceiling on individual earnings – 4½% being for superannuation benefits and the remaining 2¼% to provide other social benefits. Consistent with the 1948 NI Scheme, there was also to be an Exchequer supplement amounting to 18% of the combined contributions of employers and insured persons.

The pension emerging after the full maturity of the scheme was to provide 60% of an insured person's average earnings up to half average earnings, plus 25% of the remainder of his average earnings up to the ceiling of 1½ times average earnings. During the insured person's working lifetime, the earnings on which the scheme pension was based would be revalued to keep pace with the general rise in earnings up to pension age (65 for men and 60 for women). The broad effect of the scheme would thus be to provide a pension of about 42½% of final pay to a person on average earnings and about 37% to a person on 1½ times average earnings.[112]

The average earnings would be based on the insured person's working lifetime being the period from the beginning of the tax year containing the 19th birthday (or if later the date the scheme commenced) to age 65 (men) or 60 (women).

For the self-employed, it was considered not practicable, at least initially, to have earnings related contributions so they would contribute on the basis of a flat rate contribution (about £1.50 a week at April 1969 levels) for a pension at the level for employees earning half the average earnings.

Rights to the full new pensions would be phased in using a pro rata basis between the current scheme and the new scheme with people already on pension when the scheme started retaining their current pension. There would also be a biennial review of all pensions in payment (i.e. awarded pre or post the new scheme starting) to compensate for price rises since the last review.[113]

A fundamental feature of the Crossman scheme was the proposed partnership with occupational schemes, achieved by allowing employers with an occupational scheme to contract out their employees from part of the state scheme. Specifically, partial contracting out was to entitle employers and their employees to an abatement in the level of their contributions to the state scheme equal to 1.3% of earnings up to the scheme ceiling. In return for this, the employer would have to replace under its occupational scheme the resulting reduction in pension entitlement under the state scheme, amounting to 1% in the case of men and 0.55% in the case of women of earnings up to the ceiling. Although there was at the time much argument between the government and occupational pensions interests about the abatement terms, as they were called, it is quite probable that they would eventually have come to receive a fairly wide measure of acceptance.[114]

## 1970 general election

The economy began to recover in the summer of 1969 and in September this was reflected in a significant improvement in the trade figures.[115] In November 1969 the flat rate pension was uprated from £4.50 per week to £5.00 per week, a rise of 11.1%.[116] In January 1970 the value of the pound reached its highest point for two years when the balance of payments for 1969 disclosed a surplus of £387 million.[117] In the April 1970 budget the government introduced a package of tax concessions which, according to the Chancellor Roy Jenkins, benefited 18½ million people, two million of whom were completely relieved of the liability to pay income tax. The earnings limit for pensioners was raised.[118]

In 1970 the government enacted two pieces of tax legislation with pension provisions. The first of these was the Income and Corporations Taxes Act 1970, a consolidating Act which restated the existing law on the tax treatment of occupational pension schemes, and included all amendments of detail since 1953. The second was the Finance Act 1970, which introduced new rules for taxing occupational schemes. The effects of these rules were to liberalise, rationalise and simplify tax law relating to occupational schemes. The 'new code' of tax approval for occupational pension schemes permitted schemes to provide a tax-free lump sum at retirement equal to 1½ times final remuneration after 20 years service.[119]

The local government election results in May were very encouraging for Labour, registering a net gain of more than 400 Labour seats in England and Wales. The opinion polls revealed a groundswell of support for the Labour government and, because of the possibility that imminent price rises could dissipate this support many in the party favoured an early election. Polling day was fixed for 18 June.[120]

Although the opinion polls remained virtually unanimous right up to polling day in predicting a Labour victory, the result of the election was one of the most dramatic and unexpected electoral turnarounds of the century [121] with the Conservatives winning 46% of the total vote compared with 43% won by Labour. The Conservatives overall parliamentary majority was 30 seats[122] with Heath becoming Prime Minister. As a result, the National Superannuation and Social Insurance Bill 1970, which would have formed the legislative basis of the new state pension scheme (the Crossman scheme), was withdrawn from Parliament.

## CHAPTER SEVEN

# Conservative government 1970–74

## A change of direction in social and economic policy

In opposition the Conservatives had been developing new and relatively radical social and economic policies. At a subsequently well publicised meeting at the Selsdon Park Hotel on the outskirts of Croydon early in 1970, the Conservative Shadow Cabinet met to formulate policy for the next Conservative government. The new policies entailed a change from direct to indirect taxation in order to bring down the higher rates of income tax and a new Industrial Relations Bill, based on the principles embodied in the party's pamphlet *Fair Deal at Work*. In social services there would be a shift to greater selectivity in benefit provision with a view to concentrating resources more effectively on those in need.[1] During these policy discussions there was an overall emphasis on creating a freer market economy and a commitment, wherever practicable, to privatization. Incomes policy would be abandoned.

In a speech to the Commons introducing the new social and economic policies in October 1970, Anthony Barber, the new Chancellor of the Exchequer following the sudden death of Macleod, declared:

> We intend to adopt a more selective approach to the social services ... to confine the scope of free or subsidised provision more closely to what is necessary on social grounds.[2]

Among Barber's measures were higher charges for dentistry, spectacles, prescriptions and school meals together with the abolition of cheap welfare milk and free school milk for children between 8 and 11 years. In addition Keith Joseph at the Department of Health and Social Security removed the payment of state sickness benefit for the first three days of sickness absence.[3]

Joseph became embroiled in a controversy over a breach of the 1970 election manifesto, which contained a commitment to increase universal family allowances and claw back the benefit from those on higher incomes by decreasing tax allowances. Instead of increasing family allowances, Joseph introduced a new means tested benefit for low income families called the Family Income Supplement (FIS).[4] FIS was on the statute book by the end of the year and was seen as an expression of the Conservatives' preference for selective over universal benefit provision. It reflected the principle enunciated in Macleod and Powell's 1952 pamphlet *Social Services: Needs and Means.*

Although the Conservative government's priority in developing its new social policies was to find ways to introduce greater selectivity in the provision of benefits and other social services, the other initial reforms entailed extending some universal benefits. Social insurance pensions, at no great cost, were granted as of right to the relatively small group of pensioners aged over eighty who previously had been ineligible for the Beveridge flat rate pension. Also, at modest cost, the qualifying age for widows' pensions was reduced.[5] A more significant reform perhaps was the introduction under the NI (Old Person's and Widow's Pensions and Attendance Allowance) Act 1970 of an entirely new benefit, the Attendance Allowance, from December 1971. This benefit was payable in respect of disabled persons who were cared for at home by relatives and who needed 'frequent attention throughout the day and prolonged and repeated attention during the night'.[6] Like the previous Labour government, the new Conservative government increased the rate of employers' NI contributions to pay for improvements in benefits.[7]

In his account of the Heath government's attitude to pensions policy, Glennerster relates how it was worried by the Crossman scheme the Labour Party had nearly got on to the statute book.[8] The Crossman scheme would have created an intolerable burden on the Exchequer just at a time when the Conservatives wanted to reduce taxation. Moreover, it could have led to the accumulation of large funds from workers' contributions which would have been available to the government for investment in companies in the private sector of the economy. Furthermore the Crossman scheme, by providing better pensions (i.e. protected fully against inflation) than generally available under occupational schemes, might have threatened the viability of the latter which were themselves a valuable source of capital for industrial and commercial companies.[9]

The government's policy was quite unequivocally that occupational pension schemes provided by employers should become the principal source of retirement income for most people.[10] The Conservatives' 1970 election manifesto stated that 'everyone should have the opportunity of earning a pension related to their earnings. But ... for the great majority of people, this can and should be achieved through the improvement and expansion of occupational schemes'.[11]

In addition when describing the new pensions strategy, the manifesto had included an unexpected commitment: Our proposals will be fair to those who are now old, and also fair to those now working. The Conservatives' strategy would, unlike Labour's National Superannuation, do something for the current generation of pensioners. The manifesto said:

> Under Labour's scheme [pensioners' and workers'] pension prospects would depend upon the willingness of future generations to pay an ever increasing pensions bill through mounting taxation. Under our proposal, a growing part of the future cost of pensions will be met through genuine savings.[12]

As Hill has observed, if the statement represented a commitment to substantial increases in the pensions of current pensioners and the introduction of a funded state scheme for financing part of the pensions of current workers, it implied the imposition of significant increases in both income tax and NI contributions.[13]

The strategy could only be achieved if employers not providing occupational schemes capable of meeting this aspiration could be encouraged or required to do so. The government's solution was to propose the introduction of a reserve earnings related state scheme from which a member of an occupational scheme, which was recognised as meeting certain prescribed minimum standards, could be contracted out, or, more precisely, the member would not be enrolled in the reserve scheme.[14] These proposals, after Cabinet discussions and consultations with the occupational pensions interests (and after modifying an important point of principle that the benefits of the state reserve scheme would not after all be earnings related) were embodied in the 1971 White Paper *Strategy for Pensions*.[15]

Some historians have argued that Barber's economic strategy contained the seeds of serious recession. It is certainly true that by early 1971*, with monetary restrictions, there were signs of economic stagnation. The April 1971 budget accordingly introduced a number of reflationary measures. These included tax reductions for the year 1971–72 of £550 million, a decrease in corporation tax to 40%, an increase in child tax allowances, a cut in surtax and a general increase in NI benefits (accompanied by a rise in contributions).[16] The flat rate NI pension was uprated in September 1971 by 20% from £5 to £6 per week.[17]

However the economic benefits of the reflationary measures did not appear and throughout 1971 the economy continued to stagnate.[18] It was against this background that the White Paper was published. It indicated that the government had dropped the manifesto's commitment to pensions currently in payment. Also flat rate contributions for flat rate pensions would be abolished and earnings related contributions would be substituted as the financial basis for all NI benefits.[19] This represented the final abandonment of a fundamental Beveridge principle, his distinction between taxation and insurance contributions, namely

> Taxation is or should be related to assumed capacity to pay rather than to the value of what the payer may expect to receive, while insurance contributions are or should be related to the value of the benefits and not to capacity to pay.[20]

## Reserve Scheme

The proposal under the White Paper *Strategy for Pensions* was that every worker should have 'two pensions – a basic pension through the state scheme and an earnings related pension through a satisfactory occupational pension scheme, or failing that, a state reserve scheme.[21] Employees and employers would pay a percentage of total earnings up to a ceiling of 1½ times average earnings with both parties' percentage being lower if the employee was in a satisfactory occupational pension scheme.

The White Paper made it clear that the onus would be on each employer to decide how the second pension would be provided for each employee, namely by means of its own occupational pension scheme, which could be designed to meet any special condition relating to the employment and the terms of agreement entered into with employees, or by means of the workers' automatic enrolment in the state reserve scheme.[22]

The reserve scheme was, in Hill's view, the only serious attempt ever made in Britain to institute a funded state pensions scheme.[23] The intention was that the reserve scheme would be entirely separate from the NI Scheme and would be administered on a similar basis to an

---

* On Monday 15 February 1971, Britain converted to decimalisation. Before then, Britain's currency was in pound (£), shilling (s) and pence (d) with 12d = 1s and 20s = £1.

occupational scheme. It would be managed by an independent Reserve Pensions Board (RPB) being at arms length from government. The RPB would have responsibility for investing the assets of the Reserve Pension Fund (RPF).[24] These assets would consist of the contributions payable by employees covered by the reserve scheme and their employers together with the returns obtained from the RPF's investments. The RPB would be required to invest the assets in equities and property, but would not be allowed to purchase more than 5–10% of the equity shares of any one company. It was intended that there would be no Exchequer contributions to the RPF or any other form of government subsidy.[25]

The initial level of contributions fixed for the reserve scheme was very low. Employee contributions (in 1973 there was a significant debate in the Commons about whether such contributions should be allowable for tax purpose but concluded not[26]) were to be 1½% of total earnings up to a ceiling of 1½ times average earnings. Employer contributions were to be at the rate of 2½%. During employees' periods of unemployment, sickness or disability, industrial injuries, or maternity, no credited contributions under the reserve scheme would be awarded.

The reserve scheme pension would have two components: a pension linked to the accumulation of contributions applied to a guaranteed annuity rate based on the person's sex, plus a profit sharing element in the form of a bonus addition entirely dependent on the extent to which the RPF's investment performance exceeded what was required to support the guaranteed rate.[27] The arrangements contained the provision to provide widows pensions.[28]

Due to the lower state pension age and longer life expectancy, the women's conversion rates to pension under the reserve scheme were lower than those for men. The same principle determined the lower level of the minimum pension accrual rates for women required under the various tests for the recognition of occupational schemes.

The reserve scheme was planned to take 44 years (men) and 39 years (women) to mature, with no accelerated phasing in period like the Crossman scheme, or transfer of resources between the generations to pay full pensions to older entrants.

The Government Actuary estimated that if reserve scheme membership proved constant at around 7 million the annual income of the RPF would be around £300 million. By the end of the century (i.e. after 25 years) some £7 billion would have accrued.[29]

The reserve scheme would contribute little in the short term to reducing the number of elderly persons dependent on supplementary benefits, which was one of the most cogent reasons for extending pensions coverage in the first place, whether by means of national superannuation or through the second pension concept.[30] At the end of 1974 some 67% of those in receipt of means tested supplementary benefit were either pensioners or widow-pensioners.[31] As less than half the workforce were members of occupational pension schemes, it seemed that an underclass of elderly citizens would be perpetuated into the future.

Despite earlier criticism that contributions to Labour's superannuation scheme would have built up large funds available for backdoor nationalisation,[32] the reserve scheme was also expected to harvest large funds. Nonetheless, the government presumably felt that they were immune to such criticism because of their declared commitment to the free market economy, and more specifically because the proposed legislation would place the funds in the hands of the independent RPB and the restriction on it not to hold more than 5–10% of the equity shares of any one company. This was the safeguard against back door nationalization.

Another criticism of the proposals was that they did little to remove inequalities in the treatment of women; indeed they actually lent public sanction to them. Admittedly, the proposals envisaged an extension of the opportunity for pensions coverage to all women employees since in 1972 only 62% of men and 28% of women in employment were members of occupational pension schemes.[33] In September 1973, the government published a consultative document *Equal Opportunities for Men and Women*.[34] Its proposals had a clear application to the fields of employment and education and aimed to extend the opportunities open to women and to help remove unfair discrimination on grounds of sex. It also proposed that the legislation would set up an Equal Opportunities Commission with powers to conduct wide ranging enquiries into relative positions and opportunities for men and women.

The document, however, stated:

> As regards pensions, the government does not believe that it is necessary to require occupational pension schemes to provide benefits for women and men on the same basis; thus the Social Security Act, which has passed through Parliament in the current session, will ensure that employed women as well as employed men are covered for earnings related pensions from the start of the new arrangements in April 1975 but will not require identity of treatment. Many women will not wish to make the necessary payments. The case can best be illustrated in relation to the benefits to be provided on death. Commonly there is not the same need for a benefit to be payable to a widower on the death of his wife as to a widow on the death of her husband; and women might reasonably object to being obliged to contribute towards widowers' benefits on the same footing as men contribute towards widowhood cover.[35]

The evidence showed that the problem of poverty in old age was much greater for women than men. Due to her earlier retirement and longer life expectancy, a woman's retirement period would normally represent a greater proportion of her total life span than that of a man. It was estimated that in 1971 women accounted for 74% of the total number of retired persons in receipt of means tested supplementary benefits.[36] The earlier retirement age for women was a major obstacle to removing discrimination between men and women in pension arrangements and the only solution, it seemed, at least for future generations, would be to bring pension ages for men and women into line. There was no sound medical, social or economic reason why women should retire earlier than men.

A further defect of the proposals was the absence of any provision for death benefits in respect of female employees, both in relation to the reserve scheme and the recognition tests applicable to occupational pension schemes. Many commentators considered that the principal lack of provision for women in occupational pension schemes was the lack of dependants' benefits. The 1971 U.K. Census 1% sample tables, published in November 1973, went a long way to revealing the changing status of women in Britain and its effect on family life. Almost a half of all mothers, with children of school age or younger, were found to be in active employment. Furthermore, women were the principal economic supporters of one in five households.[37] The proportion of working mothers increased from 26% in 1961 to 40% in 1971. Over 50% of these working mothers were bringing up children entirely on their own. This statistic brought the ratio of working mothers with dependent children up to 37% in 1971 compared with 23% in 1961.[38]

Hannah records that there were concerns in the LOA and other pensions interests about the government proposal to abandon the Crossman scheme in favour of yet another fall-back scheme providing minimal benefits. With Crossman the pensions institutions and professionals had achieved acceptable contracting out terms and built a durable working consensus. They now feared that their strategy to create stability between the private and the public sectors in pension provision would be jeopardised in a new climate of uncertainty created by the Conservatives.[39] Some pensions professionals were particularly worried by Conservative radicals such as Keith Joseph and Margaret Thatcher.

According to Hannah, Joseph and Thatcher seemed 'contemptuous of the moderate, diplomatic liberalism of the actuaries and other professionals at the LOA preferring insurance brokers and company chairmen who wanted … a harder line in promoting … occupational pensions and blocking the expansion of the state scheme'.[40]

The scepticism of many pension professionals about the adequacy of the money purchase reserve scheme was linked to the relatively widespread aspiration of workers for earnings related pensions. The reserve scheme would take 40 years to mature and the only earnings related element, in any true sense, was the contributions on whose money purchase value benefits depended. They questioned how far the reserve scheme could satisfy aspirations for guaranteed earnings related pensions capable of being delivered in the shorter term.[41]

## Recession and the reversal of economic policy

In 1972, the year following the publication of the White Paper, a reversal of the government's economic policy was brought about by a series of severe difficulties; namely rising inflation, a deteriorating balance of payments and a resulting sterling crisis. The average yearly increase in retail prices had been 5.9% between 1968 and 1970 and then 8.6% in the next three years.[42] This accelerating inflation had multiple causes, most prominent being the substantial rise in labour costs resulting from large increases in negotiated wage rates after the national incomes policy was abandoned. These wage rate increases occurred during a period of low increase in productivity.[43]

The weakened economic competitiveness due to inflation and the devaluation of the US dollar in 1971 were the main reasons for the serious deterioration in the balance of payments. The balance declined from a surplus of around £300 million in 1971 to a deficit of nearly £700 million in 1972. In June 1972 a sterling crisis erupted. The value of the pound fell steeply because of a large outflow of funds partly precipitated by the deteriorating trade balance. For the first time since the 1930s the pound was allowed to float on the foreign exchange markets, although the government hastened to inform the European Economic Community (EEC) that it hoped to revert to a fixed parity before Britain's admission to membership of the EEC on 1 January 1973.[44]

Against a background of increasing labour disputes and worsening relations between the government and the trades unions because of the Industrial Relations Act, the government tried to establish a tripartite agreement with the CBI and the TUC in order to bring inflation under control.[45] When this failed in November 1972, the government's earlier policy on inflation was reversed and a statutory Prices and Pay Standstill was introduced. This measure, which virtually represented a 'last ditch' attempt to control spiralling wages, was to last for 90 days with the possibility of an extension for a further 60 days. It effectively froze the prices of most goods and services – other than imports – as well as rents, dividends and negotiated wages and salaries. The prospect of the standstill during late 1972, however, actually had the effect of stimulating further increases in prices and wages.[46]

The falling value of the flat rate NI pension in circumstances of high inflation, which caused serious difficulties for pensioners, set the pattern for annual benefit upratings which have continued to the present day and since 1974 have been enshrined in statute. Between 1961 and 1971, the uprating had been on a biennial basis and this was a policy which, until 1972, governments expected to continue.[47] In October 1972 the basic pension was increased by 12.5% from £6 per week to £6.75 per week.[48] Also in December 1972 the temporary expedient of a Christmas bonus of £10 was introduced to provide some compensation for the falling value of the pension. Compared with a weekly pension of £6.75 this was a quite significant cash sum. The bonus of £10 was again awarded in 1973 and 1974 but for the next two years was not. Thereafter to date it has been awarded each year with the bonus each time being £10.

The UK economy continued to weaken throughout 1973. Early in the year, as the first 90 day period of wage restraint ended, two new agencies, a Price Commission and a Pay Board, were established. Stage Two of the counter inflation policy came into operation at the end of March and lasted until autumn. The gas workers initiated a campaign of overtime bans and strikes in pursuit of wage claims in excess of Stage Two limits. This resulted in reductions of gas pressure in nearly four million homes and in the closure of more than 600 industrial plants.[49]

In June 1973 a serious dispute between the government and the Dockworkers severely tested the Industrial Relations Act and led to a strike by 30,000 dockers. A dispute with the miners resulted in an overtime ban and the railway men introduced a work to rule policy which seriously disrupted the operation of the railways.[50] In October, just when the government was announcing the details of Stage Three of its counter-inflation policy, the Yom Kippur War between Israel and the Arabs broke out. The Organisation of Petroleum Exporting Countries (OPEC) met in Vienna to discuss the serious problems in the supply of oil which arose in the aftermath of the war. The Arab oil producers decided on a complete oil embargo for some countries and a restriction of supplies to most of the others, including Britain which depended on foreign oil for about 50% of its energy.[51] Simultaneously Arab oil producers introduced a fourfold increase in the price of oil which has been referred to as 'the most dramatic and economically damaging global price rise in history'.[52]

For Britain this precipitated a dangerous economic and political crisis. The dependence on oil had been steadily growing throughout the previous decade, whereas reliance on coal, a source of energy produced at home, had correspondingly reduced. The sudden increase in the cost of Britain's oil imports to four times its former amount had disastrous consequences for an already deteriorating balance of payments.[53]

Despite the worsening economic situation, in October 1973 the government unexpectedly announced an immediate increase in the flat rate NI pension of 14.8% taking it from £6.75 to £7.75 per week. This 14.8% uprating was greater than the Retail Prices Index increase of 9.9%.[54] Perhaps this can be seen as a reflection, at least in part, of Joseph's real, if rarely recognised, commitment to improving social protection for the most economically vulnerable groups in society

In November 1973 the miners' union introduced a ban on overtime in support of a pay claim disallowed by Stage Three. They had also disputed for some time the policy of mine closures supported by both Labour and the Conservatives. The fuel shortage was aggravated by a ban on out of hours working by electricity power engineers and worsened after a ban on overtime by one of the railway unions which disrupted the supply of coal to power stations.

On 13 November the government declared a national state of emergency and restricted heating by electricity, other than in homes and certain other places. From 1 January 1974 the government limited the supply of electricity to industry by allowing supplies on only three days per week, effectively creating a three day working week in all industrial plants. A heating limit was imposed on commercial premises and television was required to close down at 10.30 pm.[55]

The Chancellor announced a £1.2 billion reduction in public expenditure, including reductions in health and social security expenditure of £111 milllion.[56] Nevertheless, in this troubled year the Social Security Act 1973, embodying the state reserve pension scheme, became law.

This Act represented a watershed in social policy (foreshadowed by the Crossman scheme). For the first time social objectives took precedence over purely fiscal considerations. The Act, due to come into force in April 1975, provided the legislative basis of the government's long term pension proposals[57] for a second pension for everybody, whether from an occupational scheme recognised by the new Occupational Pensions Board established by the Act or from the reserve scheme.

However, in 1973 Mrs Barbara Castle, the Labour opposition spokeswoman on social services, announced her party's intention to repeal the Act with regard to the reserve scheme when Labour was returned to office. 'We shall bring back the Crossman scheme,' she said: a significant statement at the time because of the serious debate within the party's social policy subcommittee on the form that a future state pension scheme should take. Some subcommittee members objected to the Crossman proposals on the grounds that they were not 'socialist' and that their earnings related benefits would perpetuate the inequalities and injustices of the present wage system. They argued that a greater measure of social justice could be achieved by retaining the existing social security structure, perhaps with modified contributions and increasing the flat rate retirement pension from around 20% of average earnings (at which it had more or less remained since the days of Beveridge) to 40%.

## Other strategies pursued

Because of constraints on social security expenditure, Joseph had to settle for less resources so prioritising his budget. He decided to allocate larger increases to those in receipt of long term NI benefits i.e. pensioners and persons receiving invalidity benefit, than to those in receipt of short term benefits such as the sick, short-term disabled and unemployed. This decision was made on the grounds that long term benefit recipients, because they were unable to participate in the labour market and hence in the rising living standards resulting from rising incomes, were in greater need than those on short term benefits. The latter supposedly were more likely to have some savings and presumably could defer some necessary personal expenditures until they resumed employment.[58]

The creation of a distinction between long term and short term insurance benefits, which has been consolidated by the legislation of successive governments into a permanent feature of the NI Scheme, overturned yet another Beveridge principle, namely unemployment benefit, long or short term disability benefit and basic retirement pension should be at the same rate.[59]

In addition the government's strategy of increasing selectivity in welfare provision in order to concentrate resources more effectively on those in greatest need had by 1973 led to a plethora of new means tests.[60] The family income supplement, guaranteeing to the low paid a benefit equal to half the difference between their gross pay and the level of supplementary benefit, created a noticeable poverty trap in which the take-home pay (wages and FIS combined) of low paid workers could fall as a consequence of a pay increase.[61]

This intractable problem of the poverty trap was aggravated by other means tested measures, introduced by the government to counteract child poverty and the effects of inflation. These were the national mandatory rent rebates scheme for public housing tenants and the rent allowances scheme for private tenants. The simultaneous introduction of these two policies in 1972 meant that the government was advancing two new family means tests at the same time[62] which would ensnare future generations in the poverty trap.[63]

In a debate on the 1972 Housing Finance Bill, which introduced these measures, the government was criticised from both sides of the house for developing other means tests without considering how they would interact with the already existing tests of need.[64] According to a pamphlet of the Child Poverty Action Group (CPAG) the Conservatives had institutionalised the poverty trap.[65]

The government had intended to eradicate such anomalies as the unemployment trap (i.e. where people are marginally worse off for each additional £1 of earnings as a consequence of gaining employment) and the poverty trap by rationalising the tax and benefit systems through a scheme of tax credits.[66] This scheme was intended to replace income tax allowances with a system of weekly credits which would be offset against tax due on earnings or benefits. In cases where the weekly credit exceeded the liability for tax on the earnings or the benefit, the excess would be added (as a supplementary payment) to the earnings, or the benefit.[67]

The scheme of tax credits did not apply to supplementary benefit recipients, but, as Joseph explained to the Conservative Party conference in October 1973, it would provide automatic, not means tested, weekly help to millions of those single or married with children or without children, in work or retired who are now poor or hard pressed.[68]

The proposed tax credit scheme attracted substantial criticism.[69] If the credits were to be set at a high enough level to ensure that no one would be worse off, i.e. those already gaining from family allowances and child tax allowances, it would prove a heavy financial burden on the Exchequer costing about £1.3 billion to implement.[70] If the credits were to be introduced at a lower level, in line with expenditure, it would leave many worse off financially and moreover would entail extensive administrative reform with only small gains for the poor.[71] The tax credit proposal had to be ultimately abandoned as administratively and financially impractical.[72]

Looking at the government's record between 1970 and 1974, once the initial cuts in public expenditure had been made, social policy expenditure increased very considerably thereafter.[73]

# CHAPTER EIGHT
# Labour governments 1974–79

## February 1974 general election

On 21 January 1974 the Conservative government offered the unions two alternatives to the three day industrial working week. They could have either a four-day working week or a five day working week operated on the basis of 80% of the energy supplies required for a normal five day week.[1] This had an unintended effect. Two days later the miners' union, possibly concerned that their industrial action was losing some of its impact on production, decided to ballot their members on extending the action to an all out strike. On the basis of an 80% vote in favour, the miners announced they would strike starting on 9 February.[2] Against the background of a national state of emergency and a three day industrial week, Heath felt that his government, less than four years old, needed electoral support for his counter-inflation policy with the consequence that a general election was called for 28 February.[3]

Heath's government viewed industrial action and union opposition to its counter-inflation policy as a challenge to the will of Parliament and a democratically elected government.[4] The Conservatives' election manifesto *Firm Action for a Fair Britain* undertook to remove social security benefits from strikers and their families as these benefits, representing a subsidy from the taxpayer, enabled union funds to remain undisturbed.[5] Changes in social policy would aim at creating fairness and balance in the distribution of available resources to those in need. Some of the provisions of the Industrial Relations Act would be liberalised to increase the opportunity for conciliation as opposed to legal action.[6]

Labour's election manifesto undertook to create a fundamental and irreversible shift in the balance of power and wealth in favour of working people and their families.[7] This would be achieved by measures such as a wealth tax (which was never enacted)[8], progressive taxation, an extension of public ownership and increased social spending.

The current economic indicators did not improve the Conservatives' case for re-election. Two weeks before polling day the Retail Prices Index revealed an increase in food prices of 20% during the previous 12 months. Although the unemployment figures, in the wake of the three-day week, were not as damaging as had been expected, the largest monthly trade deficit ever recorded was announced three days before the election. The size of this deficit, it was said, would have been deeply serious even had there been no rise in the price of oil.[9]

On the basis of a total poll of 78.8% of the electorate, the Conservatives received 37.9% of the vote and won 297 seats. Labour, despite only obtaining 37.1% of the vote, nevertheless won 301 seats. As an outcome of the election, no party had an overall parliamentary majority. This had not happened since 1929.[10] The Conservatives, as a consequence of their Northern Ireland policies, could no longer rely on support from the Ulster Unionist members[11] and so the balance of power in the new Parliament lay decisively with the smaller parties. The outcome of the February 1974 election seemed to foreshadow a short Parliament.

During the following weekend, Heath made a tentative bid to retain power, exploring the possibility of securing a working arrangement with the 14 Liberal members. The offer of such an arrangement was eventually declined by Jeremy Thorpe, the Liberal Leader.[12] On Monday 4 March Wilson again became Prime Minister.

During the election campaign a new social and economic compact was announced between the Labour Party and the TUC. The Social Contract was intended to replace the failed experiments by both Labour and Conservative governments in incomes policy. The central principle of the Social Contract was that in return for enhancement of the 'social wage', through increased social spending and progressive taxation, the unions would co-operate in voluntary pay restraint, entailing a yearly interval between wage settlements. In addition, the Social Contract undertook to introduce food subsidies and statutory rent controls, and to repeal the Industrial Relations Act.[13]

Wilson's third administration was historically significant for a number of reasons not least that for the first time two Cabinet members were women; Barbara Castle appointed Secretary of State for Health and Social Security and Shirley Williams appointed to the new post of Secretary of State for Prices and Consumer Protection.[14]

## Economic and social security

The Labour government's first budget on 24 March introduced increases in taxation of the order of £1.5 billion. The standard rate of income tax was increased by 3p in the pound to 33p and the thresholds, at which higher rates of income tax were payable, were lowered. Corporation tax was increased to 52% and flat rate NI contributions at higher rates were set for employers in order to provide higher social security benefits. Together with food subsidies, the principal object of the planned increase in social expenditure was the provision of higher retirement pensions.[15]

The Social Contract's terms, by their nature, entailed progress in the development of social policy. To counter disillusionment over the absence of progress in social policy, prompt action was required to resolve the seemingly intractable problems of state pension provision and child benefit policy. To address these problems, Castle, an able left-inclined Minister with a strong commitment to social service, took over the Department of Health and Social Security.[16]

As a first step, in July 1974 the flat rate NI pension was increased by 29% from £7.75 to £10 per week being 24% of average earnings,[17] consistent with Labour's commitment in the Social Contract to the trade unions. Thane recounts that the TUC, urged on especially by Jack Jones (Transport & General Workers Union General Secretary), had argued for the single person's pension to be £10 per week.[18] In line with Labour's manifesto promise, the annual review of social security benefits, both long and short term, became law.[19] Further, at each annual review, pensions and other long term benefits would now be uprated in line with earnings or prices whichever was greater. Maintaining Joseph's break with the Beveridge principle of parity between short and long term benefits, however, the legislation only uprated short term benefits in line with price rises.[20] The legislation to increase benefits, which went through all its stages in the Commons on 10 April,[21] ensured for the foreseeable future that pensioners would share in rising national income.

The 29% increase given to the flat rate NI pension was also given to the means tested supplementary benefit. Introducing the enabling legislation in the Commons, Castle said:

> There are, broadly speaking, two points of reference in our social policy. First there is the relief of poverty and its eventual abolition. Secondly, there is the aim to roll back the carpet of means testing which has now settled over social policies and which has such disincentive and humiliating effects.[22]

Having introduced the large increase in social security benefits, Castle had to consider whether to modify or repeal the Social Security Act 1973 due to come into force in April 1975. To reduce pensioners' dependence on means tested benefits, she told the Commons, there were longer term plans which would be published in a white paper before long.[23]

Bryan Ellis, a Whitehall 'insider' who contributed to designing the pension proposals, revealed that Brian O'Malley, Castle's Minister of State for Social Security, and Edmund Dell, at the Treasury, advised her against any short term adjustments to the reserve scheme. They both pointed out that adjustments would not create second pensions of sufficient adequacy to remove reliance on means tested benefits on any significant scale. Tinkering with her predecessors' scheme would only serve to delay the planning of a better and more permanent alternative.[24]

For this reason Castle announced on 7 May that the reserve scheme provisions of the 1973 Act and the accompanying contracting out requirements would not be implemented in 1975. Those measures, however, which introduced earnings related NI contributions for the provision of the basic flat rate pension, the preservation of occupational pension rights and the establishment of the Occupational Pensions Board would be implemented.[25]

The government also decided on administrative and financial grounds against implementing the Conservatives' tax credits scheme which was designed to augment without means testing the earnings or benefits of workers and pensioners on low incomes.

The occupational pensions interests, employers and pensions professionals were in general initially dismayed at the announcement of yet another major change in pensions policy, the third in six years. The Conservatives argued that the government had no logical case for abandoning the reserve scheme provisions of the Social Security Act 1973. On 1 July they tabled a censure motion that the government's action in declining to accept the legislation was likely to deprive many people of an early opportunity to secure a second pension.[26]

In the censure motion debate, Castle set out her case:

> There must be four main aims of a pensions policy. The first must be to lift everyone in retirement off supplementary benefit. The second aim must be to give women full equality. The third aim must be to make adequate provision for widowhood. The fourth should be to safeguard the value of pensions against the erosion that inflation can bring.[27]

None of these aims, she argued, would have been achieved by the reserve scheme or by the recognition conditions for occupational pension schemes. Moreover, it would not be possible to amend the arrangements to provide for the social policy aims she specified.[28]

After the debate, the Conservatives were joined by the Liberals in the division lobby and, with 280 votes cast for the censure motion and 282 against, the government just avoided censure.[29] As Ellis recounts, the debate on the censure motion had the effect of firmly putting the onus on the government to develop and publish its own pension proposals with the minimum of delay. Having set aside its predecessor's legislation for pension and tax reform, it could not contemplate entering an election campaign without first setting out its alternative proposals.[30]

In his own contribution to the debate, O'Malley referred to taking note of the best in occupational pension provision and seeing how much can be provided for others not fortunate enough to have an occupational pension.[31] According to Ellis, the new thinking on pensions was already far advanced and O'Malley's reference to matching the best in occupational pension provision suggested the direction in which such thinking was developing. Abel-Smith, one of the architects of National Superannuation, was engaged with O'Malley in designing Labour's new pension proposals which in less than two months would be published in a white paper.[32]

As a result of the March budget many business organisations were encountering liquidity problems. This situation, together with warnings of an impending serious recession due to the government's taxation policies, led Dennis Healey, the Chancellor, to introduce a second budget on 22 July. This brought into effect a number of reflationary measures.[33]

Despite the political and economic problems and the July defection to the Liberals of Christopher Mayhew, a former Labour Minister, increasing the parliamentary strength of the Liberals to 15 seats,[34] Wilson's government succeeded in surviving as a policy making minority administration. This is borne out by the significant number of legislative measures and policy statements promulgated in the summer of the short termed Parliament.[35] The Labour government continued to lead in the polls, but economic events suggested that it would not be prudent to delay seeking a new electoral mandate.

Economic indicators had not been favourable during the six months of the Parliament. Prices increased by 8% and wages by 16%.[36] The miners' strike was quickly settled on terms acceptable to the strikers. The Heath government's policy of threshold pay increases had been allowed to continue until its scheduled expiry in October. This permitted pay to rise automatically in line with cost of living increases and contributed to the rapid rise in inflation.[37] By 20 September, the Financial Times Index of Ordinary Shares had fallen from 313 points to 202 with the fall in the real value of shares between 1972 and 1974 being more severe than the collapse of share values in the stock market crash of 1929.[38]

Wilson decided to call an autumn election, and dissolved Parliament on 20 September 1974. This brought to an end the shortest parliament – a mere 184 days – since the dissolution of the third Whig parliament at Oxford in 1681.[39]

# Better pensions

Just before its dissolution, Castle presented to Parliament her White Paper *Better Pensions* outlining her pension proposals including the state earnings related pension scheme (SERPS). In its foreword she wrote:

> The proposals set out in this White Paper will fulfil the government's pledge to bring to an end the massive dependence on means tested supplementary benefit which is the sad hallmark of old age today. The new scheme will provide better pensions in retirement, widowhood and chronic ill-health. It will bring security at the end of working life to the many millions who at present lack the advantages and cover of a good occupational scheme.[40]

The essential features of the proposals – the new reform of NI – were that in return for wholly earnings related contributions, the scheme would provide earnings related pensions fully protected against inflation at all times.[41]

The new state earnings related pension scheme (SERPS) would operate in partnership with well-founded occupational schemes[42] and the terms for contracting out would be consistent with the principle that members of contracted out occupational schemes would receive pensions which were at least as good as those of full members of the state scheme.[43]

The provisions would ensure that women received full equality of treatment with men in pensions and other benefits, and adequate provision would be made for widowhood, in most cases through transfer to a deceased member's widow or widower of 100% of the member's pension entitlement.[44] The new scheme would thus meet the four aims of pension policy identified by Castle in her Commons speech on the censure motion, namely ending reliance on means testing, treating men and women equally, adequate provision for widowhood and protection against inflation. The White Paper also set out proposals for the introduction of a new benefit, i.e. earnings related invalidity benefit, which had been requested for some time by disability groups.[45]

The White Paper's proposals were embodied in 91 paragraphs, together with an Appendix containing a Memorandum *Finances of the Proposals* by Edward Johnston, the Government Actuary. Given the comprehensive and complex nature of the proposals, not least the conditions for contracting out occupational pension schemes and the economic and financial implications of the proposed reform, the White Paper represented a not inconsiderable intellectual achievement by Castle and O'Malley and their civil service team, particularly in view of the short time available for its preparation.

Although the White Paper did not contain any specific undertaking to provide an immediate substantial increase in retirement income for existing pensioners, it pointed out that raising the flat rate NI pension (by 29% to £10 per week) only nine months after the previous increase in October 1973 'was a first step towards the new pension scheme and, as such, forms part of the government's developing policy on pensions'. This was an undertaking that the new pension rates 'would maintain their relationship with the general level of earnings'.[46] Also the White Paper reaffirmed that NI pensioners had a guarantee that they would share in economic growth now that the government had undertaken a statutory obligation to uprate the basic retirement pension in line with earnings.[47] As Ellis pointed out, although the increase in the pension to £10 per week did nothing to reduce the dependence of existing pensioners, a press release accompanying the White Paper quoted Castle as saying the government would consider how, on the introduction of the new scheme and in the light of the economic situation, existing pensioners might be credited with additional pension rights.[48]

The White Paper stated that future pensioners would qualify for higher earnings related pensions under SERPS which would be phased in over 20 years. This transitional period was the same as adopted for the Crossman scheme but much quicker than that under the reserve scheme.[49]

For a contributor with a complete record of NI contributions, their pension at 65 for men and 60 for women would consist of two components: the basic pension plus the additional pension calculated as follows:

1. The basic weekly pension would represent £1 for every £1 of average weekly earnings up to a 'base level' (equal to the flat rate pension for a single person – £10 per week in 1974 terms). At this level of earnings, the basic pension would represent a 100% income replacement rate.

2. The additional pension would accrue at a rate of 1¼% of the best 20 years of revalued yearly earnings between the base level and a ceiling (equal to seven times the base level – £70 per week in 1974 terms). If the contributor was over age 45 for a man and 40 for a woman at the start of the new scheme the accrual rate would apply to the sum of the revalued yearly earnings between the base and ceiling levels. As a consequence a contributor reaching state pension age after 20 years would receive the full additional pension.[50] This additional pension became known as the state earnings related pension (SERP).

All pension rights built up and payable under the new scheme would have their value protected against inflation. The value of earnings related pension rights would be maintained during working life by revaluing up to state pension age each yearly earnings in line with the general growth in earnings. Each year following the start of payment, the basic pension would be revalued in line with the higher of the increase in the Retail Prices Index and the increase in the general level of earnings, and the additional pension would be revalued in line with the increase in the Retail Prices Index.[51]

Men and women with the same contribution record would have the same pensions, despite the differences in state pension age, and pension rights would be protected during periods spent at home looking after children or the old or sick.[52]

Widowed mothers and the majority of other widows would, subject to a specified maximum, inherit the whole of the earnings related pension accrued by their husbands.[53] A retired widow would accrue a pension based on her own earnings as well as inheriting a pension based on her husband's earnings again subject to a maximum.[54] A corresponding right would apply in the case of a man who had become a widower in retirement.[55] The discriminatory lower rate of sickness or unemployment benefit which applied to married women would be abolished by the proposed legislation.[56] The contribution option which enabled married women and some widows who worked to choose to pay the married women's reduced rate of contribution would be abolished with the existing contributors on this rate having the right to retain the option whilst remaining in employment.[57]

In addition the White Paper indicated that the flat rate invalidity pension (a long term benefit payable after 28 weeks of incapacity) would be replaced by a new invalidity pension comprising a basic pension and an additional pension, calculated in the same way as the retirement pension.[58]

## Occupational pension schemes

Previous governments, recognising the social and economic value of occupational pensions, nevertheless tried to establish arrangements under which such schemes would share with the state the responsibility for making provision for old age. This even extended to schemes which provided pension rights which accrued in fixed money terms, disregarding changes in the value of money. Such schemes clearly cannot easily be accommodated within a state pension framework which evaluates the adequacy of pension rights in terms of living standards prevailing when pensions are being paid.[59] The White Paper described these successive attempts at accommodation.

- The National Insurance Act 1959 provided for part of the state scheme to operate in fixed money terms to enable modest occupational schemes to contract out.
- The National Superannuation and Social Insurance Bill 1969 provided for partial contracting out, or 'abatement', for occupational schemes providing a pension in fixed money terms which would be deducted from a state pension fully protected against inflation.
- The Social Security Act 1973 provided an accommodation not dissimilar in principle to the National Insurance Act 1959 with the effect that the limitations of modest occupational schemes were to be imposed on the reserve scheme.[60]

If a significant proportion of occupational schemes had not developed beyond this restricted level of provision, it would have been appropriate to abandon the attempt to devise a satisfactory basis for contracting out and to encourage employers to supplement their employees' state pensions through private provision. Such a policy, which does not aim at integration of state and occupational pensions, is the common pattern of pension provision in continental European countries. It would have the merit of simplicity and would avoid the risk that improvements in the state scheme might have to be ruled out because they could not be matched by the private sector.[61]

Between 1963 and 1971, however, an increasing proportion of occupational schemes had adopted a final salary basis for calculating their members' pensions, increasing from one in eight to nearly one in two. Since 1971, the proportion of members covered by such schemes had increased to over 60% (almost 100% in the case of members of public sector schemes).[62] Eight million people were members of final salary schemes in 1971, and of these more than 7½ million were accruing pension rights calculated at the rate of 1¼% of salary for each year, with the prospect of a pension of at least half pay after 40 years service with one employer.

However most of the 2½ million manual workers in occupational pension schemes were provided with a flat rate pension entitlement for each year of service, usually amounting to less than 10p a week, i.e. less than £2 per week after 20 years service.[63] Consequently the White Paper mentioned gaps and weaknesses in occupational pension provision, one of the most significant being the virtual absence, outside the public sector, of any guarantee of inflation proofing after award, even in good final salary schemes.[64]

Nevertheless the improvement in terms of quality and quantity of provision under occupational pension schemes made it possible for a new and much more effective kind of partnership in which state and occupational schemes could combine, in a simple and logical way, to provide a total pension that would be adequate and fully protected against inflation.[65]

## Contracting out

Under the proposals, it would be open to employers with employees in membership of an occupational pension scheme meeting certain conditions to contract out these employees from part of the retirement and widow's pension elements of SERPS.[66] However no contracting out of the basic pension or the invalidity pension would be possible. Employees contracted out and their employers would pay the full NI contribution rate on lower band earnings and a reduced contribution rate on upper band earnings.[67]

To be contracted out for the employees concerned, the occupational pension schemes would have to satisfy two conditions:

> A quality condition whereby the scheme has to 'provide a member's pension based on final salary, or average salary revalued in line with the growth of earnings generally', with an accrual rate of 'at least one eightieth of pensionable salary as defined by the scheme'. This accrual rate is that which applied under SERPS for men over 45 and women over 40 at the start of the new scheme.[68]

> A quantity condition whereby the scheme has to provide a member's pension which would have to be 'at least as much as the state scheme would have paid on the upper band earnings in respect of the period of contracting out, had those same earnings been used to calculate the state pension for that period.' This minimum pension is, in effect, the pension forgone in the state scheme for which the occupational scheme has taken over responsibility and is referred to as the guaranteed minimum pension (GMP). Up to state pension age the occupational pension scheme provided full revaluation on the GMP but the revaluation of the GMP after state pension age became the responsibility of the state.[69]

Similar conditions applied in relation to widows' pensions but at the 50% level. Under SERPS the widow's pension was at the rate of 100% of the contributor's pension while under the quantity test only half of the husband's guaranteed minimum pension at the time of his death was provided. Consequently the other half is automatically provided by the state scheme so the widow would receive in total at least as much as if her husband had never been contracted out.[70] Again similar protection would apply to the widow's guaranteed minimum pension as that applying to the GMP.

For a NI contributor who was contracted out, the new state scheme continued to provide the whole of the basic and additional components of the invalidity pension, the basic components of the member's retirement pension and widow's pension, the balance of the additional component of the widow's pension and the inflation proofing after state pension age or earlier death of the NI contributor.[71]

The proposals included provisions to allow in certain circumstances a contracted out contributor to contract back into SERPS by the payment of an appropriate premium.

As a result, occupational pension schemes would share the responsibility with the state for total pension provision, instead of assuming complete responsibility for a particular element taken over from it. Ellis mentions that the idea was first aired in Lyon's paper *Social Security and Occupational Pension Schemes* presented to the Faculty of Actuaries in November 1967.[72] The paper began by clarifying what had become the usual method by which an occupational pension scheme would make provision to match part of the state pension, namely any state pension which accrued in some constant relationship to the contributions paid could be abated fully by a constant percentage abatement of the contributions.[73]

Lyon went on to argue that if, however, the accrued pensions were to be revalued according to the movement of an index of prices or earnings then a different principle would be involved. In that case it would be 'impossible to see how terms of abatement could be devised which would recompense an employer for accepting the liability to immunise [against price or earnings inflation] the equivalent pensions under an occupational scheme … There seems no escape from the conclusion that abatement should be limited to the accruing pension and that the immunizing factor should be carried by the state in all circumstances'.[74]

Although, as Ellis points out, the government did not publicly endorse Lyon's conclusions, the Crossman 1969 White Paper *National Superannuation and Social Insurance* outlined an arrangement for partial contracting out.[75] The issues of contribution and pension abatement levels were referred to a consultative body on which were represented the TUC, CBI, the nationalised industries and the pensions interests. The last of these was represented by Lyon. The later November 1969 White Paper *Terms for Partial Contracting Out of the National Superannuation Scheme* summarised, in some detail, the conclusions of the different parties represented on this body.[76] The outcome was an offer from the government of partial contracting out. Social insurance replacement pensions guaranteed under occupational schemes were set in fixed money terms without an open-ended commitment by the scheme to protect pensions from the effects of inflation when they were in payment.[77]

Despite the lack of an explicit endorsement by government of Lyon's conclusions, the evidence of subsequent events suggests that they had a profound effect on public pensions policy, both in the sixties and the seventies. The White Paper *Better Pensions* stated that 'the government have thought it right not to require contracted out schemes to guarantee to provide any increase in pensions after award. Instead the state scheme will provide for the guaranteed minimum pension … to be increased in line with prices'.[78]

## Financing the new scheme

The Memorandum by the Government Actuary on financing the White Paper's proposals showed the estimated costs on different assumptions of providing the various proposed benefits for the first 30 years of the new scheme, assuming that it would commence in April 1978. In addition it contained the estimated joint contributions (by employees and their employers) in respect of employed persons participating fully in the new scheme which would be required to balance expenditure in each 5 year period from 1978 to 2008. These contribution rates varied from an initial rate in 1978–79 of 13.6% if no persons were contracted out to 15.9% if 8 million persons were contracted out. The corresponding rates for 2003 to 2008 were 17.5% and 17.9% respectively.[79] On the assumptions stated in the document, a joint contribution of 16½% of upper band earnings (i.e. earnings between the base and ceiling level) would be required in the early years in respect of those fully participating in the new scheme if 8 million employed persons were contracted out. If a joint contribution rate of 16½% were deemed to be appropriate the employee would pay 6½% and the employer 10%.[80]

As SERPS provided an accelerated rate of accrual of benefits before maturity, it followed that the average cost of providing the pension forgone in the state scheme would fall over the years and so would the contribution reduction for contracted out employees. The Memorandum indicated that preliminary calculations showed that a total contribution reduction (commonly referred to as the rebate) in respect of employees contracted out of between 6% and 7% of upper band earnings might be appropriate for the first 5 years of SERPS. Consequently a figure of 6½% was chosen for illustrative purposes with the split being 2½% for the employee and 4% for the employer.[81]

All these figures assume that the NI Fund would continue to receive a Treasury supplement of 18% of the contribution income which for this purpose would be calculated before allowing for the reductions in the rates of contribution for employers who are contracted out. This entailed a significant increase in the Treasury supplement to the NI Fund. In 1974 terms, the Treasury supplement in the first full year would be £1,045 million instead of the £865 million that would have been paid under the Social Security Amendment Bill.[82]

## Economic and social implications

The White Paper contained a brief review of the implications of its proposals for the economy and the standard of living of retirement pensioners. The government admitted that the new scheme would entail a gradually increasing transfer of income and therefore of claims on resources from the economically active section of the community to those who have retired.[83]

This transfer was reflected in the necessity for gradually increasing contribution rates, and the taxation required to meet the Exchequer's share of the cost, in financing the improved benefits. It entailed restricting employees' take-home pay and increasing prices.[84] Therefore, the main aim was to raise the standard of living of retirement pensioners, both in absolute terms and in relation to the rest of the population.[85]

The pensioners' share of total personal consumption was estimated at the time of the White Paper to be around 10%, but the new scheme's higher standards of pension provision should, over the next 40 years, have the effect of increasing this to around 13%.[86] But as the redistribution must be within the total available at the time for personal consumption,[87] there would be a corresponding fall in the working population's share of total personal consumption of around 3%. However, on the basis of any reasonable assumption as to the rate of economic growth over this period of 40 years, the reduction would represent a very small proportion of the improvement in the standard of living of workers over the same period.[88]

The discussion is very reminiscent of a theme expressed in *National Superannuation* in 1957. On the publication of the White Paper in September 1974, the proposals received a friendly reception from the Press, the CBI and TUC and the pensions interests.[89]

In view of the controversies which had so long beset both the Crossman and Joseph proposals for state pension reform, some have been perplexed that the CBI, the TUC and the pensions interests had been so willing to accept the Castle/O'Malley proposals. A characteristic of the Castle/O'Malley scheme which particularly appealed to the pensions interests was the enlightened basis offered for contracting out. The White Paper recognised that although occupational schemes, on a final salary basis, could be expected to revalue members' benefits based on past earnings and thus meet contracting out requirements, they could not generally be expected to meet the open-ended commitment entailed in revaluing pensions already in payment.[90] As Hannah points out, Castle in effect, offered the occupational pension movement state insurance against some of these risks. Accordingly most employers found that it was a feasible and worthwhile proposition to contract out.[91]

For the trades unions and the workers they represented, SERPS was undoubtedly a very beneficial piece of pension reform, not least for the strong social framework it introduced. Within this new framework a genuine partnership between state and occupational pension schemes could flourish. That part of the unionised work force who were in good occupational schemes were gratified that, as part of the reform, a Labour government accepted the need to protect occupational pension funds and their members against intolerable levels of inflation.[92] The government had signalled that it placed a high value on occupational schemes and their contribution to the economy and to workers' security in retirement. This represented not only the renewal of the government's commitment to providing financial support to occupational schemes from general taxation through concessionary tax reliefs, but also the government's concern to encourage the improvement of the quality of these schemes and enhancement of the pension rights of their members. Such an expression of support was helpful to the occupational pensions industry and the sponsors and members of occupational schemes, for many schemes were, at the time, in severe financial difficulties following the oil crisis and the collapse in the value of their investments.[93]

For workers not in good occupational schemes, and for the more than half the workforce not in pensionable employment, there was the expectation that, in addition to their flat rate basic pension, they would under SERPS commence to accrue full earnings related pensions from 1998, with pensions based on earnings during the best twenty years of work.[94] Those workers in receipt of full-time male average earnings could expect to receive from SERPS, after the maturity of the scheme, a doubling of the level of income replacement which they would have received from the flat rate basic pension.[95] Moreover, the pension rights under SERPS, together with the basic pension, were fully portable which was particularly valuable for those who changed employment.[96]

For blue collar workers and for a high proportion of working women, the accrual of the SERPS pension on the best 20 years of earnings was particularly appropriate. For, unlike white collar workers, those employed on piecework tend to attain their earnings peak when they are in the age range 30 to 40 years, so that schemes based on final earnings disadvantage them by not reflecting the most productive phase of their working lives.[97] This feature was of great benefit to women workers whose patterns of employment and earnings were subject to considerable variation because of time away from work to have children or to care for elderly or disabled relatives. Relative to earnings, women accrued pensions at the same rate as men despite their greater longevity and earlier retiring age of 60.[98]

For all these reasons, the White Paper and the resulting legislation received a welcoming response from the trades unions and indeed from most working people, especially from those constituting more than half the working population without any prospective retirement income apart from the basic state pension.

## October 1974 general election

The election took place on 10 October 1974. Against the widespread expectation that Labour would be returned to office with a comfortable majority, they won the election narrowly with an overall majority of only three seats. The campaign had been unremarkable, except perhaps for a record number of candidates from the other parties, particularly the Liberals but also the National Front. Labour had asked for a mandate from the electorate to complete the programme of reform which they had begun. Nevertheless Labour achieved a national swing in the vote of only 2.2% from the Conservatives.[99]

Labour obtained 39.2% of the votes and 319 seats compared with the Conservatives 36.7% and 277 seats (including the Speaker). The remaining 39 of the total of 635 seats in the Commons were shared among the smaller parties. Although the result was disappointing for Labour, they nevertheless obtained a majority of 43 seats over the Conservatives. The distribution of the 39 seats among the smaller parties ensured that Labour would have sufficient parliamentary strength for the conduct of practical politics.[100]

Wilson's concern at the time was that, because of his slim overall majority (one seat less than in 1964), future by-election losses and defections would make him leader – yet again – of a minority government. By the end of 1976, the Parliamentary Labour Party would have lost three seats to the Conservatives in by-elections, and by 1979 it would lose three more to the Conservatives. There would be also three Labour defections in that Parliament.[101] Nevertheless the Labour government in October 1974 proceeded with the enactment of its legislative programme which was outlined in the Queen's Speech on 19 November.[102]

The programme included a development land tax, the phasing out of private practice in the NHS, particularly pay beds, and most controversially the establishment of Scottish and Welsh representative assemblies.[103] The impending Social Security Pensions Bill, however, was to have an easier passage.

The government was facing serious economic difficulties with average earnings increasing by 25% between the fourth quarters of 1973 and 1974. As productivity growth was minimal, this entailed an increase in labour costs of 23%. Although the government continued to try to reduce inflation through the Price Code and increased subsidies, the wages policy within the social contract clearly was not working. By January 1975 more than 700,000 people were unemployed, an increase of 25% on the figure for January 1974. Although consumer spending was falling for the first time in 20 years, the current account balance of payments deficit was the highest on record.[104]

While Wilson, winner of four general elections, was grappling with the problems of the economy, Heath in January 1975 was facing a challenge to his leadership within the Conservative Party. His personal style as well as his social philosophy (his brand of Conservatism) was disliked by many Conservatives and after losing two election campaigns in a single year there was a bid to replace him. It seemed to many the right time to rediscover a basic philosophy round which the party could unite in regaining power and a new leader would be required to take this forward. After receiving fewer votes than Thatcher in the first round of the party leadership ballot on 4 February, Heath immediately stood down. With a clear overall majority on the second ballot on 10 February, Thatcher became leader of the Conservative Party.[105]

## Social Security Pensions Bill 1975

Although the Conservatives had maintained their opposition to the Castle pension proposals throughout the election, pledging that they would re-activate their reserve pension scheme if returned to office, their strategy changed after Labour had won the election with a small majority. They decided to concentrate their efforts on obtaining changes in the government's proposed new scheme to make it easier for occupational pension schemes to co-exist with it.[106]

During the period of four months prior to the presentation of the Social Security Pensions Bill 1975 to Parliament, the Conservatives obtained two important modifications to the proposed pensions legislation. The first was for the rebate, i.e. the reduction in NI contributions for contracted out contributors, to be increased from 6½ to 7% of upper band earnings with the split being 2½% for the employee and 4½% for the employer.[107]

The second was in respect of the requirement for contracted out schemes to revalue the GMP of a member who left service in line with the general increase in earnings between the date of leaving service and retirement. As an alternative, the scheme would now have the option to revalue the early leaver's GMP at limited rate revaluation (the lower of inflation and 5% per annum based on the whole period from leaving service to state pension age) together with the payment of a premium to the state to compensate for the transfer of the liability for any excess revaluation to the state.[108]

The bill was presented to Parliament in February 1975 followed by the second reading on 18 March. Castle reaffirmed the government's position on the legislation:

> Instead of whittling down the standards of pension provision to a level that private schemes can afford, we have fixed the standards at the level necessary to remove poverty in old age, widowhood and invalidity, and then provided forms of state help to private schemes to enable them to meet the targets we have laid down.[109]

Castle stressed that the proposed new state pension framework offered a unique form of partnership between the state and private schemes which had been widely welcomed.[110] Norman Fowler, who led for the opposition, reiterated the Conservatives' commitment to occupational pension provision. He said: We must ask the crucial question of what is best for the occupational schemes and continue to seek, on their behalf, for improvements within the proposed framework. Nevertheless the opposition had taken as much advice as possible from those concerned with pensions. Their advice is overwhelmingly that we should proceed on the basis of the proposals contained in the bill.[111]

As Ellis points out, a bipartisan approach was in the making.[112] Paul Dean who had been Social Security Minister in the Conservative government between 1970 and 1974 gave unequivocal support to the measure by saying that this was the third major bill on pensions in the last six years and many of us, as had emerged already from the debate, hoped it would be the third time lucky.[113]

A note of dissent, however, was sounded by Sir George Young (Conservative MP first elected in 1974) who was concerned about the future burden of cost and the effects of inflation. He said that as a generation we have the collective effrontery to insist that our children make sacrifices on our behalf, on a scale that we are not prepared to make on behalf of the elderly today.[114]

Nevertheless the bill was given its Second Reading well within its allotted parliamentary time. As Timmins has commented: The bill which was to affect the future pensions of millions was given an unopposed second reading with fewer than a dozen MPs in the chamber.[115]

When the Standing Committee proceedings began on the bill on 8 April a bipartisan approach to the draft legislation was clearly in evidence. Kenneth Clarke reaffirmed the co-operative role of the opposition in the proceedings, stating an intention to improve the bill whilst working towards an agreed structure at the end.[116]

O'Malley had day to day responsibility for guiding the bill through the Committee stage, although Castle was present at a number of sessions. There was little dissent but some disharmony, particularly on Clause 6, providing for the two tier basis of basic and additional components of the new structure.[117] David Penhaligon expressed the concern of the Liberals that the bill offered no significant improvement in basic pension provision that would raise the current generation of poorest pensioners out of their means tested dependency.[118] O'Malley assured the Committee that the bill's transitional provisions would permit the crediting to existing pensioners of some rights to the additional pension component. Nevertheless Penhaligon divided the Committee on Clause 6 although he was eventually outvoted by eight votes to one. The bill passed through the Committee stage unchanged in all essentials.[119]

The bipartisan approach of Labour and the Conservatives can partly be explained by the fact that the Castle/O'Malley Scheme combined the best of the Crossman and Joseph proposals. According to Timmins, this reconciled Labour and the Conservatives to the new plan.[120] In his view, it generated clever innovations of its own which included the new contracting out rules. This involved Labour's acceptance of the economic and social value of occupational pension schemes and therefore of the importance of the contribution of the private sector in total pension provision. O'Malley was firmly committed to this view wanting occupational pensions to be something for which trade unions went in and negotiated.[121] It was also O'Malley who had been in the background, with his considerable technical grasp of the subject of pensions, to assist Castle to carry the more controversial aspects of the proposals through the Cabinet.[122]

The Commons passed the Social Security Pensions Bill on 12 June 1975 without a vote being taken. The bill reached the Lords for its second reading on 24 June. During the debate, Lord Banks on the Liberal benches again criticised the inadequacy of the basic pension to help poorer pensioners, but declared that the scheme embodied in the bill was preferable to the Crossman and Joseph plans.[123] Lord Byers, also a Liberal peer, who for some years had been active within the occupational pensions movement, argued that the way politicians had behaved [over state pension reform] and the many years which had been wasted 'as a result of the changes which took place' were 'intolerable from the future pensioner's point of view'. He continued by saying that if we can carry through this all-party all-interest agreement to Royal Assent it will represent an historic landmark in pensions legislation, and something of which we can all feel proud.[124]

At this later stage a technical amendment to the contracting out provisions was introduced and after some amendment was accepted. This added a third option in respect of the revaluation of the GMP of an early leaver up to state pension age with a fixed rate of revaluation (initially the fixed annual rate for leavers was 8½%). After the amendment had been accepted by the Lords on 6 August the bill received Royal Assent on 7 August 1975.[125]

When the Social Security Pensions Act 1975 reached the statute book, Lord Byers' historic landmark in pensions legislation had been achieved. The all-party all-interest coalition had enabled a Labour government to introduce a state earnings related pension scheme after twenty years of trying.[126] In this way Britain finally caught up with what a (conservative) regime in West Germany had introduced twenty years earlier.[127]

On 16 March 1976, some seven months later, the unexpected resignation of Wilson was announced. When Wilson left office in April, he was succeeded as Prime Minister by James Callaghan,[128] who dismissed Castle from the government.[129] Two days earlier, O'Malley had died prematurely aged 46.[130] SERPS was largely their creation and it came into effect two years later on 6 April 1978 with no significant change. However the 'all-party all-interest' coalition was beginning to disintegrate.

## Callaghan's Labour government 1976–79

The unexpected resignation of Wilson was announced at a time of deepening economic crisis with the value of sterling falling on the foreign exchange markets. Inflation in 1975 had risen by a higher rate than in 1974, average weekly earnings increasing by 27% and prices by 24%.[131] Against this background, the flat rate pension had been increased twice in 1975; by 16%, from £10 to £11.60 per week in April and by 14.7%, to £13.30 per week in November 1975.[132]

The last years of Wilson's leadership had seen a widening rift between the Labour left and right. Callaghan emerged as leader and Prime Minister after three ballots in a strongly contested leadership election.[133] He included in his Cabinet many of the ministers who had served under Wilson and retained Healey as Chancellor. Williams was appointed Paymaster General as well as Secretary of State for Prices and Consumer Affairs. David Ennals replaced Castle as Social Services Secretary which brought to an end the ministerial career of a great pensions campaigner who Crossman described in his diary as of prime ministerial calibre but for the fact that she was a woman.[134]

Although a new agreement on pay was concluded with the TUC in May 1976, and price controls were maintained, concern over public expenditure exacerbated the weakness of sterling, and, to prevent further falls in its value, interest rates were raised to record levels in July. A dramatic run on the pound occurred in the autumn necessitating a loan from the IMF of $3,900 million.[135] Nevertheless, in November 1976 the flat rate pension was increased by 15% to £15.30 per week.[136]

Although the 1976 sterling crisis represented the lowest point of the government's problems with the economy, by early 1977 after a number of by-election losses the Labour Party no longer had a parliamentary majority and the government was faced with the prospect of parliamentary defeat on an opposition's no confidence motion. To avoid defeat Callaghan entered into a pact with the Liberals ensuring the survival of his government. According to Sked and Cook, the Lib-Lab pact represented a constitutional precedent in that it was embodied in a formal published agreement that empowered the Liberals in Parliament to veto Cabinet legislative proposals prior to their introduction in the Commons.[137] For the Liberals this held out the hope of electoral reform.

Signs of economic recovery began to appear in 1977 as the benefits of the production of North Sea Oil began to improve the balance of payments.[138] In November 1977 the flat rate pension was uprated by 14.4% to £17.50 per week.[139] For Jack Jones, the General Secretary of the TGWU, and others active in the pensioners' movement it was an advance, but it was still not enough. He recounts that, some time previously, Callaghan had said to him that British pensioners were doing all right, to which he replied: Where do you get that idea from, Jim?[140]

Although the economic recovery continued through 1978, the government was beset by political difficulties at the end of the year. In October, at the Labour Party conference, Callaghan announced that there would be no general election that year which caused surprise to both press and public. In December the government was defeated in two divisions in the Commons, but nevertheless survived a vote of confidence the next day by 300 votes to 290.[141]

In November 1978 the flat rate pension was uprated by 11.4% to £19.50 per week.[142] Pensioners' incomes were at last rising in proportion to increases in average earnings. Worryingly for some, however, the financing of this pension entailed redistribution, although on a modest scale. At its then improved level of about 25% of average earnings, the British state pension was still among the lowest in the developed world. Nevertheless the pension's link to earnings had implications for public expenditure. This was recognised by Nigel Lawson, a member of the Shadow Treasury team, who sent a private note to Geoffrey Howe, the Shadow Chancellor, arguing that the link must be broken.[143]

Callaghan's decision not to hold an election late in 1978 was widely seen as a mistake. The Liberals had withdrawn from the pact and the government was now dependent on the support of the Scottish Nationalists who wished to safeguard the impending devolution referendum.[144]

In January 1979 the government was confronted with a wave of strikes. On 3 January a nationwide lorry drivers' strike began and was soon followed by a separate strike of tanker drivers. This was accompanied by extensive secondary picketing which spilled over into disorder on the picket lines. On 22 January one and a half million workers in the public services began a 24 hour stoppage as a protest against the government's continuing attempts to hold down public sector pay. Industrial action by water workers, ambulance drivers, sewerage staff and dustmen was 'causing widespread misery in a winter that seemed unending'. An agreement with three of the public service unions outside the 5% guideline caused the government's pay policy to collapse. On 28 March 1979 the government lost a vote of confidence in the Commons by one vote (311 votes to 310). This was the first defeat of its kind sustained by a government since 1924. The dissolution of Parliament took place on 7 April and a general election was called for 3 May.[145]

## CHAPTER NINE

# Thatcher's governments 1979–90: New direction in pension policy

In the general election campaign, the central issues unsurprisingly were the management of the economy and the appropriate role of the trades unions. The Labour Party manifesto was conspicuously moderate.[1] The Conservatives, on the other hand, promised tax reductions, but did not specify any changes they would make in social policy to finance them. There were specific pledges by the Conservatives on the sale of council houses, to halt the phasing out of pay beds in NHS hospitals and to stop the conversion of secondary schools into comprehensives. There was a commitment to reduce public expenditure overall, whilst increasing spending on law and order and defence.[2]

The Callaghan government's attempt to restore its partnership with the TUC was derisively dismissed by Thatcher as a 'boneless wonder'.[3] There was, however, an awareness across the political spectrum that the principal changes to social and pensions policy would be in economies a Conservative government might introduce.[4] Such concerns, however, had to be balanced against Thatcher's personal assurance given in a broadcast during the election campaign, supported by the election addresses of Howe and Joseph, that a Conservative government would 'maintain the purchasing power of the pension'.[5] On election day, however, pensions issues hardly figured in a public consciousness disturbed by memories of acrimonious industrial disputes and the winter of discontent.

On a total poll of 76% of the electorate, the Conservatives received 43.9% of the votes, winning 339 seats. Labour polled 36.9% of the votes, and won 268 seats. The Liberals won 11 seats experiencing a material decline in their share of the vote since the two elections of 1974 (19% to 14%).[6] This must have been disappointing in view of their increased influence on government between 1977 and 1979 as a result of the Lib-Lab pact.

The Conservatives were returned to office with an overall majority of 43 seats with Thatcher becoming Prime Minister on 4 May 1979, the first woman to hold the post.

## New economic strategy

The first Thatcher government was committed to reversing the economic decline of Britain. Thatcher believed that this entailed a break with the past and many of its social and economic practices.[7] Like Joseph, she was influenced by the views of Friedrich von Hayek (the Nobel Laureate economist), who criticised the ideal of social justice as unrealisable in a market economy and its pursuit as harmful.[8] In his view, it was not the role of government to redistribute wealth but simply to establish the conditions in which market forces could create it. State intervention in economic affairs should be kept to a minimum, although it was not inappropriate for government to provide a welfare safety net outside the market.[9]

The Conservative Party has always been a broad coalition of groups with differing views of society and the state. These different strands of Conservative thinking were well represented in all of Thatcher's Cabinets, which included traditional Tories who believed in a relatively substantial role for the state. It was perhaps this situation which prompted Milton Friedman (the Nobel Laureate economist and the academic founder of monetarism) to point out that Thatcher 'is not in terms of belief a Tory but a 19th century Liberal'.[10]

Thatcher's economic liberalism with its preference for a minimalist state did not commend itself to all her government colleagues, or even to most members of her party. In the words of Sir Ian Gilmour, a Minister, the Conservative Party is not a pressure group for capitalism, and economic liberalism because of its starkness and failure to create a sense of community is likely to repel people from the rest of liberalism.[11] Nevertheless its underlying ideas were highly influential in policy making throughout her three terms in office. Moreover, their influence on policy seems to have continued relatively undiminished during John Major's administrations and the New Labour governments which followed. It can be argued, therefore, that Thatcher's accession to office represented a watershed in the ideological currents of policy making from which emerged a new hegemony of ideas and values which were to exert a profound effect – some say irreversible – not only on social policy, including pensions policy, but in reshaping civil society.[12]

It was the Thatcher government's first budget in June 1979 which nailed its colours firmly to the monetarist mast.[13] Its strategy entailed a reduction in direct taxation (from 33% to 30% at the basic rate and from 83% to 60% at the upper rate) and a commitment to reduce the money supply. A higher threshold was also introduced for the investment income surcharge. However to ensure that cuts in direct taxation did not cause a growth in the money supply, Howe, the Chancellor, combined the split VAT rates of 8% and 12½% and increased them into a single rate of 15%. Simultaneously he announced increases in other indirect taxes.[14] These changes increased the cost of living and therefore adversely affected the less well off and so were regressive in nature.

The first budget also included a number of cuts in the real value of some social security benefits, if only at the margin, in order to bring about immediate reductions in social expenditure. Examples were unemployment, sickness and invalidity benefits, all of which were cut by 5% in real terms.[15] Concern was expressed in the Commons about breaking the election commitment to uprate the flat rate pension, and other long term social insurance benefits, in accordance with the better of earnings or prices principle, which ensured that the recipients of those benefits shared in any increase in the country's prosperity. Patrick Jenkin, the Secretary of Social Services, reassured the Commons that it remained the government's firm intention that pensioners, and other long term beneficiaries, could confidently look forward to sharing in the increased standards of living of the country as a whole.[16]

Public expenditure was reduced by £1.5 billion for the forthcoming year. Cash limits were imposed on government expenditure to produce another £1 billion cut. Controls on pay, prices and dividends were abolished and exchange controls ended in the autumn. A target was set for the money supply defined as M3 (equal to cash plus bank current and deposit accounts).

The government's economic strategy led to a steep rise in prices and increased borrowing by the banks at a time when its own income was reduced due to cuts in taxation. Government revenue was further reduced by strikes in the public services and rising unemployment. Public borrowing exerted pressure on the money supply and the Minimum Lending Rate (MLR) was increased to an unprecedented 17%.[17]

In November 1979, the government published its Public Expenditure White Paper which began with the words: Public Expenditure is at the heart of Britain's present economic difficulties. In the late 1970s, the largest item of public expenditure had been social security, which accounted for 25% of all government spending. The largest component within the social security budget was retirement pensions.[18]

Thatcher's government whilst trying to reduce public expenditure wanted the resources to curb trade unions' power, to deal with law and order problems, for defence and for the protection of overseas interests. In order to meet these commitments, disproportionate reductions in other government spending programmes would be required. The social security budget, on account of its large proportion of total public expenditure, seemed to be particularly vulnerable. This was reinforced by another government commitment, namely to end the welfare dependency culture.

However the Public Expenditure White Paper, made no specific reference to social security in general or to retirement pensions in particular.[19] The view has been expressed that, at that time, social security budgets were judged too sensitive for major direct cuts.[20] This was confirmed by the November 1979 uprating of the flat rate NI pension when the pension was increased by 19.5% from £19.50 to £23.30 per week (26% of average earnings).[21] This represented the highest point ever attained by the pension, as a percentage of average earnings, throughout its entire history either before 1979 or since.[22]

## 1980 budget

The presentation of Howe's 1980 budget to the Commons included an unequivocal statement that the better of earnings or prices method of uprating the flat rate pension was to be abandoned. After the enabling legislation had been enacted, the basis of uprating would be price inflation alone, as measured by the Retail Prices Index. The legislation was contained in the Social Security Act 1980 which specifically provided that the flat rate state pension* would be revalued by an amount not less than the increase in retail prices.[23]

This provision, read in the light of Patrick Jenkin's 1979 statement to the Commons that under the last Conservative government social insurance benefits, without any statutory link to earnings, had in fact kept pace with earnings,[24] could be held to mean that the pension, if economic conditions improved, would possibly be increased at a higher rate than price inflation.[25]

---

* If the annual uprating had continued on the previous basis, namely in line with earnings or prices whichever is the greater, then the flat rate pension in April 2008 would have been £134.75 per week instead of the actual rate of £90.70 per week

The 1980 budget introduced the government's Medium Term Financial Strategy (MTFS) which established targets for monetary growth and public expenditure. The strategy was retained throughout the subsequent economic collapse.[26] Between 1979 and 1981 yearly inflation rose to a maximum of 22% whilst industrial output fell by 16% and GDP by 5%.[27] Unemployment worsened in 1980, increasing by nearly one million, and disagreements in the Cabinet over policy started to undermine the government's objectives of reducing public expenditure, inflation and direct taxation. Increasing unemployment – approaching 3 million between 1979 and 1981 – actually gave rise to greater public expenditure and subsequent measures to curtail this only further increased unemployment.[28] Arguments in the Cabinet about the means to secure the government's economic objectives, including its goals of reforming the trades unions and privatising the nationalised industries, inevitably led to Thatcher becoming embroiled in factional strife.[29] Nevertheless she was able to declare defiantly to the 1980 Conservative Party conference in the autumn that 'the lady's not for turning'.

In November 1980 the annual uprating of the flat rate pension took place. The pension was increased by 16.5% from £23.30 to £27.15 per week. After this uprating the pension represented 24.6% of average earnings compared with 26% of average earnings in 1979.[30]

The government's preoccupation with finding quick ways to reduce social expenditure had led them to set up an inquiry into the value of pensions under the chairmanship of Sir Bernard Scott (then the deputy chairman of Lloyds Bank). The ostensible reason was public concern with the value and cost of inflation proofing public sector occupational pensions.[31] Indexation of public sector pensions under the Pension (Increase) Act 1971 (to protect the value of civil servants' occupational pensions against erosion by inflation) was proving very costly with rates of inflation close to 20% per annum.

The Scott Report was presented to Parliament in February 1981 and, perhaps disappointingly for the government, did not recommend the abandonment of inflation protection for public sector occupational pensions. Instead it advocated that inflation protection of some kind be extended to private sector occupational pensions, perhaps through government backed index linked bonds which could provide a hedge for company pension funds against inflation.[32]

The Scott Report was followed a month later by publication of the DHSS White Paper *Growing Older*. The White Paper was not so much concerned with issues affecting pensioners in general, as with social service provision and health care needs of the very old.[33]

It emphasised the primacy of economic considerations in decision making on social service provision, and that meeting social needs would in future have to depend on lower inflation and higher growth rates.[30] Similarly, pensioners would be able to share in the nation's prosperity through increased basic pensions only when economic recovery materialised.[34]

In relation to the future cost of SERPS, it was noted that, as a result of demographic trends, the long term costs would increase for both employers and tax payers.[35] This was one of the earliest public expressions of the government's concern over the long term costs of SERPS. However, as Steven Nesbitt, the social security expert, points out, similar concern over the effects on employers and tax payers of the increased costs of occupational pension provision, as a result of demographic trends, was not expressed.[36]

## Cabinet dissension

From 1979 to 1981 the steep rise in both inflation and unemployment tended to obscure some improvements in the management of the economy. Public sector borrowing for 1981–82 was actually £2 billion less than expected.[37] In relation to the Public Sector Borrowing Requirement (PSBR) this confirmed that the government's economic strategy was broadly right, and by 1982–3, the level of government borrowing as a proportion of GDP was the lowest since the 1970s.[38] By April 1981 the annual rate of inflation had fallen to 12% from more than 20% a year earlier.

Critics, however, were not slow to point out that it was actually the lack of purchasing power resulting from the increase in unemployment to over 3 million workers which had reduced inflation.[39] The 1981 budget was highly deflationary being the most vigorously anti-Keynesian budget yet.[40] In the view of the all-party Treasury and Civil Service Committee of the Commons, it represented 'a tightening of the fiscal stance'[41] at a time when the economy was already in deep recession. However a rebellion within the Cabinet had forestalled another intended series of social expenditure cuts.[42]

In July 1981 riots erupted in Brixton in South London and Toxteth in Liverpool – where CS gas was used for the first time on the British mainland to quell a civil disturbance. Civil disturbance then broke out in Manchester and riots followed in some thirty or so towns and cities elsewhere in Britain. *The Times* of 14 July 1981 reported that on her unannounced visit to Liverpool, Thatcher looked strained and she confessed that the days of the riots had been 'the worst of her premiership'.[43]

The dissension in the Cabinet however continued unabated until September 1981. Thatcher removed three social concern wets* from her Cabinet (Ian Gilmour, Christopher Soames and Mark Carlisle). Jim Prior was moved from Employment, where he was deeply concerned about the seemingly unstoppable rise in unemployment, to the Northern Ireland Office.[44] In addition Fowler succeeded Patrick Jenkin as Social Services Secretary.

## Thatcher and the National Pensioners Convention

With the support of the TUC, Age Concern and Help the Aged, the National Pensioners Convention (NPC) was formed in 1979 as an umbrella movement representing the interests of Britain's pensioners' associations. Its principal purpose is to canvass opinion among the pensioners' associations and to co-ordinate claims and make representations to Parliament and government on behalf of pensioners. A driving force in its establishment and a leading light in its development has been Jack Jones. Before his retirement as General Secretary of the TGWU in 1978, he had been active in trying to improve pension provisions for all, but was concerned at the weakness of the pensioners' organisations.[45] He wanted to continue to support working people and those who are 'too old to work but too young to die'.[46]

By 1981, the NPC had started to gain wide support and was becoming well known for its annual lobby of Parliament and deputations to leaders of the political parties. Jack Jones recounts how Thatcher was not initially inclined to meet him and the other NPC delegates with

---

* Thatcher used the epithet wets to describe those in her Cabinet who resisted cuts in social policy.[43a]

their message that the needs of 9½ million pensioner citizens should not be ignored. Their first approach was rebuffed, but it subsequently transpired that on the day they wanted to meet her she was lunching in the City. The resulting publicity ensured that she met deputations in the following years.[47]

Nevertheless the erosion of the value of the state pension in relation to average earnings and increased reliance on means testing continued. NPC delegates were repeatedly told: It's the wrong time. The burden on the working population and the taxpayers would be too great. To which Jack Jones would reply: It is never the wrong time to do justice to the retired.[48]

Thatcher, however, was not always so intransigent on pension issues. According to a newspaper report, she discovered during her early years at 10 Downing Street that Harold and Mary Wilson 'were living in straitened circumstances because of the rules governing pensions for retired Prime Ministers'. She was understandably concerned and immediately set about changing the rules in order to provide 'better pensions' for retired Prime Ministers.[49]

In November the annual uprating of the flat rate pension represented an increase of only 9% over the previous year's rate. The pension was increased from £27.15 to £29.60 per week being equal to 23.7% of average earnings.[50]

## The assault on social security

The 1982 budget was more moderate than that in 1981. The policy of reducing the value of social security benefits, however, steadily continued in 1982. The earnings related supplements (introduced by the Wilson government in 1966) to all short term social security benefits, including unemployment payments, were abolished. However, in order to maintain the government's revenue, the liability of an insured person to pay earnings related contributions was retained.[51]

The annual uprating of social security short term benefits, in accordance with price inflation, was subject to delays, freezes or only partial implementation. Lowe points out that, in 1981 and again in 1988, child benefit was frozen, and between 1981 and 1983 other short term benefits were increased by 5% less than the increase in the Retail Prices Index. Full uprating in line with price inflation was restored only after the benefits had been made taxable. This was a change of policy which secured a saving to the Exchequer of £400 million per annum in respect of unemployment insurance alone, an amount representing 10% of all unemployment benefits.[52]

In the September 1981 Cabinet reshuffle Norman Fowler succeeded Patrick Jenkin as Social Services Secretary. Fowler was more a One Nation Tory than an economic liberal and lost no time in putting a stop to Jenkin's alternative health service finance study, without consulting the Prime Minister.[53] He seemed to have settled with quiet capability into the job when a storm broke over a leaked report of the Central Policy Review Staff. This had been commissioned by Howe, the Chancellor, in the summer of 1982 after Treasury calculations suggested that if the economy only grew at an annual rate of 1%, public spending would increase significantly as a proportion of GDP. The Central Policy Review Staff had a remit to propose radical options to prevent this.[54] It was their proposals which caused Lord Hailsham to record when he read them that his hair stood on end.[55]

The options included the ending of price protection for all social security benefits, replacing the NHS with health care services underwritten by private health insurance and the termination of state funding of higher education apart from loans and a limited number of state scholarships.[56] The remaining wets in the Cabinet produced the nearest thing to a Cabinet riot in the history of the Thatcher administration[57] and forced the paper off the agenda of the Cabinet of 9 September 1982.[58] The paper was then leaked to *The Economist* which reported that the report came with the seal of approval of the Treasury and was to form the basis of a six month study of a public spending strategy for the rest of the decade.[59] Fowler was deeply angry that a proposal for the radical reform of the NHS had been put forward for consideration by the Cabinet without consultation with any health minister.[60]

According to Nesbitt, the leak disclosed firm evidence that reducing the cost of state pension provision was on the political agenda.[61] It would appear that Thatcher was reluctant to relinquish the CPRS report and its proposals until she was eventually prevailed upon to do so by a majority of the Cabinet.[62]

Despite the affair of the leaked proposals for reform of health, education and welfare, the Conservative government slowly began to recover popularity in 1982. That year, in January, Thatcher's poll rating had been the lowest of any Prime Minister since the end of the Second World War. A mere 25% of the electorate were satisfied with her premiership.[63] Unemployment continued to rise and there was little sign of economic recovery, apart from the fall in inflation which was itself seen as a partial consequence of the increase in unemployment. However, in a few weeks from April to June 1982, the Falklands War had been won. For nearly a year Conservative fortunes had been in the doldrums, the party trailing Labour and the Liberals, in third place in the opinion polls. The Falklands War victory however transformed the government's rating into a lead of 20%.[64]

In November 1982 the flat rate pension was uprated by 11% from £29.60 to £32.85 per week. The new pension rate was equal to 24.1% of average earnings.[65]

## Conflicting publications

On 27 October 1982, the Social Services Committee of the Commons published its long awaited report *Age of Retirement*. A decision to undertake the inquiry had been made in July 1981. Its purpose was to consider whether any change in pension age and the age for actually ceasing work should be made.[66] The increase in the costs of pension provision and the trend to earlier retirement were considered to be highly germane to the Committee's inquiry.[67] The high level of unemployment, and the record number of redundancies in the early 1980s, had been accompanied by an unprecedented increase in the early retirement of older workers who had no prospect of re-employment. The collection of evidence began in November 1981.[68]

The report noted that many older workers were seeking a greater measure of personal choice in the age at which they retire[69] and then went on to give a stark warning:

> Real choice must depend not only on the right to some pension, but on the ability
> to go on working and the adequacy of the pension received when work stops.

Health is perhaps the main constraint, but it is becoming increasingly difficult for older people to get jobs, and there is often considerable pressure on those over 60 who have jobs to give them up in favour of younger people.[70]

The report mentioned that the quest for flexibility in choosing the age of retirement was not confined to Britain. It cited the European Commission's statement of principles *Community Policy on Retirement Age* which aimed to influence EU member states to work towards a flexible approach to retirement age.[71] The statement of principles, issued in December 1980, had been based on an earlier recommendation concerning older workers from the International Labour Office in June 1980.[72]

The Select Committee's report suggested that consideration be given to introducing a 'decade of retirement' choice which would confer on older workers contemplating retirement a right to choose their own retirement age in any year falling within a range of ten years. The report also specified, however, that any such flexible retirement should be supported by an adequate pension to provide a minimum acceptable standard of living. This last subject was an item of protracted discussion within the Select Committee and a considerable amount of time was spent arguing in favour of higher state pension rates.[73]

On 25 October 1982 Lyon delivered his Presidential Address to the Institute of Actuaries. This was a wide ranging paper entitled *The Outlook for Pensioning* which explored the effect of anticipated demographic, social and economic trends on the future cost of pension provision. He took a cautiously pessimistic view of the cost of SERPS to future generations, believing that the increasing liabilities of the scheme would seriously burden the economy.[74]

Lyon's arguments were supported by comments made in an article, published in the same month, by Edward Johnston, the Government Actuary,[75] who had compiled the Memorandum on financing SERPS, incorporated in the 1974 White Paper *Better Pensions*. His 1982 quinquennial review of the scheme had shown that, if certain assumptions relating to prices and earnings inflation between 1985 and 2025 were borne out in practice, the change in the ratio of employed to retired sections of the population would entail an increase in Class 1 NI contribution rates of the order of 40%. This scenario was seriously at odds with the one reflected by the cost projections made at the time SERPS received parliamentary approval, a point recognised by Johnston in his article.[76]

Also in 1982 the Adam Smith Institute compiled a discreet memorandum entitled *Privatising Pensions: A Report to the Secretary of State for Health and Social Security*. The paper, because of restricted publication (it was published later in 1983), received only a limited circulation. It advocated that SERPS should be replaced by a system of personal portable pensions. This was one of the earliest published papers in Britain advocating a pension reform based on personal pensions.[77] However, although limited by its circulation, the memorandum appears to have been seminal in its influence on future developments.

Early in 1983 two further reports with conflicting recommendations on state pension policy were published. The first was the January 1983 Report of the Social Security Advisory Committee, a body of political appointees rather than politicians[78] who supported the 1975–79 pensions settlement. However in their 'espousal of an important role for the state in pension provision' they were not in accord with the direction of government thinking. Opposing any structural reform of SERPS and advocating improving the rate of the basic pension, the report was seen as taking 'the side of labour rather than that of either capital or the Treasury'.[79]

A very different view of the direction of pensions policy was taken by the second report of the Central Policy Review Staff (whose first report was leaked to *The Economist* the previous September) published in March 1983 recommending phasing out SERPS and suggesting, to counter hostile public opinion, increasing the basic pension.[80] A general election was close, and Thatcher was said to be furious at the timing of the report's publication and demanded a recall of all copies from government departments. The report also put forward recommendations on how personal pension schemes should be developed as an alternative to occupational pension schemes for some employees.[81]

In April 1983 the influential Centre for Policy Studies (CPS) produced a short and well argued paper in favour of individuals in a free society having the right to develop and manage their own personal portable pension portfolio. The paper had been prepared by a study group within the CPS led by Nigel Vinson and Philip Chappell.[82] It made a coherent case for pensions to be available in a personal, and portable, form as individually owned assets of citizens in a property-owning democracy. It was considered both socially and economically desirable for citizens of a free and market oriented society, especially because of a perceived lack of personal identification and involvement in the wealth represented by the £120 billion of pension fund assets.[83]

The case for personal portable pensions was enhanced because they would be likely to result in improved mobility of labour. The portability of the asset ensured that no financial loss would be incurred on change of employment as was the case with early leavers from occupational pension schemes. As the authors of the paper pointed out, it happened to be a beneficial and most timely by-product of our proposals that they would, over a period, also solve the early leaver problem. The authors argued for the basic state pension to be paid at a higher rate than the then current rate of 24% of average earnings without means testing.[84]

Both authors had a wholly coherent social philosophy of pension provision, which perhaps was more clearly expressed in their later writings than in the CPS paper. This was that the economic market is the legitimate institution for the creation of pension rights based on earnings from employment or on personal savings. These pension rights should ideally be vested in a fully portable, personally owned, asset with which the citizen would be able to identify as an individual (not as a member of a collective). Aside from the vagaries and inequalities of the market, however, and irrespective of employment histories, each citizen would always have a floor of social protection in retirement in the form of a universal flat rate pension, provided by the state, large enough to cover basic needs, but not so large as to discourage voluntary savings.[85]

## 1983 general election

Thatcher's government had come to power in May 1979 resolved to reverse the economic decline of Britain. Four years later this ambition had manifestly not been achieved. During the period, manufacturing production had fallen by 17.3% and the gross domestic product by 4.2%.

Unemployment had increased from 1.25 million to over 3 million, a rise of 141%. Crime was up by 28.6%.[86]

Although public expenditure overall had risen, from 41% of total output to 44%, the government had resisted calls for reflation of the economy which, almost certainly, a Labour government would have heeded with billions added to its expenditure plans. Thatcher took credit for controlling public expenditure and for bringing inflation under control. She also claimed credit for an increase in productivity, although this, like the fall in the inflation rate, may simply have been the consequence of the increase in unemployment. The new trade union laws had a moderating effect on the behaviour of the trades unions although this too may have been a partial consequence of the level of unemployment.[87] Nevertheless there seems to have emerged a new public respect for the government in the wake of the Falklands War victory. Thatcher, by early 1983, seemed to be a leader with determination to stand up to awkward realities whether at home or abroad.[88]

The Conservatives lead in the public opinion polls had been strong and consistent for several months. Thatcher decided to seek an early dissolution of Parliament and this occurred on 13 May 1983 with polling day arranged for 9 June. The Conservatives manifesto concentrated on pledges to maintain a strong defence capability and to increase economic prosperity. Economic policy would include further privatisation, reform of the trade unions and reduction of taxation and inflation.[89]

Labour, now led by Michael Foot, offered in its own manifesto *New Hope for Britain* major increases in investment in housing and public transport and greater spending on the social services. They also made firm pledges to withdraw from membership of the European Community and to abolish the Lords.[90]

Although the Conservatives' share of the vote at 42.4% was actually lower than at the 1979 election where they received 43.9%, they were returned to office with a substantially increased overall majority of 144, its largest since 1935. They won 397 seats compared with Labour 209. The Alliance Party (a coalition of Social Democrats and Liberals) obtained 23 seats. It is an interesting commentary on the British electoral system that Labour won 209 seats on the basis of 27.6% of the vote, whereas the Alliance Party's share of 25.4% of the vote only won them 23 seats.[91]

## Second Thatcher administration 1983–87

The outcome of the election secured for Thatcher a commanding position within the Conservative Party. The public's apparent acceptance of the new brand of Conservatism was promptly reflected in the composition of the new Cabinet. Francis Pym was dismissed from the post of Foreign Secretary and Howe was appointed in his place. Lawson became Chancellor of the Exchequer.[92] This led to *The Economist* publishing the following comment on 18 June:

> Mr Lawson's move to the Treasury is clearly intended to set the tone of the new government … it will be abrasive, clever, argumentative and even more at loggerheads with spending departments than usual.[93]

Among other Cabinet appointments were Michael Heseltine at Defence, Leon Brittan at the Home Office, Norman Tebbitt at Employment, and Cecil Parkinson at Trade and Industry, where he replaced the leading wet in the Cabinet, Peter Walker.[94]

On 12 June it was announced that Foot would not stand for re-election as leader of the Labour Party. In the ensuing election within that party, Neil Kinnock eventually emerged as the new Labour Leader with Roy Hattersley as Deputy Leader. The result was widely considered in Labour circles to represent a balance of Left and Right in the party.[95] In a speech at the end of the election campaign, Kinnock had said: If Thatcher wins on Thursday – I warn you not to be young; I warn you not to fall ill; I warn you not to get old.[96]

On becoming Chancellor Lawson soon discovered that public spending was growing at a faster rate than had been intended. By July 1983 he had reduced the budgets of the biggest spending departments, including Health and Education, by £500 million. At the same time he let it be known that his next target for public expenditure cuts was social security, the biggest spender of all.[97]

In his memoirs, Fowler, who had been re-appointed Social Services Secretary in the second Thatcher government, recalled that, after Lawson's initial public expenditure cuts, 'it needed no great powers of prophesy to realise that Nigel and I were on a collision course.'[98] As Timmins explains, the response of Fowler was to set up a review, the strategy he almost invariably followed to control the agenda before the Treasury or Downing Street controlled it for him.[99]

Lawson's £500 million emergency package of public expenditure cuts affected defence, employment and transport as well as health and education. They were, however, made against a background of economic recovery begun in 1982. Lawson had been the principal architect of the MTFS when he had been Chief Financial Secretary to the Treasury. The cuts were no more than limits imposed under the MTFS on the growth rate of public spending, ostensibly to reassure the City of the government's continued commitment to stringent monetary policy.[100]

In fact, Lawson's appointment as Chancellor came at a time when there was a recognisable upturn in the economy. Manufacturing productivity had increased by 12½% in 1982–83 and there was a £4 billion current account surplus on the balance of payments for that year. The yearly rate of inflation had fallen to below 4% and all the public expenditure targets had been met.[101]

## Policy and ideology

A number of commentators noted a discernible change in the nature of the government's policy after the election. Peter Young of the Adam Smith Institute, for example, refers to the re-elected government acquiring a 'sense of immortality.'[102] This gave them leave to adopt a longer term view in policy making. They were no longer concerned with preventing or controlling economic crises with the economy now being buoyed up by North Sea oil revenues.[103] The policies were no longer merely pragmatic because of the pressure to respond urgently to events. Policy justifications became more overtly ideological in character. According to Nesbitt, it had become possible for the government in general, and the Treasury in particular, to pursue policies simply because they believed them to be right.[104]

The priorities in economic policy for the second Thatcher administration had nevertheless been quite predictable. They comprised 'monetary rectitude'[105] – as was clear from Lawson's early dawn raid of cuts[106] – and reduced public borrowing, lower taxes and more privatisation. In relation to the latter, British Telecom, British Airways, British Gas and the Royal Ordinance Factories were all on the list.[107] There was, however, no possibility of delivering significant reductions in taxation unless public expenditure was kept firmly under control. The November 1983 Public Expenditure Statement committed government to maintain public spending at the 1983 White Paper level of £126.4 billion.[108] Also in November 1983 the government increased the flat rate pension by 3.7% from £32.85 to £34.05 per week being 23% of average earnings.[109]

## Fowler's Inquiry

In November, the government published its document *Reply to the Third Report from the Social Services Committee, Session 1981–82, on the Age of Retirement*. Having rebuked the Select Committee for recommending an increase in the pension levels of poorer pensioners, a subject stated to be outside the Committee's brief, the document announced that the government was to set up the Inquiry, chaired by Fowler, to study the future development, adequacy and cost of state, occupational and private provision for retirement, including the portability of pension rights, and to consider possible changes in those arrangements.[110] It started work in December 1983.

According to Nesbitt, the pensions policy debate had become dominated by an elite group of actuaries, financiers and right wing idealogues, supported at least in principle by the Prime Minister and the Chancellor of the Exchequer. The proposal that personal pensions should replace occupational pensions had been very successful in securing press and political attention. The debate appeared to be slipping out of the Secretary of State's control. The Inquiry under his own chairmanship was Fowler's attempt to regain some control.[111]

There is substantial evidence that, when the Inquiry was set up, Fowler was under considerable pressure from both Thatcher and Lawson to introduce reforms that would reduce the long term costs of SERPS.[112] Both believed that the prospective increase in the number of pensioners would result in 'an uncontrollable tide of spending'[113] unless SERPS future liabilities were reduced. Fowler, however, resented the pressure put upon him. He believed that social policy should be subject to rational appraisal and argued that the debate on any aspect of it should be responsible, realistic and open.[114] As a consequence a public disagreement emerged. On 23 November 1983, *The Times* reported that:

> Fowler [in a speech the previous night] challenged the belief of Thatcher and Lawson that public spending would have to be curbed because of long term increases in the number of pensioners.[115]

In publicly stating that the number of people over 65 years which had risen over the last 20 years would now remain more or less stable until about 2010, Fowler had undermined one of Lawson's key arguments for reducing social security pensions expenditure.[116] This evidence of dissension in the Cabinet over pensions policy was a somewhat dissonant note on which to announce a public inquiry into provision for retirement.

Early in the course of the Inquiry, the Treasury imposed a zero cost principle on all social security pension expenditures. The principle of cost neutrality was not easy to apply to the state pension system and the ancillary forms of social pension provision such as occupational schemes. The task was rendered even more difficult because the Inquiry did not have a remit to discuss tax issues, a serious impediment to the conduct of the Inquiry. Although the purpose of the Inquiry was not to present formal findings, its discussions were nevertheless intended to serve ministers in the eventual formulation of policy. The cost of tax concessions for occupational pension schemes, or personal pensions underwritten in the form of retirement annuity contracts, would be a highly relevant issue for the deliberations of the Inquiry, if there was to be discussion of any significant shift of pension provision from public sector to private sector. Any attempt, however, to raise tax issues during the Inquiry were apparently blocked by its Treasury representative.[117]

Considerable discussion was devoted to the future implications of demographic change for the cost of SERPS, and how such cost could be reduced. The Inquiry took the view that the requirements for contracting out of SERPS were a barrier to smaller employers which had to rely on the state scheme for provision of additional pensions for their employees. There appeared to be a general acceptance by members of the Inquiry of the principle that the most effective way to encourage more people to leave SERPS was by way of personal portable pensions specially designed for contracting out.[118]

Fowler was adamant that the system of personal pensions should be extended in any event as an instrument of private pension provision.[119] The system was originally established by the Finance Act 1956 with the limited tax concessions of the 1956 Act being extended by Section 226 of the Income and Corporation Taxes Act, 1970. Although generally thought of as self-employed pension contracts before the 1980s, these section 226 contracts were also available to employees in non-pensionable employment.

The personal pensions lobby had grown in strength and influence since the beginning of the 1980s. According to *The Times* of 3 September 1983, the Institute of Directors (IoD) favoured a number of proposals for pension reform which were centred on an ideological advocacy of personal pensions, i.e. pensions expressed as capital of each individual. It was claimed they would have important social and economic advantages over occupational pension schemes. There would also be political advantages in the creation of a nation of capitalists. A wider interest in the success of industry would be identified. In particular any Socialist plans to take control of pension funds would receive short shrift from 15 million owners.[120]

It is not surprising that such a perception of personal portable pensions as a useful tool to help build a people's capitalism would be shared by Conservatives of an economic liberal persuasion in the government, as well as by those others in Parliament or the country. What may be more surprising is that some ideological support for personal pensions was also forthcoming from Fowler who reputedly was more of a One Nation Tory than an economic liberal.

In Timmins' view there was an ideological element in Fowler's desire to abolish SERPS. Predictions about the long term costs of the scheme were far from certain. Whilst it was reasonable to assume that there would be a significant increase in the pensioner population, the numbers of economic contributors in the working population available to support them depended on the birth rate and future economic performance, both matters subject to speculation.[121] The ideological motive became clear when Fowler said that the state should not provide a second pension on top and certainly not an earnings related second pension as this was more generous to those on higher incomes. His view was consistent with a Tory ideology of concentrating help on those most in need.[122] It may help to explain why Fowler did not appear to attach much weight to demographic arguments[123] as suggested by his public disagreement with the Prime Minister and the Chancellor the previous November.

The main focus of the Inquiry was on reducing the cost of SERPS. There was a radical view from the Right that some finite term should be put on SERPS after which it should be abolished.[124] However opponents of this view, both inside the Inquiry and outside, had expressed the view that contributors believed that by paying NI contributions they were purchasing rights to earnings related pensions under a contract of social insurance and so would object to the idea of government reneging on its contractual obligations.[125] The more moderate view that the terms and conditions of SERPS should be modified in order to reduce its costs prevailed.

It was probably at this point that the solution of encouraging people to opt out of SERPS by purchasing a personal pension and thus reducing the ultimate cost of the scheme, may have acquired added credibility. Fowler had from the beginning believed that personal pensions should become a mainstream source of retirement provision. Evidence for this is provided by Nesbitt who cites letters sent by the DHSS, at Fowler's behest, to the IoD, as well as the CBI and the NAPF, requesting that they submit evidence to the Inquiry. The letters, by their content, seem to suggest that, for Fowler, personal pensions were the focal point of the Inquiry. The letter dated 12 December 1983 stated: The Secretary of State is anxious that the Inquiry should give priority in their consideration to the question of personal portable pensions.[126]

As Nesbitt points out, the letter describes alleged advantages of personal pensions such as conferring on employees more control over their own pensions and a greater sense of involvement in their pension scheme. It then concludes by declaring the government's sympathy with these aims and their wish to examine the consequences of achieving them through portable pensions. Such was the importance of this issue to the government that the Inquiry's complete review of state and occupational pensions was to be conducted with a bias towards personal portable pensions. The Inquiry accordingly established a Sub-Group on personal pensions. The Sub-Group consisted of three advisers – the insurance and investment entrepreneur, Mark Weinberg and the two actuaries, Stewart Lyon and Marshall Field. Its chairman was Fowler who also chaired the Inquiry's Main Team.[127]

The Sub-Group commissioned a market research survey to test public support for personal pensions. The survey allegedly showed a strong demand revealing that 80% of people not in schemes were interested in personal pensions. The point has been made by Nesbitt that with evidence of such overwhelming demand it is strange that it was felt necessary to create a generous system of incentives and NI rebates.[128]

The survey's findings were published in July 1984 within the government paper *Personal Pensions: A Consultative Document* which set out Fowler's initial proposals on personal pensions.

The principal proposals were:

- Personal pensions on a money purchase basis should be available to all employees as of right;
- The condition for contracting out of SERPS on the basis of a personal pension would be defined in terms of the contributions paid and not the benefit secured; and
- Employers should not be obliged to contribute to a personal pension except if used for contracting out purposes and then only to the extent of any employer's NI contracting out rebate with failure of the arrangement to provide an adequate income being the responsibility of the employee.[129]

The reported lack of any significant sustained critical public reaction to the personal pension proposals seems a little strange in view of the admission in the Consultative Document that the pension investment risk would transfer to any employee who contracted out of SERPS by means of a personal pension. Nevertheless the absence of public reaction helped Fowler to steer the personal pensions reform through the Cabinet, so that debate (on pensions policy within the Cabinet) would be largely focused on the future of SERPS.

The entire Inquiry, covering every aspect of the pensions debate, therefore took place under Fowler's chairmanship and so he was able to decide who could participate and how much attention each submission would receive.[130] Despite the claim that he made in the Commons in April 1984 that this was the most radical review of social security since Beveridge, its format was very different from Beveridge's review. Writing many years later Fowler explained:

> The difference between the way I did it and the way, say, the Beveridge Committee did it is that Beveridge simply made his proposals to the government. They were his proposals. He stood by them but it was the government that in the end made the decision on whether they accepted them or not. I was a government minister, my world was different. I had to make proposals, not only proposals I believed in and supported, but proposals which I could get past my colleagues. So I had to do both roles at the same time.[131]

The Inquiry concluded in January 1985 without making any policy recommendations nor was any consensus produced among its members. Among the members subsequently interviewed, however, there was a sense that the Inquiry had moved the pensions debate in a new direction.[132] Timmins has summed it up by observing that Fowler's review, at least in technical terms, represented 'symbolic change' by ending 'the cradle to grave span of the social security system'.[133]

## The 1984 budget and the miners' strike

It was widely expected that social security (the largest item of public expenditure) would be targeted in the next round of Treasury cuts. Proclaiming himself to be engaged in the most radical review of social security since Beveridge, Fowler also set up four separate reviews to examine different aspects of the entire social security system. The reviews were undertaken by a number of ministerially dominated committees,[134] conducted with painstaking care using modern computerised modelling techniques.[135] Economists in the Department of Health and

Social Security carried out studies of past trends in pensioners' incomes. These suggested that old people had fared better in income terms, provided private pension income was taken into account, than had young people with families to support. Improving the welfare of the latter accordingly became a priority of the reforms.[136]

Lawson's 1984 budget was more radical in economic terms than had been widely expected. As a result of Fowler's resistance to Lawson's demands that the social security reviews should deliver savings of £2 billion a year, Fowler would emerge from Cabinet discussions with his £40 billion social security budget almost completely intact.[137] Partly for this reason any reduction in income tax was postponed until 1985, although there was some redistribution of the tax burden by increasing the basic income tax threshold by 7% more than the rate of inflation, and abolishing the surcharge on large investment incomes.[138] Corporation tax was reduced and the shift to indirect taxation continued. The 1984 budget was described as 'the most Thatcherite hitherto'.[139]

The aim of the budget was also to reduce the PSBR from £9.7 billion in 1983–84 to £7 billion (2.25% of GDP) for 1984–85. It was hoped to keep the PSBR at that level for the next four years and then to reduce it from 2.25% of GDP to 1.75% in 1988–89.[140] However, these plans were set awry by the government becoming embroiled in the miners' strike, the most serious industrial dispute in Britain's post-war history.

The strike was precipitated by two announcements made within a few days of one another in March 1984. The first was the announcement that the Cortonwood Colliery in South Yorkshire was to close. This caused an immediate affront to the unions because the Area Director, under pressure from the office of the Chief Executive, had pre-empted the normal review procedure by saying the pit would close. The second was the announcement a few days later, on 6 March, that there was to be a cut of 4 million tonnes of capacity for 1984–85, with the assumed loss of 20 pits and 20,000 jobs.[141]

By 12 March a national strike had begun on a rolling basis, one region after another joining the strike, and within a week 90 out of 174 National Coal Board collieries were on strike.[142] Although the strike became Britain's most bitter industrial dispute since the 1926 general strike, the government's tactics were to sit back and pretend that the dispute was an ordinary one.[143] Social security benefits could only be obtained with difficulty by striking miners and their families and as a consequence the miners sought financial aid from the Soviet Union and Libya.[144] The strike went on until 5 March 1985. It caused great bitterness and cost the government £3 billion.[145] In the view of some commentators, the miners' strike inevitably failed because the National Union of Mineworkers constituted itself as a revolutionary vanguard and based its case on its own particular industrial and political perspective. It may have succeeded if a broader case had been argued 'not just for coal but for employment, social justice and a revolution in political perspectives which had narrowed, on the side of the government, to a steely-eyed faith in tight money and a loose labour market'.[146]

The government's plans to contain the PSBR at 2.25% of GDP until 1988 were thwarted by the costs it had incurred as a result of the miners' strike. Accordingly, the PSBR figures for the next two years increased. The figure for 1984–85 exceeded slightly more than 3% of GDP.[147] The flat rate pension was increased in November 1984 by 5.1% from £34.05 to £35.80 per week being 22.5% of average earnings.[148]

## Cabinet discussions on pensions policy

It has been argued that economic liberal ideology influenced Treasury policy, and there is certainly evidence for this in the 1984 Treasury Green Paper *The Next Ten Years*, which reiterated the principles that a social security system should be tailored to match the potential of the economy and not vice versa and finance must determine expenditure, not expenditure finance. This would imply support for the abolition of SERPS or, at least, its curtailment to reduce costs.[149] Fowler, as mentioned, believed that all pensions on top of the basic pension should be provided privately. Earnings related state pensions were inconsistent with a Tory ideology of targeting help at those most in need. Lawson and Thatcher were committed to the same view, although, for reasons of Treasury policy, a difference developed between them on details of the strategy for pension reform. Both Thatcher and Fowler were contemplating the outright abolition of SERPS and its replacement by mandatory private pensions to ensure that everyone was compelled to save for old age.

Despite Lawson's initial concurrence with the idea, he realised almost at the last moment (because he was distracted by preparation for the 1985 budget) that the proposed strategy for reform would have a gravely adverse impact on the PSBR.[150] The outright abolition of SERPS and its immediate replacement by a compulsory system of occupational or personal pensions would clearly have entailed an enormous cost to the Treasury in terms of the lost revenue from SERPS contributions combined simultaneously with a large increase in the cost of tax relief for private pensions. In addition, it would entail additional costs for both private industry and the public sector employers. At a time when the aim was to reduce the overall cost of social security this was not acceptable to the Treasury. This is what Lawson told MISC 111, the Cabinet Committee chaired by Thatcher which was engaged in deliberating upon the Fowler social security reviews.[151]

More acceptable to the Treasury was a strategy aimed at the gradual curtailment and phasing out of SERPS, combined with replacement by voluntary occupational schemes or personal pensions.[152] The disadvantage of this strategy of course was that the state would ultimately have to support those who failed to avail themselves of the voluntary system of retirement savings. This was a point well understood by both Thatcher and Fowler.

The serious disagreement which had occurred between Lawson and Fowler on the subject of the abolition of SERPS and the cost of lost revenue to the Exchequer (later estimated at £1 billion) was a critical development which affected the outcome of the Cabinet's discussions on pensions policy. Fowler halted the proceedings of the Cabinet Committee and there was no further discussion until a compromise solution was proposed.[153] A modified proposal for the gradual phasing out of SERPS without replacement by mandatory private pensions was developed along the lines suggested by the Treasury. Because Thatcher and Fowler were strongly committed to the outright abolition of SERPS, this was the government's preferred option which eventually emerged in the Green Paper *Reform of Social Security* published on 3 June 1985. Men under 50 years and women under 45 years would be phased out of SERPS and into private provision over a three year period with accrued entitlements to date preserved. The alternative of modifying SERPS by benefit reduction was also included. The basic pension would remain fully in force as provided for in the NI Act 1946.[154]

The proposals to abolish the additional component of SERPS outright and transfer responsibility for pension provision to employers and workers were almost universally opposed by the employers, the occupational pensions interests and by a major part of the insurance industry. The IoD concurred with the proposal because it shared the government's concern over the financial burden. However the CBI, whilst accepting the introduction of personal pensions and agreeing to curb the growth of state pension expenditure, expressed concern that the abolition of SERPS, as opposed to its modification by benefit reduction, would significantly increase business costs through the transfer to employers of a greater proportion of the overall liability for employees' retirement provision.[155] This was the point well understood by Lawson. During the consultation period an influential campaign against the abolition of SERPS was mounted by the poverty lobby and groups representing the elderly, including the NPC.

The CBI's response was to put forward an alternative basis for the modification of SERPS in preference to its abolition. It was suggested that the basis of calculation of the SERPS additional pensions should be linked to lifetime earnings instead of the best 20 years. Moreover, the SERPS pension payable to a surviving spouse should be reduced from 100% to 50% of the deceased spouse's pension. Because of the widespread opposition by the employers and the pensions industry to the abolition of SERPS, the government's proposal for the outright abolition was withdrawn,[156] with the government publishing its pension reform White Paper *Programme for Action* in December 1985.

## 1985 and 1986 budgets

In January 1985 the government was confronted by an incipient crisis in the value of sterling, when the pound slumped almost to parity with the dollar. Interest rates were increased by 2% and as a result the pound rallied on the exchange markets and was rapidly appreciating in value by budget day.[157]

In the 1985 budget, the basic income tax thresholds were increased by 10% which was twice the rate of inflation and NI contributions for lower paid workers were substantially reduced from 9% to rates in a range from 5 to 7%. These two changes, introduced in the budget, substantially improved the take-home pay of lower paid workers.[158]

The upper earnings limit on employers' NI contributions was abolished outright, thus transforming employers' NI contributions, in the view of some, into an open ended payroll tax. Because of the reduced rates of contribution for lower paid employees estimated as 8.5 million workers, it was calculated that employers overall would be about £900 million better off as a result of the changes. The PSBR outcome for 1985–6 was £5.9 billion, considerably less than the 1985 target of £7 billion.[159]

The flat rate pension was increased in November 1985 by 7% from £35.80 to £38.30 per week being 22.4% of average earnings.[160]

In the 1986 budget, the standard rate of income tax was reduced by a penny, but more significant reductions in income tax had to be postponed because of a large fall in the price of oil which adversely affected Treasury revenues from North Sea oil.[161]

## Modification to SERPS

In December 1985 the government published its pension reform White Paper *Programme for Action* setting out its proposals for modifying SERPS with the Social Security Act 1986 implementing them into law with effect from 6 April 1988, ten years after SERPS had been introduced. The modifications to SERPS are summarised briefly as follows[162]:

1. Contributors reaching state pension age before April 2000 would continue to accrue a SERPS additional pension calculated at the rate of 1.25% of 'revalued' earnings for the best years in the scheme up to a maximum of 20 years.

2. The rate of accrual of the SERPS additional pension after April 1988, for contributors retiring between April 2000 and April 2010 would be tapered to reflect the period of the contributor's membership of SERPS before and after April 1988.

3. Contributors retiring after April 2010 would receive a SERPS additional pension based on 20% of revalued lifetime average earnings in the scheme.

4. After April 2000 a surviving spouse would only be entitled to receive a SERPS pension equal to 50% of the deceased spouse's pension.

5. From April 1988 a contributor to an Appropriate Personal Pension Scheme could contract out of the SERPS additional pension. An Appropriate Personal Pension Scheme is a personal pension arrangement which is deemed to have met the required defined contribution test for contracting out and in recognition of which an appropriate scheme certificate has been granted by the Inland Revenue NI Contributions Office.[163]

The Social Security Act 1986, together with the Financial Services Act 1986 and the Building Societies Act 1986, provided for the launch of the contracted out personal pension regime from 1 July 1988. From that date, it would be illegal for an employer to require employees to become members of an occupational scheme as a condition of employment. The regulatory framework for this regime was established by the Financial Services Act 1986.[164]

In 1987 legislation was introduced to give effect to a system of contracting out rebates and incentives. The NI rebate for contracting out of SERPS, for the period 6 April 1988 until 5 April 1993, was 5.8% (2.0% employee and 3.8% employer) of earnings between the lower and upper earnings limits. In addition to the rebate, a 2% contracting out incentive rebate, based on the same level of earnings, was paid directly into the employee's Appropriate Personal Pension Scheme.[165]

## The end of cradle to grave social security

The Social Security Act 1986 finally brought to an end the 'cradle to grave span of the social security system' by abolition of two of Beveridge's universal benefits.[166] These were the £25 maternity grant and the £30 death grant. Neither benefit had been uprated by any government for years and the Act now formally replaced them with means tested benefits targeted at the very poor.[167] Supplementary Benefit was replaced by Income Support, a new benefit which had a scale of automatic additions to the basic rate to allow for the cost of children or a disabled person. Family Income Supplement was replaced by Family Credit, a more generous benefit to supplement the earnings of low paid working families.[168]

Rules were introduced under the Act to place the assessment of entitlements based on the claimant's income to each of the different means tested benefits on a consistent basis. This replaced the former complex system.[169]

An unexpected provision in the Act was the requirement that all means tested benefit recipients would have to pay an amount equal to 20% of the local authority household rates (or the flat rate community charge or poll tax soon to be introduced) for which they would have been liable. This was to ensure that people on benefit appreciated the value of the services provided by their local authority.[170]

One of the most controversial reforms was the creation of the *Social Fund*, designed to replace the system of discretionary payments which had been available under the supplementary benefits scheme to help people with specific needs, such as furniture grants, the number of which had increased three and a half times between 1978 and 1983.[171] The aim of the Social Fund was to cap the budget which had increased from £44 million in 1981 to £220 million by 1984.[172] 70% of all expenditure was to be in the form of interest-free loans, but strict cash limits applied to the sums which local social services could allocate in any year.[173] As Timmins notes, the Social Fund, at least, brought about the end of tribunals considering whether or not a claimant was entitled to a 'grant for a hot water bottle'.[174]

## 1987 general election

In the spring of 1986 there were signs of the reversal of economic decline. The new economic agenda overturned the old order of financial crises, prices and income policies, the rescue of corporate failures, industrial conflict and countless strikes. Instead there was an economic regime of monetary rectitude, balanced budgets, free enterprise, private ownership and lower income tax. The political power of the trade unions had been curbed and substantial sectors of the economy had been privatised.[175] Moreover, with the privatisation of British Telecom and British Gas, a 'shareholder democracy' was created.

The economic indications, apart from unemployment, were all favourable. Low inflation and low interest rates had given rise to economic growth, which in turn increased tax revenues providing scope for reductions in income tax and even some relaxation in the control of public spending. By the summer of 1986 economic growth in Britain was the highest in Europe at 3%. Buoyant Treasury revenues enabled Lawson in the autumn to increase public expenditure in the 'politically vulnerable areas of health and education' with £7.5 billion of the additional cash to be spent in 1987–88, the year of the general election, and £5.5 billion the following year.[176] The legislative measures to reduce expenditure on state pensions – a very much less politically vulnerable area of social service provision – were safely on the statute book well before the election.

During the previous decade the annual uprating had occurred each November. The government, in two stages, changed the month to April so that it was in line with the tax year although linking the increase in the pension to the rise in the Retail Prices Index over the year to the September preceding the April. Consequently in July 1986 the flat rate pension was increased by just 1% from £38.30 to £38.70 (an increase of 40 pence) per week. In April 1987, a few weeks before the general election, the pension was again increased, this time by 2.1% to £39.50 per week.[177] Over this nine months period the flat rate NI pension had been reduced from 21% to 19.9% of average earning.[178]

The election campaign was uneventful apart perhaps from Labour's introduction of the 'red rose' theme. No impression, however, was made on the Conservative's lead in the polls. On election day 11 June the Conservatives, with 42.2% of the vote and 375 seats compared with Labour 30.8 % of the vote and 229 seats, won an overall majority of 100 seats.[179]

## Thatcher's third term

The re-election in 1987 of a Conservative government under Thatcher for a third successive term presaged a further round of market liberal policies entailing cuts in public expenditure.

Although Thatcher reshuffled her Cabinet on 13 June, most of the major posts were unchanged. These included Howe as Foreign Secretary, Hurd as Home Secretary and, significantly but not surprisingly, Lawson as Chancellor of the Exchequer.[180] For Fowler, who moved to Employment, the election represented 'release from the longest period of service of any Secretary of State for Social Services'.[181] His successor was John Moore who had worked in the US and was reputedly an economic liberal. However, the legislation following Fowler's social security reviews was already on the statute book although still to be implemented and so there was no immediate scope for any radical new agendas on pensions or social security. In the reshuffle John Major obtained his first Cabinet position as Chief Secretary to the Treasury.[182] He had entered Parliament only in 1979 when Thatcher first became Prime Minister,

A central feature of the Queen's Speech on 25 June was the proposed replacement of the household rating system by the new (later controversial) flat rate community charge (commonly called the poll tax). The reduction of the basic rate of income tax to 25% was also announced.[183] The growth of nominal (money) GDP had been contained to an average of 8% per annum between 1982 and 1986 (compared with an annual average rate of 15% through most of the 1970s). PSBR now represented 1% of GDP.[184]

In April 1988 the flat rate pension was uprated by 4.2% from £39.50 to £41.15 per week being 18.8% of average earnings.[185] During the same month the government's radical legislation to reduce state pensions expenditure came into force. The measures to reduce the cost of SERPS were long term, aiming to halve the estimated cost in the year 2033 from £25 billion a year to £13 billion.[186] However, the incentive payments and NI rebates introduced to encourage contributors to opt out of the SERPS additional pension by means of their own personal pension scheme was to succeed well beyond the government's expectations. It had been assumed for the purposes of The Personal and Occupational Pension Schemes (Incentive Payments) Regulations 1987 that 500,000 people would contract out by means of personal pensions. In that case, it was predicted that in the tax year 1989/90 the cost to the Treasury would be £800 million.[187] By 1993, however, no doubt encouraged by the media campaigns, more than five million people had opted out of SERPS by means of a personal pension.[188] The effect of the unexpectedly large number of people who took this course, was to completely undermine the 'zero cost principle' imposed by the Treasury.

## Lawson's 1988 budget

Lawson's 1988 budget was tax cutting with the upper rate of income tax being reduced from 60% to 40% and the basic rate from 30% to 25%. The total amount given away by this budget was £4 billion in the first year.[189]

The tax cutting budget soon attracted the criticism that it was ill timed. After the debacle of the world stock markets in the autumn of 1987 (when the FTSE All-Share Index fell from 1222.12 on 5 October 1987 to 784.81 on 10 November 1987 with the capitalisation falling over the same period from £464.6 billion to £299.3 billion, a fall of roughly a third), the US tightened its monetary policy.[190] Britain's economy was also subject to inflationary pressure, and Lawson, many thought, should have followed the US lead.[191] The Commons was told that government revenue was now in surplus by no less than £14.4 billion. The balance of payments deficit only reflected the strength of the economy which was on course for growth.[192]

Lawson had also turned his attention to remedying two problems which were regarded as continuing failures to implement 'true Thatcherite ideology'. The first was mortgage interest tax relief, and the other was 'the over generous' tax status of the occupational pensions industry.[193]

His attempt in the 1988 budget to limit tax relief on mortgage interest payments, which was costing the Treasury approaching £8 billion a year, proved disastrous. His announcement that as from 1 August (for the convenience of the Inland Revenue) relief would be limited to only one person in each household led to a stampede of couples seeking properties before expiry of the period during which multiple tax relief would still be available and caused a rise in house prices for the year of between 30 and 50%.[194]

The Treasury also started to curtail its expenditure on tax reliefs granted by the Inland Revenue to tax approved occupational pension schemes by restricting the limit of surplus (i.e. the excess of the value of the assets over liabilities of the scheme) that could be retained in the scheme, with any excess surplus losing tax relief on its investment income. In assessing the surplus the scheme actuary had to use a prescribed set of assumptions as laid down by the Revenue with the surplus limit being equal to 5% of the scheme liabilities. This test was carried out at each actuarial valuation of the scheme which occurred no less frequently than every 5 years. Because of the favourable financial positions that occupational pension schemes enjoyed at that time, this legislation encouraged schemes in surplus to increase benefits and/or to reduce contributions (including contribution holidays) with the contribution reductions being mainly enjoyed by the sponsoring employers. In a minority of cases, there was a repayment of excess surplus to the sponsoring employer, but such refunds were subject to a non recoverable tax charge of 40%. Any refunds were then treated as a trading receipt for corporation tax purposes.

It has been suggested that Lawson even contemplated withdrawing tax relief from the investment income of occupational pension schemes. However Cabinet colleagues considered this a step too far and he relented. The next stage in the curtailment of occupational pension scheme tax reliefs was announced by Lawson in his 1989 budget speech (the last before his resignation) and introduced by the Finance Act 1989. This was the introduction of an earnings ceiling of £60,000 per annum (to be uprated in line with prices, not earnings) for assessing maximum benefits above which tax reliefs on employees' contributions and investment income would be curtailed.[195] This restriction only applied to new entrants of their employer's occupational pension scheme. A similar limit on salary ranking for pension provision already applied to personal pensions. However, a subsequently introduced new age related scale of contribution rates qualifying for tax reliefs, with the carry forward and carry back rules relating to unused tax reliefs, alleviated the effects of the restriction.[196]

The pensionable earnings ceiling, known later as the pensions cap, caused much concern within the NAPF, as evidenced by the publication in May 1989 of their pamphlet *Truth, Honour and Democracy: The Finance Bill 1989.*[197]

Realising the futility of trying to persuade the Thatcher government to abandon the policy entirely, the NAPF embarked on a strategy of trying to persuade them to uprate the earnings ceiling in line with earnings rather than prices, which would have prevented the number of prospective pensioners affected by the regulation from significantly increasing over the years. The initial pensions cap of £60,000 per annum represented about five times average earnings. However as the NAPF pamphlet pointed out, during the previous 25 years (1964 to 1989) average earnings had moved steadily ahead of prices. During the previous 10 years (1979 to 1989) they had outstripped prices by 2% a year. If the process continued, it was argued, then in 30 years' time, the pensions cap would have declined by around a half in 1989 earnings terms.[198]

The NAPF appeared to be incensed that the Chancellor had broken the undertaking that he had given in his 1989 budget speech that any fundamental reform of the tax treatment of pension funds would be preceded by a green paper. The NAPF in their pamphlet stated that they feared profoundly for the security of future generations in old age, for the time honoured traditions of our parliamentary procedures and for democracy itself[199] and that in time, ordinary working people would find they are losing out.[200]

The NAPF's' pamphlet also referred to pressures constantly brought to bear on the government by right-wing policy advisers to remove pension tax reliefs altogether, supposedly because such reliefs inhibit the spread of popular share ownership.[201] The Pensions Management Institute (PMI) also expressed concern about what they saw as the progressive withdrawal of tax reliefs 'not just for high earners but for an increasing proportion of the working population'.[202]

By curtailing pension tax reliefs at the higher levels of provision, Lawson had removed a significant social subsidy from the retirement incomes of high earners. Nevertheless, in their efforts to encourage a public debate on the issue, the occupational pensions interests and the TUC went beyond their purely functional role of trying to protect the legitimate interests of their members. By inviting discussion on a measure passed into law, and, as they believed, without being subject to the full scrutiny of traditional parliamentary procedures, they saw themselves as acting in the public interest.

It could be argued that if the measure had been designed to achieve a more even balance between the future needs for pension provision of citizens with a labour market value and the present needs for pension provision of citizens without a labour market value, then it could have been seen as an equitable instrument of social policy. This, however, was never discussed nor was it likely that there had ever been any intention to earmark the increase in Treasury revenue from curtailing occupational pension tax reliefs for the purpose of increasing the value of the basic state pension. It is highly probable that such increase in Treasury revenue was simply offset against Treasury revenue forgone by according costly NI rebates and incentive payments to personal pensions. This episode, together with the abolition in 1989–90, of the Exchequer's contribution to the NI Fund – for so long a part of the institutional framework for financing social security in Britain – did not seem to auger well for the poorer of Britain's 'two nations in retirement'.

## ERM

In the spring of 1989, after the episode of the curtailment of pension tax relief, annual inflation reached 8.3% and the current account deficit of the balance of payments increased to more than £19 billion.[203] Since 1985, Lawson had been a convert to the Exchange Rate Mechanism (ERM) of the European Monetary System.[204] The official government position however was that Britain would enter the ERM only 'when the time was ripe'. Nevertheless, as the economy started to go further into recession in June 1989, Lawson and Howe jointly informed Thatcher that they 'would not continue in office unless a specific commitment to join the ERM was made'. By September 1989 she had dismissed Howe as Foreign Secretary and in October Lawson resigned. Major was appointed Chancellor.[205]

Major, supported by the new Foreign Secretary, Douglas Hurd, urged entry to the ERM as the only way to reassure the foreign exchange markets. Thatcher reluctantly agreed on entry in October 1990, just before the Conservative Party conference. Because of Iraq's invasion of Kuwait, inflation had climbed to over 10%, as Britain entered the ERM beset by strong inflationary pressures and the economy in recession.[206]

## Margaret Thatcher resigns

Thatcher's standing with the electorate had already been severely undermined by the riots which had erupted immediately after introduction of the poll tax. 'Downing Street was attacked and the South African Embassy set alight'.[207] The government seemed engulfed by endless controversy over the EEC and national sovereignty, and by November 1990, the boom created by Lawson's 1988 give-away budget had turned to bust. Mortgage rates had reached 15% and unemployment was again rising. Labour had a 20 point lead in the opinion polls.[208]

After Thatcher returned from a summit meeting on European monetary and political union, declaring that she would never countenance a single European currency, Howe, in a scarcely coded Commons speech of resignation as Leader of the House, signalled a revolt.[209] This led to Thatcher's leadership being challenged by Heseltine on Europe and the poll tax. A ballot was called. After failing to secure sufficient votes on the first ballot to avoid a second, Thatcher withdrew from the contest. On 22 November 1990 she announced her resignation. In the second ballot on 27 November, Major emerged as the new leader of the Conservative Party and became Prime Minister.[210]

Looking over Thatcher's Premiership, the basic state pension had increased from £19.50 to £46.90 per week. However its relative value had declined from 25% of average earnings in 1979 to only 18% in 1990.[211] According to Lowe, pensions had suffered the most swingeing cut in value; the overall cost of the pension was reduced by one third, delivering an estimated saving to the Exchequer between 1980 and 1992 of £43 billion.[212]

# Personal pensions

Also over this period, the government had encouraged the rapid growth of the personal pension market, especially with regard to using the product as the vehicle to contract out of SERPS. The total cost to the Treasury in respect of NI rebates and incentive payments for personal pensions, calculated by the National Audit Office for the period up to April 1993, amounted to £9.3 billion. Against this has to be offset the savings of £3.4 billion in respect of SERPS pensions that would no longer be provided. The net cost to the Treasury incurred by the pension reform for this period up to 1993 was therefore £5.9 billion.[213] As Nesbitt points out:

> A scheme designed to relieve future tax payers of the intolerable future cost of SERPS has ended up costing twice as much as it is likely to save.[214]

Many people, to their longer term financial detriment, allowed themselves to be persuaded, on the basis of bad sales advice, to decline or to opt out of membership of their employer's occupational scheme as a consequence of the introduction of the new provisions under the Social Security Act 1986[215] or to transfer benefits out of their employer's occupational scheme on leaving service.[216]

Whether the reasons for the launch of personal portable pensions were primarily ideological or pragmatic, their use as an instrument of policy to reduce state pensions expenditure resulted in a substantial social and economic cost for people as citizens and taxpayers, the consequences of which are significant. From a market liberal perspective, advocates of opting out of SERPS or occupational pension schemes by way of personal portable pensions could take some comfort from Friedman's dictum that those of us who believe in freedom must believe also in the freedom of individuals to make their own mistakes.[217]

Barbara Waine in her article *A Disaster Foretold? The Case of the Personal Pensions*, presents well documented evidence for the view that the problems with personal pensions which surfaced in the 1990s had been anticipated earlier by pension professionals in responding to the 1985 Green Paper *Reform of Social Security*.[218]

She cites, in particular, the responses of the CBI and the Institute of Actuaries, both of which had expressed doubts about the final investment returns of 'individual speculative investments' such as personal pensions.[219] They had, moreover, also expressed concerns about the transaction costs, which could absorb an unreasonable proportion of individuals' savings for retirement, particularly where these are at the minimum level.[220] Perhaps the most incisive comment, quoted by Waine, is a statement from the Reed Stenhouse response: 'we accept that the proposals will give personal freedom to the consumer – they will certainly not give value for money to the consumer'.[221]

The government did try to provide some consumer protection to the purchasers of personal pensions as can be seen from the complex regulatory framework introduced by the Financial Services Act 1986. Although personal pensions had been available since the Financial Services Act 1956 they were, prior to 1988, marketed as retirement annuity contracts to the self-employed (hence the name 'self-employed annuities' associated with the 1954 Millard Tucker proposals from which they originated).

As Nesbitt points out, this is a group of consumers who can be expected to have the financial knowledge to make an informed judgement in purchasing a personal pension. If they lacked sufficient market information, they would certainly have had access to independent professional advice.[222] In contrast, a high proportion of personal pension purchasers after 1988 would have neither the financial knowledge nor recourse to reliable independent advice to make an informed judgement about their retirement provision. However, the need for regulation to protect consumers was at odds with the government's preference for open competition and regulation by market forces. As a result, a compromise emerged in the form of a system of self-regulation imposed on pension providers and financial advisers[223] which failed to give sufficient consumer protection. By 1997 the pensions industry was forced to review 2.5 million cases of potential mis-selling of personal pensions during the period 1988–94. This was primarily life assurance salesmen persuading a new generation of consumers to purchase personal pension plans rather than joining or remaining in (i.e. not opting out) of their employer's schemes and so, in many cases, losing the benefits of the employers' contributions going forward. By 30 June 2002, 98% of the cases had been completed and it was estimated that the final pension review costs being borne by personal pension providers and financial advisers was £11.5 billion in redress with a further £2 billion arising in the administration costs incurred in carrying out the review.[224]

One of the most informed and coherent papers that raised searching questions about the social and economic consequences of the pension reforms of Social Security Act 1986 was the Centre for Economic Policy Research Discussion Paper by Hannah, published exactly two years before the reforms were implemented.[225] The paper was an attempt to examine the 'government's new proposals for personal portable pensions and of the parallel reduction of the benefits in the state earnings related pension scheme … in the light of historical evidence on the behaviour of pension savings'.[226]

As Hannah argued, the flexibility and choice demanded by the government's pension reform will, if it is to be based on personal pensions, inevitably have a social cost. A state pension system, operated within the framework of the general tax-collecting mechanism, without the contracting out option, can have a ratio of administrative expenses to cash flow as low as 1% compared with personal pensions as marketed to the self-employed at that time (with expensive investment and benefit options and high sales commissions and marketing costs) as high as 20% of contributions.[227]

Hannah's researches indicated that even medium sized employer sponsored collective occupational schemes (consisting of a few hundred members) could have expense ratios of about 6% of cash flow and the large occupational schemes (consisting of thousands of members) which cover the great majority of the members of occupational schemes, as low as 2%.[228] From this, it may be concluded that a shift from public to private provision, if operated collectively, would result in no great increase in administrative costs, whilst perhaps facilitating the achievement of a more flexible operational framework. If, however, the proposed shift to private provision were to be by way of personal pensions on an individual basis, then expense ratios would increase dramatically because of the higher administrative and selling costs associated with personal pensions.

Hannah also drew attention to the fact that higher selling costs are generally the consequence of greater competition in ill informed markets[229] such as those likely to be dominated by personal pension consumers from all walks of life. This is a situation which is in direct contrast with those markets dominated by well informed consumers, such as pension fund managers and trustees (often acting on the advice of fee remunerated professional consultants), where greater competition tends to lead to improved performance and lower costs.

The introduction of the government's pension reforms centred on personal pensions led to the cost of retirement provision being increased with adverse social and economic effects. In his paper Hannah concluded that increased private pension provision on such a basis would have serious consequences, reducing resources available for the support of the elderly with an increase in employment in the financial services sector instead.[230]

Since the 1990s, charges on individual pension plans have fallen. This is partly as a result of customer awareness increasing after the Financial Services Act 1986 regulations came into force requiring investment businesses to disclose commissions and charges to customers and partly with the introduction of plans with low capped charges, such as Stakeholder plans. However it is still true that collective schemes are less expensive to operate than individual arrangements.[231]

Writing nearly ten years after Hannah's paper, Waine concluded that the reforms were leading to significant under provision for retirement:

Although Conservative governments since the 1980s have sought to remake pensions in such a way as to secure their ideological objectives of individual property ownership and independence there is little evidence that these objectives will be achieved. However, there are considerable indications that the attempt will create problems for a future generation of the retired as the ideology is likely to mean a reduced level of pension and dependence upon means tested benefits.[232]

## CHAPTER TEN

# Major's governments 1990–97

On 27 November 1990 Major replaced Thatcher as the leader of the Conservative Party and became Prime Minister. He appointed Norman Lamont as Chancellor of the Exchequer with ambitions to be a tax reforming one. Economic policy, however, was now largely subject to the constraints and exigencies of ERM membership. As a result the recession, which had begun in the early autumn of 1990, was prolonged until the middle of 1992, becoming the longest recession in the post-war period. Unemployment was again approaching three million and there was a large rise in social security expenditure. The PSBR was officially forecast to be £28 billion, but in reality was probably nearer £40 billion.[1]

The advent of Major as Prime Minister seemed to augur well for a more sympathetic approach to social policy than that which had characterised his predecessor. The welfare state he proclaimed, in an interview in *The Independent*, was an 'integral part of the British Instinct'.[2] One of his final actions as Chancellor was to unfreeze child benefit which had not been uprated for the last three years of Lawson's chancellorship. During his first winter as Prime Minister there was a spell of bitterly cold weather. Learning that there had been a delay in 'cold weather payments', he ordered that there should be advance payment of the benefit in anticipation of cold weather rather than a payment in arrears after the event.[3]

The government publicised its aim to create standards in schools, hospitals and other public services of sufficient quality to deter people from the belief that the private sector should be their natural choice for education and healthcare, if they could afford it. Eventually a Citizen's Charter was introduced to define the standards of service all consumers of welfare had the right to expect.[4] Such an attempt to guarantee the standards of public services was certainly capable of interpretation as a negation of Thatcherite market liberal philosophy. The Charter soon drew the protest from Nicholas Ridley, one of Thatcher's staunch supporters, that welfare was for those in true need; in other words for those 'who could not afford private health, education or housing'.[5]

The issue of a public service in pension provision received no attention. For the Major government that issue seemed already to have been settled by the Thatcherite social policy agenda. According to Timmins, at the end of the Thatcher era, middle income citizens had not actually been encouraged to abandon the key public services of health and education because they found their concerns being addressed. Only in state pensions, where large numbers of people had opted out of SERPS, and in social housing, where following the policy of council house sales (which as for occupational and personal pensions had significant financial incentives), the service had degenerated into a safety net for those on very low incomes, had the state 'really been rolled back'.[6] The Citizen's Charter, however, even in relation to health and education, came to be viewed as a 'talismanic reform'[7] because the economic recession which Major had inherited led to resourcing problems.

## Beginning the long recession

Lamont's first budget was somewhat deflationary despite the recession and tax changes that included an increase in VAT to 17.5%, and the abolition of mortgage tax relief for higher rate income tax payers – leading to increased mortgage payments for nearly a million people – did not help.[8] The basic state pension was increased by 10.9% in April 1991 from £46.90 to £52.00 per week being 18.3% of average earnings.[9]

Unemployment continued to increase in 1991. On 16 May Lamont told the Commons that it was a price well worth paying to get inflation down.[10] The recession deepened. Home repossessions which had reached 40,000 in 1990 rose to 75,000 in 1991. Another 1.7 million home owners were faced with negative equity, i.e. the situation when the market value of the home is less than the mortgage on it. More than a quarter of a million people were six months in arrears on mortgage payments.[11]

The 1992 budget was intended to have a political character because it was election year. It needed to provide a contrast with Labour's tax raising policies.[12] This was not without difficulty as government spending was increasing due to the recession. Social security expenditure had risen sharply at a time when Treasury revenues were falling.[13] Lamont, unable to reduce taxes before the election, displayed some ingenuity by introducing a new tax band of 20% on the first £2,000 of taxable income, announcing a Conservative policy of increasing this band until it became the standard rate of income tax.[14] The basic state pension in April 1992, the month of the general election, was uprated by 4.1% from £52.00 to £54.15 per week being 17.8% of average earnings.[15]

## 1992 general election

During the 1980s there had been a stark reversal of the post-war trend towards greater social equality in Britain with a substantial growth of inequality in the distribution of income and wealth.[16] At the level of social and economic policy, this was a not unexpected outcome. Nor was it without any ideological underpinning. Thatcher had expressed the view that opportunity has no meaning 'unless it includes the right to be unequal'.[17] The rich might have become richer but some of the wealth would, in time, 'trickle down' to the less affluent. In 1988 Thatcher told the Commons that everyone had benefited from the increasing prosperity.[18] However the official statistics later revealed that, whilst the income of the top 10% of households had risen by 62% in real terms since 1979, the income of the bottom 10% of households had fallen by 6%. In real terms, the income of this group of the population continued to decline with the fall being 14% by 1990 and 17% by 1992, the year of the election.[19]

Labour, for reasons of principle, morality and credibility, accordingly felt that they had to go into the election with their 1987 manifesto child benefit and pension pledges intact, although, in their leader's words it revealed that they were willing to make commitments for redistribution that nobody else was willing to make.[20] The pledges to restore the value of child benefit and increase the basic state pension as well as to restore the pension's link with earnings were the two spending commitments to survive Labour's social policy review. This had been conducted under the chairmanship of John Smith, the Shadow Chancellor, who chaired their economic equality working party after 1987.[21]

In March 1992 Smith prepared his shadow budget largely on the basis of Labour's two main election pledges relating to child benefit and pensions. By then the pension commitment meant an increase of £7 per week on the basic state pension to make up the difference between price inflation and earnings inflation after 1987. According to Timmins, Smith's shadow budget was drafted to raise the £3.3 billion required for their provision. During the election campaign they began to be seen as the wrong priorities. There was by then much greater concern among the electorate about health and education, with the pension pledge seeming unexciting, as it had been around so long.[22] However, precisely because of the expected costs of implementing the child benefit and pension pledges, Labour could only commit to additional spending on health and education of £1 billion and £600 million respectively.[23]

For the first time perhaps since 1979, there was belief among Labour supporters that an election victory was within reach. The Conservatives seemed equally confident, although the opinion polls seemed to suggest that a hung parliament would be the outcome. Having rid themselves of the notorious poll tax, the Conservatives unleashed an onslaught on Labour's tax plans, with the claim that Labour's election pledges would entail additional public expenditure of £37.9 billion.[24]

The Conservatives, with their election posters featuring Labour's tax bombshell and stark warnings that tax increases would affect all incomes over £21,000 per annum (at the time average yearly earnings were £15,800), won their fourth successive general election victory with an overall parliamentary majority of 21 seats.[25] The Conservatives share of the poll was 41.9% which gave them 336 seats. Labour received a share of the poll of 34.4%, winning 271 seats. Although the Liberal Democrats received 17.8% of the vote, they only obtained 20 seats. There was a swing to Labour from the Conservatives of 3.9%.[26]

## Time for a rethink

The Conservatives' election victory under Major in 1992 represented something of a watershed in the development of British social policy. Labour had entered the election with its child benefit and pension pledges as its main welfare commitments, with £3.3 billion of Smith's shadow budget earmarked for their cost.[27] This, as Timmins argues, was an extremely mild version of tax, spend and redistribute,[28] and yet it had been decisively rejected by an electorate ostensibly aspiring to higher 'low tax' incomes and more interested in higher public spending on health and education.

Even before 1992, analysts of voting behaviour had detected 'populist suspicions' about social expenditure which could be exploited by a Thatcherite government introducing promised tax cuts.[29] This posed a problem of electability for Labour because of the party's historical commitment to universalism in benefit provision.

In social policy universalism had been the dominant ideology of the Labour Party[30] since its foundation as a parliamentary party in 1906. This unequivocal commitment to universalism is traceable to the roots of the labour movement in the 1880s in its determination to remove poor law stigma, forever associated with means tests and welfare selectivity. Concerns about other harmful consequences of means testing, such as moral hazard and the penalty on thrift, which may originally have been expressed by Liberals, later reinforced Labour's commitment to universalism.

After the 1992 election, Bryan Gould, who emerged as a challenger for the Labour leadership, suggested that perhaps universalism needed to be reassessed. Labour had alienated, in his view, a large section of the electorate, by appearing to cap their aspirations for higher incomes and better living standards. For less well off members of this group, the party should help to provide a path to wealth creation.[31] Other groups of the population had been uninterested in the promise of higher state pensions and child benefit. Their aspirations would have been better served by improved services in health and education.

If Labour was to be electable it had to find ways of responding to the social and economic preferences of the majority of voters. Yet how was this to be reconciled with the party's supposedly 100 year old commitment to the principle of equality of citizenship in welfare provision, subject only to such provision being biased towards the poor and other deprived groups. This last point was emphasised by Anthony Crosland, the Labour Cabinet Minister, in 1975:

> First an overriding concern for the poor, the deprived and generally the underdog, so that, when considering the claims on our resources, we give an exceptionally high priority to the relief of poverty, distress and social squalor. Secondly a belief in equality.[32]

On this principle, Labour's stance on child benefit and pensions at the 1992 election was understandable. Child benefit had been frozen between 1981 and 1983 and again between 1987 and 1989, a prelude to its eventual destruction.[33] In 1992 the basic state pension was 17.8%[34] of average earnings, this being lower than that in 1948 when the country was still recovering from the Second World War and its sequel the 'Financial Dunkirk'. Surveys of poverty in the early to mid 1990s, including the Joseph Rowntree Foundation *Inquiry into Income and Wealth* carried out by John Hills in 1995, revealed high concentrations of poverty among old people, particularly among those in the very old age group (aged 75 or more) who had a high dependency on state pensions.

By contrast the investment of public resources in the expansion of state education, which had begun with the Education Act 1944, had been prodigious. The Education Act 1988, enacted towards the end of Thatcher's last term, represented a radical move to transform Britain's still relatively elitist higher education system into a system of mass higher education. Although the number of university or polytechnic students had increased more than twofold since publication of the 1963 Robbins Report on expanding higher education, this still meant that only 15% of eighteen year olds were entering higher education. The intention behind the Act was to have one in three eighteen year olds entering higher education by 1999, compared with the one in eight in 1979. The government's target was reached earlier in 1993 when 31% of eighteen year olds enrolled in higher education with the number of full-time students increasing from around 700,000 in 1988 to well over a million by 1993.[35]

This was entirely consistent with the supply-side priorities of economic policy[36] – namely the notion of targeting expenditure on channelling the poor into the production side of goods and services rather than delivering welfare benefits to the poor alone. These priorities can be seen in the Conservative's social policy of expanding higher education and in New Labour's social policy of ending child poverty. This may help to explain why social expenditure on state pensions in Britain has generally been a low priority in social policy, particularly since 1979.

In fact, a significant number of policy makers have argued that social policy should somehow always be consistent with the supply-side priorities of economic policy. Macnicol sheds some light on this. The guiding principle of policy makers, he says, has been to minimise redistribution.[37] Many people believe in the need for better pensions, but are unable to come to terms with the income redistribution required to finance them. Policy makers argue that social expenditure on pensions should have a low priority, not only because it would entail radical redistribution, but also because it was wasteful to divert resources towards those citizens who had no future labour market value.[38] Any policy decision based on such a view, in Macnicol's words, violates the idea of equality of citizenship through welfare,[39] or social service provision. A consequence of such a view was that it undermined the contributory social insurance principle which, as Beveridge expressed it, gives the right to benefits in return for contributions with all citizens being treated equally.[40]

Macnicol also points out that 'social capital' or 'reproduction of labour' arguments have influenced some historical judgements about social policy. He cites, as an example, a comparatively recent comment that the decision of the post-war Labour government to award full state pension immediately made little economic sense because it would have been far more logical to invest in the future, rather than to reward the past workforce.[41] Such an economic calculus of social service expenditure would presumably have to discount the value of the services, including war services, rendered by this past workforce which contributed to the survival of the British state and the security and well being of its future citizens. It accords no recognition to the principle that some claims to justice, like claims on capital, can only be redeemed in the future. Macnicol concludes with the observation that a great test of any society's welfare intentions is whether it is prepared to support its retired citizens, who have no future social capital value.[42]

The notion that social expenditure on services for the young is a more efficient use of public resources than providing services for the old, because the young, unlike the old, have a future labour market value, led Peter Laslett, the historical sociologist, to comment, as long ago as 1977:

> Since it is the elderly who have lived and worked through the time of educational expansion it could be said that they have been paying the bill, but not sharing the benefits... Equity suggests that persons of all ages should have equal shares in the social fund, but the young have had a monopoly in that very considerable part that goes to education.[43]

A further method for limiting the redistributive effect of social policy was by increasing the use of means testing as a device for delivering benefits kept at a subsistence level. For example, at the time of the introduction of the basic state pension in 1948, there had been about a million people receiving means tested social assistance benefits. Of these about 53,000 were unemployed persons, the rest were pensioners. By 1993 those in receipt of means tested income support benefits had increased more than fivefold to 5.6 million. With the addition of dependants, more than 20% of the population were reliant on means tested benefits.[44]

After the 1992 election Smith succeeded Kinnock as Labour Leader. As a response to its defeat at the polls, the party set up a Commission on Social Justice. Smith, whilst professing his personal belief in and commitment to universal provision in child benefit and state pensions, nevertheless announced that it would be a task of the Commission to address such painful issues as the balance between universal and selective benefits.[45]

## Major's second administration 1992–97

In 1990 when he became Prime Minister, Major had spoken of his wish to create a nation at ease with itself.[46] By 1992 the recession, for which Major bore little blame, had deepened into an economic and fiscal crisis on the scale of the mid 1970s.[47] Unemployment continued to rise, necessitating increased social security expenditure. The budget deficit, predicted by Lamont in his 1992 pre-election budget to reach £28 billion, actually grew to £46 billion. Of this at least £13 billion represented the cost of social security payments to the unemployed.[48] Later in the year Britain was forced out of the ERM due to an unstoppable run on the pound.

Up until 1993, non-tax paying investors, including occupational pension schemes, were able to claim back the tax paid on dividends from companies in which they owned shares. This tax was assessed at 25% but in the March 1993 budget, Lamont reduced the relief from 25% to 20%. This reduced the dividends that occupational pension schemes and other lower rate or non-tax payers received. The Treasury estimated that the saving to the Exchequer of this reduction in tax credits would be £1 billion a year. With his 1993 budget, Lamont's tenure at the Treasury was coming to an end and he was replaced by Clarke in May 1993.

The budget deficit, expected to rise to £50 billion in 1993, became the source of deep divisions in the government over welfare expenditure. During his first speech as Chancellor in June 1993, Clarke had protested that he had no interest in dismantling the welfare state.[49] This was four months after Michael Portillo, Chief Secretary to the Treasury had announced fundamental long term reviews of social expenditure, targeting social security, health and education. The declared objective was to identify areas where better targeting can be achieved, or from which the public sector could withdraw altogether.[50] In addressing the Commons, Portillo must have had very much in mind that spending, in Timmins' words, on the 'five giants' of social security (Want), health (Disease), education (Ignorance), housing (Squalor) and personal social services (Idleness) amounted to nearly £160 billion, almost two thirds of government expenditure.[51]

As Timmins points out, the welfare state seemed to be under review in a way previously unparalleled. To Labour MPs who enquired about the services that might be withdrawn, Portillo replied with Smith's own words about the remit of the Commission on Social Justice that 'we should be prepared to re-examine everything. I've not ruled anything out of court'. He went on to say that if Labour could 'think the unthinkable' so could the government. In November Portillo suggested that it would be prudent for those then under 40 to make their own private provision for pensions rather than rely on the basic state pension,[52] for if it continued to be uprated in accordance with price inflation, it would by 2020 be nugatory.[53]

In December 1993 Lilley, then Secretary of State for Social Security, told a Young Conservatives' conference that individuals, families and companies will, in the welfare society of the future, have to undertake a greater share of provision.[54] Five MPs belonging to the Thatcherite 'No Turning Back Group' published a pamphlet *Who Benefits? Re-inventing Social Security* setting out proposals for the abolition of SERPS and the provision for NI contributors irreversibly to opt out of the basic state pension. The pamphlet declared that ultimately the state may provide no insurance of its own.[55] Clarke, the Chancellor, intervened with the comment that the basic state pension was an integral part of the welfare state, that individuals would not be allowed to opt out of it and it would not become solely for those who cannot provide for themselves.[56]

At this precise point in the public debate, the Joseph Rowntree Foundation and the London School of Economics jointly published Hills' informative document *The Future of Welfare: A guide to the debate.* It summarised the conclusions of extensive research on welfare state expenditures from 1974 and projected into the 21st century.[57] It noted that the future of the entire welfare state was under review, that for the government Portillo is leading a review of the main public spending areas, including social security, health and education, and for the opposition, Labour's Commission on Social Justice is covering the same areas and issues.[58]

The document showed that, over the last 20 years or so up to 1993, Britain's welfare spending has been stable as a share of GDP. That share – about a quarter of GDP – is below that of most other European countries.[59] The document concluded that there is no 'demographic time bomb',[60] neither is spending 'spiralling out of control', rather: There are upward pressures: the ageing populations; SERPS; and higher basic pension entitlements. But, even if benefit levels kept up with overall living standards, the total net effects on public finances over the next fifty years [to 2043] would add up to an addition of about 5% of GDP.[61] This level still leaves a real choice about the future of the welfare state.[62]

For those who wished to defend the welfare state and the universal basic pension from their critics and detractors, the following passage in the document was a source of encouragement and hope:

> We could maintain or even improve provision in relation both to need and contemporary living standards, accepting a slow rise in the share of welfare spending in GDP and hence in the taxes or contributions required to pay for it. The rise implied by maintaining services while the population ages would not take Britain's welfare spending above the share of national income already spent in most other European countries.[63]

Commenting on the document, Will Hutton, in *The Guardian*, wrote that, in terms of an ageing population, Britain is in one of the least problematic situations of any Western industrialised country. After a projected peak in 2030, Britain's demographic profile will begin to get younger. If pensions were again to be uprated in line with earnings, the cost would increase from the 1993 figure of 4.1% of GDP to a peak of 7.4% and then again start falling.[64]

Despite Hills' findings, Lilley carried a stage further Portillo's campaign for radical reductions in welfare spending. Publishing projections showing that the growth of social security expenditure had exceeded, and would continue to exceed, growth in the economy as a whole, Lilley argued that such expenditure had gone beyond the nation's ability to pay.[65]

## Influential proposals on future state pension provision

In April 1994 the basic state pension was uprated by 2.7% from £56.10 to £57.60 per week being 17.7% of average earnings.[66] In his document *The Future of Welfare: A guide to the debate*, Hills pointed out that if uprating the state pension in line with price inflation continued, the pension would become trivial in relation to contemporary incomes. Even if earnings growth does not exceed 2% per annum, the pension would be less than 10% of average earnings by 2030. He questioned whether it was feasible to have basic state pension and pensioner income support levels halved relative to contemporary living standards[67] Between 1992 and 1994 proposals for state pension reform emerged from a variety of sources.

Dilnot and Johnson in their paper *What pension should the state provide?* argued that with the increase in the members of SERPS and occupational and personal pension schemes, a universal state pension was no longer required. Instead they suggested resources should be concentrated on the poorest pensioners by providing them with a means tested higher pension thus blending the basic state pension with income support. The authors admit, however, that such a policy would extend the savings trap in which there is no incentive to save, the so-called penalty on thrift.[68]

In their paper *A Unified Funded Pension Scheme (UFPS) for Britain*, Falkingham and Johnson suggested establishing a funded pension scheme invested in the private sector for all citizens. This would replace the state pension scheme financed by current contributions on a pay as you go basis which could disadvantage future generations who would have to bear the cost of pensions of an earlier generation.[69] The proposal would entail every individual building up a private personal pension fund. Individuals unable to build up an adequate pension fund would be aided by a capital transfer from taxation.

All pensions, however, represent a transfer of resources from one group of the population to another, because as Falkingham and Johnson point out elsewhere, saving for old age, whether public or private, funded or unfunded, involves the accumulation of a claim on the goods and services produced by future generations of workers.[70]

Any argument that pre funding is likely to provide greater security or equity than pay as you go financing is not easy to substantiate. Indeed, the principal argument in favour of France's system of repartition – a collective system of occupational pensions financed on a pay as you go basis – is the greater security it affords, by the spread of risk over generations.[71] This is also true at the micro-economic level. A pensioner, through pay as you go financing, has a claim on human capital (the earning power of future workers) at a time when his, or her, own human capital is low or non-existent. Without that claim the assets will, either directly or indirectly, be entirely dependent on tradable assets in financial markets.[72]

Townsend and Walker proposed in a Fabian Society paper restoring earnings indexation to the state pension together with an immediate 10% increase in the amount of the pension.

The cost of earnings uprating and the 10% augmentation would be met by the withdrawal of subsidies and rebates to personal pensions, the removal of specified tax allowances and reducing the amount of the earnings cap for occupational pension schemes. SERPS would be restored to its original 1978 basis with the requirement for higher contributions from employers.[73]

In another Fabian Society paper, Frank Field and Matthew Owen proposed a new role for the state in pension provision, to design and establish a legal framework to facilitate universal pension provision through the private sector. The pension provided would then be underpinned by a state guarantee to ensure a minimum level of provision – suggested to be at least 20% more than the then current basic state pension (in 1993 the minimum being proposed would be at least 21% of average earnings).[74]

Under the arrangement a statutory duty would be imposed by an obligation on employers to pay a contribution of 6% of gross salary into a private sector stakeholder's money purchase scheme and on employed persons to pay a contribution of 4% of gross salary into the same scheme. The state would 'make up' the contributions of unemployed persons, full and part-time carers and non-working parents caring for young children, the level of contribution being determined by special rules appropriate to circumstances.[75]

Further the proposals would entail the phased replacement of the entire Beveridge NI pension system. The authors argued that as universal private pension provision became established (over approximately 25 years) the need for a flat rate pension 'for every affluent pensioner would be called into question'. In addition the tax relief on occupational pension schemes lump sum and capital gains from asset investment (estimated at £9.5 billion per annum) would be abolished. Also there would be provisions for staggered levies to apply to 'claw back' some of the pension entitlement above a minimum level from affluent pensioners.[76]

The market would be encouraged to offer a wide variety of personal pension scheme products and providers for contributors to choose from. As Field's later book *Making Welfare Work* states, there would in addition be a National Savings Personal Pension Plan for contributors, invested in equities and bonds, with an open market option allowing purchase of an annuity at retirement from the contributor's preferred competitive provider.[77]

Another series of proposals for pension reform emanated from the *Commission on Wealth Creation and Social Cohesion* established by the Liberal Democrats under the chairmanship of Lord Dahrendorf (philosopher and social liberal, holding a number of positions during his career including being a European Commissioner 1970–74). First, the state pension would be uprated in accordance with a formula to ensure a higher rate of annual increase than price inflation but a lower rate than earnings inflation. In addition a SERPS pension would be paid to poorer pensioners who were too old to join the scheme at its inception. Secondly, all private pensions would be universalised by the requirement that every employed person over age 25 and their employers would contribute to an occupational or personal pension scheme. Alternatively they could contribute to a National Pension Saving Scheme to give additional choice to contributors. Transfer to this scheme would be permitted for those already in occupational or personal pension schemes.[78]

The Institute for Public Policy Research published a paper recommending improvements to the level of the basic state pension to provide a minimum retirement income for all.

The paper also advocates a reform of SERPS to make it more attractive, better understood, and valued by the membership. Industry wide schemes for both blue and white collar workers should be introduced to encourage the provision of adequate pensions for all employed persons.[79]

The Adam Smith Institute issued a paper arguing that the principle of allowing people to opt out of SERPS into private provision in return for a reduction in NI contributions should be extended to the basic state pension. Similar financial incentives should be offered to encourage contributors to opt out of the basic state pension into private schemes.[80]

As their contribution to the pensions debate, Age Concern's document *A Report on Income and Pensions in Retirement* contained detailed information on pensioners' incomes and assets at the time and a profile of the financial position of older people. There was also a review of the then current pension systems encompassing state, occupational and personal schemes and a critical analysis of the principal proposals for pension reform which emerged during the debate.[81]

Age Concern's proposals were that a flat rate, non-means tested pension should remain as the foundation for income in retirement and that this is the only way to ensure that an adequate income is available to the vast majority of older people without recourse to means tested pensioner income support benefits.[82]

They endorsed the Beveridge principle (without mentioning Beveridge) that an adequate basic pension provides an incentive to make additional private provision because of the knowledge that the state pension will not be withdrawn because of having a private pension.[83] Owing to public scrutiny by the National Audit Office, there is an element of security present in the state pension which is absent from other systems. Moreover, as contributions are collected with income tax, the state pension system is cheaper to administer than any private pension system.[84]

Acting on the premise that an income in retirement should be adequate to cover not only basic needs but also to prevent social exclusion, Age Concern also explored the concept of adequacy. Taking into account research conducted by the Family Budget Unit,[85] they suggested that an individual minimum income of one third of average earnings should be the aim.[86] Age Concern's main proposals were that the basic state pension should be increased and its link with average earnings should be restored to maintain its value in relation to the incomes of the general population.[87] Better coverage under the state pension system should be provided for disadvantaged groups such as women raising families when SERPS started in 1978.[88]

The final and possibly the most influential set of proposals for pension reform to emerge between 1992 and 1994 were from Labour's arms-length Commission on Social Justice which had been established by Smith. It reported in October 1994, three months after Tony Blair was elected leader of the Labour Party following the sudden death of Smith. As Timmins has commented, it proved to be no new Beveridge plan.[89]

The appointment of the Commission by Smith together with the comment in his leadership address that no policy must be regarded as out of bounds for the searching review the Labour Party must now mount,[90] had been widely interpreted as a loss of nerve by Labour over its commitment to welfare and redistribution.[91] Some, however, saw it as an exploration of ways to reinstate the importance of the public sector, and to enable an active state to reassert a public interest in the face of market liberation.[92]

The report was launched by Blair, who neither endorsed nor rejected its more radical proposals. It argued that restoring the pension's link with earnings would be too expensive, estimating the cost at £9 billion a year, and that restoration of the link to earnings would not help pensioners on income support.[93] It recommended that the basic state pension should be subsumed into a new, earnings linked, but means tested, income guarantee for the elderly. This, in Timmins' view, effectively resulted in means testing all pensioners.[94]

It is interesting to compare the Commission's estimated cost of restoring the state pension link with earnings at £9 billion, with Field's estimate of £11.2 billion, quoted in *Private Pensions for All*, for increasing the state pension to the level at which income support and housing benefit would have ceased to be payable. This, of course, would have represented a much more substantial reform of the basic pension than restoring the earnings link.[95] Later in his paper, Field wrote that according to the Inland Revenue's estimates the cost of tax relief on private pension funds' lump sums and capital gains amounted to £9.5 billion. He then indicated that if these two reliefs were to be withdrawn the resulting savings of £9.5 billion would help to pay for the Treasury grant to the NI Fund to finance the universal minimum pension advocated in his paper.[96] Such a Treasury saving would have been equally available to improve the basic state pension.

## Equalisation of state pension ages

Although Thatcher's last government had been committed, at least by 1988, to the principle of equal state pension ages for men and women, it was not until after publication of a white paper by Major's second administration in December 1993 that enabling legislation for a common pension age was introduced in the Pensions Act 1995. Although state arrangements were exempt from the EU equalisation legislation, nevertheless the catalyst for the legislation on equalising state pension ages may have been the landmark ruling of the European Court of Justice (ECJ) in the case of Barber v Guardian Royal Exchange in May 1990. This judgement, relating to employers' schemes, ruled that men and women should be provided by their employers with equal pension benefits at the same age. The logical consequence of the judgement was that in equity men and women should have the same pension ages although it was left unclear by the ruling whether employers could equalise pension ages by raising the pension age for women to the pension age of men.[97]

It was not until September 1994, however, that the ECJ ruled, in another case, that pension ages in employers' schemes could be equalised upwards, but only in respect of future pensionable service.[98]

The Pensions Act 1995 provides for equalisation of state pension ages to be phased in over a period from 6 May 2010 to 6 March 2020. In the case of women who were born on or after 6 April 1955, the state pension age will be 65 instead of the current women's state pension age of 60. In the case of women who were born on or after 6 April 1950 but before 6 April 1955, the state pension age is an intermediate age between 60 and 65, determined in accordance with the Act's provisions.[99]

## New Labour

In July 1995, Blair made a speech to the Fabian Society as leader of the Labour Party which he had now consciously and conspicuously dubbed New Labour,[100] reminiscent of the way Bill Clinton had rebranded his party in the US as the New Democrats. In his speech Blair argued that it had been a great mistake for the political Left in Britain to allow a rift to develop between themselves and the 1906 New Liberals who had created the original 'ambulance' form of the welfare state. Blair said that Labour should value the contribution of these New Liberals and not just Attlee, Bevan or Crosland.[101]

In 1996 New Labour's policy document *Security in Retirement* was published. A section entitled *The Future of SERPS* contained the following statement: We have already suggested that SERPS could not easily or sustainably be rebuilt in its original form. New funded pension schemes could provide better returns for the same contribution level for many people.[102]

Castle, the principal architect and Cabinet sponsor for SERPS in the mid 1970s, responded to the policy document with a denunciatory article in the Fabian Review, protesting that SERPS had been pushed 'to the bottom of the pile'.[103] In the same article Castle also criticised the party's interim manifesto *New Labour, New Life for Britain* which contained no commitment to restoring the earnings link for the basic state pension, but promised a new framework for funded second tier pension provision.[104]

New Labour, in Castle's view, seemed to have accepted that an annual earnings linked uprating could no longer be afforded and that it would be necessary to fall back on some form of means tested pension entitlement on the lines proposed by the Commission on Social Justice. She took the view that New Labour had been frightened off restoring the earnings link by the alleged cost, which the Commission estimated as £9 billion a year. She pointed out that, in quoting this figure, the Commission must have assumed that the pension would be immediately restored in full to its 1979 level by an incoming Labour government which had not been expected. She believed that the link should be restored for future upratings which she estimated would cost half a billion pounds in the initial years. This she indicated would at least bring pensioners more into line with the rest of society.[105]

Castle's article was accompanied by the publication of a pamphlet *We CAN afford the Welfare State* she had written with Peter Townsend, which challenged New Labour's assumptions about welfare reform. The pamphlet was a spirited defence of social insurance arguing that the state pension is 'not a handout'. All workers and their employers have to contribute and, in return, workers earn pension rights guaranteed against erosion by inflation. Such a pension would not be available from any private scheme at the same price, which is why 6 million people still cling to SERPS.[106]

The pamphlet was also a spirited attack on means testing pointing out that it is a disincentive to earn or save and an affront to human dignity. Income support costs £5.45 per week to administer for each recipient whereas the state pension costs 45p per week for each recipient, and, according to DSS figures, the cost of means tested benefits was rising more rapidly than those which were not means tested.[107]

These views were strongly reiterated by the 86 year old Castle in an impassioned speech delivered during the pensions debate at the Labour Party conference in the autumn of 1996.

As a result of the fresh thinking – or 'thinking the unthinkable' – about pensions and the social services enjoined on Labour, some divisions on welfare policy had begun to appear in the party. As Lowe has observed, it was the ideals of the democratic socialists which gave the British welfare state its unique international reputation. Founded on the principle of state intervention, it was no mere corrective for market failings. It was the means of creating a more equal and fair society.[108]

The idea of social insurance continued to have its supporters. For example, David Piachaud of the LSE attempted to clear up a common misconception. In a Fabian pamphlet *What's wrong with Fabianism?*, he argued that the social security budget should not be viewed simply as a sum of money for the Treasury, to allocate as it considers appropriate. A significant part of the budget is made up from NI contributions which individuals are more willing to pay than income tax as they perceive that in due course they are getting benefits for their contributions. If the social insurance benefits for which the contributions pay are 'phased-out', then contributors would have to make provision elsewhere and therefore be unable or unwilling to make the same contributions to the state. Accordingly, the 'pot of gold' to improve means tested benefits would have been lost.[109]

In Timmins' view, it was Blair who had changed the language of welfare for Labour. He argued that socialism was a set of principles and beliefs that should be concerned with ends, not means.[110] In an article published in the *New Statesman* shortly after becoming leader, Blair insisted that Labour had been out of office for 15 years because Society changed and we refused to change with it.[111] This kind of rhetoric and the welfare reform proposals caused some resentment, even anger, on the party's left, but a general election was approaching and much hope throughout the party had been invested in Blair as the leader who would bring Labour electoral success.[112]

## Stakeholding – the elusive concept

During 1996 the word stakeholding, which had entered the welfare debate some years earlier, came into evermore frequent usage with the connotation of making the economy more efficient and society more cohesive in the longer term[113] The term, which originated in the vocabulary of economics, refers to the status of all the parties (i.e. the 'stakeholders') that have a financial or other interests in a company. These stakeholders cover shareholders, creditors, bond holders, employees, customers, management, the community and government. In this context, the debate is about how to recognise and cater for these different interests and how to resolve conflicts between them.[114]

In the political debate, stakeholding was concerned with how to make companies work better, and how to make societies less alienated and fragmented. Stakeholding was the title of the economics section of Labour's *Road to the Manifesto*.[115] Blair made a number of speeches with titles such as *The Stakeholder Economy* and *The Stakeholder Society*.[116] In a speech in Singapore in January 1996, Blair defined the stakeholder economy as one in which opportunity is available to all, advancement is through merit, and from which no group is set apart or excluded. The speech was seen as a non-specific re-defining of Labour's commitments to reduce unemployment, reform welfare, improve education and build trust between government and business.[117]

Will Hutton's book *The state we're in* sets out a different view of stakeholding. It combined a radical critique of the outcomes of Thatcherism with arguments for a stakeholding society which would give everyone a clear stake, from employees in their firms to people in their pensions, with the aim of bringing about an economically productive and socially inclusive society.[118] He argued that the challenge is to create a new financial architecture in which private decisions produce a less degenerate capitalism. He also wanted a commitment to reform the British state and to clear away hereditary privilege, unfair electoral systems and concentrations of power.[119]

This was not attractive to New Labour and they sought to distance themselves from Will Hutton's idea of stakeholding. A leading Labour spokesman commented that New Labour was 'on the sane end of stakeholding not the Hutton end'.[120] In a speech in Derby after his return from Singapore, Blair nevertheless used the concept of stakeholding to criticise the government for denying people a stake in the country although the accusation was supported by little detail.[121] New Labour were as averse to intervening in business,[122] to remodel corporations and strengthen corporate governance to facilitate authentic stakeholding, as they were to introducing radical reforms to public institutions. For New Labour, the task of empowering stakeholders consisted in equipping citizens, particularly the young, to find a place and establish a stake in a social and economic environment beset by constant and rapid change, which is largely globally determined and which government is powerless to reform in order to moderate the impact and pace of change.[123]

This perception led Blair and his Shadow Chancellor, Gordon Brown, to advocate social policies which gave priority to education and training to develop vocational skills. This set the course once again for giving precedence to meeting the needs of those in society who were seen to have a future labour market value over those, such as pensioners and the chronically disabled, who clearly did not. At the 1996 Labour Party conference Blair said in his leadership address, 'ask me my three main priorities for government and I will tell you: education, education, education'. As Lowe commented this was a mantra to be endlessly repeated at the 1997 election when questions were asked about the party's main aims.[124] The leadership of New Labour had taken the party a long way from believing, as Crosland had, that the priorities in the allocation of a Labour government's resources should be 'the relief of poverty, distress and social squalor'.[125]

## The Conservative plan to privatise state pensions

In March 1997, a few weeks before the general election, Peter Lilley unveiled Basic Pension Plus, a plan which, if implemented, would probably have become, as Timmins argues, the biggest and most spectacular privatisation of them all, transferring to the financial market the £33 billion total current liability for the basic state pension and the remainder of SERPS for the next generation of pensioners.[126] Under the plan, new entrants would receive rebates of the NI contributions required to be invested in privately funded personal pension arrangements.[127] On Lilley's calculations the market would provide higher levels of retirement income. For example, a personal retirement fund of £130,000 should provide a pension of £175 per week compared with the then current level of the basic state pension[128] of £61.15 per week (to be increased to £62.45 the following month).[129]

It was claimed that the Basic Pension Plus proposal would offer the next generation 'genuine security through a real fund for its pensions'.[130] Critics pointed out that historical evidence shows that the advance funding of pensions does not necessarily provide greater security than pay as you go financing. The system of funded private pensions, developed in France in the 1930s, was destroyed in the 1940s by the military occupation and subsequent inflation. The French government had to introduce levies on the working population to rescue the elderly whose savings had vanished.[131]

Prudence would suggest that a reasonable balance should be maintained between capitalisation and pay as you go in order to obtain a broad spread of risk. Perhaps it is just because there is a lack of total faith in the long term security of funded pensions that Lilley's proposal provided for a guarantee that, where pension funds had under-performed, the state would supplement the pension emerging to the equivalent of the state pension.[132] No such guarantee would apply to funds supposedly providing the SERPS replacement pension. Basic Pension Plus would have taken 40 or more years to mature and, in terms of 1996 prices, would have removed £40 billion pounds from public expenditure – the largest item in such expenditure. It was estimated that the cost of the rebates would be of the order of £7 billion per annum by 2040.[133]

Under the proposal, pension contributions would not receive tax relief, but the pensions provided would be payable free of tax. The unveiling of the radical proposals of Basic Pension Plus in the Commons stunned the New Labour leadership who, in the words of Timmins, discovered that it was Lilley, not themselves, who had been thinking the unthinkable.[134]

## CHAPTER ELEVEN

# New Labour in government

## 1997 general election

In the campaign which began in April 1997, Basic Pension Plus, despite serious divisions over welfare policy in the government, remained the Conservatives' key proposal for pension reform. Labour's manifesto was cautious on welfare reform. The moderate proposals for welfare expenditure in their 1992 manifesto were believed to have lost them that election. A major aim in 1997 was to ensure that Labour could not be criticised for their tax and spending plans. They put forward five pledges (reproduced on the party membership card). They undertook not to increase income tax rates and to remain within the Conservatives' published long term spending plans (which, it subsequently transpired, the Conservatives would not have adhered to if returned to office). Their other commitments were to reduce school class sizes to 30 for 5 to 7 years olds, reduce NHS waiting lists by ensuring that 100,000 patients received earlier treatment and to get 250,000 under 25s (considered to be the most employable) off state benefits and into work. This New Deal was New Labour's first move in welfare policy.[1]

The five pledges, however, reflected the new image of the Labour Party, after its re-branding as New Labour, as a party of financial prudence and pragmatism. Its leadership had carefully prepared the party for this election during the preceding three years. There were the instructive conclusions of the Commission on Social Justice proposing a more targeted approach to welfare. In 1995 there was the triumphant, perhaps largely symbolic, replacing of Clause 4 of Labour's constitution, with its commitment to the common ownership of the means of production, distribution and exchange, by a pledge of 'equal opportunity' and 'social justice'.[2] In 1996 there was the opportunity to learn from the successful US experience of supply side welfare policy following the introduction of President Clinton's new deal.[3]

An even more pervasive influence in the Labour Party of the 90s was the third way. This was an idea which seemed to have originated in the US Democratic party early in the decade,[4] and was developed into a coherent and sophisticated social philosophy by Anthony Giddens in his book *Beyond Left and Right* published in 1994. The idea was that of a third way between free-market conservatism on the one hand and national protectionist socialism on the other.[5] It entailed the adaptation of social democracy to a political environment dominated by global finance and communications which had severely limited the scope of national governments to act independently.[6]

Labour entered the election campaign with a substantial lead over the Conservatives in the opinion polls. The lead was sustained throughout the campaign and by the end of polling day it was clear that Labour had won the election with a landslide majority. The eventual majority was 179,[7] the largest in the 20th century. The electorate seemed to have responded to New Labour's vibrant campaign theme 'Things can only get better'. But despite the size of the majority, perhaps the extent of the electorate's support was not quite what it seemed. The turnout was the lowest in any election since 1935.[8] In 1997 Labour obtained 43.2% of the votes cast compared with Attlee's victory in 1945 when Labour obtained 48% of the vote based on a higher turnout. In fact, when the Attlee government lost power at the 1951 election it did so after receiving a 48.8% share of the vote.[9]

## The first Blair administration 1997–2001

In his first speech as Prime Minister, delivered at Labour's election victory party a little after 5 a.m. on 2 May 1997, Blair told his supporters and the country that 'We have been elected as New Labour and we will govern as New Labour'.[10]

As widely expected Brown became Blair's Chancellor of the Exchequer. One of his first acts in that office was to cede responsibility for monetary policy to the Bank of England. Blair had declared in the party's election manifesto that 'We will be the party of welfare reform' with one of the first Cabinet appointments being that of Harriet Harman as Secretary for Social Security. She had the reputation of being a Labour moderniser saying that 'work is the best form of welfare'.[11] Field became her Minister for Welfare Reform. Field's post was not in the Cabinet and at first he declined it believing he needed the senior post of Secretary of State if he was to deliver welfare reform.[12]

In July 1997 Brown presented his first budget as Chancellor. He announced that approved pension funds would no longer be able to reclaim the 20% tax credit on dividends in respect of their investments. The withdrawal of this tax concession to pension funds, estimated to save the Treasury £11.7 billion over three years, was described as a reform to boost investment. The reform, according to Brown, was needed as the present system of tax credits encourages companies to pay out dividends rather than reinvest their profits. In his speech to the Commons, Brown offered the justification that:

> Many pension funds are in substantial surplus and at present many companies are enjoying pension holidays, so this is the right time to undertake a long needed reform. So with immediate effect, I propose to abolish tax credits paid to pension funds and companies.[13]

Brown without any compunction as a Labour Chancellor had removed from workers' pension funds what many saw as a valuable state subsidy, an act which, eight years earlier, a tax reforming Conservative Chancellor had been persuaded was a step too far. The NAPF Chairman described the 'reform' as the biggest attack on funded pension provision since the war, removing over £50 billion of extra pension contributions from public and private sector employees over the next 10 years. Even Robert Maxwell, he added, took only £400 million.[14]

This, however, was only one of a raft of 'positive reforms'. Government revenue was also boosted by a windfall tax on privatised utilities, which brought in £5.2 billion of extra revenue.[15] This was earmarked for the New Deal. The Commission on Social Justice, consistent with the philosophy of the third way, had addressed not just the consequences, but also the causes of need, and a Social Exclusion Unit was set up in 1997 to identify and remove the causes of deprivation.[16] The active welfare state – to activate claimants off welfare and into work – had been launched to cut the bills of social and economic failure' and to 'release resources for education and health.[17]

There was no mention in the budget of an increase in the basic pension or indeed of increases in any benefits. Roy Hattersley, who had been deputy leader of the party under Kinnock accused the New Labour leadership of 'apostasy' on poverty and equality. In the article *Why I'm no longer loyal to Labour*, published in *The Guardian*, he argued that without benefit increases the poor would remain in poverty.[18]

Brown's response was that New Labour were committed to addressing 'the causes of poverty – unemployment, low skills and low wages – not simply the consequences.'[19] Peter Mandelson, one of the principal architects of New Labour's victory, conceded in a speech in August 1997, that his party's 'message of opportunity' must sound hollow to poor pensioners, but 'our first efforts must be to help individuals who can escape their situation to do so'.[20] Perhaps more memorable was his plea at that time to 'judge us after ten years of success in office. For one of the fruits of that success will be that Britain has become a more equal society.'[21]

At the end of September 1997, just before the Labour Party conference, 54 social scientists, including members of the Commission on Social Justice, wrote to the *Financial Times*, accusing the Labour government of having 'erased redistribution from the map altogether, despite the massive redistribution from poor to rich achieved by the Conservatives'.[22] The source of their disquiet was the failure of New Labour to improve the value of state pensions and other benefits.

The government's decision not to abandon the reduction in lone parent's benefit caused a revolt to erupt in the Commons in November. 47 Labour MPs voted against the government and another 13 abstained. A junior minister resigned and it was left to Harman, on her own on the front bench, to defend the policy while Blair was giving 'a Downing Street party'.[23] The next proposed reform was to make it more difficult for disabled people to claim incapacity benefit which would enable substantial savings to be channelled into education and health. Timmins records that as New Labour 'prepared to celebrate its first Christmas in office, disabled people chained themselves to the Downing Street gates'.[24]

During the government's first year, the philosophy of the third way which had so influenced New Labour's thinking on social policy after the 1992 election defeat now entered the broad stream of political discourse after a high-powered seminar hosted by Hillary Clinton and Blair.[25] This was followed by the publication simultaneously of Tony Blair's pamphlet The Third Way: new politics for a new century and Giddens' The Third Way: the renewal of social democracy. The term was defined by Giddens as a popular name for a theory of social justice and individualism in the context of the global economy.[26]

## Welfare reform

Brown, the Chancellor, began to introduce his own innovations in welfare cash benefits. In November 1997 he introduced a winter fuel payment of £20 for all households with someone over 60, with the amount increasing to £50 in the case of recipients of income support. In addition cold weather payments to recipients of income support continued to be paid for any period of 7 days when the temperature was freezing or below or it was forecast to be that cold.

He also announced that Family Credit would be replaced in October 1999 with a Working Families Tax Credit. The new benefit, which was to be more generous than Family Credit, would be received through the pay packet, like earned income tax credit in the US, and not claimed by the mother.[27] In this way it would be seen as a reward for being in work, which reflected New Labour's supply-side priorities in social policy.[28]

As promised at the 1986 Labour conference when Castle made her passionate speech for better state pensions, the government announced that it would carry out its Pension Review with 25 organisations and individuals associated with pensioners and pensions being invited to participate in a full review of UK pension provision.

Many submissions were made with the Review team having meetings with a number of the submitters to discuss further their ideas. One of these was the NPC who wanted to ensure that the views of today's pensioners were at the heart of the review process.[29]

Its submissions were wide ranging and detailed covering the basic state pension, the second pensions, older pensioners, financing of national insurance and stakeholder pensions. The recommendations included:

- Restoring the earnings link to the basic state pension
- Over a period of five years, restoring the rate of the basic state pension to the amount it would have been, if it had continued to be uprated in line with earnings since 1980.
- Awarding SERPS credits to older pensioners.
- Increasing the 25p age addition* – £20 was considered to be a reasonable aim.
- Disallowing money purchase arrangements to be used for contracting out.[30]

Six meetings between NPC representatives and Ministers were held to discuss these submissions. Four were held with John Denham, Minister for Pensions, and one with Harman and Denham, with the final meeting being held with Brown, an indication perhaps that it was Gordon Brown who had the final say on pensions.[31]

In March 1998 a little after Brown's budget, the Green Paper *A New Contract for Welfare* was published.[32] This, after numerous revisions, embodied Field's proposals for welfare reform which he had been working on for some months. When it was published, however, it appeared to contain little that Brown had not already announced and no specific proposals on pension reform.[33] During the paper's preparation there seems to have been some discord between Field and the Chancellor with Brown considering that pensions was an issue over which he should have control.[34] Field would apparently 'demand where Brown's ideas for pensions were'[35] and Brown would criticise Field for lack of progress over the paper – this seems to have been impeded by 'exchanges between No 10, No 11 and the Social Security Department'.[36] There was friction too between Harman, the Secretary of State, and Field. Both had to resign from the government in July 1998 although Field was offered a post in another department which he declined[37] with Alistair Darling moving from the Chief Secretary to the Treasury to the Secretary of State for Social Security.

---

* The National Insurance Act 1971 introduced extra pension provision for the over 80s. The age addition since inception has been 25p per week. Further if the person receives either no or less than the full entitlement to a basic state pension then a non contributory pension is payable provided the residence conditions are met. At April 2008, this amounts to £54.35 per week.

During 1998, there had been an extensive debate within government about introducing compulsory retirement saving. There was substantial evidence that those of working age were in general not saving enough to provide an adequate income to support their retirement. Timmins reports that Blair was in favour of employees being compelled to save more for retirement. This was consistent with his 'rights and responsibilities' agenda and could reduce the burden on the state for pension provision.[38] However neither Blair nor Brown wanted to compel employers to contribute more to the pension arrangements of their employees because of the negative effect they believed this would have on the creation of employment opportunities.[39] This clearly was the reason why there was no requirement for employers to contribute to stakeholder pensions taken out by their employees.

It would appear that the idea of compulsory retirement saving was only abandoned after evidence had been presented to Blair that the families of low paid workers, and even the families of moderately paid workers which included larger numbers of children, would suffer deprivation if the breadwinner was compelled to invest more in retirement provision.[40] The social and economic conditions which made it difficult, or impossible, for some groups in society to save for retirement, which Blair was reminded of in 1998, were precisely those which, more than 100 years earlier, had been brought to the attention of the Royal Commission on the Aged Poor 1893–95 by Hardy and other witnesses.[41] The lack of capacity of the poor for thrift has always been an issue and in the cases of Chamberlain in the 1920s and Beveridge in the 1940s resulted in their insistence on the need for a regular Treasury supplement in the financing of the state pension system.

## A new contract for welfare: Partnership in pensions

In December 1998, Darling was ready to publish his Green Paper *A New Contract for Welfare: Partnership in pensions*.[42] According to the paper, the broad principle behind the government's proposals for welfare reform was 'work for those who can and security for those who cannot'. The slogan was probably part of Field's legacy. Of particular interest was the statement: People who work all their lives should not have to rely on means tested benefits when they retire.[43] The proposals were substantial with Glennerster commenting that British willingness to tear up pension schemes at will every few years leaves foreign observers gasping.[44]

The government's proposals for pension reform were in three main areas as follows:

### 1. Reform of means tested Income Support

The paper states that the basic state pension will remain a key building block of the pension system and will continue to be increased at least in line with prices.[45]

In accordance with the 1994 recommendations of the Commission on Social Justice, the basic state pension would only be guaranteed to increase at the rate of price inflation. This presumably meant that the government had accepted the Commission's argument that restoring the pensions link with earnings would be too costly and 'would not help pensioners claiming income support'.[46] This maintained the policy introduced by the Conservative government in 1980.

Help would be provided to pensioners claiming income support and to future poorer pensioners through a minimum income guarantee. Its aim was to ensure that all pensioners received a decent income in retirement.[47] In April 1999 Income Support for pensioners was renamed the Minimum Income Guarantee (MIG). The amount of the MIG from that date was £75 per week for a single pensioner compared with the basic state pension which, at the same time, was uprated from £64.70 per week to £66.75, being 16.4% of average earnings. A higher rate of MIG was payable for eligible recipients aged 75 and over.[48]

According to the Green Paper, the MIG would be increased in future as resources allow, with the aim of increasing the benefit in line with earnings growth so that all pensioners can share in the rising prosperity of the nation.[49] It was pointed out that the MIG would be unable to provide all pensioners with a share in the nation's rising prosperity because it was a means tested benefit only for claimants. If the basic state pension continued to rise only in line with prices an increasing gap would emerge over time between that rate and the MIG.

## 2. State Second Pension Scheme replacing SERPS

A state second pension (S2P) Scheme would start to replace SERPS from April 2002.[50] Pension rights already accrued under SERPS would not be affected by the reform. S2P has three salary bands between the lower and upper earnings levels and within each band benefits are built up at different rates of accrual. The target pension varies from 40% of earnings for the low earnings band (those earning less than £9,000 per annum at the time – approximately half average earnings) to 20% of earnings for the high earnings band (those earning at or in excess of £18,500 per annum at the time – approximately average earnings). As a result those in the high earnings band would be no better off under S2P than under SERPS. In addition for those in the low earnings band their S2P benefits are deemed to be based on earnings of £9,000 per annum.[51] Carers in certain categories and disabled persons who are unable to accrue S2P benefits from paid employment would be credited with S2P accruals as if they were 'low earners'. Consequently the main beneficiaries of S2P are the low earners. It achieved the government's objective of lifting future low income pensioners out of poverty while the proposed reform of Income Support (the Minimum Income Guarantee) would do the same for today's poor pensioners.[52]

A person who built up a lifetime of pension accruals in S2P would be entitled to a pension amounting to a little more than the means tested retirement income support benefit payable to poorer pensioners. However, as Glennerster points out, because the S2P pension does not increase in line with earnings after retirement, whereas the means tested benefit does, the amount of the former will soon be overtaken by the latter. As a result S2P pensioners with full pension entitlement would 'fall back into means tested support not long after retiring'.[53]

S2P was enacted into law by the Child Support, Pensions and Social Security Act 2000 and came into effect for accruals from April 2002 with contracting out of S2P being permitted.

## 3. Stakeholder pensions

The Green Paper's third main proposal for pensions reform was the introduction of a system of stakeholder pensions. The government's aim for this proposal was to introduce more flexible value for money pension schemes providing more efficient access to pensions and promoting the habit of saving. These pensions are essentially personal pensions with a statutory limit on management charges. The annual management charge was capped at 1% of the fund under management (although this was increased subsequently to 1.5% for the first ten years of a stakeholder pension contract taken out after April 2005).[54]

All employers (other than those with fewer than five employees or offering employees a qualifying personal pension or occupational pension scheme) are required to provide access to a nominated stakeholder pension scheme. Employers are also required to offer the facility to deduct stakeholder pension contributions from the employees' pay, although they are not required to contribute to the pension. Decision trees, published by the Financial Services Authority, were made available to enable potential investors in stakeholder pensions to decide whether to take out such a pension without seeking independent financial advice.[55] In fact, one of the aims of stakeholder pensions is to increase private pension provision, particularly for those on incomes of between 50% and about 125% of average earnings.[56] The legislation governing stakeholder pensions was embodied in the Welfare Reform and Pensions Act 1999.

Many made submissions during the Green Paper's consultation period for the Green Paper including the NPC. The NPC's conference in January 1999 unanimously agreed that the submissions of the pensioners' movement to the Pension Review had been totally ignored.[57] In the NPC's view, the proposals in the Green Paper:

- did not address the needs of today's pensioners, nor seriously those of the working population;
- offered nothing, beyond means tested provision, for today's poorest and oldest pensioners;
- did not adequately address the pension needs of women as carers;
- would provide a pension above the poverty level only for the better off who are able to save and invest, instead of increasing and strengthening national insurance to provide a decent retirement income for all.[58]

The NPC called for an alternative policy from the government which recognised the rights of today's pensioners, made adequate provision for the future and was not biased against state provision.[59]

## SERPS survivors pensions fiasco

Early in 1999 the Benefits Agency discovered, to the government's embarrassment, that the 'halving' of SERPS widow's and widower's pensions, due to take effect in 2000, had not been mentioned in the Agency's leaflets. Although legislation to give effect to the reduction had been passed by the Conservative government in 1986, the leaflets had not been updated.[60] As a result, retired couples or those on the point of retirement learned of a reduction in an earned benefit of which they should have had 14 years notice. Accordingly, the government, in the face of a threatened court action by Age Concern and warnings from a Parliamentary Select Committee of an 'administrative disaster', agreed to a partial postponement of the benefit reduction at an estimated cost of £12 billion over 50 years.[61]

## Pledge on child poverty

In March 1999 Blair went to Toynbee Hall* to announce the 'historic aim' of 'ending child poverty within a generation'.[62] Both Timmins and Lowe consider the pledge to be extremely astute politics. By concentrating resources on those with a future labour market value, it was consistent with the supply-side priorities of economic policy.[63] No child was to be in a family earning less than half average income. Public support for redistribution to poorer families and pensioners might be limited, but few would object to its use to eradicate poverty among children.[64]

## National Minimum Wage

The April 1999 budget announced the National Minimum Wage. Its initial rate was £3.60 per hour (£5.52 per hour in 2008) with a lower rate applying to younger workers, which some thought to be far too modest. In addition Brown announced that the New Deal to induce people to work by ensuring work paid by granting tax credits[65] and initially funded by windfall taxes was now to be consolidated into a permanent policy.[66] The government's message was abundantly clear and made explicit by the Chancellor: Your responsibility is to seek work. My guarantee is that if you work, work will pay.[67]

Brown also announced in his budget a 1% cut in income tax, a £12 billion increase for education over four years, a twofold increase in finance for housing association homes ('building for the poor') and some £800 million for neighbourhood renewal. After two years of prudent public spending, the Chancellor was able to claim that his 'prudence with a purpose' was delivering a sound economy.[68] As Timmins observed, the one group 'conspicuously missing from this three year settlement' were the elderly.[69]

In April the basic state pension was increased by 3.2% from £64.70 to £66.75 per week, i.e. 16.4% of average earnings.[70]

As promised in the budget, Working Families Tax Credit was introduced in October 1999. This guaranteed to any person in full-time work with children an income net of tax of £10,400 per annum,[71] about half average earnings.[72] By 2000 the policy of increasing cash benefits and tax credits to eradicate child poverty had added up to a third to the annual income of poor families.[73] Nevertheless in 2000 Britain still had one of the highest rates of child poverty (after housing costs) in Europe at 32% compared to 13% in Germany and 12% in France with the EU average being 20%. As poverty can never be completely eradicated, the government's new declared aim was the lowest rate of child poverty in Europe. But this would require a major reallocation of resources.[74] Poverty, for this purpose, was defined as living below 60% of the contemporary median income level, after housing costs.

---

* Toynbee Hall is a charity, founded in 1884 by Canon Samuel Barnett and based in Tower Hamlets in the East End of London, producing practical innovative programmes for young people and families, adults, and older people to meet the needs of local people, improve social conditions and enable communities to fulfil their potential.

## Incapacity benefit, state pension and Pension Credit

Incapacity benefit was one of the two major universal long term benefits. The other was the basic state pension. The government believed that the relative laxity of the test of incapacity, which determined whether a person was eligible for the benefit, could encourage fraud and dependency. Accordingly, a more stringent test of incapacity was introduced in 1999. This aimed to determine the degree of capacity of a person to do some kind of work rather than their incapacity to do any kind of work.[75] It enabled resources to be transferred from the less disabled to the more severely disabled and to children.[76] The reform was opposed by 67 MPs.

An element of means testing was eventually introduced for the first time in relation to a NI benefit. A portion of incapacity benefit was clawed back for each £1 of private ill-health pension or disability income insurance the claimant received. As Lowe has observed: The disabled were one of the government's less favoured groups of claimants.[77]

In April 2000 the basic state pension was increased by 75 pence per week to £67.50 per week. Although calculated in accordance with the formula, namely the annual increase in the Retail Prices Index up to September 1999 (i.e. an increase of 1.1%),[78] the discretion within the legislation to grant a higher amount was not applied, especially when the economy at the time was buoyant and increases in earnings outstripped prices by a considerable margin. The response to the increase was anger and widespread resentment among pensioners who, with some justification, felt that they had been excluded from a share in rising prosperity.[79]

The acrimony could easily have been avoided, if the government had taken note of the reaction of Parliament to the previous December announcement of the proposed pension increase. This was when 106 MPs, including 64 Labour members, signed a Liberal Democrats' early day motion in protest at the 'miserly increase'.[80]

The resentment of pensioners and disquiet in the party and the unions led to a revolt over state pensions at the Labour Party conference in October 2000. At the conference Castle, almost 90, made a powerful speech setting out a strong case for the restoration of the earnings link as she had done four years earlier at the 1996 conference. At that time the New Labour leadership avoided a confrontation over its pension policy by promising to institute a Pension Review which it did on returning to government in 1997.[81]

At the 2000 conference Castle had the full backing of the unions and pensioners lobby. The conference vote on restoring the earnings link to the basic state pension was won. However conference votes do not determine Labour policy. In his conference speech, Brown had argued that our priority cannot be that the wealthiest get exactly the same as the neediest.[82] Blair in his keynote address felt constrained to mention the issue on account of the vote, declaring that he could not agree to restoring the earnings link because it would impose an intolerable economic burden on future generations.[83]

The preference of New Labour for selectivity over universality in state pension provision had been successful in its policy of targeting redistribution of resources on poorer pensioners. The policy nevertheless was causing some resentment among slightly less poor pensioners who failed to qualify for means tested support by having small amounts of savings, or a minimal private pension. They were no better off for having saved than they would have been if they had not saved. The government had to concede that one of the consequences of means testing was the penalty on thrift. This also ran counter to its policy of encouraging lower paid workers to save for retirement through stakeholder pensions.[84]

The Labour Party conference vote on pension reform, together with the growing resentment over the administration of the MIG, led to the government reassessing its retirement income support policy. In November 2000 it published *The Pension Credit: a consultation paper*.[85] The document was prefaced by the government's commitment to ensure that all pensioners share in the rising prosperity of this country, with more help for those on low and modest incomes than ever before.[86] In this introductory statement there was more than an echo of New Labour's 1996 commitment to ensure that all pensioners, today and tomorrow, share fairly in the increasing prosperity of the nation.[87]

A significant increase in the MIG for younger pensioners was announced in the paper. The benefit was to be increased from £78.45 per week in 2000/01 to £92.15 per week from April 2001[88] with the assurance that the 2002 increase would be above earnings inflation. The effect was to increase the MIG rate for younger pensioners to the rate for older pensioners, resulting in a simpler non-age related scale. Older pensioners accordingly did not benefit from this increase to the same extent as younger pensioners.[89]

The paper announced some modification for the 2001 and 2002 pension upratings with the basic state pension increasing by £5 a week in April 2001 and £3 a week in April 2002, so increasing the pension to £75.50 a week by 2002. For Timmins there was an irony in the 2001 increase being precisely that pledged by Labour at the 1992 election which was summarily abandoned by Brown afterwards.[90] It represented an increase of 7.4% in the pension compared to the RPI increase of 3.3% and in the Average Earnings Index of 4% for the year to September 2000.[91] The corresponding percentages for the 2002 increase were 4.1%, 1.7% and 4.4% respectively.

The paper indicated that the proposed above inflation increases in the basic state pension for 2001 and 2002 were awarded to give immediate extra support to pensioners on low and modest incomes ahead of the introduction of a new benefit, which would also be means tested, and would be called the Pension Credit.[92] This benefit superseded the MIG from 2003 as the new form of income support for poorer pensioners comprising of two elements – the Guarantee Credit, like the MIG, being that required to uplift the pensioner's income to the standard minimum guarantee and the Savings Credit provided a further top-up to reward a pensioner aged 65 and over who has built up a modest income for retirement whether in the form of a second pension or savings.

Under the means testing rules which applied to the MIG, any income from a second pension (i.e. a private pension or SERPS) was taken into account in full in calculating the benefit. In other words, every £1 of weekly income from the second pension resulted in a £1 reduction in the MIG benefit. The Savings Credit amounts to 60p for every pound of pension (such as occupational pensions and SERPS) and income from savings by which the pensioner's income is above the level of the savings credit threshold (i.e. the full rate of the basic state pension) and below the standard minimum guarantee. For every pound of income a pensioner has above the level of the standard minimum guarantee, the Savings Credit is reduced by 40p to a minimum of nil.[93]

The recipient's income is augmented by the Pension Credit being the sum of the Guarantee Credit and the Savings Credit. As a consequence, even when the recipient's income before Pension Credit is in excess of the standard minimum guarantee, a Savings Credit may still be payable.

Consequently the additional income supplement provided by the Savings Credit is subject to a maximum. The pensioner only receives this maximum if the person's weekly income of the basic state pension, second pensions and that from savings is equal to the standard minimum guarantee. In 2003–04, the weekly standard minimum guarantee was £100 (about 21% of average earnings) for single pensioners and £154 for pensioner couples so the maximum Savings Credit in 2003–04 was £13.80 a week for a single pensioner and £18.60 a week for a pensioner couple. However, as the NPC pointed out, most qualifying pensioners would receive much less than the maximum Savings Credit.[94]

The proposals in the consultation paper revealed that the government was aware of some of the negative aspects of means testing. The claims procedure for the Pension Credit would be simpler than that for the MIG, and, in order to reduce stigma, means tests for entitlement to benefit would be conducted less frequently than had been the case with the MIG.[95] The Pension Credit was introduced into law by the State Pension Credit Act 2002 and came into effect in October 2003.

It is unsurprising that many pensioners experienced perplexity as they struggled to understand the complexity of the new benefit. The introduction of Minimum Income Guarantee – a title invented not by the Department of Social Security, but by the Chancellor[96] – has been referred to as 'one of the great milestones' in the history of the first New Labour administration.[97] Its aim was to eliminate poverty among pensioners which income support had failed to do. However it had to be said that the MIG, initially reflected a restricted definition of poverty and, on the government's own admission, penalised pensioners with modest savings.[98] Martin Hewitt, a social policy analyst, cited by Lowe, described these attempts to lift pensioners out of poverty as taking on the guise of a Heath-Robinson cartoon as the problems of means testing are addressed by bolting on further means testing mechanism to produce what could only be called an unwieldy and unworkable structure.[99]

In a pamphlet published early in 2001, the NPC pointed out that, despite the promise made in the Green Paper *Partnership in Pensions* that action would be taken to ensure that everyone who is entitled to MIG received it, only 82,000 of the estimated 500,000 pensioners entitled to but not receiving it had now made successful claims.[100] Despite this situation, New Labour's faith in the efficacy of mass means testing, not simply as a measure to meet the needs of the current generation of poorest pensioners, but as a permanent feature of pensions policy was undiminished. It was estimated that Pension Credit would more than double the number of pensioners dependent on means tested support so covering half of all pensioner households, or about 5.5 million pensioners in 2003. The policy was a reversal of policies pursued throughout most of the post-war era to reduce the dependence of pensioners on means tested benefits.[101]

The NPC also deplored the government's intention to abolish from April 2001 the higher rates of means tested support, introduced in the early seventies, to meet the needs of pensioners over 80 years.[102] The Savings Credit only applied to income above the full amount of the basic state pension. Therefore pensioners with less than a full contribution record and therefore receiving a reduced amount of basic state pension being payable – mainly women – would not be rewarded for every pound of income from savings, second pension or even earnings. Statistical records showed that 51% of all women pensioners did not qualify for the full state pension. In such cases every £1 of income that would be required to increase income up to the basic pension rate would be deducted from the Guarantee Credit entitlement just as it had been deducted from the MIG.[103] The NPC pamphlet also criticises the Pension Credit for its distributional effects and the rules proposed to ensure that recipients of the benefit, previously entitled to means tested housing benefit and council tax benefit, continue to do so. These rules, argued the NPC, would inevitably result in a significant increase in means testing.[104]

Brown was approaching his fifth budget, the last one before the general election. On the premise that major elements of social policy were an integral part of economic policy, Brown and the Treasury had exerted a dominance over even the details of welfare reform, especially pensions.[105] According to Timmins, Brown's budgets had by 2001 delivered a distribution of the fruits of growth in favour of the less well off. Pensioners and households with children were the main beneficiaries, each gaining about £5 billion.[106]

This is echoed by Lowe, who goes on to argue that pensioners had even gained more than children. He lists the four main sources of public income from which pensioners benefit: the basic state pension – around 16% of average earnings; winter fuel allowance and free TV licences for over 75s; housing benefit and council tax benefit; and MIG introduced in 2000 and transformed into Pension Credit in 2003.[107] The first two are universal with the other two means tested.

As Lowe commented, pensioner poverty has not been eradicated, although the number of pensioners in poverty declined from 27% to 24% between 1997 and 2001.[108] Pensioners had gained £5 billion from Brown's distribution, but in a £900 billion plus economy,[109] this was hardly a seismic shift of resources.

The 2001 pre-budget report from HM Treasury announced that the rate of the MIG and its successor, the Guarantee Credit, would be increased in line with earnings growth throughout the next parliament i.e. after the 2001 general election.[110] The report also announced that the basic state pension would be increased by at least £100 a year in April 2003. In fact it was increased by £1.95 per week (i.e. £101.40 pa) to £77.45 per week. Since the increase in the Retail Prices Index was 1.7% for the year up to September 2002 – the measurement date usually used for the uprating – the actual increase in the pension of 2.6% was the third successive above price inflation annual increase in the pension In addition, the report contained a declaration of intent to increase the rate of the basic state pension in subsequent years annually by the higher of 2.5% and annual increase in the RPI.[111] This declaration of intent concerning the uprating of the basic state pension, however, was not enacted into law although to date the government has honoured it.

On account of these changes in the method of uprating pensioners' incomes it could be argued that the government met its commitment as embodied in the Pension Credit consultation paper, to ensure that all pensioners share in the rising prosperity of this country, with more help for those on low and modest incomes than ever before. However there was no undertaking that the share of all pensioners in rising prosperity would be proportional to that of wage earners, or even to that of poorer pensioners, but it would be a share provided that the yearly increase in the Retail Prices Index remained below 2.5%.

## 2001 general election

Pensions were not a significant issue at the 2001 general election.[112] There was discussion about university tuition fees in England which had become an issue after Scotland solved the problem in its own way.[113] All political debate, however, was 'ideology-lite', a result perhaps of the primacy accorded to the economic market in the social policy preferences of all three main parties. The Conservatives certainly had some difficulty in finding 'clear blue water' by which to distinguish themselves politically from New Labour.[114]

Between 1997 and 2001 there was more convergence between the ideas and policies of the two parties on welfare reform. This is evident from New Labour's policies, such as the New Deal to get people into work, which are firmly focused on supply-side measures to improve the efficient working of the market.[115] The old Labour ideal of the social democratic state had transmuted into the 'social investment state'.

New Labour's dominant campaign theme was to continue with the implementation of its programme of economic efficiency and social justice, and to start the second stage of building its active welfare state. The Conservatives had little recourse but to commit broadly to New Labour's health and education plans and to advance tentative proposals for tax relief on medical insurance premiums and for a watered-down version of Lilley's basic pension plus.[116]

Turnout in the election at 59.4% was the lowest of any election since 1918.[117] Labour's share of the vote was 40.7% and 413 seats, compared with the Conservatives 31.7% and 166 seats and the Liberal Democrats 18.3% and 52 seats. The outcome for Blair's Labour Party was a parliamentary overall majority of 167 seats,[118] a landslide victory with the support of just over 24% of the electorate.

## What is poverty?

During their first term in office, Blair and Brown had held broadly similar views on the priorities in pension provision. In responding to the pressures from an ageing society, attention had to be focused on the poorest pensioners. This entailed a greater role for means tested retirement income provision for the current pensioner population. For those in work and the future work force, however, the leaders of New Labour believed there had to be a greater reliance on the private sector in pension provision.[119]

But the dwindling state pension, combined with the government's new means tested retirement income support policies, had made only a small impact on pensioner poverty. This was at least in part due to the poverty standard being applied, namely the European Union measure of 60% of the median income of the member state. This is calculated after housing costs are deducted from the individual's and the median incomes. The measure is dynamic because, as with all measures of relative poverty, the poverty line moves in step with median income.[120] Use of this standard for compiling official statistics led to a dispute during the election about definitions of poverty.

Brown had claimed in the election that New Labour's policies had reduced the number of children living in poverty (estimated in 1998–9 as 4.5 million) by 1.2 million. However it was revealed by the official statistics immediately afterwards that the real number was in fact much lower at 0.5 million. It transpired later that Brown's figures had been based on a 'static' measure of poverty, rather than a 'dynamic' measure like the EU's standard.[121]

Later, in 2004, the official British standard was changed having the effect of reducing the number of children in poverty at a stroke by 900,000. This entailed a change in the basis of calculation from after housing costs to before housing costs, which in areas of high housing costs might underestimate the true extent of poverty.[122] Why the change from the EU measure was made is not clear in view of the government's declared aim to reduce the rate of child poverty in Britain to the lowest rate in Europe. According to the EU's preferred measure (60% median contemporary income after housing costs), 33% of UK children were in poverty in 1998–9 reducing in three years to 30%. The corresponding figures for pensioners were 27% and 22%.[123] Low income figures published by the DWP in *Households below average income 2001–02* document showed that in 2001–02 there were still over 2 million older people living in poverty on the EU's preferred measure.[124]

Many including Age Concern recommended that the government should establish clear targets for abolishing pensioner poverty in line with the commitment on child poverty. In support of this, the DWP in the above mentioned publication commented that pensioners are the demographic group most likely to have a persistently low income. This renders them extremely vulnerable to deprivation.[125]

There are other income standards for measuring poverty, in addition to those mentioned above. The most common examples are the minimum income levels established for means tested income support under social assistance schemes and the World Bank's somewhat arbitrary and widely criticised $1, $2 or $4 per day standard.[126] They are considered to be useful for their simplicity and for their comparability with similar international standards. However, because income standards are unrelated to criteria of need or deprivation, the poverty thresholds established by reference to them are considered to be arbitrary compared with those based on an objective measure of human needs, such as *household budget standards*. These are specified baskets of goods and services which, when priced, represent particular living standards. Budget standards, regularly updated, are useful indicators of human needs. The idea was developed by Rowntree in his study of poverty in York in 1901. The methodology was used by Beveridge in calculating social security benefit levels for his 1942 report. It has also been used to determine the US poverty line since the 1960s.[127]

When politicians refer to lifting people out of poverty they are often referring to lifting their income above the level at which they would qualify for means tested income support. The MIG (£92.15 per week in 2001–02) if used as a measure of poverty is of course lower than the 60% of median contemporary income measure used by the DWP in establishing that over 2 million elderly people were in poverty in 2001–02. That income measure was then about £170 per week. How many people would have been in poverty at that time according to the lower MIG measure? It is therefore surprising that, in a written answer to a parliamentary question on 30 November 2000, the Pensions Minister, Jeff Rooker, wrote:

As a result of the measures outlined in the pre-budget report, over 2 million pensioners will benefit from the MIG in 2001–02; this will increase to 2.2 million in 2002–03.[128]

Actual DWP figures showed that in May 2002, 1,746,000 people aged 60 or more (single pensioners or couples) were receiving the MIG on account of their low incomes. It was estimated by the DWP that in 1999–2000, the year in which the MIG was introduced, between 22% and 36% of pensioners entitled to income support, did not claim it.[129] Whatever the reasons may have been for not claiming the benefit – stigma or the complexity of the claiming process – this situation has led people to question New Labour's pension policy.

In the March 2002 issue of *Accountancy*, John Shuttleworth, an actuarial partner of PricewaterhouseCoopers, although acknowledging the relative strength of occupational pension schemes and private pension provisions in the UK supported by generous tax incentives by the state wrote:

> The government is keen to boast of the UK's low spend on state pensions. It is already the lowest in the European Union (half the EU average, at just 5% of GDP). In spite of our adverse demographics, we are the only member state where the spend is expected to fall over the next few decades. Some boast![130]

## Decline of occupational pension schemes

In 2000–01, the DWP revealed that 69% of pensioner households depended on state benefits for at least 50% of their income.[131] In these circumstances the feasibility for the state to reduce its role in retirement income provision could be questioned. This had certainly been the objective of all Conservative governments since the Second World War. It was also the declared intention of the New Labour government that by 2050 a significantly higher proportion of retirement income will come from occupational schemes, and other forms of funded private provision, than from the state.[132]

In the government's view, however, the problem was not the current generation of pensioners. There may be less than complete take up of pensioners' full range of entitlements – perhaps as many as a third did not claim – but the government was convinced that the intensity of the poverty of pensioners, the extent to which their incomes were below the poverty threshold (however defined) was typically very low.[133]

The problem was the prospective pension entitlements of those currently in work. While occupational pension schemes had been in surplus from high share values prior to the end of the 20th century and encouraged by the statutory restrictions on 'excessive surpluses', sponsoring employers had adopted a mixture of taking reductions in contributions including holidays, improving members' benefits and in relatively few cases taking a refund. However starting in the 1990s occupational pension schemes were hit by the combination of no longer being able to reclaim tax credit on dividends from 1997, the stock market collapse after 2001 and the effect of low inflation resulting in virtually all benefits – some forced onto schemes by legislation – becoming contractual, so adversely affecting solvency. This in turn resulted in more legislation attempting to provide appropriate protection and progressively more stringent accountancy requirements in assessing the financial position of such schemes within the sponsoring employers' own accounts. As a result, surpluses quickly disappeared with substantial deficits on the balance sheet of the sponsoring companies appearing.[134]

The eventual response of most organisations was to reduce the pension promises made to new staff and, in some cases, those to existing staff in respect of future pension accruals. This was usually accomplished by closing final salary schemes (schemes under which pensions are based on service and earnings at or near retirement age) to new entrants, and sometimes to all future accruals.[135]

Two thirds of private sector final salary schemes had been closed to new entrants by 2003.[136] In their place, many employers offered their employees membership of schemes administered on a defined contribution (DC) basis, i.e. schemes under which the benefits depended on the money purchase value of the contributions paid by, and in respect, of the employees. This had the effect of transferring both the investment risk and the longevity risk to the employee until an annuity was purchased with the available accumulated fund at retirement. Formerly, both these risks had been borne by the employer.[137] Although the reduction in final salary pension provision has occurred to a limited extent in the public sector, most has occurred within the private sector.

In the summer of 2002 Blair became increasingly concerned about the general decline in the quality of occupational pensions and about the collapse of final salary schemes. He held a series of meetings on the pensions situation with the Treasury and the DWP. Realising that the situation had serious implications for the long term security of retirement income provision, he resolved that a green paper to address the problem should be published by the autumn.[138]

Although the Treasury agreed, in principle, with the idea of a green paper they 'wanted to dominate its content'. Profound differences of view emerged in the discussions concerning the Treasury's policy of means testing and the Pension Credit. Blair realised that a far reaching and fundamental review of the entire pensions issue was required and he proposed a long term commission to find the way forward. He had in mind a cross-party consensus on pension provision which would, unlike that of 1975, last for fifty years.[139]

Brown originally opposed the idea of an independent review, but eventually consented provided the commission's terms of reference were restricted to private pensions and the subject of state pension was excluded.[140] A fundamental issue which the commission would address was whether or not contributions to private pension arrangements should be made compulsory.[141]

## New pension proposals

In December 2002, the government finally published its Green Paper *Simplicity, security and choice: Working and saving for retirement*. In the Foreword, the government's belief was expressed: Pensions saving should be based on partnership with employees, employers, pension providers and government all working together.[142]

The proposals related generally to occupational and other forms of private pension provision rather than to state provision. The paper states that the government is determined to do more to promote employment among those aged 50 and over and that a number of commentators have recommended that the government should raise the age at which people can start to draw their state pensions. These commentators and others have argued that an increase in state pension age could change attitudes and encourage more people to work in later life, but that the primary challenge is to ensure that people can keep working until 65. It also notes that increasing state pension age would disproportionately affect lower income people who rely more on state benefits in retirement. The document concludes with the statement that overall, while recognising the arguments in favour of an increase in state pension age, the government believes that the arguments against are more compelling, principally because our approach is based on choice. Presumably in order to encourage workers to defer their retirement in order to prolong their working life, the proposals included improving the benefits, including the introduction of a lump sum deferment payment, available to those who defer receipt of their state pension beyond state pension age.[143]

Finally the Green Paper announced the establishment of the Pensions Commission with the terms of reference to keep under review the regime for UK private pensions and long term savings and to make recommendations to the Secretary of State for Work and Pensions on whether there is a case for moving beyond the current voluntarist approach.[144]

The Commission had a team of three commissioners under the chairmanship of Adair Turner*. His appointment was uncontroversial but, in Anthony Seldon's view, sowed the seeds of future conflict. It was apparently immediately obvious to Turner and his two fellow commissioners, Jeannie Drake† and John Hills‡, that it was impossible to remedy what was wrong in the private pension system without also looking at the state system.[145] This is confirmed by Glennerster who comments that like Beveridge before them they decided that the specific narrow question of compulsion they had been set could not be discussed without looking much more widely.[146]

The Green Paper was published alongside the Inland Revenue's proposals to simplify the tax treatment of occupational and personal pension arrangements. These proposals were implemented by the Finance Act 2004 and came into force on 6 April 2006 (A Day). The new pensions tax regime replaced the previous tax regimes. The new regime is based on two allowances within which members can receive tax advantaged benefits. The first is the lifetime allowance being an overall limit on an individual's tax privileged retirement savings (for the tax year 2008–09 this is £1,650,000) and the other the annual allowance being an annual limit on an individual's 'total pensions input' (for the tax year 2008–09, this is £235,000). There are a number of transitional provisions aim to protect benefits accrued prior to A Day.

---

* During the Commission's period of operation, Adair Turner (Chairman) was Vice Chairman of Merrill Lynch Europe, a director of United Business Media plc and chair of the Low Pay Commission. Shortly before his appointment to the PC, he had been appointed as an independent cross bench peer in the House of Lords. He was a former Director General of the CBI. Currently amongst other positions he holds, he is the chair of the Committee on Climate Change and from September 2008 will be the chair of the Financial Services Authority.

† Jeannie Drake was and still is the Deputy General Secretary for the Communication Workers Union having completed her term as president of the TUC shortly before her appointment as a Commissioner.

‡ John Hills was and still is the Professor of Social Policy and Director of the ERSC Research Centre for Analysis of Social Exclusion (CASE) at the London School of Economics.

Benefits for an individual above the lifetime allowance can be provided but such benefits lose the tax privileges.[147]

## Age Concern's response

In March 2003, Age Concern published a detailed paper in response to the Green Paper's proposals.[148] Whilst conceding that the paper includes useful and important measures, Age Concern expressed disappointment that its scope falls short of the wide reaching review of pensions that is needed, and does not provide for a long term pensions settlement clearly setting out the roles of the state, employers, individuals and the financial services industry.

Age Concern's paper noted that the proposals offered little in the way of improving the economic condition of current pensioners. Whilst supporting the proposals to establish an independent Pensions Commission, it made the pointed comment that the Commission's remit should include state as well as private provision. Age Concern identified three recurrent themes in their response:

- The role of the state pension, and the need for an adequate non-means tested state pension which is crucial to avoid poverty and to encourage savings and work;
- Any system of voluntary pension provision, with a range of options, must be accompanied by a clear advice strategy, if it is to succeed; and
- Pension policies must suit men and women and take into account the needs and circumstances of all sections of our diverse community.[149]

Age Concern argued for retention of the voluntarist approach to pensions saving, stressing that they do not feel that the case has been made for increased compulsion. They maintained that 'there should be a balance between state pay as you go and private pension provision'.[150]

Although DWP low income figures showed that in 2001–02 there had been an increase in the incomes of less well off older people, the figures also reveal that there are still over 2 million older people living in poverty. Age Concern accordingly recommended that targets should be established for abolishing pensioner poverty in line with the commitment to abolish child poverty. They felt it was important to remind the government that, although improving the state pension would inevitably result in a commitment to increased expenditure, direct public spending on pensions in the UK is low compared with other countries in the developed world.

The Age Concern paper was both wide ranging and comprehensive in its coverage of the social and economic issues affecting retirement, not only for the current generation of pensioners, but for the present and future workforces as well. At the heart of the paper was the need of all people to have an adequate income in retirement that facilitates healthy and active lifestyles and for older people to have appropriate opportunities to work.[151]

In the following month, April 2003, the basic state pension was set to rise by 2.6% from £75.50 to £77.45 per week. It was a rise above inflation but it only represented 15.9% of average earnings. It was difficult for pensioners and their organisations to understand how a £900 billion plus economy would be put under strain by linking the increases to such a low level universal pension to earnings.[152] Yet the Chancellor and the Treasury were adamant that restoring the pensions link to earnings was unaffordable. However, pensions, for a time, faded from the public consciousness with the American and British invasion of Iraq in March 2003.

# Pensions Commission's first report

From 2004, according to Seldon, Blair began to view pensions as 'a legacy issue'. He saw the Pensions Commission as a potential source of material for his legacy and for the 2005 general election campaign. At the 2004 Labour Party conference in the autumn, Blair in his speech seemed to be arguing that means testing had been taken too far and that income support for the elderly should be centred on a basic state pension. Brown apparently disagreed.[153]

The Commission took verbal and oral submissions as well as commissioning research. Its first report *Pensions: Challenges and Choices* was published in October 2004. Its introduction states that the report presents 'the findings of an analysis of the UK pensions and retirement savings system'.[154] It contains a detailed description of the current situation, existing trends and the challenges to be met. Specific recommendations on pensions policy were not made as they were to be set out in the second report planned for autumn 2005. Glennerster, described the report 'as one of the best examples of public policy analysis of any state paper since the Second World War'.[155]

In the chapter on demographic change, the report noted that increasing life expectancy, combined with a forecast low birth rate, will, between 2004 and 2050, entail a near doubling in the percentage of the population aged 65 years and over. Accordingly, the Commission indicated that society and individuals must choose between four options.

A. Pensioners will become poorer relative to the rest of society;
B. Taxes/national insurance contributions devoted to pensions must rise;
C. Private savings must rise; or
D. Average retirement ages must rise.[156]

The Commission concluded that if pensioners are not to become poorer, it is necessary to choose any two or three of the remaining options in combination, because there are significant barriers to solving the problem through any one of the other three options alone. In other words some mix of higher taxes/national insurance contributions, higher private savings and later average retirement is required.[157]

In the Commission's opinion, the UK pension system appeared in the past to work well because one of the least generous state pension systems in the developed world was complemented by the most developed system of voluntary private funded pensions. However the Commission recognised that some specific groups were poorly provided for although they reaffirmed that the percentage of GDP transferred to pensioners is comparable to other countries.

A valuable contribution to increasing public awareness of an impending crisis in retirement income provision was made by the Commission underscoring the fact that the benefits provided by state, occupational and personal pension systems had been in decline since the early 1980s.

> The state plans to provide decreasing support for many people in order to control expenditure in the face of an ageing population and the private system is not developing to offset the state's retreating role. Instead it is in significant decline.[158]

The Commission also expressed concern that the level of funded pension saving is falling rather than rising to meet the demographic challenge. It noted that stakeholder schemes have not reversed the trend with the vast majority of small company stakeholder schemes being empty shells with no contributing members. Further it noted that 65% of companies with 5–12 employees had nominated a stakeholder supplier, but only 4% were making contributions'.[159]

The report noted that pension right accrual is becoming still more unequal, and risk is being shifted to individuals sometimes ill-equipped to deal with it. It was estimated by the Commission that 75% of all members of defined contribution schemes had contribution rates lower than required to provide an adequate retirement income. Also women pensioners were poorer than men and any effective pension system for the future must ensure women accrue both state and private entitlements in their own right. It went on to say that any muddle-through option would result in less socially equitable and less economically efficient outcomes than a consciously planned response to the problems we face.[160]

The Commission identified three possible ways to achieve adequacy:
(i)   revitalisation of the voluntary system; and/or
(ii)  significant changes to the state system; and/or
(iii) an increased level of compulsory private pension saving.[161]

An analysis of possible change along these three ways would be the focus of the Commission's conclusions in its second report planned for autumn 2005.

## 2005 general election

As the New Labour leadership began to prepare early in 2005 for the forthcoming general election there were already signs of conflict over the party's pension policy. According to Seldon, the Pensions Commission, having delivered its first report, seemed close to recommending the restoration of the earnings link to the basic state pension. This in the view of a senior Minister would 'light the Chancellor's blue touch paper'. The idea of restoring the link was supported by many in the party, and it has been suggested that Brown did not want to appear to be opposing it outright.[162]

Both the Conservatives and Liberal Democrats made election manifesto commitments to restore the earnings link. Labour studiously refrained from making any such commitment. It adopted the stance that it had set up the Commission as an independent review body to conduct a wide ranging inquiry into all aspects of pension provision and retirement savings, and for the time being it would only be prudent to await its recommendations. On social policy all the parties were confronted with the 'public opinion ambivalence' of the British electorate which 'demands European levels of welfare state provision' combined with 'United States low levels of taxation'.[163]

The election was won by Labour with 35.2% of the vote, a decrease of 5.5 percentage points compared with 2001. It was the lowest share of the vote of any governing party since 1923 and the lowest won by any party to gain a majority since 1832. With the low turnout of 61.3% of the electorate, it meant that Labour had won the election with the support of only 20% of the electorate, a record low level of support for a winning party. Nevertheless, the electoral system provided them with an overall parliamentary majority of 66 seats.[164]

# Blair's third term 2005–2007

In 2001 the EU had extended the open method of co-ordination to pensions by inviting Member states to prepare national strategy reports describing how they were developing their own policies for adequate and sustainable pension provision. The first set of reports was submitted in September 2002 with an update report issued in July 2005.[165] In preparing these reports the government invited members of the Partnership Group including Age Concern and NPC to comment on draft copies of the document. The update report sets out the current stage of the government's reforms and reiterates its *Principles for reform: The national pensions debate* which it first published in February 2005. The principles are:

* Pension system must tackle poverty effectively
* Opportunity to build an adequate retirement income should be open to all
* Affordability and economic stability must be maintained
* Pension system should produce fair outcomes for women and carers
* Reform should seek to establish a system that people understand
* Reform should be based around as broad a consensus as possible[166]

It is significant that a 2005 British Election Study showed that whilst 55% of the public considered that the government had handled the economy very or fairly well, only 20% considered that it had handled pensions likewise. This was one point lower than for Iraq.[167]

Blair confided in his staff at Number 10 that pensions reform would be one of his key third term priorities. According to Seldon, during the summer Blair refined his thinking on pensions at a series of meetings at Chequers. Blair concluded that people should be given a simple base pension from the state, sufficient to keep them out of poverty, while allowing them freedom to build up personal retirement savings on top.[168] Few would fail to recognise the similarity of this to Beveridge's universal pension for subsistence, which would leave individuals free without disincentive to build upon their basic entitlement pensions from employment and personal savings. Blair's idea was that the subsistence state pension could be partly financed from resources released by increasing the state pension age.[169]

In September and October 2005, Blair had a series of meetings with the Commissioners to discuss these ideas. Seldon recounts that on 2 November 2005, Blunkett who had been appointed to the DWP at the beginning of the third term, was succeeded in the post by John Hutton. This was just three weeks before publication of the Pensions Commission's second report with its policy recommendations. According to one source, DWP officials dreaded the Treasury condemning the proposals as unaffordable and wrong.[170]

A letter from Brown to Turner, leaked to the *Financial Times,* criticised the Commission's figures, and suggested that any recommendations the Commission made to link the pension to earnings would be unacceptable. The furore which preceded the report's publication on 30 November had no discernible effect on the Commissioners or on the recommendations set out in the Commission's report.[171]

# Pensions Commission's second report

The second report *A New Pensions Settlement for the 21st Century*[172] followed on from the analysis and trends of pension provision in the UK as set out in its first report. It commences with a summary of an extended and deepened version of that analysis. On the basis of the extended analysis, the Pensions Commission went on to identify a number of objectives which have to be met in order to create a new pensions settlement.

These objectives include preventing the spread of means testing; closing the gap in current state pension provision for people with interrupted careers and caring responsibilities; maintaining employer involvement in good quality pension provision; and overcoming the barriers which deter voluntary private pension provision. Another objective, which most current pensioners would probably have taken for granted given the modest level of public expenditure entailed, was maintaining the improvements in the relative standard of living of the poorest pensioners which the present means tested approach has achieved.[173]

Meeting these objectives required two key elements of reform, namely:

1. Creation of a low cost national funded pension savings scheme into which individuals will be automatically enrolled but with the right to opt-out, with a modest level of compulsory matching employer contributions, and delivering the opportunity to save for a pension at a low annual management charge

2. Reform to make the state system less means tested and closer to universal than it would be if current indexation (i.e. in line with price inflation) arrangement was continued indefinitely. In order to achieve this while maintaining the standard of living of the poorest pensioners it will need to be more generous on average.[174]

Like Beveridge, the Commission was proposing that the state should provide a non-means tested universal minimum income at a level which would reduce significantly the role of means testing. This would serve as a platform on which pensions from employment and private savings could be built. The only difference would appear to be one of emphasis. The Commission advocated reforms to the state system in order to underpin private saving. Beveridge proposed a universal state pension for subsistence, treating 'the poorer man and the richer man alike' so that they were free without disincentive to build on it with private saving. Perhaps the difference in emphasis merely reflects the differences between the economic liberal and the social liberal attitudes to the market and to state provision.[175]

The Commission recommended that the basic state pension should be re-indexed to average earnings. A more generous basic pension would be created over time by the earnings related second pension (SP2) evolving into a flat rate top up of the basic state pension. There is a preference for this gradual and evolutionary approach over the alternatives of a single unified state pension, introduced immediately at a high enough level to ensure that most present and future pensioners were free of means testing. The former would evolve from the system as it exists in 2005 whereas the latter would require an immediate and significant increase in public expenditure. To provide the improvements in the state pension system taxes and/or contributions and/or state pension age would have to rise.[176]

In the short term, the reduction in state pension costs due to the planned raising of the women's pension age to 65 under the Pensions Act 1995 would partly offset the cost of increasing the basic pension. In the longer term, the cost would be met in part by raising the state pension age. This could rise in stages to 67 or 68 by 2050, on the assumption that the increase in life expectancy over the same period continued to correspond to the estimates of improved longevity. This more sustainable state pension system is essential to cope with increasing life expectancy and to prevent the spread of means testing to most of the pensioner population. If the present pension system continued unaltered, the Commission estimated that 70% of pensioners would be entitled to claim the means tested Pension Credit by 2050.[177]

The Commission also proposed that state pension rights should accrue by virtue of being resident in the UK and not on the basis of contribution records or eligibility for credits. This would transform the state pension into 'a citizen's pension', thus bringing to an end the system of social insurance pensions established in 1925 by extending Lloyd George's 1911 '9d for 4d' health and unemployment insurance schemes. Concerns would be expressed about the Citizens Pension precisely because it undermined the contributory principle that has represented the moral underpinning as well as the economic basis for universal entitlement. It was the contributory principle which above all distinguished the pension from poor law relief.[178]

These proposed reforms to the state pension system would underpin the Commission's recommendation for a National Pension Savings Scheme (NPSS) funded by 4% of employees' pay with their employers being required to contribute a further 3%. Tax credits would add another 1% so making a total contribution of 8% of pay. All employees would be automatically enrolled in the NPSS unless members of a good occupational scheme. Their contributions would be deducted through the PAYE tax system unless they elected to opt out. The proposal thus maintains the 'convention of voluntarism', relying on inertia to operate against opting-out, except in the case of workers who are members of a contracted out occupational scheme. The recommendation of auto-enrolment is based on a study of pension schemes in the US, with and without auto-enrolment, which suggests that few workers would opt out of the NPSS.[179]

Sums contributed to the NPSS would be available for investment in a range of approved schemes. The NPSS would transfer the sums received to the scheme of the contributor's choice. Contributions would accumulate in an individual account established for each contributor and contributors would be encouraged to supplement the sums in their savings accounts with voluntary additional contributions. Payroll deductions would, on the basis of economy of scale, facilitate a low annual management charge (e.g. 0.3%, or less).[180]

The furore, which had preceded the publication of the report, did not subside for long. The Commissioners, in particular Turner, had become embroiled in what has been described as the most contentious issue of the day: restoring the earnings link to the state pension. This he advocated simply on the grounds that the pension's value was falling in relation to earnings. This brought more pensioners into poverty and so into means testing, which in turn was a discouragement to saving by the working population.[181]

A trilateral working group, composed of officials from the Treasury, DWP and the Prime Minister's Office, started to examine the Commission's proposals in order to prepare the government's response. Work began in December 2005 and continued into March 2006. The group's conclusions were to be presented to Blair and Brown on 15 March, but on 13 March an entirely unexpected event occurred. Without warning Brown put forward an alternative plan for pension reform. The plan had been devised for him by the Treasury, presumably acting in isolation, and he wanted to announce it in the budget on 22 March.[182]

Brown's alternative plan omitted the proposal to restore the earnings link, but included a guaranteed above price inflation increase in the pension between 2010 and 2020. It also provided for a limitation in the growth of means tested retirement income support. It was adjudged overall to fall far short of the Commission's proposals. According to Seldon, Brown invited the Commissioners to the Treasury in order to 'explain why his own proposals were superior'. After examining them Turner wrote to the Chancellor 'begging to differ'.[183]

Pemberton, Thane and Whiteside have examined how the government responded to the challenge posed by the Commission's proposals. In their view the battle which raged in Whitehall, although seen through 'the prism of conflict between Blair and Brown', was in reality a familiar and traditional pattern of British pension policy making. At its centre is the struggle of the Treasury to contain long term expenditure on pensions.[184] It is a struggle re-enacted many times in the history of British state pensions since 1899, when Sir Michael Hicks-Beach rejected Arthur Balfour's proposals to the Cabinet on the grounds that all state pension proposals are 'socialistic' and too costly for tax payers.[185]

## Pensions Commission's final report

The third and final report *Implementing an integrated package of pension reforms*[186] of the Pensions Commission was published on 4 April 2006. As the title suggests, the main content of the report dealt in some detail with structural, statistical and administrative aspects of the reforms. For example, it discussed the possible impact of a NPSS on private sector labour costs. It also analysed the Commission's 'preferred option', modelled with state pension age increasing to 68 by 2050, and shown alongside DWP long term public expenditure projections (Pre-Budget report 2005) in terms of state pension and pensioner benefit expenditure as a percentage of GDP.

Also included in the final report is a summary of the opinion poll results on automatic enrolment in the NPSS (1) with the choice to opt out and (2) without the choice to opt out. Nearly 80% of respondents favoured (1). The report commented on some of the reactions to the proposals in the first and second report. The marketing side of the insurance industry considered, for example, that the Commission's conjectural annual management charge for the NPSS was too low a figure, and also suggested that voters would not want their retirement savings handled by a government quango. They offered to set up an alternative retirement savings facility. The report therefore also reviews the features of 'choice and competition' in alternative models comprising (a) the NPSS, (b) the Association of British Insurers (ABI) Partnership Pensions Scheme and (c) the National Association of Pension Funds (NAPF) Super Trusts.[187]

It seems that shortly before publication of the government's proposals, Blair and Brown held a series of meetings to consider them 'line by line' with some parts of the final text not agreed until immediately before publication. This included the sentence:

> Our objectives subject to affordability of the fiscal position will restore the earnings link by 2012 or by the end of the parliament at the very latest.

The date 2012 was a compromise suggested by John Hutton. Commenting some time after publication of the White Paper, the NPC pointed out that 'if we wait until 2012, 3 million of today's pensioners will have already died.'[188]

## White Paper

The White Paper *Security in retirement: towards a new pension system*[189] was published on 25 May 2006. The launch took place at a breakfast meeting in the pillared room at Number 10 presented jointly by Blair, Brown and Hutton. The last vestiges of Treasury resistance had probably dissolved at the prospect of over 70% of pensioners claiming means tested Pension Credit by 2050.[190] The White Paper's main proposals were:

### 1. Restoration of the earnings link to the basic pension

The basic state pension would rise in line with average earnings by 2012, subject to the caveats of affordability and the fiscal position, but in any event by the end of the next parliament. In introducing the measure from 2012 the government had not followed the Pensions Commission's recommendation that the earnings link should be restored in 2010 and, as Pemberton et al pointed out, the Treasury caveats leave scope for a future government to backtrack on this commitment. The choice of 2012 would generate savings over the long term (as a link will be restored at a lower level of average earnings than would otherwise have been the case). As a result, however, a larger number of pensioners would remain dependent on means tested income support, and it is likely that many of these will continue in poverty because they will not claim.[191]

### 2. Enhancing the basic pension

The earnings related second pension (S2P) would gradually be transformed into a flat rate top-up pension in addition to the basic state pension.

### 3. Reform of the contributory principle

Although the proposal of substituting a citizen's pension, based on a residence qualification, for the basic state pension, as recommended by the Commission, was not adopted by the government, there were proposals for radically reforming the contributory principle to qualify for the basic state pension. The present qualifying condition of 44 years for men and 39 years for women for entitlement to a full basic pension would be reduced to 30 years of contributions. A weekly NI credit will be awarded to carers of children aged less than 12. This would replace the annual credit under the Home Responsibilities Protection scheme (HRP). The system of credits for those caring for the disabled will be improved by the granting of credits to those caring for 20 hours per week instead of the current requirement of 35 hours per week.[192]

Further for those reaching state pension age after 6 April 2010 with less than 30 years (with no minimum years applying) they would be entitled to a thirtieth of the full basic state pension for each qualifying year accrued.

The state pension reforms are not retrospective in their effect so the White Paper, in the long tradition of pension white papers, offered current pensioners very little. As Pemberton et al point out, the government's proposals do not address the present problems of the very large number of women with existing histories of disrupted past contributions and low earnings.[193]

### 4. Increasing state pension age

The state pension age would be increased from 65 to 66 in 2024 (brought forward at the Treasury's instigation from 2030 as proposed by the Commission), with further increases to 67 in 2034, and to 68 in 2044.[194]

### 5. Personal Savings Accounts

The government endorsed the Commission's proposal for a NPSS, although the White Paper included little on detail. It does, however, introduce a change of language from that of the Commission, referring to 'personal savings accounts'. However, as proposed by the Commission, employees would contribute a minimum of 4% of earnings in the band between approximately £5,000 and £33,000 per annum. Matching employers' contributions of 3% would be phased in at the instigation of employers, over three years (with an extension of the transition period, if required). A further 1% would be contributed by the state through tax relief. Enrolment of employees would be automatic, but with an option to opt-out. Employers operating appropriate pension schemes would be entitled to do the same. Voluntary participation by self-employed and unemployed persons would be encouraged.[195]

In the months preceding publication of the White Paper, some opposition to the Commission's NPSS proposals had arisen from parts of the financial services industry. There was also some concern in the Treasury at the idea of a state sponsored retirement savings scheme with funds invested in the stock and bonds market, in case there was expectation that the Government would act as guarantor of asset values in a market collapse. The White Paper accordingly announced that the government would conduct further analysis of the NPSS as a delivery model for the personal accounts scheme as well as considering industry alternatives in order to achieve the right balance between value for money for the taxpayer and value for money for savers.[196] As a result, a further White Paper: *Personal accounts: a new way to save* was published on 12 December 2006.

## Reactions to the White Paper

Whilst there were reports in the media and elsewhere of a broadly favourable response to the White Paper, as there had been to the Pensions Commission's proposals, there were nevertheless concerns in the City and, as noted, in the financial services industry, at the prospect of a large state sponsored pension fund with an estimated membership of between 6 and 10 million persons.[197] There was also not inconsiderable disappointment in the organisations representing the elderly and pensioners at the proposals for reform of the state pension system. Although the government is committed to introducing, subject to the caveats of affordability and the fiscal position, some longer term improvements in the state pension, there is little or nothing in the White Paper or in the Commission's recommendations to improve the financial position of current pensioners. According to the NPC, if the state pension's link to earnings is restored in 2012, it will increase the pension by just £1.40 per week more than if the pension had remained linked to prices.[198]

# An illusory impression of improvement!

Perhaps the most coherent and well argued set of criticisms of the proposals in the White Paper, and the Pensions Commission's recommendations were those that appeared in a collection of essays contributed by a group of historians and social policy analysts, including Jay Ginn.[199] In her view, the Commission had produced an excellent analysis but disappointingly cautious proposals. The Commission's first report was quite unequivocal about pensions inequality among women:

> Women pensioners in the UK today are significantly poorer than men. This reflects both labour market features (lower employment rates, lower average earnings, and more part-time work) and specific features of the UK's state pension system.[200]

The Commission returned to the theme in its second report by stating that it had been explicitly asked by government to recommend how pension system reform can help address the problems which people with interrupted paid work records and caring responsibilities (in particular women) have faced in the past and still face to a degree today. The Commission claimed that several of its proposals would be particularly beneficial for women and carers.[201]

As Ginn points out, however, in spite of the rhetoric of paying attention to women's needs, the pensions problem for women – how to build adequate independent pensions while undertaking the socially important tasks of child rearing and elder-care – persists because of the continuing inadequacy of state pensions. Her essay concludes with the pointed observation that older women, who are one of the poorest groups in Britain, would gain almost nothing from the recommendations.[202] Further Debora Price has carried out research looking at different cohorts on a pensions simulator developed by the Department for Work and Pensions and concluded:

> By proposing a complex system that retains means testing to prevent poverty in old age and relies heavily on income in retirement linked to income during the working life for replacement rates in old age, gender inequality in income in later life will continue to reflect the large disparities in men's and women's incomes during the working life.[203]

Elsewhere it was observed in the above mentioned collection of essays that even so the Commission's proposals met strong Treasury resistance (one Whitehall official is quoted as saying: The Chancellor immediately engaged in a deliberate attempt to undermine and discredit the Commission's calculations). The proposals only became acceptable after modification, by adjustment of the timescales, to meet Treasury objectives.[204] The earnings link is not to be restored in 2010, as recommended by the Commission, but in 2012, provided there are sufficient resources at the time. The increase in state pension age to 66 is not to take place in 2030, as the Commission recommended, but in 2024. Some commentators believe that more could have been done to raise the incomes of the poorest pensioners who will otherwise remain dependent on means tested income support.[205] The Treasury, however, plans to offset the savings it has gained against the expenditure incurred by introducing the White Paper's proposals. These are expected to add 0.9% of GDP to public expenditure on pensions by 2020. However, 'savings elsewhere, chiefly gleaned' – and there is irony in this – 'from changes in women's state pension age, will allow overall pension spending to be kept at the present level of 5.2%'. For women, the scheme endorsed by the Treasury 'offers an illusory impression of improvement. It may be affordable but it is palpably socially unjust'.[206]

## The empty budget of 2007

The Chancellor's statement that the means tested Pension Credit would be raised by £5 per week from April 2007 elicited a less than enthusiastic response from pensioners' organisations. The NPC issued a statement that around '10m of Britain's pensioners will feel betrayed by today's 'empty' budget for failing to address … the consistently low level of the state pension, the cost of fuel and energy bills and the continuing burden of council tax'. In the NPC's view the Chancellor's announcement about uprating the Pension Credit 'masks the real fact' that in 2007 the state pension will only rise by just over £3 to £87.30 per week, and passed over the inconvenient truth that 'around 1.8m older people don't even claim the Pension Credit despite being entitled'.[207] The point was also made that the annual winter fuel allowance of £200 had not been uprated since 2003.* Moreover, in the 2005 general election campaign all three major parties promised to alleviate, in one way or another, the burden of council tax on pensioners. To meet this commitment the government introduced a £200 council tax rebate per pensioner household. This was only payable once, before being withdrawn by the Chancellor in 2006. The fact that it has never been reinstated as council tax bills continue to rise, putting more pressure on low income pensioners, is, according to the NPC, even more evidence that pensioners' concerns are being ignored.[208]

## Pension Credit non take up estimates

The DWP's estimates, published in March 2007, showed that among all pensioners eligible for the Pension Credit in the year 2005–06, the take up range was between 60% and 69% with some 1.2 to 1.7m people entitled but not claiming the benefit. The overall amount of benefit unclaimed was between £1.6bn and £2.5bn. Of the 2.6m pensioners receiving the Pension Credit, about 1.5m were single women. The range of single women pensioners estimated to be entitled to the benefit but not claiming it was between 570,000 and 880,000.[209]

## New legislation

On 26 July 2007 the Pensions Act 2007 received its Royal Assent. This Act legislated for the reforms to the state pension system set out in the 2006 White Paper *Security in retirement: towards a new pension system*. The Bill was published on 29 November 2006 and completed its passage through the Commons at the end of April 2007. Pensioners' organisations, led by the NPC, had been engaged throughout the month in lobbying MPs and peers to amend the Bill to provide for restoration of the earnings link to the universal state pension with effect from April 2008, and simultaneously for the pension to be increased to the standard minimum guarantee

---

* In the first half of 2008, the government announced that for the winter 2008–09 only there would be an additional payment of £50. For households with someone aged 80 or over the additional payment would be £100.

under the Pension Credit. However, during the final debate on the Bill in the Commons, Ministers resorted to a procedural device to prevent any amendments from being discussed.[210] In July 2007, as expected, Blair resigned as Prime Minister and gave up his seat in Parliament. Brown succeeded him as Prime Minister with Brown making Darling his Chancellor.

The campaign for pensions reform gained a new impetus when on 24 July 2007 Kelvin Hopkins MP put down an early day motion in the Commons, on behalf of the NPC, calling for a 'Pensioners' Charter of Rights'. The motion, receiving the support of another 63 MPs, was expressed in the following terms:

> That this House draws attention to the Pensioners' Charter of Rights created by the NPC; expresses in particular its strong support for the Charter's demands for the state pension to be set above the official poverty level for all men and women, and for all long term and social care to be provided free; and calls on the government to respond positively to the Charter's contents'.[211]

It was accompanied by the public call to all who supported the Charter to write to their MPs and ask them to sign the motion when they returned to Westminster after the summer parliamentary recess.[212]

The government's announcement on 18 October 2007 of a 3.9% increase in the basic state pension from April 2008 brought about further protests and demands from the pensioners' organisations. The NPC released a statement reminding the government that their new Pensions Act does nothing to improve the condition of the current generation of pensioners beyond telling them to wait until 2012 for the restoration of the link with earnings and in the meantime condemning them to a retirement on means tested benefits. The statement added that by 2012, 3m of today's pensioners will be dead and means tested Pension Credit (£119 per week) fails to reach 1.8m poor pensioners reluctant to claim because the system is so complicated and demeaning.[213]

The NPC, on behalf of the pensioners' organisations, called on the government to provide a state pension set above the poverty level at £119 per week, the 2007–08 level of the Pension Credit. The pension should then rise in stages until it reaches the government's preferred measure for the poverty level i.e. 60% of median contemporary income before housing costs (in 2007–08 terms, £134 per week).[214] This, it will be recalled, was the official measure of poverty adopted by the government in 2004, when in estimating child poverty Brown departed from the then official measure (based on the EU standard) of 60% of median contemporary income after housing costs.

The Pensions Minister, Mike O'Brien, indicated in his written parliamentary answer of 9 October 2007 that

> We have made good progress in tackling pensioner poverty. Since 1997, the number of pensioners living in relative poverty, based on a threshold of 60% of contemporary median income after housing costs, has fallen by 1.1 million, from 2.9 million to 1.8 million in 2005–06. Raising the level of the basic state pension to the level of the Guarantee Credit is estimated to reduce the number

of pensioners below 60% median income after housing costs by around 200,000 based on 2007–08 benefit rates.[215]

The Pensions Act 2007 dealt with the first phase of the government's reform to the UK pensions system with the second Pensions Bill published on 5 December 2007 and once enacted it will implement the proposals of the White Paper *Personal Accounts: a new way to save* with its measures aimed at encouraging greater private pension provision.

## Inadequate NI contribution record

In a written parliamentary answer,[216] the government minister, Dawn Primarolo, gave an analysis of the NI contributions for 2004–05. This showed that 14.87 million men between ages 16 to 65 were paying a mean NI contribution of £1,500. The corresponding figures for women between ages 16 and 60 were 11.25 million and £1,010. Looking at the 2004–05 UK population in these age brackets, very roughly a third of both male and females were not making NI contributions. The information does not indicate how many of these people not making NI contributions were employed in receipt of less than the lower earning limit (for 2004–05 this was £77 per week) or receiving credits.[217] O'Brien, in a further written parliamentary answer, published a table showing that some 754,000 women aged between 60 and 69 in 2003–04 had, in their own right, contribution records insufficient for them to be entitled to any part of the basic state pension. However this does not mean that they would not receive a basic state pension as they may be entitled to this based on their husband's NI contribution record.[218]

Nevertheless the government is concerned that a significant number of citizens within their working life are not maintaining an adequate NI contribution record to safeguard their entitlement to the full basic state pension. In another written parliamentary answer, Primarolo indicated that 3.7 million letters were issued in 2004 for the 2002–03 tax year to advise insured persons that they had a gap and indicating a voluntary contribution (see Appendix 2) could be made. The numbers of such letters in the following two years have been 3.2 million and 4.7 million.[219] Although asked for the information, the minister could not indicate how many payments together with their amounts had been made. However because of the interplay with the Pension Credit it may not be to the individual's benefit in making such contributions.

This has been further complicated by the change in the eligibility conditions for a full basic state pension for those reaching state pension age on or after 6 April 2010. This change reduced the number of qualifying years to 30 for both men and women. This change was forewarned in the White Paper *Security in retirement: Towards a new pensions system* published on 25 May 2006. As a consequence the government announced on 16 January 2007 that where individuals have continued to make voluntary NI contributions since 25 May 2006 but would have chosen not to do so had they been aware of the government's intention to reduce the number of qualifying years required for a full basic state pension to 30, they may be entitled to a refund.[220]

## Surplus in the NI Fund

As the schedule in Appendix 2 shows the NI Fund has always been in credit since its inception in July 1948. In the first 20 years the Fund's balance (i.e. the accumulation of receipts less payments and commonly called the surplus) had been between £1 billion and £1.5 billion. Over the next 20 years it had grown to £8 billion and was £38 billion at 31 March 2007. The Government Actuary has estimated that the surplus could increase further to £115 billion by 31 March 2013 – this being in excess of the payments for that year.[221] However these estimated figures are dependent on the actual experience adhering closely to the assumptions adopted, with differences being able to affect the position significantly.

A number of commentators have made the point that with the increasing surplus effectively part of the NI contributions, it is a form of direct taxation so providing the Treasury with a convenient source of additional revenue which it is reluctant to relinquish. As a consequence they argue that the receipts and payments should move more into equilibrium so that the Fund's surplus is only that necessary for the smooth operation of the Fund.[222]

O'Brien's written parliamentary answer of 21 April 2008, quoted below, is interesting as it shows the government thinking concerning the surplus and the extent to which the basic state pension could increase if the balance were to be used for that purpose.

When national insurance contributions are made, a proportion of them go directly to help fund the NHS, while the rest are paid into the NI Fund. The NI Fund pays out contributory benefits to which people who have paid sufficient contributions are entitled, such as the basic state pension, incapacity benefit and contribution-based jobseeker's allowance.

National insurance contributions and associated social security benefits operate within the government's fiscal rules designed to ensure sound public finances and when there is a surplus, it is invested in public services. Any surplus of contributions over social security benefits in any one year (the NI Fund's surplus) is not therefore an extra resource available to spend.

As the Government Actuary's latest report on the draft Social Security Benefits up-rating and Contributions Re-rating Orders notes, the excess of income over payments each year is the difference between two large numbers and so quite small percentage changes in either of them results in a large percentage change in the surplus income. This, in turn, could have a significant effect on the NI Fund's surplus.

However, if the equivalent of the NI Fund's annual excess of receipts over payments projected by the Acting Government Actuary for the years 2009–10 to 2012–13 were paid in its entirety to recipients of the basic state pension, this would lead to an estimated percentage increase in the basic state pension of around 24% in 2009–10 and around 6% in the years 2010–11 to 2012–13. Any increase in basic state pension expenditure has a cumulative impact on government spending going forward.[223]

What makes the NI Fund's surplus of such pointed relevance to the issue of affordability of better state pensions is that many workers and pensioners take the view that the Fund consists entirely of their contributions. Like the social insurance sceptics who were suspicious of Chamberlain's scheme in 1925, they do not believe that employers really pay social insurance contributions. This scepticism interestingly gains some credibility from modern analysis of labour costs which classifies the employer's social security contributions, in accountancy jargon, as a non-wage employment cost, together with the costs of occupational pensions and other employee benefits. Like the worker's pay, they are taken into account in assessing the total cost of the job.

Given the status of employer's contributions as an element in the employment package, it is at least understandable that many workers and pensioners view the NI Fund's surplus as generated entirely by workers' compulsory social insurance savings. For the same reason, one can perhaps see why they may feel that the government's unwillingness to use the surplus to provide adequate state pensions – a purpose for which the Fund was intended – is an affront to social and economic justice.

## Economic crisis and 2008 budget

In the second half of 2007, the UK economy was beginning to experience serious problems against a background of higher world commodity prices, in particular oil and gas, and the start of an international banking crisis. These factors contributed in causing the world's stock markets to be volatile and continue to do so.

By late summer, the imprudent lending in the mortgage market lead to a crisis of confidence in the mortgage provider, Northern Rock with its share price crashing and depositors withdrawing their savings. The government stepped in to provide loans and other government guarantees and tried to facilitate a take-over of the company. With no suitable suitor being found, the government nationalised Northern Rock in February 2008.

A shake-up of capital gains tax the previous autumn had already led to big concessions in January 2008 to entrepreneurs furious about the adverse impact it would have on the formation and development of new businesses. The Treasury then backed away from plans to tax the offshore wealth of rich foreigners who claimed non-domiciled tax status in the UK. As a result, in March 2008, Darling's first budget made no radical changes. He announced an increase in expenditure designed to fight child poverty, an increase in the winter fuel payments for the pensioner's household (£50 if the household has someone aged 60–79 or £100 if the household has someone aged 80 or over) but only for 2008/9 and a rise in the taxes on alcohol and vehicles.[224]

Darling, in his budget, reaffirmed that the 10% lowest tax band would be abolished from April 2008 as had been announced in the March 2007 budget, this being the last one of Brown as Chancellor. However, during the passage of the Finance Bill, substantial opposition within Parliament grew to its abolition, in particular from a significant number of Labour backbenchers led by Frank Field. Their concern was that this change would affect adversely many on low incomes. This pressure resulted in the government announcing in June a number of concessions, costing £2.7 billion,[225] to compensate for the adverse effects in abolishing the 10% rate. With these concessions, the Finance Act 2008 received the Royal Assent on 21 July 2008.

Darling made more headlines in August when he said that the economic times were the worst in 60 years which caused more anxiety. In August 2008, there was a general acceptance that there were many problems but commentators were not in agreement about their extent. Such problems included:

- house prices falling rapidly (11% over 12 months) after the unsustainable boom in prices during the previous few years.
- new mortgage approvals being substantially lower with July 2008 figures being some 71% lower than a year ago.
- the UK suffering from high household indebtedness.
- consumer price inflation increasing – as measured by the Retail Prices Index, it went up by 5% in the year to July 2008 with higher food (up 12.2% over the same period), energy and transport prices.
- falling sterling pushing up the costs of imports.
- the mortgage and banking difficulties.
- the uncertainty effect of the US Presidential election being held later in November.

There have been gloomy forecasts from the Bank of England and various think tanks. On August 13, Mervyn King, the Bank's Governor, warned that the next year would be a difficult one with inflation high and output broadly flat. The economy, he said, was undergoing a painful readjustment due to the unique combination of the credit crisis and the shock of higher inflation. After a long period of sustained economic growth, Britain was teetering on the brink of recession.[226]

In June 2008, official figures showed that the number of pensioners below the poverty line in the UK had risen substantially during 2006/7 by 300,000 to 2.5 million, the first time the number had increased since 1998.[227] Some upward movement was thought likely but the size of the increase was much higher than expected. The Joseph Rowntree Foundation published a report in July,[228] based on a new way of comparing wealth and poverty across Britain, that showed a widening gap between the rich and poor to levels of inequality that had not been seen for over 40 years. The report indicated that households in already wealthy areas tended to become disproportionately wealthier and that many rich people lived in areas segregated from the rest of society. At the same time, more households had become poor over the previous 15 years, but fewer had become very poor.

## Raising the state pension age

Various people were interviewed for an article in *The Times* to celebrate the 100th anniversary of the Old Age Pensions Act 1908. It is worth reiterating the points that a number of them made. Lord Turner, the architect of the recent pension reform to increase state pension age progressively to 68, considered that if the value of the state pension was to be protected, the retirement age would have to rise again, assuming continued increases in life expectancy. He expected the state pension age to rise to 70 if the basic state pension was to survive until the end of the 21st century. Even adopting that age, he believed that people would still be able to enjoy a lengthy period in retirement. Increasing the age to 70 would be back to the state pension age of the 1908 scheme. Mervyn Kohler, from Help the Aged, whilst accepting the principle that links state pension age with life expectancy, urged more flexibility. Chris Grayling, the Shadow Work and Pensions Secretary, did not oppose Turner's view, indicating that more and more governments are going to see retirement as a process not occurring at a single age with people having more flexibility in choosing when to retire. Finally from the article, Neil Duncan-Jordan, a spokesperson for the National Pensioners Convention, pointed out that some groups in society, especially low paid manual workers, have life expectancies much lower than professional groups. Their life expectancy is not much beyond 70 or 75. Five years is not exactly the 'lifetime in retirement' people have been promised. He indicated that the differences in life expectancy should be taken into account when deciding on the state pension age.[229]

## Pensioners' campaign marking 100 years of state pension

During 2008, Britain's largest pensioners' organisation, the NPC, ran a twelve month campaign to mark a century of the state pension and to demand a £40 per week increase in the basic state pension.

The reasons for the campaign were summed up by Joe Harris, the NPC's general secretary:

> We owe the original pension pioneers a great debt of gratitude for securing the very first state pension that sought to end the threat of the workhouse for millions of older people. But a 100 years on and we still have over 2 million pensioners living below the poverty line and many more struggle to make ends meet. In fact, today's state pension is worth even less in relation to average wages than it was in 1908.[230]

# CHAPTER TWELVE
# Learning from the past

## Introduction

It is of more than passing interest that this history of 100 years of social pension provision should begin and end with a campaign for an adequate retirement income for the elderly. At the end of the 19th century, there was a gulf between the well off with good incomes and inherited wealth and the poor, dependent on the poor law for survival in old age. We can still observe this division in our more affluent current age. There is a considerable income gap between those who enjoy a prosperous retirement with a substantial pension and the less well off who are dependent on the basic state pension with its declining value and means tested Pension Credit. Before the state pension was introduced 100 years ago, around a quarter of the older population were dependent on the poor law to avoid absolute destitution. Although living standards overall have improved, there are still 2.5 million pensioners (roughly a quarter) living below the poverty line.[1] The current basic state pension is worth less today as a percentage of average earnings than it was when the first old age state pension at 5s per week was paid to the first pensioners on 1 January 1909.[2]

At the root of both campaigns, separated by more than 100 years, is the still unresolved question of the extent to which it is the state's role to ensure adequate social pension provision for the elderly. This raises a number of associated questions:-

- How can a decent standard of living be ensured for those who can no longer work?
- How should the costs of paying for the elderly to have an adequate standard of living in retirement be split between the individuals themselves, their employers and the state?
- What responsibility should each working generation accept to provide pension benefits, out of general taxation, for the generation in retirement?
- In what ways should today's pensioners benefit from current productivity and economic growth?
- Should provision differ depending on how prudent or reckless people have been with their money?
- Should a state pension sufficient to live on be paid on a universal basis, or should there be reliance on self provision and restriction of state spending with targeting of those in need on a means tested basis?
- At what age should the payment of a state pension commence and what flexibility and choice should be allowed?
- How should entitlement to a universal state pension be earned – on the basis of a NI contribution record or as a citizen's right?
- What should be the entitlement of those who rear children, take care of elderly relatives or become unemployed?

- How can we fund state benefits and, at the same time, encourage thrift and savings?
- Most fundamentally, how do we determine what is an adequate income and what level of cost is affordable to provide such benefits?

## The major issues that have affected state pension scheme developments over the last 100 years

The legislation for the first state scheme, the Old Age Pensions Act 1908, was only eight pages long and written in clear English. Today we have a complicated pensions and benefits system, perhaps the most complex of any country in the world,[3] and yet we are still tackling the same questions. The first state pension was designed to give a minimum standard of living to the 'aged deserving poor'[4] who would otherwise be destitute. At that time, there were approximately two million people over age 65 in Britain, of whom two thirds were estimated to be in want (but many were not eligible for poor law relief) and 'for the most part simply suffering from the sin of living on'.[5] However, in order to keep down the cost the non-contributory state scheme only provided a pension to those of good character in need aged 70 and over. The aim was not to pay a comfortable income in retirement to everyone, but rather to provide a safety net of a national minimum amount to enable the survival of the deserving poorest. There was some concern at the time that the prospect of a pension for their closing years 'will disincline the poor' to continue to work or make savings provision for themselves.[6] In 1905, the National Committee of Organised Labour pointed out that many of those who had saved were no better off when they were no longer able to work as they could not obtain any poor law relief until their savings had been spent, whereas those with no savings received poor law relief straightaway. Pensions were payable subject to a test of need which stigmatised claimants, penalised thrift and possibly led to moral hazard.

In 1925, the first contributory state pension scheme was introduced. It provided an entitlement to a pension from age 65 in return for making contributions. In 1940, the retirement age for women was reduced to 60. The pension was still at a low level and not intended to be sufficient to live on by itself. A means tested income to the elderly poor who had not been able to provide for themselves continued alongside.

In the early decades of the 20th century occupational pensions began to develop, but this reinforced a division in society between the significant part of the population who were poor and relied on the state pension and public assistance and the remainder who were better off, some in regular long term employment with an occupational pension scheme and others who were the beneficiaries of inherited wealth. Titmuss referred to this as creating 'two nations in old age'.[7] From the beginning, occupational schemes in general did not provide significant benefits for women and low paid, part-time or temporary workers.

The Beveridge Report (1942) proposed a radical development of the role of the state in pension provision. Its key principles were:
- a state pension sufficient to live on;
- a pension based on contributions by the employed and their employers, the self-employed and the non-employed together with a supplement from general taxation;
- the same pension entitlement for everyone; and
- rich and poor treated the same.

When it was introduced in 1948 it was on a pay as you go basis, i.e. current benefits to the elderly were paid from current contributions by and in respect of those in work. The flat rate pension, in order to contain costs, was set below the subsistence level recommended by Beveridge but nevertheless was meant to provide an income adequate for those lacking other resources and low enough to encourage voluntary additional saving. Enhanced benefits were paid to those in retirement by those in work with the scheme being essentially redistributive between generations. It was not otherwise significantly redistributive as it relied on flat rate contributions to pay for flat rate benefits.

In 1948 National Assistance was introduced throughout Britain in the form of means tested benefits which replaced the poor law. The stigma of means testing resulted in low take up, a key issue even today.

As the economy grew in a time of fuller employment and people became better off, occupational pensions expanded. Before the Second World War there were around 2.5 million people in occupational schemes with this increasing to about 6 million in 1953 and then to around 12 million in 1967 being approximately 50% of the workforce by the 1960s.[8]

Primarily to raise additional revenue, the Conservatives introduced the graduated pension scheme in 1961. For the first time, it added to the basic state pension a small earnings related pension in return for additional earnings related NI contributions on top of flat rate NI contributions. Future accrual of benefits under this scheme ceased in 1975. The principle of paying flat rate contributions for a flat rate state pension, so treating everyone the same, continued until 1975 when earnings related contributions were introduced for the flat rate pension. The effect of the change was redistributive towards the low paid. Also in 1975, following all-party agreement, Labour passed the legislation which resulted in the state earnings related pension scheme (SERPS) which started in April 1978. This retained the basic state pension and added, for an employed contributor, a new earnings related pension linked to the contributor's earnings related contributions. Under SERPS, before its level of benefits was downgraded by the Social Security Act 1986, accrual of pensions was based on earnings during the best 20 years of work, resulting in a doubling of the level of income replacement which workers on average earnings would have received from the flat rate basic pension. It therefore benefited women, carers and other groups who might have a restricted career of paid employment.

A key principle which has driven pension policy through the Thatcher years and into the New Labour era has been the concentration on directing government spending into areas which would increase employment and the national income and cutting expenditure in areas which are seen as non-productive. Private provision and individual saving for old age was identified with 'independence' and therefore seen as morally good whereas state welfare was seen as a burden.[9] Although the Thatcher government elected in 1979 declared its firm intention to improve pensioners' living standards, it reduced the basic state pension in real earnings terms by changing its indexation from the increase in earnings to that of prices. At the November 1979 uprating, the last before the earnings link was broken, the basic state pension represented 26% of average earnings but by 2008 it had fallen to just below 16% of average earnings.

In 1986 SERPS benefits were cut by reducing the accrual rate and linking benefits to career average earnings instead of the best 20 years of earnings. In 2002, the state second pension scheme (S2P) was introduced to replace SERPS. It is partly redistributive and benefits low earners and some categories of carers and disabled workers. In effect, it operates like a flat rate supplement to the basic state pension and takes low income pensioners out of poverty and above the means testing minimum level. However, this relief is temporary as the uprating of S2P benefits, once in payment, are linked to the rise in prices rather than earnings.

The introduction of the state pension scheme in 1908 and the subsequent reforms of 1925 and 1948 did much to improve the income in retirement for the then generations of elderly people. Recent pension reforms have concentrated more on providing pensions savings vehicles (either state, occupational or private) for future generations of retirees with the living standards of current retirees being overlooked, apart from some changes to means tested entitlements.

## The recent decline in state and occupational pensions

Recent Conservative and New Labour governments have sought to shift the burden of pension provision away from the state and towards employers and individuals making their own provision. The reduction in the value of state benefits relative to earnings is creating under-provision because occupational and other forms of private pension provision are not expanding to fill the gap. A spate of scandals, crises and changes to the legislation relating to pensions has generated a lack of confidence in the pensions system among employers and individuals.[10]

Many private sector employers have switched their schemes from relatively generous final salary schemes to money purchase schemes with lower employer contributions, which are likely to pay out lower benefits. Deficits in final salary occupational schemes caused by falling stock market returns, reduction in tax benefits and more onerous funding regulations have resulted in three quarters of private sector final salary schemes being closed to new entrants by 2008. Of these, 8% are closed to future accrual of benefits with this percentage expected to increase to over 40% within a further five to ten years.[11]

This has resulted in quite a divergence between the private and public sectors in the occupational pension provision being provided. As the main part of this continuing final salary pension provision within the public sector is funded from general taxation, this imbalance may not be sustainable.

New Labour has continued the policy introduced by the Conservatives of down-grading the level of the state pension and relying on means tested income support to help the poorest pensioners. In 2005, it was estimated that, compared to 1997, between 810,000 and 1.5 million fewer pensioners were in poverty than would have been the case without Pension Credit.[12] The Pensions Act 2007 makes it mandatory for the Pension Credit guarantee rate to be increased annually in line with earnings. This ensures the poorest receive around a quarter of average earnings through a combination of the state pension and Pension Credit. The 2007 Act also provides for the basic state pension to be uprated in line with earnings but this change will not be made before 2012 at the earliest. There is no intention to restore the pension to its 1979 level relative to average earnings. The declared objective is to ensure that by 2050 a significantly higher proportion of people's retirement income will come from occupational and other forms of private pension provision rather than from the state.

In 2006, the New Labour government published two Department for Work and Pensions White Papers (*Security in Retirement: towards a new pensions system* and *Personal Accounts: A new way to save*) which set out the details of the government's proposed National Pension Savings Scheme (NPSS). The scheme is based on a system of personal accounts with cash accumulation of individual employee's contributions and matching employer contributions that are mandatory if the employee remains opted in. Employers will be able to substitute the NPSS arrangement with their own provision, provided it is 'good enough'. It has similarities with the Joseph state reserve scheme (which reached the statute book but was repealed before implementation by the Labour Government in 1975 and replaced by SERPS). The funds built up in NPSS will be entirely under the management of investment banks and insurance companies. It is hoped that automatic enrolment will significantly increase take up as employees will be included in the scheme unless they take specific action to opt out.

During the last 30 years, governments have been concerned about the increasing costs of providing pensions and care services to an ageing population. The need to support British economic competitiveness in a global economy has brought a new approach towards pension provision. We are seeing a shift

- from state to private provision
- from collective to personal provision
- from pay as you go financing to advance funding (or capitalisation).

There has been no reduction in NI contribution rates leaving an increasing burden for the next generation which is expected to pay for a poorer value state pension and to make more individual provision for their own retirement.

## Moral choices

As Titmuss pointed out 50 years ago,[13] society needs to decide what it believes is socially just and then to blend principle with pragmatism to produce a framework which is economically and politically viable. In deciding upon solutions we cannot avoid making moral choices. One question has dominated all others over the last 100 years – to whom should state pension benefits be paid? In 1908, it was decided to pay the state pension only to the deserving poor. The aim was to pay benefits to those of good character with an annual income not exceeding £31.50 – this limit was later increased. As a consequence, loafers and wastrels and those who had been in prison in the previous ten years were excluded initially. In 1925, the contributory principle was introduced. Pensions were to be paid to all in return for contributions under a social insurance scheme. The 1942 Beveridge Report wanted a universal state pension sufficient to live on paid for by flat rate NI contributions. In the 1950's, Macleod and Powell (and others) attacked the concept of universalism and argued that no social service should be provided without a test of need so that the state would not waste resources by providing benefits to those who do not need them.

Today, after 100 years of the state pension scheme, the argument that the state should only intervene as a last resort seems to dominate political thinking. This was very much the situation in the 19th century under the poor law. The result is that the UK has a very large number of current pensioners dependent on means tested income support. In 1891, the actuary, Hardy, expressed concern about the pauperisation of 'a deserving class of citizens' and that over 40% of aged persons 'became chargeable to the poor rates'.[14] Although standards of poverty have changed since 1891, and are now related to contemporary median incomes, it was estimated that by 2008 40% of pensioners could qualify for the current form of means tested income support, the Pension Credit.[15] There is even greater concern that, without more reform of the state pension, the proportion of pensioners entitled to means tested income support could further increase.

There is the added predicament of the estimated up to 1.8 million pensioners who, although entitled to claim, do not claim the Pension Credit.[16] This is likely to be because of the complexity of the claiming process and the stigma associated with being dependent on state benefits.  In addition, some pensioners may only be entitled to small amounts and may not consider it worthwhile to claim. The low take up of means tested benefits was an issue in the 19th century with the poor law and has continued to be a problem throughout 100 years of the state pension scheme.

Means tested benefits, as well as being costly to administer, are ill-designed to relieve the poverty of future pensioners because they are a powerful disincentive to accumulate savings and build up pension rights in an occupational or private pension scheme. Although the current Pension Credit provisions are intended to mitigate the extent of this disincentive, it is still very much in existence. As a result the debate on the appropriateness of means tested benefits continues. The NPC is campaigning for a £40 per week increase in the basic state pension to provide a better pension for all. Although the government plans to re-introduce the earnings link sometime between 2012 and 2015, the basic state pension will continue to decline in value in relation to earnings in the meantime. To support those in need, there will be a growth in means tested benefits.

## A pension adequate to live on

The basic state pension provides pensioners with an income of just below 16% of average earnings. A 2007 study[17] showed that this is the lowest level in Europe with the average for all European Union countries being 57%. Even the Netherlands, which has the second-lowest level, provides a state pension nearly double the UK figure. The study also shows that the UK has one of the highest retirement ages in Europe at an average of 62.2 years, with 57% of people aged between 55 and 65 still working. The study concluded that the 'inadequacy' of the UK's state pension system is 'beyond question'.

At the heart of the problem has been the policy introduced by the Conservatives under Thatcher, who cut the link between average earnings and pensions in 1980 and the unwillingness of successive governments until recently to reverse it. However this reversal will not take place before 2012 and will not restore the value lost over the previous 32 years. Since 1979 annual pension increases have been tied to retail price inflation and the basic state pension has fallen from 26% to just below 16% of average earnings in 2008. At present, it is only the lowest earners, where the government has specifically targeted Pension Credit, whose combined state benefit is anywhere near the level of state pension provided by any other EU country.

In Scandinavia general taxation funds universal state benefits and services. In other countries, such as France and Germany, benefits are related to social insurance contributions. This contrasts with the UK and the USA, where public policy is leaving much to the private sector and the individual when it comes to pension provision, with only a residual role for the state. Even then, social security pension rates are higher in the USA than in the UK.[18]

The UK only spends 4.2% of GDP[19] on state pensions which is under half of that of most of our EU neighbours.

## Increasing longevity

Life expectancy at birth has improved from roughly 50 years in 1908 to about 80 years in 2008.[20] As we are living longer and entering the workforce later, primarily because of the extension to the period of full-time education, the age at which we can afford to retire will increase. It is clear that there is a limit to the burden the older generation can put on the working population.

When the state pension age was set at 65 for men (i.e. the 1925 Scheme), people did not live as long as now, so pensioners spent a much smaller proportion of their lives in retirement than is currently experienced. Although legislation has been passed which means future pensioners will retire later, the proportion of their lives they spend in retirement or semi-retirement is expected to remain much the same as at present. One of the questions that needs to be addressed is whether the current balance between working life and retirement is fair and financially sustainable. Since the cost of providing welfare is a prime concern to policy makers, a more open discussion is necessary about the trade off between the cost of provision, the level of state pension and the period over which it is paid.

Despite the fact that only 5% of the population in 1908 was over age 65 (the age initially proposed for the 1908 Scheme), the state pension age was set at 70. Now 19% of the population has reached the current state pension age (65 for men and 60 for women).[21] Over the decade 2010 to 2020 the women's state pension age will be gradually increased to 65 so becoming equalised again with that of the men. After that the state pension age for all will be increased to 66 in 2024, 67 in 2034 and 68 in 2044. On recent projections, as the state pension age increases, it is possible that the percentage over the revised age will remain at around 20% of the population at the time that the revised state pension age comes into effect.[22]

It seems clear that some alteration to the state scheme is necessary to deal with future demographic change. Society needs to consider the degree to which this should be at the expense of current pensioners who have paid their NI contributions and so believe they have earned the right to a state pension adequate to support life, good health and a reasonable degree of personal autonomy, or current workers (and future pensioners). Increasing the state pension age for future pensioners and increasing the level of the basic state pension in real terms would benefit the current generation of pensioners, but would be at the expense of the current and future working population. Existing legislation increasing the state pension age attempts to deal with the future demographic change but the changes do not come into effect for some years and will only affect future retirees. Concerns are already being expressed that the planned changes are not sufficient.

## Inequalities

Occupational pensions have proved beneficial for those with access, mainly middle and high income earners and those with relatively stable or traditional employment patterns. They have provided good pensions in the public sector. Part-timers, some of the low paid earners, those in casual or temporary employment and those in small organisations in the private sector have been disadvantaged. In the past, jobs done by women were only half as likely to offer an occupational pension scheme as those done by men.

Employee contributions are tax deductible and part of the pension can be taken as a tax-free lump sum. The lump sum is a regressive tax benefit, of particular benefit to high earners. The distribution of scheme membership means the tax relief on contributions also appears regressive. Alan Walker and Liam Foster in their review *A Century of Pension Policies in the UK* commented that over one fifth of the contributions to private pensions came in the form of tax relief with high earners, who get tax relief at their highest marginal rate, benefiting the most. At least half the tax relief on contributions went to the richest 10% of tax payers (two thirds to the top 20%) with only 1% of the tax benefit going to the bottom 10% of earners. Whilst occupational pensions can make an important contribution to reducing pensioner poverty they are a source of perpetuating income and status differences into old age.[23]

John Shuttleworth, an actuary, drew attention to this point in an article in the magazine *Accountancy* in 2002. Although on pensions as a whole, public and private together, the UK spends roughly the EU average, he pointed out that:

> To be sure, our spend on state pensions is half the EU average, but all that is happening is that the half of the UK workforce who are not in tax-subsidised occupational pensions are losing out.[24]

As Jay Ginn pointed out:

> Paying a universal pension at the 2002 threshold for means testing (£109 per week, or 22% of average national earnings) would cost an extra £7.3 billion net in the first year ... The increase in cost is only one third of the amount spent to incentivise savings through private pensions. In 2005 the net cost of tax relief on private pension contributions was £21 billion, or 1.8% of GDP.[25]

Increasing reliance on means testing, and abandonment of universal provision, has been made with the aim of producing an affordable welfare state. Since 1979 the debate about pensions has focused almost entirely on the increasing cost of an ageing population in the context of maintaining economic efficiency. A 1993 government report argued that demographic change, combined with longer life expectancy, would increase the number of pensioners from 10.4 million to a projected 15.5 million by the year 2030.[26] Despite studies from a number of sources, notably Hills[27] on social security expenditure and Warnes[28] on the demography of ageing, who questioned the accuracy of the assumptions, the Conservative government at the time – against little or no opposition – used them to justify cuts in benefits and care services for elderly people.

The reduction in state pension benefits in real earnings terms and the tax relief provision for pension savings that are mostly made by the well off has had the effect of widening the gap between the rich and the less well off in retirement. The inequalities that exist during people's working lives are perpetuated into old age.

## Paying for the state scheme

The Conservative government in 1979 declared that pensioners could look forward to sharing in the increased standard of living of the whole country.[29] New Labour's 1998 Green Paper *Partnership in Pensions* proclaimed that 'all pensioners should share fairly in the increasing prosperity of the nation'.[30] However, the guiding principle of policy makers has been to limit redistribution between generations and, until the S2P reforms, between income groups. Many people believe in the need for better pensions, but are unable to come to terms with the income redistribution that would be required to finance them. Social expenditure on pensions 'should have a low priority', not only because it would entail radical redistribution, 'but also because it was wasteful to divert resources towards those citizens who had no future labour market value'.[31] As Macnicol has pointed out, any policy decision based on such a view violates 'the idea of equality of citizenship through welfare'.[32] In Beveridge's language, contributory social insurance entails the exercise of duties (contributions) and rights (benefits) which arise from 'the solidarity of free and equal citizens'.[33]

Macnicol's view is that 'social capital' or 'reproduction of labour arguments' have influenced some historical judgements. He cites, as an example, a comparatively recent comment that the decision of the post-war Labour government to award full pensions immediately made little economic sense because it would have been far more logical to invest in the future, rather than to reward the past workforce. He concludes with the observation that 'a great test of any society's welfare intentions is whether it is prepared to support its retired citizens, who have no future social capital value'.[34]

The notion that social expenditure on services for the young is a more efficient use of public resources than providing services for the old, because the young, unlike the old, have a future labour market value, led Peter Laslett to comment, as long ago as 1977: 'Since it is the elderly who have lived and worked through the time of educational expansion it could be said that they have been paying the bill, but not sharing the benefits… Equity suggests that persons of all ages should have equal shares in the social fund, but the young… have had a monopoly in that very considerable part that goes to education'.[35]

This issue needs to be considered when looking at the current generation of pensioners. What promises were made to them and how should they be honoured? Most have worked all their lives after leaving education. They have raised their children and paid their taxes and their NI contributions during their working lifetime. Many contribute significantly to the economy in retirement by providing care for the young and the elderly and other non paying work and by continuing to pay their taxes. In the main, they believe that as a result they should be able to look forward to an adequate state pension and a secure retirement. However, the value of their state pension continues to be eroded in real terms.

The original (and Beveridge's) 'contributory principle' meant that those who paid into the scheme were entitled to benefits based on their contribution record and, in theory, the monies were collected in the NI fund and used only to pay NI benefits. More recently, the link between NI contributions and benefits has been broken. NI contribution income has risen over recent years in line with wages whereas the basic state pension increases have been linked to prices and have therefore grown at a slower rate. As Hills has shown, NI contributions now represent around 6.5% of national income but contributory benefits and pensions being paid out have fallen to around 5% of national income. NI contributions are no longer earmarked to provide NI benefits; to a large degree they are just another method of raising taxes, with the excess of contributions received over benefits paid used to fund general government expenditure. The promise of getting a reasonable pension linked to contributions paid into a national insurance scheme has been abandoned, with each new generation of pensioners getting poorer value for money based on the contributions they have made throughout their working lives.[36]

In the short term if the current basic state pension were significantly increased, it would have to be paid for by those currently in employment, with arguably more burden falling on those with higher incomes. This would be redistributive between the generations and between the well off and those on lower incomes.

In the longer term, what are the implications of trying to provide a flat rate state pension for all at a level adequate to meet pensioners' basic needs? A number of proposals have been put forward aimed at achieving this. For example, Hills[37] has argued that 'if we were more honest and explicit about what recent reforms are trying to achieve' we could use them to work towards providing a contributory state pension close to 'the current means tested minimum, whilst not giving extra to those with higher lifetime earnings'. He suggested that we 'unwind Britain's belated excursion into earnings related state pensions' and adapt the accrual rules for SERPS and S2P over time to work towards integrating them to produce a single state pension 'as close as possible to the current means tested minimum' which would again become a flat rate amount:

> Crucially…. most people's private pension receipts would return to being an add-on to the flat rate state pension… The spread of means testing within the state pension system would be reduced, so that at the margin people would retain the benefits of their additional saving, restoring much clearer incentives for additional private provision.[38]

This point was also made in the Actuarial Profession's response to the White Paper, *Security in Retirement – towards a new pensions system.*

This is an alternative to the current pensions structure which relies, in the main, on individual and employer provision backed up by means tested benefits and with only limited pension provision by the state. A flat rate universal state pension that ensured an adequate minimum income level as a right could require higher contributions, even if state pension ages were increased more than currently proposed. If the contributions were fully earnings related, then such a solution would be more redistributive than at present. Even after 100 years, we are still debating the level of the state pension and who should pay for it. What obligation is there on the current generation to pay for state pension benefits to those in retirement? To what extent should we use the state pension scheme to redistribute income and wealth in society?

## Sustainability and affordability

All party agreement in 1975 resulted in SERPS gaining parliamentary approval after 20 years of Labour party attempts to reform state pension provision. Britain had no more than caught up with what a (conservative) regime in West Germany had introduced 20 years before. Since 1975 there have been a significant number of pensions bills enacted with that associated with the Pensions Act 2007 currently going through its parliamentary stages. The Pensions Act 2007, with provisions not expected to be implemented for some years, may mark the start of a period of some stability in pensions legislation. However, there is still not complete consensus about the operation of auto-enrolment into pension saving. Political viability will be a major factor in the Act's success, but changes of government between the two major parties have resulted in the widely acknowledged proclivity of the British political class 'to tear up pension schemes at will every few years'.[39] Pensions by their nature are long term commitments. Employees paying contributions at age 20 may still be drawing their pensions 70 years later. Political consensus on the way ahead would provide increased stability and continuity and allow individuals and employers to plan for their old age with more confidence. Britain seems likely to experience a period of uncertainty in the years ahead, particularly if consensus is not achieved.

The economic efficiency arguments underpinning the pensions policies of the New Labour government since 1997 have been broadly in line with those of their predecessor Conservative governments in making a narrow definition of affordability a key objective of pension reform. Whilst still in opposition in 1996, New Labour issued its policy document *Security in Retirement* stating that 'SERPS could not easily or sustainably be rebuilt in its original form' and that 'new funded pension schemes could provide better returns for the same contribution level for many people'.[40]

In recent times, on the grounds of affordability, state provision has changed its emphasis from universal to means tested. This change has undermined the intended purpose of the universal basic state pension, making it necessary for its purpose to be clearly defined for the future. In the past, the basic state pension has benefited millions and we believe there is strong consensus outside of Parliament that it should continue to be the bedrock of pension policy.

## Security in old age

New Labour has given a commitment to reducing the number of older people in poverty, but also to reducing the state spending on pensions by shifting more of the burden on to private provision.[41] The main method by which New Labour has sought to improve the living standards of the poor in retirement has been through spending £10 billion on the Pension Credit scheme and by increasing the range of other benefits such as free eye tests, TV licences and winter fuel payments. 'The means test, which was the hated legacy of the poor law and still deters hundreds of thousands of pensioners, has been one of the cornerstones of New Labour policy'.[42] This policy has reduced the numbers of elderly below the poverty line, but suffers because of poor take up.

Entitlement to the full basic state pension is also problematic, as this is linked to each person's contribution record. Whilst in employment, except for those with earnings below the lower limit (£105 per week for the tax year 2008–09 – there are over one million women in this category), NI contributions are payable based on each person's earnings. However when not in employment the payment of NI contributions is voluntary (£8.10 per week for the tax year 2008–09). There is provision for people not in employment for certain reasons (e.g. low earners, students, carers, the unemployed, etc) to receive credits so reducing the period during which NI contributions must be made to secure the full basic state pension.

People without sufficient NI contributions receive a reduced entitlement. The government writes to them prior to retirement to warn them of the potential risk and to suggest the payment of voluntary NI contributions. However, many do not take up this option. (The Pensions Act 2007 changes have major consequences to the value proposition for paying voluntary contributions.)

The erosion of the value of the state pension (in relation to earnings) and the decline in final salary occupational pension schemes puts an increasing burden on individuals to make provision for themselves. The government would like to see an increase in the sale of private pension arrangements into which individuals contribute (with, following the most recent proposals, some quasi-compulsory contributions from their employers). These funds are invested in the stock market which places all the risks related to investment performance and the level of pension income that can be generated from the fund at retirement on the individual. Consequently those saving for retirement have to contend with much more uncertainty than would be the case if these risks were picked up by the state or by occupational defined benefit schemes.

Because state pensions are funded from public resources with the risks shared by the whole of society, they are not directly exposed to the hazards of the economic market or the possible depredations of fund sponsors or managers as are occupational schemes. Moreover, by their direct claim on human capital (the earning power of workers) on behalf of citizens, state pensions can be endowed with greater stability and security than occupational pension schemes which, either directly or indirectly, are entirely dependent on tradable assets in financial markets.

Social insurance has been a great provider of stability and social cohesion in our society and has provided some protection for the poor and disadvantaged.[43] In the modern volatile world, it seems unquestionable that there is an important continuing role for social insurance to provide good basic standards for all in health, care and pensions. There is a loss to society and an increase in risk and instability if the state restricts itself to a residual role – providing last resort means tested benefits to the poor. It is significant that, despite all the legislative changes over the last 100 years, the social insurance element of the state pension scheme has survived, even though, as a proportion of average earnings, the basic state pension is substantially less than it was in 1948. For 60 years the basic state pension and the contributory principle have resisted a number of moves for their abolition, and at least one attempt in the mid-1990s to secure public support for privatisation. The contributory social insurance system has withstood the criticisms of left and right because of the support of the contributors themselves who, by payment of their contributions, are accruing pension rights under a social insurance contract. The value of this to the security and stability of UK society should not be underestimated.

## The challenge for the future

The 100 years history began and has ended with popular campaigns for adequate retirement income for the elderly. It is clear that despite the achievements in pension reform, there is much that still needs to be done to build an affordable and sustainable system that ensures everyone receives an adequate income in old age. It is also clear that no pension reform is likely to be politically viable for the long term without public acceptance and long term cross-party agreement about the role of the state in pension provision.

The erosion of the value of the basic state pension and the growth in the number of pensioners receiving Pension Credit crystallises the balance between the key choices of:

**social insurance**   where all contribute (or are credited with contributions) during their working lives to a fund and so all members of society have a right to a pension in retirement sufficient to meet their basic needs;

and

**means tested benefits**   where resources are targeted to focus expenditure where it is really needed. However, based on past and current experience, the delivery of such benefits causes significant problems.

100 years after the first state old age pension was legislated for in the UK, we believe that the lessons and experience of the past can and should be used to mould the future development of state pensions in this country.

# Outline of provisions of the main legislation affecting state old age pensions

## Old Age Pensions Act 1908

Non-contributory means tested state pensions for the population aged 70 and over.

It granted a pension to every person, male and female, who fulfilled and continued to fulfil the following conditions:-

1. The person had attained age 70;
2. For at least 20 years up to the date of receipt of pension, the person had been a British subject with a residence in the United Kingdom;
3. The person's yearly means did not exceed £31 10s. There were complex provisions involved in the calculation of the yearly means including:-
   a. the yearly value of any benefit, advantage or privilege enjoyed by the person;
   b. if the person was one of a married couple living together in the same house, the means of that person is not less than half the total means of the couple; and
   c. not allowing the person directly or indirectly to dispose of any income or property in order to meet the means test;
4. Except in certain circumstances, the person was not in receipt of poor law relief during any time in the two year period to 31 December 1910;
5. The person had not habitually failed to work (except in the case of those who had continuously for 10 years up to age 60 made provision for their future old age, sickness, infirmity or loss of employment by payments to friendly or other societies or trade unions. If the exception applied to the husband then it was treated as automatically applying to his wife provided the married couple were living together);
6. The person had not been detained in a pauper or criminal lunatic asylum; and
7. The person had not been imprisoned without the option of a fine – this disqualification applied for 10 years following release from prison.

Unlike the receipt of poor law relief, there was no loss of voting rights as a consequence of receiving the old age pension. The pension was paid each Friday with the rate being: –

| Where the yearly means of the pensioner as calculated under the Act | Rate of pension per week |
| --- | --- |
| do not exceed £21 | 5s |
| exceed £21 but not £23 12s 6d | 4s |
| exceed £23 12s 6d but not £26 5s | 3s |
| exceed £26 5s but not £28 17s 6d | 2s |
| exceed £28 17s 6d but not £31 10s | 1s |
| exceed £31 10s | no pension |

All claims were determined by the pension authorities. These were (1) pension officers appointed by the Treasury from among Inland Revenue officers; (2) a central pension authority (i.e. the Local Government Board) or (3) local pension committees for every county and significant sized boroughs and urban districts.

The Old Age Pensions Acts of 1911 and 1919 amended the conditions to be satisfied in order to be entitled to a pension. The 1919 Act also increased the rate of pension from 2 January 1920 as follows:-

| Where the yearly means of the pensioner as calculated under the Acts | Rate of pension per week |
| --- | --- |
| do not exceed £26 5s | 10s |
| exceed £26 5s but not £31 10s | 8s |
| exceed £31 10s but not £36 15s | 6s |
| exceed £36 15s but not £42 | 4s |
| exceed £42 but not £47 5s | 2s |
| exceed £47 5s but not £49 17s 6d | 1s |
| exceed £49 17s 6d | no pension |

# Widows', Orphans' and Old Age Contributory Pensions Act 1925

Contributory pensions for 65 to 70 year olds and maintenance for widows.

This Act built onto the framework of the Old Age Pensions Acts 1908, 1911 and 1919 with those covered being the same as under the National Insurance Act 1911 as amended by the National Health Insurance Act 1924.

The National Insurance Act 1911 established two compulsory and contributory schemes of insurance against ill health and unemployment. The first scheme, which came into operation on 15 July 1912, provided for the payment of sickness, disablement and maternity cash benefits and for a general practitioner and certain medical benefit for the insured person. With certain exceptions, this scheme covered all those between the ages of 16 and 70 who were employed under a contract of service in manual labour or in non manual employment if receiving a rate of remuneration not exceeding £160 a year. The National Health Insurance Act 1919 raised the remuneration limit to £250 a year with this being increased further to £420 a year as from January 1942.

The other scheme, which commenced also in July 1912, was initially a limited compulsory and contributory insurance arrangement against unemployment in certain skilled industries in which marked fluctuations in employment were known to occur (e.g. building, shipbuilding, iron founding). It initially covered about 2¼ million workers with it being extended in 1916 to cover a further 1½ million workers. The Unemployment Insurance Act 1920 superseded the original scheme and extended unemployment insurance to cover over 11 million workers, including non manual workers. Also the 1920 Act raised the remuneration limit to £250 a year with this being increased further to £420 a year as from September 1940.

The Widows', Orphans' and Old Age Contributory Pensions Act 1925 provided the first compulsory and contributory state pension scheme for those covered by the National Health Insurance Scheme (including those who had been insured under the compulsory scheme and elected to become voluntary contributors). As a consequence of this legislation, the system of tripartite insurance introduced by the National Insurance Act 1911 was extended to pensions (the three parties being the wage earner, the employer and the Exchequer). In 1926 the main weekly rates of contributions for employed persons were as follows:-

| | Men | | | | Women | | | |
|---|---|---|---|---|---|---|---|---|
| | Employee | Employer | Exchequer | Total | Employee | Employer | Exchequer | Total |
| | s  d | s  d | s  d | s  d | s  d | s  d | s  d | s  d |
| Unemployment | 7 | 8 | 6¾ | 1  9¾ | 6 | 7 | 5¼ | 1  6¼ |
| Health | 4½ | 4½ | – | 9 | 4 | 4½ | – | 8½ |
| Pensions | 4½ | 4½ | – | 9 | 2 | 2½ | – | 4½ |
| **Total** | **1  4** | **1  5** | **6¾** | **3  3¾** | **1  0** | **1  2** | **5¼** | **2  7¼** |

In addition to the annual Exchequer supplement as indicated in the table above, there was an initial Exchequer single contribution to extinguish past years benefit accrual.

The benefit provisions of the 1925 Act came into force in three stages:-
1. As from 4 January 1926, pensions at the rate of 10s a week (with allowances for young children) became payable to the widows of insured men dying on or after that date, while in the case of motherless children orphans' pensions at the rate of 7s 6d a week became payable to their guardians;
2. As from 2 July 1926, old age pensions at 10s a week were granted, without any question of means, to persons then over age 70, or who attained that age between such date and 2 January 1928 – if they had been insured under the National Health Insurance scheme prior to attaining 70;

3. As from 2 January 1928 and subject to an adequate contribution record, a weekly pension of 10s was paid to an insured person then between 65 and 70 and to each insured person reaching age 65. The wife of an insured man received a pension as a concomitant of her husband's insurance, when she attained age 65 or as soon thereafter as her husband reached that age.

There was also the provision for the limited duration of pension payments to certain people who would have been entitled to a contributory pension if the scheme had been in force before 1926.

## Old Age and Widows' Pensions Act 1940

The state pension age for women reduced to 60 so that from 1 July 1940 the state pension of 10s a week was payable as from age 60, instead of 65, to an insured woman and to the wife of an insured man who had himself attained age 65.

The Act also provided a system of supplementary pensions from August 1940 whereby pensioners and widows who were in need were able to apply to the Assistance Board for supplementary allowances. For a pensioner without other resources, the normal weekly rates, inclusive of the contributory or non-contributory pension, were 19s 6d for a single person living alone and £1 12s for a married couple where both were pensioners.

## National Insurance Act 1946

Universal social insurance system – flat rate benefits for flat rate NI contribution.

This legislation introduced what is commonly called the Beveridge Scheme and which became effective from July 1948.

Covered the whole population over school leaving age and under state pension age (65 men & 60 women) divided into three classes; employed, self-employed and non-employed – *insured persons*. Married women on or after marriage elected whether or not to pay contributions appropriate to the class to which they belonged. Modified conditions of insurance applied also to a number of special groups (e.g. armed forces, seamen and students).

Contributory: Weekly flat rate contributions by insured persons but students, persons on earnings not exceeding £104 a year or sundry other special groups elected whether or not to contribute. Contributions were not payable by the employed while unemployed and by the employed and self-employed while incapacitated for work due to sickness or injury.

Employers paid a weekly contribution for all their employees even if the employee had elected not to contribute. In addition, for all insured persons, the Exchequer made a supplement in respect of every contribution paid.

The table below shows the contribution rates for adults from July 1948 with somewhat lower contributions applicable to insured persons under age 18:-

|  |  | Weekly contribution† | | Exchequer Supplement | |
|---|---|---|---|---|---|
|  |  | s | d | s | d |
| Payable by employed persons* | Men | 4 | 7 | 1 | 1 |
|  | Women | 3 | 7 | – | 10 |
| Payable by their employers* | Men | 3 | 10 | 1 | 0 |
|  | Women | 3 | 0 | – | 9 |
| Total for employed persons | Men | 8 | 5 | 2 | 1 |
|  | Women | 6 | 7 | 1 | 7 |
| Self-employed persons | Men | 6 | 2 | 1 | 1 |
|  | Women | 5 | 1 | – | 11 |
| Non-employed persons | Men | 4 | 8 | – | 9 |
|  | Women | 3 | 8 | – | 7 |

* The contributions for employed persons with weekly earnings of 30s or less were lower (by 1s 11d for men and 1s 5d for women) with the employer paying the reduction so that the total contributions were unaltered.
† Includes sums of 10d (men) and 8d (women) – the employers' share for employed insured people being 1½d – which are transferred to the Exchequer to meet a small part of the cost of the NHS.
‡ The weekly stamp for an employed person was the sum of the contribution shown in the table above and the contribution payable under the Industrial Injuries Scheme. The latter contribution amounted to 8d (men) and 6d (women) split equally between the insured person and the associated employer.

Subject to the contributor having a full contribution record, weekly pension at the rate of £1 6s payable at or after attaining state pension age (65 men & 60 women) upon retirement from regular work with provisions for deferring it. From age 70 (men) and 65 (women) the pension as uplifted to allow for the period of deferment must be taken without the retirement condition applying. A married man drawing a pension from age 65 with a dependent wife under age 60 received an additional 16s per week; if the wife was over 60 and not at work this sum was paid as a pension to her. The wife's pension was payable at £1 6s per week if she was herself insured with a full contribution record. Until the beneficiary attained age 70 (men) and 65 (women), the pension was reduced if earnings are more than £2 a week. There was an additional pension of 7s 6d if the pensioner had a dependent child.

Special provisions applied to persons who first became insured at the outset of the scheme (5 July 1948) and were then within 10 years of state pension age. Such persons were not entitled to a pension until 5 July 1958. If they reached state pension age before that date they could elect at that age to cease contributing so forfeiting the right to a pension and instead received a refund of that portion of their contributions relating to the pension with interest.

The Act also provided for unemployment, sickness, maternity and widows benefits as well as guardian's allowance and death grant.

## National Assistance Act 1948

Extended and consolidated means tested safety net.

## National Insurance Act 1959

It introduced the graduated pension scheme.

From April 1961, insured persons were required to pay weekly flat rate contributions appropriate to their class with each employed person and associated employer also paying a further graduated contribution of 4¼% of the person's earnings between £9 and £15 a week (maximum weekly contribution of 4s 10d). Although the total graduated contribution made by both parties was 8½% of the person's earnings between £9 and £15 a week, the amount of the graduated pension was calculated by reference to the graduated contributions paid by the insured person. The graduated pension was 6d per week for each £7 10s of graduated contributions (men) and 6d per week for each £9 of graduated contributions (women) i.e. a unit of graduated pension. On reaching state pension age the insured person received the sum of the basic state and graduated pensions.

Where employed persons over the age 18 were members of an occupational scheme which satisfied certain conditions, the employer could apply for them to be treated as being in non-participating employment. This meant, in essence, that while in non-participating employment, the employees and employer concerned would not pay the graduated contributions but would have to make a higher flat rate contribution.

In June 1963 the upper limit for the graduated scheme was raised to £18 per week with employees in non-participating employment still being able to contract out fully from the graduated element. However although the upper limit for the graduated scheme was further increased the upper limit for contracting out was not increased any further. In addition the graduated rate of contribution was increased a number of times.

Before the accrual of benefits under the graduated scheme ceased in April 1975, the upper limit was £62 per week so the earnings band was between £9 and £62 per week (maximum weekly contribution of £2.91) with the maximum pension accrued from 14 years of graduated contributions being £3.10 a week.

Graduated pension in payment and the value of graduated units which had been earned by people who are still of working age were initially not subject to increase. However, since the November 1978 uprating, the pension in payment and the value of the unit have been increased in line with price inflation. For a contributor reaching state pension age in the tax year 2008–09, the multiplier is £0.1098 per week compared to the initial multiplier of 6d (£0.025).

## Social Security Act 1973

This Act made NI contributions fully earnings related, closed the graduated scheme to future accrual of benefits, introduced further provisions covering occupational pensions including the establishment of the Occupational Pensions Board and legislated for the contributory reserve pension scheme under a Reserve Pension Board for not recognised pensionable employment. However the reserve pension scheme legislation was repealed before it was implemented.

# National Insurance Act 1974

The annual uprating of the basic state pension became the better of prices or earnings.

# Social Security Pensions Act 1975

The Act introduced the state earnings related pension scheme (SERPS) to provide an 'adequate' pension, which would lift all pensioners off means tested benefits. It also introduced provisions for the equality of treatment of men and women in pensions and other benefits.

SERPS commenced from April 1978 with the state pension becoming the sum of two components – the basic pension (i.e. the flat state pension as previously applied) and, for employed persons only, the additional pension (earnings related). Once in payment, the basic component was uprated annually by the better of prices or earnings with the additional pension being subject to annual price increases.

The additional pension was calculated by taking an 80th of the best 20 years of revalued relevant earnings from April 1978. This was calculated by converting back the contributor's NI contributions to his earnings (up to the upper earnings limit) for each tax year from April 1978. Each of these earnings was then revalued to the year before attaining state pension age in line with average earnings. The best 20 of these earnings (or all of them if less than 20) were then selected with each of them being reduced by the lower earnings limit that applied at the contributor's state pension age. They were then added together to become the best 20 years of revalued relevant earnings.

Widow's and widower's pensions were determined on a compatible basis.

The new arrangement permitted partial contracting out in respect of the additional component provided the employed person's occupational scheme met a test that contained two elements, one being a quality and the other a quantity condition – for the latter, the scheme had to promise to pay at least a minimum pension (the Guaranteed Minimum Pension) to each participating employee. The purpose of the test was to ensure that there would be no loss in benefits by contracting out.

For contracting out employees, the NI contributions were reduced by the rebate which was initially 7% (2½% employee and 4½% employer) of earnings between lower and upper earnings limits.

The legislation also abolished the married women's reduced rate for new cases from April 1977 but women already paying the reduced rate immediately before April 1977 were able while continuing in employment to retain their right to pay the reduced rate with consequential loss of benefits.

# Social Security Act 1980

State pension uprating to be based on prices only.

# Social Security Act 1986

Cutback SERPS to reduce costs, coupled to encouraging a more varied and flexible occupational and personal pension arrangements.

It modified SERPS in several ways including abolishing the best 20 years provision and reducing the accrual rate for future service. Once fully implemented, the maximum additional pension would be 20% of average revalued annual earnings between lower and upper earnings limits. The Act also reduced by 50% the amount that widows can inherit from April 2000.

It also made a number of important changes in non state pension arrangements including the provisions on the protection of pensions in payment, altering the contracting out provisions so permitting money purchase pension arrangements to contract out, introducing the government paid incentive payments to appropriate contracted out arrangements, introducing personal pensions and provisions for voluntary membership of and opting-out of occupational pension schemes.

## Pensions Act 1995

Equalisation of state pension age at 65 for men and women with the women's state pension age gradually increasing from 60 to 65 over a 10 year period from April 2010. As a result all people born after 6 April 1955 have a state pension age of 65.

From April 1997, various changes to the provisions for contracting out of SERPS were made including the introduction of age related rebate rates, the cessation of the future accrual of Guaranteed Minimum Pensions and the Reference Scheme Test replacing the previous conditions for a salary related occupational pension scheme to contract out.

There were changes also to the regulations applying to occupational pension schemes partly to cope with the aftermath of the Maxwell affair (where Robert Maxwell, the proprietor of the Mirror Group, had used the group's pension schemes' assets to finance his business interests and once these interests had failed the pension schemes became insolvent) and partly because of the European Court of Justice judgement in the case of Barber (occupational pensions are treated as pay with benefits in respect of service after 17 May 1990 to be equal).

## Child Support, Pensions and Social Security Act 2000

Replaced SERPS with the state second pension (S2P) – weighted towards those contributors whose lifetime earnings are low.

S2P replaces SERPS with effect from 6 April 2002 with any SERPS entitlement earned to that date being protected. S2P has 3 salary bands between the lower and upper earnings limits and within each band benefits are built up. Currently the target pension varies from 40% of earnings for the lowest salary band to 20% of earnings for the highest salary band. Consequently low earners will build up a S2P entitlement higher than under SERPS and at a greater rate than individuals earning higher salaries.

In addition certain carers and disabled people not accruing S2P through employment obtain S2P credits as if they are a low earner.

## State Pension Credit Act 2002

Guaranteed minimum income with tapered benefits for all age 60 and over

The Act introduced the Pension Credit replacing the Minimum Income Guarantee (MIG) from October 2003. The Pension Credit comprises two elements; (a) the Guarantee Credit which replaced effectively the MIG and (b) the Savings Credit.

The Guarantee Credit is that necessary to increase the recipient's income to the standard minimum guarantee. It is granted to men and women at or over the age which is the minimum qualifying age for women to receive the basic state pension. For a pensioner without additional needs, the Guarantee Credit granted will bring the recipient's income to the standard minimum guarantee which for the year 2008/09 is £124.05 per week for a single person and £189.35 per week for a couple.

The Savings Credit rewards those pensioners aged 65 and over who have built up a modest income for retirement whether in the form of a second pension or savings. The Savings Credit amounts to 60p for every pound of pension (such as occupational pensions and SERPS) and income from savings that the pensioner's income is above the level of the savings credit threshold (i.e. the full rate of the basic state pension) and below the standard minimum guarantee. For every pound of income a pensioner has above the level of the standard minimum guarantee, the Savings Credit is reduced by 40p to a minimum of nil. The savings credit threshold for the year 2008/09 is £91.20 per week for a single person and £145.80 per week for a couple (i.e. the full rate of the basic state pension).

The recipient's income is augmented by the Pension Credit being the sum of the Guarantee Credit and the Savings Credit. As a consequence, even when the recipient's income before Pension Credit is in excess of the standard minimum guarantee, a Savings Credit may still be payable.

With the introduction of Pension Credit, the government gave a commitment to uprate the standard minimum guarantee each year in line with average earnings until 2008. The Pensions Act 2007 made this basis of uprating the standard minimum guarantee a mandatory requirement from 2008 and beyond.

## Pensions Act 2007

The Act put into law the reforms set out in the May 2006 White Paper *Security in retirement: towards a new pension system* and included:-

- State pension age to increase by one year per decade between 2024 and 2046 with each change phased in over two consecutive years in each decade. This change will affect anyone born after 5 April 1959 with people born after 5 April 1978 having a state pension age of 68.
- For those reaching their state pension age from 6 April 2010, the number of years needed to qualify for the full basic state pension to reduce from 44 years for men and 39 for women to 30 qualifying years in both cases. A person with less than 30 years qualifying years (with no minimum years applying) to be entitled to a thirtieth of the full basic state pension for each qualifying year accrued.
- From 6 April 2010 the removal of the restriction that the spouse or civil partner must be in receipt of a state pension in order that the other person can qualify for a state pension on that person's contribution record.
- New crediting arrangements to allow a parent, a registered foster parent or a carer (as defined in the legislation) to build up in certain circumstances an entitlement to a basic state pension and for their spouse or civil partner to build up an entitlement based on these credits.

- From a date still to be announced but expected to be no later than by the end of the next Parliament, the basic state pension to be uprated annually in line with earnings rather than prices. In addition the link between the amount of the lower earnings limit and the weekly rate of the basic state pension will be broken with any future increase in the lower earnings limit being at the discretion of the Treasury.
- The annual uprating of the Pension Credit standard minimum guarantee in line with average earnings became a mandatory requirement from 2008 and beyond.
- S2P to be restructured on a phased basis from 2009 into a flat rate top-up to the basic state pension. Accrual on the lower band to be replaced with a flat rate accrual. The other two bands being merged in 2010 with the future accrual rate being 10% and the upper earnings limit applying to these bands being frozen. With time this merged band will disappear. These changes will have an effect on the contracted out rebate for defined benefit schemes.
- On a phased basis, contracting out for occupational and personal pension schemes that contract out on a money purchase basis to be abolished.
- The provisions for establishing the Personal Accounts Delivery Authority whose task is to undertake the preliminary work necessary for the establishment of a personal accounts scheme. Further legislation currently going through Parliament will establish the personal accounts scheme with the planned commencement date being 2012.

Source:   Office for National Statistics, *Pension Trends*, 2005 edition, Figure 1.1, Pensions legislation timeline, 1990 to 2004, HMSO
Old Age Pensions Acts 1908, 1911 & 1919
Social Insurance and Allied Services Report 1942 (Cmd 6404) Appendix B
Report by the Government Actuary on the Financial Provisions of the National Insurance Bill, 1946 (Cmd 6730)
Report of the Committee on the Economic and Financial Problems of the Provision for Old Age (Cmd 9333)
Report by the Government Actuary on the Financial Provisions of the National Insurance Bill 1959 (Cmd 629)
Report by the Government Actuary on the Third Quinquennial Review issued 20 November 1964
Report by the Government Actuary on the operation of the Social Security Acts in the period 6 April 1975 to 5 April 1980 issued July 1982.
Explanatory Notes to State Pension Credit Act, HMSO, 2002.

# An outline of the history of the National Insurance Fund and the current basic state pension scheme

## Origins

The National Insurance Fund was established in 1911, reformed in 1948 and assumed broadly its current form in 1975, when the separate Industrial Injuries Fund and National Insurance (Reserve) Fund were merged with it. In this note, reference to the Fund is to the combination of the above three funds.

The Schedule at the end of the appendix summarises the accounts of the Funds from 1 July 1948. From 1948, its income has come from three main sources:-

- National Insurance contributions paid by individual contributors and, if employed, their employers;
- The state (in the form of an Exchequer supplement or Treasury Grant); and
- Investment income (interest plus net profit on investment transactions) in respect of the assets held by the Fund.

The National Insurance Scheme is financed on a pay as you go basis with the contributions set at a level broadly necessary to meet the expected benefits expenditure in that year, after taking into account any other payments and receipts, and to maintain a working balance. Changes in contribution levels in response to the needs of the Fund take time to implement and therefore a working balance is necessary because the Fund has no borrowing powers.

The amounts received by and paid out of the Fund, and the resulting balance, depend on legislation, which is the responsibility of government ministers. As a result, the benefits provided by the Fund have changed over the period from 1 July 1948 with the principal benefit throughout being the retirement state pension – basic, graduated (based on contributions paid on earnings between April 1961 and April 1975) and additional pension (based on contributions paid after April 1978 i.e. SERPS and S2P).

In setting contribution rates, the government ministers are required to have regard to changes in the general level of earnings, the state of the Fund and payments expected to be made from it in the future (Sections 141 and 143 of the Social Security Administration Act 1992).

# National Insurance contributions

Since the scheme was introduced in 1948, there have been three categories of contributors – employed, self-employed and non-employed. By paying the appropriate National Insurance contribution relative to the contributor's status of employment throughout the working life (age 16 to state pension age) the contributor accrues a full contribution record.

Details of the contribution rates for the various categories are given below. Part of the contributions is to meet part of the cost of the National Health Service. For the initial years, the total contributions were paid to the Fund with the National Health Service allocation of contributions being transferred out of the Fund. Since then this allocation has been made before the contributions are paid into the Fund. The schedule shows the contributions net of the National Health Service allocation. This allocation was £18.4bn in 2005–06 and £18.9bn in 2006–07.

A. **Employed** – These contributors and their employers pay Class 1 contributions which since the 1970s have been on an earnings related basis. A contributor's earnings are split into a number of ranges with each range being linked to a contribution rate. Details for the years 2007–08 and 2008–09 are as follows:-

|  | 2007–08 | 2008–09 |
|---|---|---|
| Lower earnings limit | £87 per week | £90 per week |
| Upper earnings limit | £670 per week | £770 per week |
| Primary threshold | £100 per week | £105 per week |
| Secondary threshold | £100 per week | £105 per week |
| Employee's contribution rate on earnings between primary threshold and upper earnings limit[1] | 11% | 11% |
| Employees' contribution on earnings above the upper earnings limit | 1%[2] | 1%[2] |
| Employer's contribution rate on earnings above secondary threshold | 12.8% | 12.8% |

Notes
1. If the employee is contracted out, the rebate on earnings on which contributions are payable up to the upper earnings limit is:-

|  | | |
|---|---|---|
| Employee's | 1.6% | 1.6% |
| Employer's – salary-related schemes | 3.7% | 3.7% |
| Employer's – money purchase schemes | 1.4% | 1.4% |

2. To be credited solely to the National Health Service.

If a contributor earns less than the primary threshold, the person does not pay any contribution but nevertheless will have notional contributions added to the contributor's record as long as the earnings are at least as much as the lower earnings limit.

B. **Self-employed** – The self-employed pay a flat rate Class 2 contribution unless the contributor's earnings are below the small earnings exception. In addition, there is an earnings related Class 4 contribution depending on the level of profits. Details for the years 2007–08 and 2008–09 are as follows:-

|  | 2007–08 | 2008–09 |
|---|---|---|
| Class 2 rate | £2.20 per week | £2.30 per week |
| Small earnings exception | £4,635 p.a. | £4,825 p.a. |
| Lower profits limit | £5,225 p.a. | £5,435 p.a. |
| Upper profits limit | £34,840 p.a. | £40,040 p.a. |
| Rate applying on earnings between lower and upper profits limit | 8% | 8% |
| Rate applying on earnings above upper profits limit | 1%* | 1%* |

*To be credited solely to the National Health Service

**C. Non-employed** – Class 3 contributions (2007–08: £7.80 per week, 2008–09: £8.10 per week) are voluntary contributions which a person can pay if payment of a compulsory contribution as an employee or self-employed person is not required to be made – for example, if the person's earnings are low or the person is working or living abroad – or the person is not entitled to credits in order to ensure a full contribution record.

If the contributor has paid or been credited with some contributions in a tax year but not enough to count towards the pension conditions, the HM Revenue and Customs has for some years contacted the person to indicate how much is needed to make up that year's contributions. If the contributor elects to pay these contributions then the payment must be made by the end of the sixth tax year following the one in which they were due.

The following table indicates the split in the National Insurance contributions (after deduction of the National Health Service share) between the classes for the five years to 31 March 2007:-

| Figures in £ million | 2002–03 | 2003–04 | 2004–05 | 2005–06 | 2006–07 |
|---|---|---|---|---|---|
| Employed –sum of employees' & employers' contributions | 56,544 | 56,732 | 59,639 | 64,434 | 66,161 |
| Self-employed |  |  |  |  |  |
| – flat rate contributions | 295 | 243 | 220 | 305 | 309 |
| – earnings related contributions | 1,516 | 1,542 | 1,621 | 1,527 | 1,631 |
| Voluntary contributions | 67 | 70 | 90 | 136 | 111 |
| Total contributions | 58,422 | 58,587 | 61,570 | 66,402 | 68,212 |

## Married women

A married woman with an adequate contribution record can claim her basic state pension when she reaches age 60. If she is not entitled to a pension on her own contribution record or her basic state pension is less than roughly 60% of her husband's basic state pension then, once her husband starts to draw his basic state pension, the wife will be entitled to the above maximum amount (i.e. roughly 60% of her husband's basic state pension) together with her entitlement to graduated and/or additional pension based on her contributions.

In addition if the wife is below age 60 when the husband claims his basic state pension and subject to a restriction in respect of her earnings then the husband receives the married couple's pension which is equal to his own basic state pension plus the above maximum amount.

Because of the provisions for a pension based on the husband's contribution record to be payable to a married woman, the scheme from its inception in 1948 permitted a married woman to opt out of the scheme by electing to pay a reduced contribution (commonly referred to as the married women's reduced contribution). However by doing so the period during which the option is exercised (this includes periods when not in paid employment) does not count towards the eligibility conditions for a basic state pension.

The right to elect to pay reduced contributions was abolished from 6 April 1977 although women already paying the lower rate at that time could continue to do so but would lose the right if they did not have paid work for two tax years or became divorced. For the tax year 2008–09, the reduced rate of contribution is 4.85% on earnings between the primary threshold and upper earnings limit and 1% on the excess earnings above the upper limit if employed. No contributions are due if self-employed.

## National Insurance credits

National insurance credits are added to the person's contribution record under certain circumstances including:

- while unemployed and registered for Jobseeker's Allowance;
- while incapable of work subject to having a medical certificate;
- while unable to work because the contributor is receiving the Carer's Allowance while looking after someone who is disabled;
- starting credits – from age 16 to 19 if the record would otherwise be insufficient;
- men aged 60 to 64 who are not receiving earnings unless they are abroad for more than six months during the tax year;
- Home responsibilities protection – started in April 1978 and protects the pension rights from that date onwards of someone caring for a child or a sick or disabled person unless she is a married woman or widow who has exercised in that tax year to pay the married women's reduced contributions. The maximum period for home responsibilities protection is 20 years.

These credits effectively reduce the number of years a person has to pay National Insurance contributions in order to get the full amount of benefit.

From April 2010 there will be a number of changes in the credits provision including a new carer credit and abolishing the 60–64 credits for men not in employment.

# State pension age

The state pension age depends on the person's date of birth as follows:-

|  | State pension age |
|---|---|
| A woman born before 6 April 1950 | 60 |
| A woman born on or after 6 April 1950 but before 6 April 1955 | phased to 65 |
| A woman born on or after 6 April 1955 but before 6 April 1959 | 65 |
| A man born before 6 April 1959 | 65 |
| A man or woman born on or after 6 April 1959 but before 6 April 1960 | phased to 66 |
| A man or woman born on or after 6 April 1960 but before 6 April 1968 | 66 |
| A man or woman born on or after 6 April 1968 but before 6 April 1969 | phased to 67 |
| A man or woman born on or after 6 April 1969 but before 6 April 1977 | 67 |
| A man or woman born on or after 6 April 1977 but before 6 April 1978 | phased to 68 |
| A man or woman born on or after 6 April 1978 | 68 |

# Eligibility for the full basic state pension

The eligibility conditions for the full basic state pension to be granted are very complex.

For a person who reaches state pension age before 6 April 2010, the following two conditions need to be met:-

1. Actual National Insurance contributions (not credits) have been paid in any one year. This condition must be satisfied through the contributor's own contribution record or that of the contributor's spouse or civil partner; and

2. The contributions and the credits that have been granted cover roughly 90% of the contributor's working life between age 16 and 65 (males) and 60 (females). The contributor's own contribution record can be combined with the contributor's former spouse's or civil partner's record if the contributor (a) is widowed, (b) is the surviving civil partner of a partner who has died, (c) is divorced or (d) has dissolved the civil partnership.

For a person who reaches state pension age on or after 6 April 2010 the two conditions become:-

1. To qualify for a pension the person has paid or has been credited with contributions for at least one year; and

2. To obtain a full pension, the person must have at least 30 years of a combination of paying contributions and credits.

Since December 2005 same sex couples have been able to register a civil partnership. State pension provisions that previously only applied to husbands and wives now also apply to registered civil partners. However where provisions apply only to women, such as the married women's pension, rules will only be extended to civil partners and married men when the state pension age starts to be equalised for men and women in April 2010.

## Basic state pension

Provided that the contributor meets the eligibility conditions, a full basic state pension is payable from state pension age. There are provisions for deferring the pension.

For a person not satisfying the conditions, a reduced rate of pension is payable. For a person reaching state pension age before 6 April 2010, the contributor's contribution record must cover at least 25% of the required years (this is around 11 years for a man and around 10 years for a woman and for a person with the minimum number of years required the state pension would be 25% of the full rate). For a person reaching state pension age on or after 6 April 2010 with less than 30 years of paid and credited contributions, the accrual of the basic state pension is a thirtieth for each year. This means that a person with a 10 year contribution record on reaching state pension age would receive a pension of a third of the full rate.

For the year starting April 2008, the full weekly rates are:-

| | |
|---|---|
| Single person | £90.70 |
| Wife on husband's contributions | £54.35 |
| Married couple on husband's contributions | £145.05 |
| Married couple/civil partners if both paid full contributions | £181.40 |

with an extra 25p per week payable when the pensioner attains age 80.

## Uprating of the basic state pension

The 2007 Budget report specified that the basic state pension is to increase each April by 2.5% or the 12 month rate of the Retail Prices Index for the previous September. At a date still to be announced but not earlier than 2012 and not later than the end of the next Parliament, the basic state pension will thereafter be increased annually in line with average earnings.

## Exchequer payments

Initially following the commencement of the scheme in 1948, the Exchequer made two separate payments to the Fund. The first was its share of the National Insurance contribution and the second was to meet the inception costs. The amounts of these payments for the first few years are as follows:-

| Period to | 31/3/49[1] | 31/3/50 | 31/3/51 | 31/3/52 |
|---|---|---|---|---|
| Exchequer payment | | | | |
| – Share of NI contributions | £71m | £102m | £102m | £87m |
| – Cost of inception | £26m | £40m | £44m | 24m |
| Total Exchequer payment | £97m | £142m | £146m | £111m |

1. The figures are in respect of the nine months to 31 March 1949

As shown by the table below, the Exchequer supplement associated with the contribution rates started to be reduced from April 1981 with the supplement being abolished by the Social Security Act 1989 starting with the 1989–90 financial year.

| Tax year | Exchequer supplement rate as % of the NI contributions of insured persons and employers before contracting out rebates and deductions of statutory sick, maternity, etc pay | Exchequer supplement as % of net contribution income after allowing for deduction of contracting out rebate |
|---|---|---|
|  | % | % |
| 1980–81 | 18.0 | 22.7 |
| 1981–82 | 14.5 | 17.3 |
| 1982–83 | 13.0 | 15.9 |
| 1983–84 | 13.0 | 15.8 |
| 1984–85 | 11.0 | 13.7 |
| 1985–86 | 9.0 | 10.4 |
| 1986–87 | 9.0 | 10.8 |
| 1987–88 | 7.0 | 8.7 |
| 1988–89 | 5.0 | 6.0 |

The Social Security Act 1993 introduced the Treasury Grant. It enables money provided by Parliament to be paid into the Fund if the government considers it expedient to do so in order to maintain the level of the Fund. By statute, the Treasury Grant has a cap of 20% for 1993–94 and 17% for subsequent years of the estimated benefit expenditure for that tax year.

In assessing the Treasury Grant for 1993–94, the Government Actuary decided that it should be, as a minimum, that necessary for the estimated balance in the Fund at the end of that year to be equal to a sixth of that year's benefit expenditure. This remains the recommended minimum level by the Government Actuary to ensure that a reasonable working balance in the Fund is maintained.

Treasury Grants totalling £20 billion were made between 1 April 1993 and 31 March 2000 but since then the Government Actuary's view each year has been that it would not be necessary for any Grant to be made.

## Fund's assets

The Fund's balance has risen from £887 million as at 1 July 1948 to £38,220 million as at 31 March 2007. Up to 31 March 2006, the balance was invested in government and government guaranteed stocks by the Commissioners for the Reduction of the National Debt (CRND). However, following a review by the HM Revenue and Customs, the Treasury and CRND, a change to the Fund's investment strategy was approved in December 2006 with the change resulting in lower administrative charges to the Fund. The change was effected in January 2007 when all the Fund's gilt holdings were sold and the proceeds placed into the Debt Management Account Deposit Facility. In future, the Fund's assets held in this facility are expected to earn a rate of interest close to the Official Bank of England Rate (Base Rate).

With this change the book value and the market value of the balance at the year end will be the same from 31 March 2007.

## Government Actuary's role

The Government Actuary is required under Sections 142(1), 147(2) and 150(8) of the 1992 Social Security Administration Act (as amended by the Social Security Contributions (Transfer of Functions, etc) Act 1999) to report on the likely effect on the Fund of the government's annual changes in NI benefits and contributions that come into force the following April. This report is laid before Parliament around the turn of the year before the April date and debated alongside the relevant orders with approval of both Houses being required. In the report, the Government Actuary is required to express his view on the necessity for a Treasury Grant to be made to the Fund in the forthcoming financial year.

The Government Actuary's latest report (Cm7312) on the government's changes to the NI benefits and contributions was tabled in January 2008 alongside the statutory instruments *Social Security Benefits Up-rating Order 2008* and *Social Security (Contributions) (Re-rating) Order 2008* that cover the financial year 2008–2009. The Government Actuary's report includes an estimate of the Fund's position over the years to 31 March 2013 (this is given in the following schedule).

The Government Actuary is also required under Section 166 of the Act to report every five years on the long term financial estimates of the Fund. The latest quinquennial report was laid before Parliament on 27 October 2003 and an update provided on 23 December 2004.

In determining the financial estimates, the Government Actuary has to adopt a set of assumptions, some of which are specified by the government. Consequently the estimates of future benefit payments and contributions, both very large figures, are sensitive to changes in a number of these assumptions (such as the level of employment and earnings). Therefore differences between the expected and the actual future position could have a very significant effect on the excess of receipts over payments in any future years.

Sources:   The statutory accounts of the National Insurance Fund from 1 July 1948 to 31 March 2007.
   *Report by the Government Actuary on the drafts of the Social Security Benefits Up-rating Order 2008 and the Social Security (Contributions) (Re-rating) Order 2008* (Cm 7312). The report was issued in January 2008.
   Booklet *State pensions – your guide* published October 2007 by The Pension Service, part of the DWP.
   Office for National Statistics note on *Uprating of benefit payments* issued on 16 October 2007.
   http://dmo.gov.uk/index.aspx?page=CRND/CRND_Portfolio/NIFIA

**SCHEDULE – Accounts of the National Insurance Fund** – All figures in £ million

| Period to 31 March | 1949 | 1950 | 1951 | 1952 | 1953 | 1954 | 1955 | 1956 | 1957 | 1958 | 1959 | 1960 | 1961 |
|---|---|---|---|---|---|---|---|---|---|---|---|---|---|
| **Receipts** | | | | | | | | | | | | | |
| Contributions | 277 | 391 | 390 | 406 | 439 | 474 | 482 | 570 | 590 | 615 | 757 | 775 | 778 |
| Exchequer payments | 97 | 142 | 146 | 111 | 72 | 77 | 78 | 100 | 105 | 110 | 176 | 181 | 183 |
| Investment income | 18 | 27 | 33 | 34 | 24 | 46 | 56 | 51 | 54 | 58 | 59 | 62 | 65 |
| Other receipts | 4 | 5 | 4 | 4 | 5 | 2 | 1 | 0 | 0 | 0 | 1 | 1 | 1 |
| Total receipts | 396 | 565 | 573 | 555 | 540 | 599 | 617 | 721 | 749 | 783 | 993 | 1,019 | 1,027 |
| **Less Payments** | | | | | | | | | | | | | |
| Retirement pension | 176 | 249 | 249 | 275 | 316 | 334 | 348 | 433 | 448 | 482 | 617 | 657 | 677 |
| Other benefits | 87 | 129 | 133 | 130 | 167 | 176 | 174 | 200 | 209 | 237 | 312 | 308 | 307 |
| Administration | 22 | 26 | 25 | 27 | 30 | 31 | 31 | 32 | 36 | 38 | 41 | 45 | 45 |
| PP payments | 0 | 0 | 0 | 0 | 0 | 0 | 0 | 0 | 0 | 0 | 0 | 0 | 0 |
| Other payments | 0 | 0 | 0 | 10 | 3 | 7 | 4 | 5 | 6 | 5 | 7 | 9 | 5 |
| Total payments | 285 | 404 | 407 | 442 | 516 | 548 | 557 | 670 | 699 | 762 | 977 | 1,019 | 1,034 |
| Excess of receipts over payments | 111 | 161 | 166 | 113 | 24 | 51 | 60 | 51 | 50 | 21 | 16 | 0 | -7 |
| **Closing balance** | | | | | | | | | | | | | |
| Book value | 998 | 1,159 | 1,325 | 1,438 | 1,462 | 1,513 | 1,573 | 1,624 | 1,674 | 1,695 | 1,711 | 1,711 | 1,704 |
| Market value | 1,019 | 1,104 | 1,270 | 1,253 | 1,346 | 1,463 | 1,488 | 1,349 | 1,417 | 1,361 | 1,150 | 1,403 | 1,334 |

| Period to 31 March | 1962 | 1963 | 1964 | 1965 | 1966 | 1967 | 1968 | 1969 | 1970 | 1971 | 1972 | 1973 | 1974 |
|---|---|---|---|---|---|---|---|---|---|---|---|---|---|
| **Receipts** | | | | | | | | | | | | | |
| Contributions | 972 | 1,009 | 1,172 | 1,266 | 1,552 | 1,599 | 1,740 | 1,923 | 2,044 | 2,339 | 2,642 | 3,139 | 3,741 |
| Exchequer payments | 199 | 200 | 225 | 233 | 297 | 303 | 316 | 359 | 371 | 420 | 512 | 578 | 623 |
| Investment income | 58 | 68 | 62 | 51 | 73 | 69 | 78 | -13 | 70 | 67 | 69 | 73 | 91 |
| Other receipts | 2 | 1 | 1 | 0 | 2 | 1 | 1 | 2 | 0 | 3 | 5 | 5 | 3 |
| Total receipts | 1,231 | 1,278 | 1,460 | 1,550 | 1,924 | 1,972 | 2,135 | 2,271 | 2,485 | 2,829 | 3,224 | 3,795 | 4,458 |
| **Less Payments** | | | | | | | | | | | | | |
| Retirement pension | 784 | 807 | 959 | 1,015 | 1,238 | 1,272 | 1,385 | 1,543 | 1,627 | 1,778 | 2,045 | 2,369 | 2,752 |
| Other benefits | 360 | 402 | 464 | 471 | 571 | 619 | 738 | 779 | 828 | 853 | 1,020 | 1,096 | 1,246 |
| Administration | 49 | 55 | 61 | 62 | 68 | 72 | 81 | 84 | 97 | 110 | 129 | 140 | 159 |
| PP payments | 0 | 0 | 0 | 0 | 0 | 0 | 0 | 0 | 0 | 0 | 0 | 0 | 0 |
| Other payments | 8 | 10 | 12 | 13 | 16 | 17 | 19 | 18 | 21 | 23 | 31 | 37 | 42 |
| Total payments | 1,201 | 1,274 | 1,496 | 1,561 | 1,893 | 1,980 | 2,223 | 2,424 | 2,573 | 2,764 | 3,225 | 3,642 | 4,199 |
| Excess of receipts over payments | 30 | 4 | -36 | -11 | 31 | -8 | -88 | -153 | -88 | 65 | -1 | 153 | 259 |
| **Closing balance** | | | | | | | | | | | | | |
| Book value | 1,734 | 1,738 | 1,702 | 1,691 | 1,722 | 1,714 | 1,626 | 1,473 | 1,385 | 1,450 | 1,449 | 1,602 | 1,861 |
| Market value | 1,363 | 1,470 | 1,442 | 1,345 | 1,353 | 1,412 | 1,225 | 1,010 | 945 | 1,032 | 1,114 | 1,225 | 1,195 |

**SCHEDULE – Accounts of the National Insurance Fund** – All figures in £ million

| Period to 31 March | 1975 | 1976 | 1977 | 1978 | 1979 | 1980 | 1981 | 1982 | 1983 | 1984 | 1985 | 1986 | 1987 |
|---|---|---|---|---|---|---|---|---|---|---|---|---|---|
| **Receipts** | | | | | | | | | | | | | |
| Contributions | 5,023 | 6,184 | 7,730 | 8,559 | 8,969 | 10,314 | 12,377 | 13,836 | 16,044 | 17,502 | 18,757 | 20,511 | 22,024 |
| Exchequer payments | 847 | 1,133 | 1,387 | 1,537 | 1,976 | 2,343 | 2,848 | 2,433 | 2,591 | 2,807 | 2,597 | 2,163 | 2,412 |
| Investment income | 134 | 193 | 281 | 387 | 443 | 542 | 607 | 588 | 496 | 490 | 520 | 541 | 610 |
| Other receipts | 7 | 4 | 0 | 0 | 23 | 99 | 177 | 199 | 262 | 291 | 244 | 281 | 294 |
| Total receipts | 6,011 | 7,514 | 9,398 | 10,483 | 11,411 | 13,298 | 16,009 | 17,056 | 19,393 | 21,090 | 22,118 | 23,496 | 25,340 |
| **Less** | | | | | | | | | | | | | |
| **Payments** | | | | | | | | | | | | | |
| Retirement pension | 3,578 | 4,791 | 5,651 | 6,592 | 7,593 | 8,814 | 10,541 | 12,127 | 13,550 | 14,615 | 15,302 | 16,521 | 17,817 |
| Other benefits | 1,518 | 2,021 | 2,415 | 2,793 | 3,089 | 3,429 | 4,352 | 5,117 | 5,061 | 5,102 | 5,528 | 5,788 | 6,188 |
| Administration | 223 | 335 | 344 | 355 | 395 | 442 | 601 | 707 | 720 | 716 | 808 | 810 | 738 |
| PP payments | 0 | 0 | 0 | 0 | 0 | 0 | 0 | 0 | 0 | 0 | 0 | 0 | 0 |
| Other payments | 54 | 48 | 60 | 65 | 68 | 78 | 104 | 96 | 85 | 76 | 106 | 62 | 183 |
| Total payments | 5,373 | 7,195 | 8,470 | 9,805 | 11,145 | 12,763 | 15,598 | 18,047 | 19,416 | 20,509 | 21,744 | 23,181 | 24,926 |
| Excess of receipts over payments | 638 | 319 | 928 | 678 | 266 | 535 | 411 | -991 | -23 | 581 | 374 | 315 | 414 |
| **Closing balance** | | | | | | | | | | | | | |
| Book value | 2,499 | 2,219 | 3,147 | 3,825 | 4,091 | 4,626 | 5,037 | 4,046 | 4,023 | 4,604 | 4,978 | 5,293 | 5,707 |
| Market value | 1,954 | 2,323 | 3,432 | 4,149 | 4,454 | 4,505 | 5,145 | 4,098 | 4,361 | 5,001 | 5,227 | 5,921 | 6,225 |

| Period to 31 March | 1988 | 1989 | 1990 | 1991 | 1992 | 1993 | 1994 | 1995 | 1996 | 1997 | 1998 | 1999 | 2000 |
|---|---|---|---|---|---|---|---|---|---|---|---|---|---|
| **Receipts** | | | | | | | | | | | | | |
| Contributions | 24,265 | 27,119 | 29,229 | 30,699 | 32,328 | 33,467 | 34,942 | 37,726 | 39,850 | 41,682 | 45,542 | 48,831 | 50,593 |
| Exchequer payments | 2,135 | 1,653 | 0 | 0 | 0 | 0 | 7,589 | 6,280 | 3,575 | 1,902 | 941 | 3 | 2 |
| Investment income | 596 | 778 | 1,040 | 996 | 1,109 | 925 | 470 | 364 | 444 | 474 | 466 | 651 | 715 |
| Other receipts | 340 | 276 | 177 | 2,793 | 1,220 | 1,242 | 1,309 | 736 | 690 | 799 | 869 | 750 | 856 |
| Total receipts | 27,336 | 29,826 | 30,446 | 34,488 | 34,657 | 35,634 | 44,310 | 45,106 | 44,559 | 44,857 | 47,818 | 50,235 | 52,166 |
| **Less** | | | | | | | | | | | | | |
| **Payments** | | | | | | | | | | | | | |
| Retirement pension | 18,648 | 19,238 | 20,697 | 22,699 | 25,543 | 26,706 | 28,183 | 28,745 | 29,963 | 31,995 | 33,557 | 35,575 | 37,705 |
| Other benefits | 6,145 | 6,159 | 6,303 | 6,991 | 8,520 | 9,492 | 10,281 | 10,520 | 10,178 | 9,726 | 9,035 | 8,864 | 8,510 |
| Administration | 802 | 866 | 857 | 980 | 1,202 | 1,332 | 1,555 | 1,280 | 1,180 | 1,038 | 1,041 | 1,021 | 817 |
| PP payments | 0 | 289 | 2,434 | 2,069 | 2,452 | 2,654 | 2,860 | 1,957 | 1,961 | 1,998 | 2,052 | 1,656 | 2,574 |
| Other payments | 160 | 193 | 217 | 264 | 399 | 347 | 318 | 325 | 269 | 199 | 262 | 450 | 399 |
| Total payments | 25,755 | 26,745 | 30,508 | 33,003 | 38,116 | 40,531 | 43,197 | 42,827 | 43,551 | 44,956 | 45,947 | 47,566 | 50,005 |
| Excess of receipts over payments | 1,581 | 3,081 | -62 | 1,485 | -3,459 | -4,897 | 1,113 | 2,279 | 1,008 | -99 | 1,871 | 2,669 | 2,161 |
| **Closing balance** | | | | | | | | | | | | | |
| Book value | 7,288 | 10,369 | 10,307 | 11,792 | 8,333 | 3,436 | 4,549 | 6,828 | 7,836 | 7,737 | 9,608 | 12,277 | 14,438 |
| Market value | 7,823 | 10,595 | 9,836 | 12,123 | 8,580 | 3,728 | 4,605 | 6,765 | 7,863 | 7,890 | 10,245 | 13,491 | 15,190 |

## SCHEDULE – Accounts of the National Insurance Fund – All figures in £ million

| Period to 31 March | 2001 | 2002 | 2003 | 2004 | 2005 | 2006 | 2007 | 2008 | 2009 | 2010 | 2011 | 2012 | 2013 |
|---|---|---|---|---|---|---|---|---|---|---|---|---|---|
| **Receipts** | | | | | | | | | | | | | |
| Contributions | 54,312 | 56,718 | 58,422 | 58,587 | 61,570 | 66,402 | 68,212 | 74,806 | | | | | |
| Exchequer payments | 0 | 0 | 0 | 0 | 0 | 0 | 0 | 0 | | | | | |
| Investment income | 851 | 1,113 | 1,422 | 1,257 | 1,255 | 1,364 | 1,846 | 1,854 | | | | | |
| Other receipts | 932 | 869 | 1,023 | 1,535 | 1,616 | 1,530 | 1,285 | 1,667 | | | | | |
| Total receipts | 56,095 | 58,700 | 60,867 | 61,379 | 64,441 | 69,296 | 71,343 | 78,327 | 85,236 | 88,499 | 94,317 | 100,326 | 106,535 |
| **Less** | | | | | | | | | | | | | |
| **Payments** | | | | | | | | | | | | | |
| Retirement pension | 38,669 | 41,887 | 44,252 | 46,256 | 48,787 | 51,377 | 53,786 | | | | | | |
| Other benefits | 8,258 | 8,510 | 8,592 | 8,541 | 8,224 | 8,352 | 8,269 | | | | | | |
| Total benefits | 46,927 | 50,397 | 52,844 | 54,797 | 57,011 | 59,729 | 62,055 | 65,700 | | | | | |
| Administration | 1,165 | 839 | 1,241 | 1,754 | 1,480 | 1,424 | 1,433 | 1,489 | | | | | |
| PP payments | 2,772 | 2,764 | 3,276 | 3,771 | 3,441 | 2,515 | 3,020 | 2,543 | | | | | |
| Other payments | 390 | 349 | 606 | 505 | 488 | 472 | 874 | 698 | | | | | |
| Total payments | 51,254 | 54,349 | 57,967 | 60,827 | 62,420 | 64,140 | 67,382 | 70,431 | 74,358 | 77,748 | 80,987 | 84,351 | 88,822 |
| Excess of receipts over payments | 4,841 | 4,351 | 2,900 | 552 | 2,021 | 5,156 | 3,961 | 7,896 | 10,878 | 10,751 | 13,330 | 15,975 | 17,713 |
| **Closing balance** | | | | | | | | | | | | | |
| Book value | 19,279 | 23,630 | 26,530 | 27,082 | 29,103 | 34,259 | 38,220 | 46,116 | 56,994 | 67,745 | 81,075 | 97,050 | 114,763 |
| Market value | 20,304 | 24,333 | 27,675 | 27,652 | 29,585 | 34,839 | 38,220 | | | | | | |

Note
Figures for years ending 31 March 2008 and onwards are estimates from the report by the Government Actuary on the drafts of the Social Security Benefits Up-rating Order 2008 and the Social Security (Contributions) (Re-rating) Order 2008 (Cm 7312). For all other years, the figures are from the statutory accounts of the National Insurance Fund from 1 July 1948 to 31 March 2007.

## Schedule – Notes on the Accounts of the National Insurance Fund

- On 5 July 1948 the Fund received the assets from the prior funds amounting to £887 million.

- The column headed '1949' shows the figures for the nine month period from 1 July 1948 to 31 March 1949. All other periods are twelve months.

- The separate Industrial Injuries and National Insurance (Reserve) Funds were merged with the National Insurance Fund on 1 April 1975 in accordance with section 44 of the Social Security Act 1973. The figures given for years to 31 March 1975 are the aggregate in respect of all three funds. On transfer, the assets of the wound up funds were taken in at market value which resulted in the book value as at 31 March 1976 reducing by £599 million.

- Contributions are net of the allocation to the National Health Service.

- The row 'Other receipts' is made up of a number of items with the main ones being (1) the government compensation payments to the Fund from 1 April 1990 for the loss of revenue due to contribution receipts being reduced by recoveries of statutory sick, maternity, adoption and paternity pay (to 31 March 2007 these payments total £15 billion with that for the year to 31 March 2007 being £1.2 billion); and (2) State Schemes premiums made to the Fund from 1 April 1978 in respect of employed persons who cease to be covered in certain specific circumstances by a contracted out pension scheme (to 31 March 2007 these payments total £5 billion with that for the year to 31 March 2007 being £74 million).

- The row 'Other benefits' covers the benefits other than the state retirement pensions provided under the Funds. These benefits change from time to time with those for the year to 31 March 2007 being (1) incapacity benefits – £6.683 billion; (2) bereavement benefits including widow's and widower's benefits – £0.799 billion: (3) Jobseeker's Allowance – £0.482 billion; (4) maternity allowance – £0.176 billion; (5) Christmas bonus for pensioners – £0.127 billion and (6) other benefits – £0.002 billion.

- The row 'PP payments' are the payments in respect of employed earners with a contracted out personal provision. A 'minimum contribution' in respect of that provision is made from the Fund.

- The row 'Other payments' is made up of a number of items with the main ones being (1) transfers to Northern Ireland National Insurance Fund (to 31 March 2007 these payments total £5 billion with that for the year to 31 March 2007 being £0.630 billion) and (2) net redundancy payments (to 31 March 2007 these payments total £3 billion with that for the year to 31 March 2007 being £0.204 billion).

- Book and market values as at 31 March 2007 onwards are the same as the assets since January 2007 are held in the Debt Management Account Deposit Facility.

- At the time of producing his report, the Government Actuary only had provisional accounts for period to 31 March 2007 which showed the Fund's value at £38,173 million.

- Figures for the years from 31 March 2007 are estimates based on a set of assumptions as specified in the Government Actuary's report. Consequently the estimates of future benefit payments and contributions, both very large figures, are sensitive to changes in a number of these assumptions (such as the level of employment and earnings). Therefore differences between the expected and the actual future position could have a very significant effect on the excess of receipts over payments in any future years.

# Profile of William Beveridge

William Beveridge was born in Bengal, India, on 5 March 1879, his father being a judge in the Indian civil service. After studying at Charterhouse and Balliol College, Oxford, he became a lawyer.

Early in his life, he became interested in social service, becoming a Sub-warden of Toynbee Hall between 1903 and 1905 when he became a leader writer for the Morning Post. As a result, he was considered to be the country's leading authority on unemployment insurance. His prominence increased during the Liberal government of 1906–14 when he was asked by David Lloyd George to advise on old age pensions and national insurance. In 1909, he joined the Board of Trade and was appointed by Winston Churchill as the first director of Labour Exchanges so helping to organise the implementation of the national system of labour exchanges and to influence the contents of the National Insurance Act 1911.

During the First World War, he was involved in mobilising and controlling manpower. After the war, he was knighted and made the permanent secretary to the Ministry of Food. In 1919, he left the civil service becoming the Director of the London School of Economics where he remained until 1937 when he was appointed Master of University College, Oxford. During his academic career, Beveridge served on several commissions and committees on social policy.

In June 1941, after a brief period as an Under-Secretary in the Ministry of Labour, he was appointed the chairman of an inter-departmental inquiry to consider the co-ordination of social insurance (Committee on Social Insurance and Allied Services). As the other members of the Committee were civil servants with potentially a conflict of interest, the government and Beveridge agreed that the resulting report would be that of Beveridge alone. His report *Social Insurance and Allied Services* was published in December 1942 with his second report *Full Employment in a Free Society* issued in 1944.

Later that year, he became a member of the Liberal Party and was elected to the Commons as the member for Berwick-upon-Tweed. However his membership of the Commons was brief losing his seat at the 1945 election. In 1946 he was created Baron Beveridge of Tuggal (in the County of Northumberland) eventually becoming the Liberal leader in the Lords. He died at home on 16 March 1963 (aged 84).

Beveridge was a workaholic with it being reported that, as he sat up in bed while working on his latest project, his last words were 'I have a thousand things to do'.

During his career, the paths of many of the influential people of the 20th century crossed that of Beveridge; for example Harold Wilson, later to become Prime Minister, worked as a research assistant of Beveridge indicating in his *Memoirs: 1916–1964* that '[he] found [Beveridge] a devil to work for... ruthless at getting at the facts and drove me as hard as he drove himself'.

# APPENDIX 4
# Statistics

## CONTENTS

# 100 Years of State Pension

## GREAT BRITAIN – POPULATION PROFILES – 1901 TO 1951

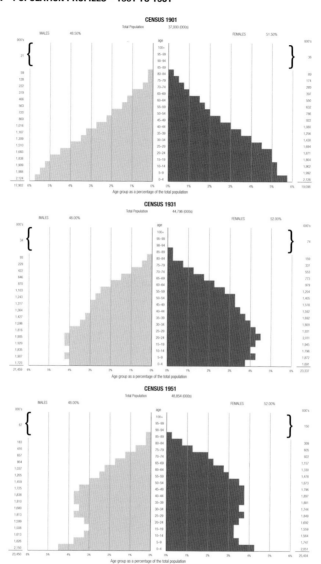

# GREAT BRITAIN – POPULATION PROFILES – 1971 TO 2001

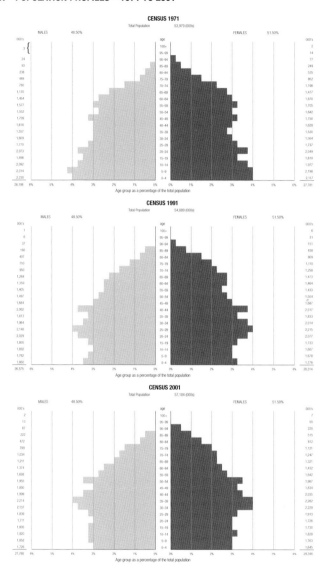

# 100 Years of State Pension

## GREAT BRITAIN – POPULATION PROFILES – 2011 TO 2081

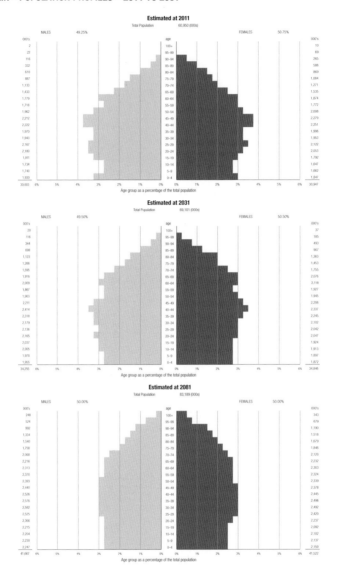

Notes
1. The United Kingdom consists of Great Britain (England, Scotland and Wales) and Northern Ireland. Northern Ireland came into existence in 1922. Its population has increased from approximately 1 million in 1901 to 1.7 million in the 2001 census and estimated to be just over 2 million in 2031 and 2081.
2. Assumption for the estimated population 2011, 2031 & 2081 (2006-based set of national population projections). Fertility – Long-term average number of children per woman 1.84. Mortality – Period expectation of life at birth in 2031 – Males 82.7: Females 86.2. Net migration – Annual long-term assumption – +190,000

Source:   1991 Census – Table 1 & Historical Tables – Table 5 www.histpop.org   http://www.statistics.gov.uk/StatBase/Expodata/Spreadsheets/D6797.xls
www.statistics.gov.uk/census2001/population_data.asp   http://www.gad.gov.uk/Demography_Data/Population/2006

## LIFE EXPECTANCY

### Male – Age

| Year Period[1] | 0 L | 0 P | 0 H | 20 L | 20 P | 20 H | 60 L | 60 P | 60 H | 65 L | 65 P | 65 H | 70 L | 70 P | 70 H | 90 L | 90 P | 90 H |
|---|---|---|---|---|---|---|---|---|---|---|---|---|---|---|---|---|---|---|
| 1901 | | 48.6 | | | 43.0 | | | 13.5 | | | 10.8 | | | 8.4 | | | 2.6 | |
| 1931 | | 58.7 | | | 46.8 | | | 14.4 | | | 11.3 | | | 8.6 | | | 2.6 | |
| 1961 | | 68.1 | | | 50.6 | | | 15.1 | | | 12.0 | | | 9.3 | | | 3.0 | |
| 1991 | | 73.4 | | | 54.5 | | | 17.9 | | | 14.3 | | | 11.2 | | | 3.5 | |
| 2001 | | 75.9 | | | 56.7 | | | 19.9 | | | 16.1 | | | 12.6 | | | 3.8 | |
| 2011 | 78.9 | 79.2 | 79.6 | 59.6 | 59.8 | 60.2 | 22.5 | 22.7 | 23.0 | 18.5 | 18.7 | 19.0 | 14.8 | 15.0 | 15.2 | 4.1 | 4.2 | 4.3 |
| 2031 | 81.0 | 82.9 | 84.9 | 61.8 | 63.4 | 65.4 | 24.4 | 25.9 | 27.5 | 20.4 | 21.8 | 23.3 | 16.7 | 17.9 | 19.3 | 5.2 | 5.9 | 6.6 |
| 2051 | 81.0 | 85.2 | 89.3 | 61.6 | 65.6 | 69.7 | 24.4 | 27.8 | 31.3 | 20.5 | 23.6 | 26.9 | 16.7 | 19.5 | 22.6 | 5.3 | 6.8 | 8.7 |
| **Cohort[2]** | | | | | | | | | | | | | | | | | | |
| 2001 | 80.9 | 87.6 | 96.3 | 61.4 | 65.8 | 71.5 | 23.6 | 24.3 | 25.3 | 19.1 | 19.5 | 20.1 | 14.5 | 14.7 | 15.1 | 3.9 | 3.9 | 3.9 |
| 2011 | 81.0 | 88.9 | 99.2 | 61.6 | 67.2 | 74.4 | 24.3 | 25.9 | 27.7 | 20.2 | 21.3 | 22.8 | 16.4 | 17.2 | 18.2 | 4.3 | 4.5 | 4.6 |
| 2031 | 81.0 | 91.4 | 104.7 | 61.6 | 69.6 | 79.9 | 24.4 | 27.8 | 32.1 | 20.5 | 23.3 | 26.9 | 16.7 | 19.1 | 22.0 | 5.3 | 6.1 | 7.2 |
| 2051 | 81.0 | 93.9 | 109.6 | 61.6 | 72.0 | 85.2 | 24.4 | 29.8 | 36.8 | 20.5 | 25.2 | 31.3 | 16.7 | 20.8 | 26.1 | 5.3 | 7.0 | 9.5 |

### Female – Age

| Year Period[1] | 0 L | 0 P | 0 H | 20 L | 20 P | 20 H | 60 L | 60 P | 60 H | 65 L | 65 P | 65 H | 70 L | 70 P | 70 H | 90 L | 90 P | 90 H |
|---|---|---|---|---|---|---|---|---|---|---|---|---|---|---|---|---|---|---|
| 1901 | | 52.4 | | | 45.8 | | | 15.0 | | | 12.0 | | | 9.2 | | | 2.9 | |
| 1931 | | 62.9 | | | 49.9 | | | 16.5 | | | 13.1 | | | 10.0 | | | 3.0 | |
| 1961 | | 74.0 | | | 56.0 | | | 19.1 | | | 15.3 | | | 11.8 | | | 3.3 | |
| 1991 | | 79.0 | | | 59.7 | | | 22.1 | | | 18.1 | | | 14.5 | | | 4.4 | |
| 2001 | | 80.6 | | | 61.2 | | | 23.3 | | | 19.2 | | | 15.3 | | | 4.4 | |
| 2011 | 82.6 | 82.8 | 83.0 | 63.1 | 63.3 | 63.6 | 25.0 | 25.2 | 25.4 | 20.8 | 20.9 | 21.1 | 16.7 | 16.8 | 17.0 | 4.5 | 4.6 | 4.7 |
| 2031 | 85.1 | 86.4 | 87.6 | 65.6 | 66.8 | 68.0 | 27.4 | 28.4 | 29.5 | 23.1 | 24.0 | 25.1 | 18.9 | 19.8 | 20.8 | 5.7 | 6.2 | 6.8 |
| 2051 | 85.1 | 88.4 | 91.6 | 65.6 | 68.7 | 71.9 | 27.4 | 30.1 | 33.0 | 23.1 | 25.7 | 28.4 | 19.0 | 21.4 | 23.9 | 5.8 | 7.2 | 8.8 |
| **Cohort[2]** | | | | | | | | | | | | | | | | | | |
| 2001 | 85.0 | 91.0 | 98.7 | 65.5 | 69.4 | 74.4 | 26.6 | 27.2 | 28.0 | 21.8 | 22.2 | 22.7 | 16.8 | 17.0 | 17.3 | 4.4 | 4.4 | 4.4 |
| 2011 | 85.1 | 92.1 | 101.3 | 65.6 | 70.5 | 76.9 | 27.2 | 28.5 | 30.0 | 22.8 | 23.7 | 24.9 | 18.6 | 19.3 | 20.1 | 4.7 | 4.8 | 4.9 |
| 2031 | 85.1 | 94.3 | 106.2 | 65.6 | 72.7 | 81.9 | 27.4 | 30.4 | 34.1 | 23.1 | 25.6 | 28.7 | 19.0 | 21.0 | 23.6 | 5.8 | 6.5 | 7.4 |
| 2051 | 85.1 | 96.5 | 110.8 | 65.6 | 74.8 | 86.7 | 27.4 | 32.2 | 38.4 | 23.1 | 27.3 | 32.8 | 19.0 | 22.7 | 27.5 | 5.8 | 7.4 | 9.6 |

Notes

1. Expectations of life shown above have been calculated in two ways:-
   Period life expectancy at a given age for a given year is the average number of years a person would live, if he or she experienced the particular area's age-specific mortality rates for that time throughout his or her life. It makes no allowance for any known or projected changes in mortality in later years. Cohort life expectancies are calculated using age-specific mortality rates which allow for known or projected changes in mortality in later years. Consequently they are regarded as a more appropriate measure of how long a person of a given age would be expected to live, on average, than period life expectancy.

2. For years up to 2006 the actual experience has been used. Current annual improvements in mortality rates vary considerably by age and sex. For the above table, the mortality projections assume that for most ages these improvements will gradually converge to common 'target rates' of improvement, at each age and for both sexes, by the year 2031, and continue to improve at that constant rate thereafter. However, these mortality projections also assume that those born in the years 1923 to 1940 (cohorts which have consistently experienced relatively high rates of mortality improvement over the last 25 years) will continue to experience higher rates of mortality improvement than the rest of the population.
   The target rate assumptions are as follows:
   Principal Projection (col P) – 1% annual improvement at 2031, thereafter annual improvement remaining at 1%. For those born between 1923 and 1940 rates of annual improvement in and after 2031 will rise to a peak of 2.5% a year for those born in 1931 and then decline back to 1% a year for those born in 1941 or later.
   High Variant Projection (col H) – 2% annual improvement at 2031, thereafter annual improvement remaining at 2%. For those born between 1923 and 1940 rates of annual improvement in and after 2031 will rise to a peak of 3.5% a year for those born in 1931 and then decline back to 2% a year for those born in 1941 or later.
   Low Variant Projection (col L) – 0% annual improvement at 2031, thereafter mortality rates remaining constant. For those born between 1923 and 1940 rates of annual improvement in and after 2031 will rise to a peak of 1.5% a year for those born in 1931 and then decline back to 0% a year for those born in 1941 or later.

Source: Years 1901, 1931, 1961 & 1991 – English Life Tables No 7, 10,12 & 15
Years 2001 and onwards – ONS & GAD websites

# 100 Years of State Pension

## PAUPERISM IN THE POPULATION IN THE LATE 19TH CENTURY

Table 1 – Proportion of paupers in England and Wales compared with the population

| Year | Number of indoor poor | % of population | Number of outdoor relief | % of population | Total number of poor | % of population |
|------|------|------|------|------|------|------|
| 1849 | 133,513 | 0.77 | 955,146 | 5.50 | 1,088,659 | 6.27 |
| 1852 | 111,323 | 0.62 | 804,352 | 4.47 | 915,675 | 5.09 |
| 1862 | 132,236 | 0.66 | 784,906 | 3.90 | 917,142 | 4.56 |
| 1872 | 149,200 | 0.66 | 828,000 | 3.63 | 977,200 | 4.29 |
| 1882 | 183,374 | 0.71 | 604,915 | 2.32 | 788,289 | 3.03 |
| 1892 | 186,607 | 0.64 | 558,150 | 1.92 | 744,757 | 2.58 |

Source:   Report of the Royal Commission on the Aged Poor 1895 page ix para 12

Table 2 – Age profile of paupers by number and percentage of population in age group

| Age | Population 1891 census | Indoor poor Number | % | Outdoor relief Number | % | Total poor Number | % |
|------|------|------|------|------|------|------|------|
| **One Day Count** | | | | | | | |
| Under 16 | 10,762,808 | 51,611 | 0.5 | 177,567 | 1.6 | 229,178 | 2.1 |
| 16–65 | 16,867,116 | 77,415 | 0.5 | 125,756 | 0.7 | 203,171 | 1.2 |
| Over 65 | 1,372,601 | 63,352 | 4.6 | 205,045 | 14.9 | 268,397 | 19.5 |
| Total | 29,002,525 | 192,378 | 0.7 | 508,368 | 1.7 | 700,746 | 2.4 |
| **Split of over 65** | | | | | | | |
| **On totals** | | | | | | | |
| Males | 606,587 | 37,803 | 6.2 | 59,707 | 9.8 | 97,510 | 16.0 |
| Female | 766,014 | 25,549 | 3.4 | 145,338 | 18.9 | 170,887 | 22.3 |
| **By age – both sexes combined[3]** | | | | | | | |
| 60–65 | 772,879 | | | | | 41,180 | 5.3 |
| 65–70 | 571,947 | Breakdown of the statistics not shown | | | | 62,240 | 10.9 |
| 70–75 | 417,914 | in the Royal Commission's report | | | | 77,708 | 18.5 |
| 75–80 | 233,333 | | | | | 60,879 | 26.1 |
| 80+ | 149,407 | | | | | 44,860 | 30.0 |
| **Twelve Months' Count** | | | | | | | |
| Under 16 | 10,762,808 | 111,782 | 1.0 | 441,805 | 4.1 | 553,587 | 5.1 |
| 16–65 | 16,867,116 | 232,284 | 1.4 | 385,299 | 2.3 | 617,583 | 3.7 |
| Over 65 | 1,372,601 | 114,144 | 8.3 | 287,760 | 21.0 | 401,904 | 29.3 |
| Total | 29,002,525 | 458,210 | 1.6 | 1,114,864 | 3.8 | 1,573,074 | 5.4 |
| **Split of over 65** | | | | | | | |
| **On totals** | | | | | | | |
| Males | 606,587 | 68,490 | 11.3 | 95,140 | 15.6 | 163,630 | 26.9 |
| Female | 766,014 | 45,654 | 6.0 | 192,620 | 25.1 | 238,274 | 31.1 |

Notes

1.  The one day count details of the number of poor are mainly based on 1 January 1892 with those on a twelve months' count being based on the year to 25 March 1892 (i.e. Lady Day). The higher the ratio of the year's count to that of the day count shows the temporary nature of that relief.
2.  The outdoor relief figures include those receiving medical relief only. The report provides a breakdown for those over age 65 which showed that roughly 2% of both the male and female population were in receipt of medical relief only during the 12 months to 25 March 1892.
3.  The figures of the paupers' age profile are based at 1 August 1890.

Source:   Report of the Royal Commission on the Aged Poor 1895 para 21 page xii, para 22 page xiii and Table III page cvi

# POPULATION PROFILE OF THE UK IN 2006/07
## QUINTILE DISTRIBUTION OF INCOME BY VARIOUS FAMILY AND HOUSEHOLD CHARACTERISTICS
## WORKING-AGE ADULTS – ONE OR MORE ADULTS IN THE FAMILY IN PART-TIME OR FULL-TIME WORK

| | Before Housing Costs | | | | | After Housing Costs | | | | | Overall total in category |
|---|---|---|---|---|---|---|---|---|---|---|---|
| | Net equivalised disposable household income | | | | | Net equivalised disposable household income | | | | | |
| | Bottom quintile | Second quintile | Middle quintile | Fourth quintile | Top quintile | Bottom quintile | Second quintile | Middle quintile | Fourth quintile | Top quintile | |
| | m | m | m | m | m | m | m | m | m | m | m |
| **Total** | 6.1 | 5.7 | 6.8 | 8.2 | 9.0 | 6.8 | 5.7 | 6.8 | 7.8 | 8.7 | 35.8 |
| Split by:- | | | | | | | | | | | |
| **A. Economic status of household[1]** | | | | | | | | | | | |
| All adults in work | 1.3 | 2.4 | 4.3 | 6.3 | 7.6 | 1.5 | 2.6 | 4.3 | 6.1 | 7.4 | 21.9 |
| At least one adult in work but not all | 2.2 | 2.3 | 2.1 | 1.7 | 1.3 | 2.5 | 2.3 | 2.1 | 1.5 | 1.2 | 9.6 |
| Workless households | 2.6 | 1.0 | 0.4 | 0.2 | 0.1 | 2.8 | 0.8 | 0.4 | 0.2 | 0.1 | 4.3 |
| **B. Gender by number of adults in the family and work status[2]** | | | | | | | | | | | |
| Males | | | | | | | | | | | |
| Couple, in work | 1.1 | 1.5 | 2.1 | 2.9 | 3.4 | 1.2 | 1.5 | 2.2 | 2.8 | 3.3 | 11.0 |
| Couple, workless | 0.6 | 0.2 | 0.1 | 0.1 | 0.0 | 0.6 | 0.2 | 0.1 | 0.1 | 0.0 | 1.0 |
| Single, in work | 0.4 | 0.6 | 0.9 | 1.2 | 1.3 | 0.4 | 0.6 | 0.9 | 1.2 | 1.3 | 4.4 |
| Single, workless | 1.0 | 0.5 | 0.4 | 0.2 | 0.1 | 1.1 | 0.5 | 0.3 | 0.2 | 0.1 | 2.2 |
| Total males | 3.1 | 2.8 | 3.5 | 4.4 | 4.8 | 3.3 | 2.8 | 3.5 | 4.3 | 4.7 | 18.6 |
| Females | | | | | | | | | | | |
| Couple, in work | 1.0 | 1.5 | 2.0 | 2.7 | 3.3 | 1.2 | 1.6 | 2.0 | 2.5 | 3.2 | 10.5 |
| Couple, workless | 0.5 | 0.2 | 0.1 | 0.0 | 0.0 | 0.5 | 0.2 | 0.1 | 0.0 | 0.0 | 0.8 |
| Single, in work | 0.4 | 0.7 | 0.9 | 0.9 | 0.8 | 0.5 | 0.7 | 0.9 | 0.9 | 0.7 | 3.7 |
| Single, workless | 1.1 | 0.5 | 0.3 | 0.2 | 0.1 | 1.3 | 0.4 | 0.3 | 0.1 | 0.1 | 2.2 |
| Total females | 3.0 | 2.9 | 3.3 | 3.8 | 4.2 | 3.5 | 2.9 | 3.3 | 3.5 | 4.0 | 17.2 |
| **C. Pension provision** | | | | | | | | | | | |
| Employer organised pension only | 0.6 | 0.9 | 1.8 | 2.9 | 4.0 | 0.5 | 1.1 | 1.9 | 2.9 | 3.8 | 10.2 |
| Self arranged personal pension only | 0.5 | 0.5 | 0.6 | 0.7 | 0.9 | 0.5 | 0.4 | 0.6 | 0.7 | 1.0 | 3.2 |
| Self arranged stakeholder pension only | 0.0 | 0.0 | 0.0 | 0.1 | 0.2 | 0.0 | 0.1 | 0.0 | 0.1 | 0.1 | 0.3 |
| Combination of employer organised and self arranged pensions | 0.1 | 0.1 | 0.2 | 0.4 | 0.5 | 0.1 | 0.1 | 0.2 | 0.4 | 0.5 | 1.3 |
| Not contributing to a non-state pension | 4.9 | 4.2 | 4.2 | 4.1 | 3.4 | 5.7 | 4.0 | 4.1 | 3.7 | 3.3 | 20.8 |
| Total | 6.1 | 5.7 | 6.8 | 8.2 | 9.0 | 6.8 | 5.7 | 6.8 | 7.8 | 8.7 | 35.8 |

Notes applying to all the Population Profile of the UK in 2006/07 tables
1. Within households, pensioners are excluded from the classifications if they are not working, and are included if they are working. For example, a household with a pensioner in work, but a working-age person not in work, would be in the At least one adult in work, but not all category. A household with all working-age adults in work and a pensioner not in work would be categorised as All adults at work.
2. In work is defined as one or more adults in the family in part-time or full-time work
3. The population figures given for benefit receipt do not sum to the total of all pensioners as they are not mutually exclusive groups since people can receive more than one benefit
4. Appendix C of The Institute for Fiscal Studies' report Poverty and Inequality in the UK:2008 issued in June 2008 indicates that the Family Resources Survey (FRS) on which the HBAI is based was under counting, both the number of families in receipt of tax credits and the amount paid out. On Pension Credit, FRS appeared to be recording two thirds of the beneficiaries receiving Pension Credit (around 64% of single pensioner recipients and 70–80% of pensioner couple recipients). The report indicates that this under-reporting of Pension Credit will lead pensioner poverty to be overstated if it is those pensioners whose true income places them just over the poverty line who are failing to report their receipts
5. Numbers are rounded to nearest 100,000 with a number of people, in excess of zero, included in all categories

Source:    DWP's Households Below Average Income (HBAI) series, published on 10 June 2008. The HBAI series takes household income as its measure of living standards and is derived from the Family Resources Survey (FRS), a survey of around 28,000 households in the UK.

## POPULATION PROFILE OF THE UK IN 2006/07
### Quintile distribution of income by various family and household characteristics
### PENSIONERS – A PERSON OF STATE PENSION AGE OR ABOVE (65 FOR MEN, 60 FOR WOMEN)

| | Before Housing Costs | | | | | After Housing Costs | | | | | Overall total in category |
|---|---|---|---|---|---|---|---|---|---|---|---|
| | Net equivalised disposable household income | | | | | Net equivalised disposable household income | | | | | |
| | Bottom quintile | Second quintile | Middle quintile | Fourth quintile | Top quintile | Bottom quintile | Second quintile | Middle quintile | Fourth quintile | Top quintile | |
| | m | m | m | m | m | m | m | m | m | m | m |
| **Total** | 2.8 | 3.1 | 2.3 | 1.6 | 1.1 | 1.7 | 3.2 | 2.4 | 2.1 | 1.5 | 10.9 |
| Split by:- | | | | | | | | | | | |
| **D. Economic status of adults in family** | | | | | | | | | | | |
| One or more working | 0.1 | 0.2 | 0.5 | 0.4 | 0.4 | 0.1 | 0.2 | 0.4 | 0.4 | 0.5 | 1.6 |
| No one working | 2.7 | 2.9 | 1.8 | 1.2 | 0.7 | 1.6 | 3.0 | 2.0 | 1.7 | 1.0 | 9.3 |
| **E. Age** | | | | | | | | | | | |
| 60–64 | 0.4 | 0.4 | 0.3 | 0.3 | 0.3 | 0.2 | 0.4 | 0.4 | 0.3 | 0.4 | 1.7 |
| 65–69 | 0.5 | 0.7 | 0.6 | 0.5 | 0.3 | 0.4 | 0.7 | 0.5 | 0.6 | 0.4 | 2.6 |
| 70–74 | 0.5 | 0.7 | 0.5 | 0.3 | 0.2 | 0.3 | 0.7 | 0.5 | 0.4 | 0.3 | 2.2 |
| 75–79 | 0.6 | 0.5 | 0.4 | 0.2 | 0.1 | 0.3 | 0.6 | 0.4 | 0.3 | 0.2 | 1.8 |
| 80–84 | 0.5 | 0.5 | 0.3 | 0.2 | 0.1 | 0.3 | 0.5 | 0.4 | 0.3 | 0.1 | 1.6 |
| 85+ | 0.3 | 0.3 | 0.2 | 0.1 | 0.1 | 0.2 | 0.3 | 0.2 | 0.2 | 0.1 | 1.0 |
| Total | 2.8 | 3.1 | 2.3 | 1.6 | 1.1 | 1.7 | 3.2 | 2.4 | 2.1 | 1.5 | 10.9 |
| **F. Family type** | | | | | | | | | | | |
| Couple living with others | 0.1 | 0.1 | 0.2 | 0.1 | 0.1 | 0.1 | 0.1 | 0.2 | 0.1 | 0.1 | 0.6 |
| Couple living alone | 1.4 | 1.5 | 1.2 | 0.9 | 0.8 | 0.8 | 1.6 | 1.3 | 1.2 | 0.9 | 5.8 |
| Single living with others | 0.1 | 0.2 | 0.2 | 0.1 | 0.1 | 0.1 | 0.2 | 0.1 | 0.2 | 0.1 | 0.7 |
| Single living alone | 1.2 | 1.3 | 0.7 | 0.4 | 0.2 | 0.7 | 1.3 | 0.8 | 0.6 | 0.4 | 3.8 |
| Total | 2.8 | 3.1 | 2.3 | 1.5 | 1.2 | 1.7 | 3.2 | 2.4 | 2.1 | 1.5 | 10.9 |
| **G. Gender** | | | | | | | | | | | |
| Male | 1.0 | 1.2 | 0.9 | 0.5 | 0.5 | 0.6 | 1.2 | 1.0 | 0.7 | 0.6 | 4.1 |
| Female | 1.8 | 1.9 | 1.4 | 1.0 | 0.7 | 1.1 | 2.0 | 1.4 | 1.4 | 0.9 | 6.8 |
| **H. Pensions receipt** | | | | | | | | | | | |
| Couple | | | | | | | | | | | |
| No occupational/personal pension | 0.6 | 0.4 | 0.2 | 0.1 | 0.1 | 0.5 | 0.5 | 0.2 | 0.1 | 0.1 | 1.4 |
| Only one with occupational/personal pension | 0.7 | 0.9 | 0.7 | 0.4 | 0.4 | 0.4 | 0.9 | 0.8 | 0.6 | 0.4 | 3.1 |
| Both with occupational/ personal pensions | 0.2 | 0.4 | 0.5 | 0.4 | 0.4 | 0.1 | 0.3 | 0.5 | 0.5 | 0.5 | 1.9 |
| Total | 1.5 | 1.7 | 1.4 | 0.9 | 0.9 | 1.0 | 1.7 | 1.5 | 1.2 | 1.0 | 6.4 |
| Single | | | | | | | | | | | |
| No occupational/personal pension | 0.7 | 0.7 | 0.3 | 0.2 | 0.1 | 0.5 | 0.8 | 0.4 | 0.2 | 0.1 | 2.0 |
| Occupational/personal pension | 0.6 | 0.7 | 0.6 | 0.4 | 0.2 | 0.2 | 0.7 | 0.5 | 0.7 | 0.4 | 2.5 |
| Total | 1.3 | 1.4 | 0.9 | 0.6 | 0.3 | 0.7 | 1.5 | 0.9 | 0.9 | 0.5 | 4.5 |
| **I. Benefit receipt of family[3]** | | | | | | | | | | | |
| Disability Living Allowance | 0.2 | 0.4 | 0.4 | 0.2 | 0.0 | 0.1 | 0.3 | 0.4 | 0.3 | 0.1 | 1.2 |
| Attendance Allowance | 0.1 | 0.4 | 0.4 | 0.2 | 0.1 | 0.1 | 0.3 | 0.4 | 0.3 | 0.1 | 1.2 |
| Pension Credit4 | 0.6 | 0.8 | 0.4 | 0.2 | 0.0 | 0.3 | 1.0 | 0.4 | 0.2 | 0.1 | 2.0 |
| Housing Benefit | 0.2 | 0.8 | 0.3 | 0.2 | 0.0 | 0.3 | 0.8 | 0.3 | 0.1 | 0.0 | 1.5 |
| Not in receipt of any benefits listed above | 1.8 | 1.5 | 1.4 | 1.1 | 1.1 | 1.1 | 1.6 | 1.5 | 1.4 | 1.3 | 6.9 |
| Total | 2.9 | 3.9 | 2.9 | 1.9 | 1.2 | 1.9 | 4.0 | 3.0 | 2.3 | 1.6 | 12.8 |

## POPULATION PROFILE OF THE UK IN 2006/07
## COMPOSITION OF LOW-INCOME GROUPS BY VARIOUS FAMILY AND HOUSEHOLD CHARACTERISTICS
## WORKING-AGE ADULTS – ONE OR MORE ADULTS IN THE FAMILY IN PART-TIME OR FULL-TIME WORK

| | Before Housing Costs<br>Net equivalised disposable household income | | | After Housing Costs<br>Net equivalised disposable household income | | | Overall total in category |
|---|---|---|---|---|---|---|---|
| | 50%<br>m | 60%<br>m | 70%<br>m | 50%<br>m | 60%<br>m | 70%<br>m | m |
| **Total** | 3.4 | 5.3 | 7.8 | 5.3 | 7.3 | 9.2 | 35.8 |
| Split by:- | | | | | | | |
| **A. Economic status of household**[1] | | | | | | | |
| All adults in work | 0.7 | 1.0 | 1.8 | 1.1 | 1.7 | 2.4 | 21.9 |
| At least one adult in work but not all | 1.1 | 1.9 | 2.9 | 1.8 | 2.7 | 3.6 | 9.6 |
| Workless households | 1.6 | 2.4 | 2.9 | 2.4 | 2.9 | 3.2 | 4.3 |
| **B. Gender by number of adults in the family and work status**[2] | | | | | | | |
| Males | | | | | | | |
| Couple, in work | 0.6 | 1.0 | 1.6 | 0.9 | 1.4 | 1.9 | 11.0 |
| Couple, workless | 0.4 | 0.5 | 0.6 | 0.4 | 0.6 | 0.6 | 1.0 |
| Single, in work | 0.2 | 0.3 | 0.5 | 0.4 | 0.5 | 0.6 | 4.4 |
| Single, workless | 0.6 | 0.9 | 1.1 | 1.0 | 1.2 | 1.5 | 2.2 |
| Total males | 1.8 | 2.7 | 3.8 | 2.7 | 3.7 | 4.6 | 18.6 |
| Females | | | | | | | |
| Couple, in work | 0.6 | 1.0 | 1.3 | 0.9 | 1.3 | 1.7 | 10.5 |
| Couple, workless | 0.3 | 0.4 | 0.5 | 0.4 | 0.5 | 0.6 | 0.8 |
| Single, in work | 0.2 | 0.3 | 0.6 | 0.3 | 0.5 | 0.8 | 3.7 |
| Single, workless | 0.5 | 0.9 | 1.2 | 1.0 | 1.3 | 1.5 | 2.2 |
| Total females | 1.6 | 2.6 | 3.6 | 2.6 | 3.6 | 4.6 | 17.2 |
| **C. Pension provision** | | | | | | | |
| Employer organised pension only | 0.2 | 0.4 | 0.6 | 0.4 | 0.6 | 0.8 | 10.2 |
| Self arranged personal pension only | 0.3 | 0.4 | 0.5 | 0.4 | 0.5 | 0.6 | 3.2 |
| Self arranged stakeholder pension only | 0.0 | 0.1 | 0.1 | 0.1 | 0.1 | 0.1 | 0.3 |
| Combinations of employer organised and self arranged pensions | 0.1 | 0.1 | 0.1 | 0.1 | 0.1 | 0.1 | 1.3 |
| Not contributing to a non-state pension | 2.8 | 4.5 | 6.3 | 4.5 | 6.1 | 7.5 | 20.8 |
| Total | 3.4 | 5.5 | 7.6 | 5.5 | 7.4 | 9.1 | 35.8 |

# 100 Years of State Pension

**POPULATION PROFILE OF THE UK IN 2006/07**
**Composition of low-income groups by various family and household characteristics**
**PENSIONERS – A PERSON OF STATE PENSION AGE OR ABOVE (65 FOR MEN, 60 FOR WOMEN)**

| | Before Housing Costs | | | After Housing Costs | | | Overall total in category |
|---|---|---|---|---|---|---|---|
| | Net equivalised disposable household income | | | Net equivalised disposable household income | | | |
| | 50% | 60% | 70% | 50% | 60% | 70% | |
| | m | m | m | m | m | m | m |
| **Total** | 1.4 | 2.5 | 3.8 | 1.1 | 2.1 | 3.4 | 10.9 |
| Split by:- | | | | | | | |
| **D. Economic status of adults In family** | | | | | | | |
| One or more working | 0.1 | 0.1 | 0.2 | 0.1 | 0.1 | 0.2 | 1.6 |
| No one working | 1.3 | 2.4 | 3.6 | 1.0 | 2.0 | 3.2 | 9.3 |
| **E. Age** | | | | | | | |
| 60–64 | 0.1 | 0.3 | 0.4 | 0.1 | 0.3 | 0.4 | 1.7 |
| 65–69 | 0.3 | 0.5 | 0.8 | 0.2 | 0.4 | 0.7 | 2.6 |
| 70–74 | 0.3 | 0.5 | 0.8 | 0.2 | 0.4 | 0.6 | 2.2 |
| 75–79 | 0.3 | 0.5 | 0.8 | 0.2 | 0.4 | 0.7 | 1.8 |
| 80–84 | 0.2 | 0.4 | 0.6 | 0.2 | 0.3 | 0.6 | 1.6 |
| 85+ | 0.2 | 0.3 | 0.4 | 0.2 | 0.3 | 0.4 | 1.0 |
| Total | 1.4 | 2.5 | 3.8 | 1.1 | 2.1 | 3.4 | 10.9 |
| **F. Family type** | | | | | | | |
| Couple living with others | 0.0 | 0.1 | 0.1 | 0.0 | 0.1 | 0.1 | 0.6 |
| Couple living alone | 0.6 | 1.2 | 1.9 | 0.5 | 1.0 | 1.7 | 5.8 |
| Single living with others | 0.1 | 0.1 | 0.2 | 0.1 | 0.1 | 0.2 | 0.7 |
| Single living alone | 0.7 | 1.1 | 1.6 | 0.5 | 0.9 | 1.4 | 3.8 |
| Total | 1.4 | 2.5 | 3.8 | 1.1 | 2.1 | 3.4 | 10.9 |
| **G. Gender** | | | | | | | |
| Male | 0.4 | 0.8 | 1.4 | 0.4 | 0.7 | 1.2 | 4.1 |
| Female | 1.0 | 1.7 | 2.4 | 0.7 | 1.4 | 2.2 | 6.8 |
| **H. Pensions receipt** | | | | | | | |
| Couple | | | | | | | |
| No occupational/personal pension | 0.3 | 0.5 | 0.7 | 0.3 | 0.5 | 0.7 | 1.4 |
| Only one with occupational/personal pension | 0.3 | 0.6 | 1.0 | 0.2 | 0.5 | 0.9 | 3.1 |
| Both with occupational/personal pensions | 0.1 | 0.2 | 0.3 | 0.1 | 0.1 | 0.2 | 1.9 |
| Total | 0.7 | 1.3 | 2.0 | 0.6 | 1.1 | 1.8 | 6.4 |
| Single | | | | | | | |
| No occupational/personal pension | 0.5 | 0.7 | 1.0 | 0.4 | 0.7 | 1.0 | 2.0 |
| Occupational/personal pension | 0.2 | 0.5 | 0.8 | 0.1 | 0.3 | 0.6 | 2.5 |
| Total | 0.7 | 1.2 | 1.8 | 0.5 | 1.0 | 1.6 | 4.5 |
| **I. Benefit receipt of family[3]** | | | | | | | |
| Disability Living Allowance | 0.1 | 0.1 | 0.2 | 0.1 | 0.1 | 0.2 | 1.2 |
| Attendance Allowance | 0.0 | 0.1 | 0.2 | 0.0 | 0.1 | 0.2 | 1.2 |
| Pension Credit[4] | 0.3 | 0.6 | 0.9 | 0.2 | 0.5 | 0.9 | 2.0 |
| Housing Benefit | 0.0 | 0.2 | 0.4 | 0.2 | 0.4 | 0.7 | 1.5 |
| Not in receipt of any benefits listed above | 1.0 | 1.6 | 2.4 | 0.8 | 1.3 | 1.9 | 6.9 |
| Total | 1.4 | 2.6 | 4.1 | 1.3 | 2.4 | 3.9 | 12.8 |

## RATE OF BASIC STATE PENSION FROM 1909

| Date of uprating | Rate of basic state pension £pw | Increase over previous rate % | Change in RPI between upratings % | Real value of pension at date of uprating | Average real value of pension between upratings | Rate as a percentage of average earnings % |
|---|---|---|---|---|---|---|
| | | | | £pw at Apr 2008 prices | | |
| Jan 1909 | 0.250 | | | 15.55 | 11.27 | 18.0 |
| Jan 1920 | 0.500 | 100.0 | 135.5 | 13.21 | 16.79 | 11.5 |
| Jul 1948 | 1.300 | 160.0 | -2.2 | 35.14 | 33.32 | 18.5 |
| Sep 1951 | 1.500 | 15.4 | 18.4 | 34.23 | 32.89 | 18.0 |
| Sep 1952 | 1.625 | 8.3 | 6.7 | 34.75 | 33.55 | 18.0 |
| Apr 1955 | 2.000 | 23.1 | 7.5 | 39.77 | 37.21 | 17.5 |
| Jan 1958 | 2.500 | 25.0 | 13.0 | 44.00 | 43.25 | 19.0 |
| Apr 1961 | 2.875 | 15.0 | 4.8 | 48.28 | 46.27 | 18.5 |
| May 1963 | 3.375 | 17.4 | 7.8 | 52.60 | 51.55 | 20.0 |
| Mar 1965 | 4.000 | 18.5 | 5.8 | 58.94 | 55.84 | 20.5 |
| Oct 1967 | 4.500 | 12.5 | 8.9 | 60.87 | 57.38 | 20.5 |
| Nov 1969 | 5.000 | 11.1 | 11.5 | 60.65 | 56.30 | 19.5 |
| Sep 1971 | 6.00 | 20.0 | 16.5 | 62.48 | 60.41 | 20.9 |
| Oct 1972 | 6.75 | 12.5 | 8.5 | 64.78 | 62.44 | 21.1 |
| Oct 1973 | 7.75 | 14.8 | 9.9 | 67.69 | 64.09 | 21.3 |
| Jul 1974 | 10.00 | 29.0 | 13.5 | 76.96 | 72.93 | 24.0 |
| Apr 1975 | 11.60 | 16.0 | 17.7 | 75.86 | 71.30 | 21.5 |
| Nov 1975 | 13.30 | 14.7 | 11.7 | 77.87 | 73.14 | 24.6 |
| Nov 1976 | 15.30 | 15.0 | 15.0 | 77.90 | 72.35 | 23.8 |
| Nov 1977 | 17.50 | 14.4 | 13.0 | 78.84 | 75.96 | 24.9 |
| Nov 1978 | 19.50 | 11.4 | 8.1 | 81.30 | 75.64 | 24.7 |
| Nov 1979 | 23.30 | 19.5 | 17.4 | 82.76 | 76.34 | 26.0 |
| Nov 1980 | 27.15 | 16.5 | 15.3 | 83.62 | 79.17 | 24.6 |
| Nov 1981 | 29.60 | 9.0 | 12.0 | 81.42 | 78.73 | 23.7 |
| Nov 1982 | 32.85 | 11.0 | 6.3 | 85.05 | 83.45 | 24.1 |
| Nov 1983 | 34.05 | 3.7 | 4.8 | 84.08 | 82.36 | 23.0 |
| Nov 1984 | 35.80 | 5.1 | 4.9 | 84.24 | 81.73 | 22.5 |
| Nov 1985 | 38.30 | 7.0 | 5.5 | 85.46 | 84.62 | 22.4 |
| Jul 1986 | 38.70 | 1.0 | 1.7 | 84.92 | 83.56 | 21.0 |
| Apr 1987 | 39.50 | 2.1 | 4.4 | 83.04 | 82.29 | 19.9 |
| Apr 1988 | 41.15 | 4.2 | 3.9 | 83.23 | 80.88 | 18.8 |
| Apr 1989 | 43.60 | 6.0 | 8.0 | 81.63 | 79.48 | 18.2 |
| Apr 1990 | 46.90 | 7.6 | 9.4 | 80.23 | 77.96 | 17.8 |
| Apr 1991 | 52.00 | 10.9 | 6.4 | 83.61 | 82.52 | 18.3 |
| Apr 1992 | 54.15 | 4.1 | 4.3 | 83.49 | 83.30 | 17.8 |
| Apr 1993 | 56.10 | 3.6 | 1.3 | 85.39 | 84.85 | 17.7 |
| Apr 1994 | 57.60 | 2.7 | 2.6 | 85.48 | 84.80 | 17.7 |
| Apr 1995 | 58.85 | 2.2 | 3.3 | 84.52 | 83.92 | 17.4 |
| Apr 1996 | 61.15 | 3.9 | 2.4 | 85.75 | 85.13 | 17.4 |
| Apr 1997 | 62.45 | 2.1 | 2.4 | 85.50 | 84.15 | 17.0 |
| Apr 1998 | 64.70 | 3.6 | 4.0 | 85.15 | 84.55 | 16.5 |
| Apr 1999 | 66.75 | 3.2 | 1.6 | 86.47 | 85.87 | 16.4 |
| Apr 2000 | 67.50 | 1.1 | 3.0 | 84.92 | 84.32 | 15.9 |
| Apr 2001 | 72.50 | 7.4 | 1.8 | 89.63 | 89.23 | 16.1 |
| Apr 2002 | 75.50 | 4.1 | 1.5 | 91.96 | 91.02 | 16.0 |
| Apr 2003 | 77.45 | 2.6 | 3.1 | 91.47 | 90.83 | 15.9 |
| Apr 2004 | 79.60 | 2.8 | 2.5 | 91.73 | 90.54 | 15.8 |
| Apr 2005 | 82.05 | 3.1 | 3.2 | 91.64 | 90.93 | 15.9 |
| Apr 2006 | 84.25 | 2.7 | 2.6 | 91.75 | 90.00 | 15.7 |
| Apr 2007 | 87.30 | 3.6 | 4.5 | 90.96 | 89.56 | 15.9 |
| Apr 2008 | 90.70 | 3.9 | 4.2 | 90.70 | | 15.9 |

Notes
1. On Monday 15 February 1971, Britain converted to decimalisation. Before then, Britain's currency was in pound (£), shilling (s) and pence (d) with 12d = 1s and 20s = £1.
2. Basic state pension is the full amount payable to a single person.
3. Average real value of pension between upratings is the single pension for the period uplifted by the RPI for April 2008 and divided by the average RPI during the period between upratings.

Principal source   DWP: The Abstract of Statistics for Benefits, National Insurance Contributions, and Indices of Prices and Earnings – 2007 Edition – Table 5.1

# 100 Years of State Pension

## STATE BENEFIT EXPENDITURE VERSUS GROSS DOMESTIC PRODUCT

| Year to 31 March | Retirement pension – basic | Retirement pension – earnings related | Total retirement pension | Pension Credit | Other benefits paid by DWP | All benefits paid by DWP | Gross Domestic Product | %age of Gross Domestic Product | | |
|---|---|---|---|---|---|---|---|---|---|---|
| | | | | | | | | Total Retirement Pension | Pension Credit | All benefits paid by DWP |
| | £bn | £bn | £bn | £bn | £bn | £bn | £bn | % | % | % |
| 1951 | 0.249 | 0 | 0.249 | 0.000 | 0.362 | 0.611 | 14 | 1.8 | 0 | 4.5 |
| 1956 | 0.433 | 0 | 0.433 | 0.000 | 0.509 | 0.942 | 20 | 2.2 | 0 | 4.8 |
| 1961 | 0.677 | 0 | 0.677 | 0.000 | 0.713 | 1.390 | 26 | 2.6 | 0 | 5.3 |
| 1966 | 1.238 | 0 | 1.238 | 0.000 | 1.084 | 2.322 | 36 | 3.4 | 0 | 6.4 |
| 1971 | 1.778 | 0 | 1.778 | 0.000 | 1.859 | 3.637 | 53 | 3.4 | 0 | 6.9 |
| 1976 | 4.791 | 0 | 4.791 | 0.000 | 4.547 | 9.338 | 111 | 4.3 | 0 | 8.4 |
| 1981 | 10.533 | 0.008 | 10.541 | 0.729 | 11.388 | 22.658 | 237 | 4.5 | 0.3 | 9.6 |
| 1986 | 16.380 | 0.141 | 16.521 | 1.371 | 23.876 | 41.768 | 363 | 4.5 | 0.4 | 11.5 |
| 1991 | 21.973 | 0.726 | 22.699 | 2.305 | 31.475 | 56.479 | 565 | 4.0 | 0.4 | 10.0 |
| 1996 | 27.741 | 2.222 | 29.963 | 3.888 | 54.856 | 88.707 | 731 | 4.1 | 0.5 | 12.1 |
| 2001 | 33.938 | 4.731 | 38.669 | 4.095 | 58.602 | 101.366 | 965 | 4.0 | 0.4 | 10.5 |
| 2006 | 43.203 | 8.174 | 51.377 | 6.426 | 58.044 | 115.847 | 1,241 | 4.1 | 0.5 | 9.3 |
| 2011 | 54.402 | 13.243 | 67.645 | 8.119 | 65.735 | 141.499 | 1,632 | 4.1 | 0.5 | 8.7 |

Notes
1. All monetary figures are at cash prices
2. The benefits expenditure data are for Great Britain and for people living abroad whose benefits are paid by the DWP (and its predecessors). The costs of administering the benefits are excluded.
3. The column Pension Credit encompasses the Guaranteed and Savings Credits and the prior arrangements i.e. National Assistance, Supplementary Benefit, Income Support and Minimum Income relating to the over 60s
4. Non pension benefit figures are not strictly comparable over time as provision for certain items has moved from benefits and directly provided services to benefits and tax allowances and tax credits and vice versa.
5. Gross Domestic Product relates to the whole of the United Kingdom. Northern Ireland benefit expenditure accounts for approximately an additional 0.4% of GDP.

Source:  DWP: The Abstract of Statistics for Benefits, National Insurance Contributions, and Indices of Prices and Earnings – 2007 Edition – Table 7.1
http://www.hm-treasury.gov.uk/economic_data_and_tools/gdp_deflators/data_gdp_index.cfm
http://www.dwp.gov.uk/asd/asd4/expenditure.asp

# INFLATION – RETAIL PRICES & AVERAGE EARNINGS INDICES FROM 1901

| January of year | Retail Prices Index | | Average Earnings Index | |
|---|---|---|---|---|
| | Index | Annual change % | Index | Annual change % |
| 1901 | 3.2 | 1.3 | 0.3 | 1.2 |
| 1902 | 3.2 | 0.9 | 0.3 | 0.1 |
| 1903 | 3.2 | 0.9 | 0.3 | 0.4 |
| 1904 | 3.3 | 0.9 | 0.3 | 0.2 |
| 1905 | 3.2 | -0.9 | 0.3 | 0.5 |
| 1906 | 3.2 | 0.0 | 0.3 | 1.4 |
| 1907 | 3.3 | 3.1 | 0.3 | 2.2 |
| 1908 | 3.4 | 3.0 | 0.3 | 0.7 |
| 1909 | 3.4 | 0.0 | 0.3 | 0.1 |
| 1910 | 3.5 | 0.9 | 0.3 | 1.0 |
| 1911 | 3.5 | 0.9 | 0.3 | 1.6 |
| 1912 | 3.6 | 3.7 | 0.4 | 2.3 |
| 1913 | 3.6 | 0.0 | 0.4 | 3.1 |
| 1914 | 3.6 | -1.9 | 0.4 | 1.0 |
| 1915 | 4.0 | 11.2 | 0.4 | 15.8 |
| 1916 | 4.9 | 22.7 | 0.5 | 13.7 |
| 1917 | 5.9 | 22.2 | 0.6 | 27.9 |
| 1918 | 6.7 | 12.1 | 0.8 | 24.1 |
| 1919 | 7.9 | 18.9 | 0.9 | 14.2 |
| 1920 | 8.1 | 2.3 | 1.0 | 15.4 |
| 1921 | 9.5 | 17.8 | 0.9 | -6.1 |
| 1922 | 6.9 | -27.6 | 0.8 | -19.4 |
| 1923 | 6.4 | -7.2 | 0.7 | -7.0 |
| 1924 | 6.4 | -0.6 | 0.7 | 1.4 |
| 1925 | 6.5 | 1.7 | 0.7 | 0.8 |
| 1926 | 6.3 | -2.8 | 0.7 | -2.2 |
| 1927 | 6.3 | 0.0 | 0.7 | 1.8 |
| 1928 | 6.1 | -4.0 | 0.7 | -1.2 |
| 1929 | 6.0 | -0.7 | 0.7 | 0.2 |
| 1930 | 6.0 | -0.5 | 0.7 | -0.7 |
| 1931 | 5.5 | -7.9 | 0.7 | -1.9 |
| 1932 | 5.3 | -4.0 | 0.7 | -1.7 |
| 1933 | 5.1 | -3.4 | 0.7 | -0.6 |
| 1934 | 5.1 | 0.0 | 0.7 | 1.1 |
| 1935 | 5.2 | 0.8 | 0.7 | 1.5 |
| 1936 | 5.3 | 2.7 | 0.7 | 2.3 |
| 1937 | 5.4 | 2.8 | 0.7 | 2.4 |
| 1938 | 5.7 | 5.3 | 0.8 | 3.5 |
| 1939 | 5.6 | -2.6 | 0.8 | 2.7 |
| 1940 | 6.3 | 12.4 | 1.0 | 26.5 |
| 1941 | 7.1 | 12.6 | 1.1 | 9.6 |
| 1942 | 7.2 | 2.0 | 1.2 | 7.5 |
| 1943 | 7.2 | -0.4 | 1.3 | 11.3 |
| 1944 | 7.2 | 0.0 | 1.4 | 6.0 |
| 1945 | 7.3 | 1.4 | 1.3 | -1.4 |
| 1946 | 7.3 | 0.6 | 1.4 | 2.6 |
| 1947 | 7.4 | 0.5 | 1.5 | 9.3 |
| 1948 | 7.6 | 3.7 | 1.6 | 9.5 |
| 1949 | 8.0 | 4.6 | 1.7 | 4.2 |
| 1950 | 8.3 | 3.6 | 1.8 | 4.6 |
| 1951 | 8.6 | 3.9 | 2.0 | 10.1 |
| 1952 | 9.7 | 13.0 | 2.1 | 7.8 |
| 1953 | 10.1 | 4.4 | 2.3 | 6.1 |
| 1954 | 10.3 | 1.4 | 2.4 | 6.6 |
| 1955 | 10.7 | 4.1 | 2.6 | 9.3 |
| 1956 | 11.2 | 5.1 | 2.8 | 7.9 |
| 1957 | 11.7 | 4.4 | 3.0 | 4.7 |
| 1958 | 12.2 | 3.6 | 3.1 | 3.4 |
| 1959 | 12.4 | 2.1 | 3.2 | 4.5 |
| 1960 | 12.4 | -0.4 | 3.4 | 6.5 |
| 1961 | 12.6 | 2.2 | 3.6 | 6.0 |
| 1962 | 13.2 | 4.6 | 3.8 | 3.6 |
| 1963 | 13.6 | 2.7 | 3.8 | 1.5 |
| 1964 | 13.8 | 1.9 | 4.1 | 7.9 |
| 1965 | 14.5 | 4.6 | 4.3 | 4.9 |
| 1966 | 15.1 | 4.4 | 4.7 | 9.3 |
| 1967 | 15.7 | 3.7 | 4.9 | 4.3 |
| 1968 | 16.1 | 2.6 | 5.2 | 6.1 |
| 1969 | 17.1 | 6.2 | 5.6 | 7.7 |
| 1970 | 17.9 | 5.0 | 6.1 | 8.9 |
| 1971 | 19.4 | 8.5 | 7.0 | 14.8 |
| 1972 | 21.0 | 8.2 | 7.6 | 8.6 |
| 1973 | 22.6 | 7.7 | 8.7 | 14.5 |
| 1974 | 25.3 | 12.0 | 9.3 | 6.9 |
| 1975 | 30.4 | 19.9 | 12.5 | 34.4 |
| 1976 | 37.5 | 23.4 | 15.1 | 20.8 |
| 1977 | 43.7 | 16.6 | 16.8 | 11.3 |
| 1978 | 48.0 | 9.9 | 18.4 | 9.5 |
| 1979 | 52.5 | 9.3 | 20.5 | 11.4 |
| 1980 | 62.2 | 18.4 | 24.7 | 20.5 |
| 1981 | 70.3 | 13.0 | 29.2 | 18.2 |
| 1982 | 78.7 | 12.0 | 32.4 | 11.0 |
| 1983 | 82.6 | 4.9 | 35.2 | 8.6 |
| 1984 | 86.8 | 5.1 | 37.6 | 6.8 |
| 1985 | 91.2 | 5.0 | 40.3 | 7.2 |
| 1986 | 96.2 | 5.5 | 43.6 | 8.2 |
| 1987 | 100.0 | 3.9 | 47.0 | 7.8 |
| 1988 | 103.3 | 3.3 | 51.1 | 8.7 |
| 1989 | 111.0 | 7.5 | 55.8 | 9.2 |
| 1990 | 119.5 | 7.7 | 60.9 | 9.1 |
| 1991 | 130.2 | 9.0 | 66.5 | 9.2 |
| 1992 | 135.6 | 4.1 | 71.2 | 7.1 |
| 1993 | 137.9 | 1.7 | 73.8 | 3.7 |
| 1994 | 141.3 | 2.5 | 76.1 | 3.1 |
| 1995 | 146.0 | 3.3 | 78.9 | 3.7 |
| 1996 | 150.2 | 2.9 | 81.2 | 2.9 |
| 1997 | 154.4 | 2.8 | 84.9 | 4.6 |
| 1998 | 159.5 | 3.3 | 89.0 | 4.8 |
| 1999 | 163.4 | 2.4 | 93.0 | 4.5 |
| 2000 | 166.6 | 2.0 | 99.0 | 6.5 |
| 2001 | 171.1 | 2.7 | 103.4 | 4.4 |
| 2002 | 173.3 | 1.3 | 106.4 | 2.9 |
| 2003 | 178.4 | 2.9 | 109.9 | 3.3 |
| 2004 | 183.1 | 2.6 | 118.2 | 7.6 |
| 2005 | 188.9 | 3.2 | 123.3 | 4.3 |
| 2006 | 193.4 | 2.4 | 127.2 | 3.2 |
| 2007 | 201.6 | 4.2 | 133.3 | 4.8 |
| 2008 | 209.8 | 4.1 | 138.4 | 3.8 |

Base level – Retail Prices Index (RPI): January 1987 = 100; Average Earnings Index: Average 2000 = 100

Source:    DWP: The Abstract of Statistics for Benefits, National Insurance Contributions, and Indices of Prices and Earnings – 2007 Edition – Tables 1.1 & 3.1
Department of Employment and Productivity; British Labour Statistics, Historical Abstract, 1886–1968 (1971) – Tables 11, 12, 13, 56, 88, 89 & 90.
Website – www.measuringworth.org

# REFERENCES

## CHAPTER ONE
### Before 1908

1   Pat Thane, *Old Age in English History*, pages 165–193, Oxford University Press, 2002.

2   D Thomson cited in Thane, op cit, page 165.

3   K D M Snell cited in Thane, op cit, page 165.

4   Thane, op cit, page 102.

5   Maurice Bruce, *The Coming of the Welfare State*, page 32, B T Basford Ltd., London 1968.

6   Thane, op cit, page 102.

7   Report by Sir William Beveridge, *Social Insurance and Allied Services*, page 211, Appendix B, para 2, Cmd 6404, London HMSO, November 1942.

8   Thomas Paine, *Agrarian Justice*, frontpiece & page 6, printed by W Adlard, Rue Menilmontant, Paris, reprinted for T G Ballard, No 7 Little May's Buildings, St Martins Lane; and Evans and Bone, No 120 Holborn Hill London, 1797.

9   *Blackwell Dictionary of Social Policy*, editors: Pete Alcock, Angus Erskine, and Margaret May, page 103, Blackwell, Oxford 2002.

10  Ibid, page 278.

11  Maurice Bruce, op cit, pages 89–153.

12  Thane, op cit, page 172: Table 9.3 *Indoor paupers over age 65.*

13  Ibid, pages 194–195.

14  John Macnicol, *The Politics of retirement in Britain 1878–1948*, page 119, Cambridge University Press, 1998.

15  Ibid, page 118.

16  Ibid, pages 116–117.

17  Ibid, pages 120–123.

18  Ibid, page 122.

19  Ibid, pages 61–62.

20  Report of the Royal Commission on the Aged Poor 1895, Vol III, page 705, evidence no. 12774.

21  Report of the Royal Commission on the Aged Poor 1895, Vol III, page 705, evidence no. 12775.

22  Macnicol, op cit, page 62.

23  Report of the Royal Commission on the Aged Poor 1895, Vol III, page 705, evidence no. 12775 & Vol I, page lxxv, para 303.

24  Macnicol, op cit, page 63.

25  Thane, op cit, pages 196–197.

26  Ibid, page 197.

27  Pat Thane, *The 'Scandal' of Women's Pensions in Britain: How did it come about?*, pages 78–79, in Hugh Pemberton, Pat Thane and Noel Whiteside *Britain's Pensions Crisis: History and Policy*, British Academy Occasional Paper 7, Oxford University Press, 2006.

28  Thane, *Old Age in English History*, op cit, page 197 and W H Dawson cited therein.

29  Ibid, pages 173–174 and C Booth cited therein.

30  Bruce, op cit, page 124.

31  Thane, op cit, page 174.

32  Ibid, page 174, and E P Hennock cited therein.

33  Ibid, page 174, and T S and M Simey cited therein.

34  Ralph Price Hardy *Old Age Pensioning* 3, page 4, a paper read before the County of London Poor Law Officers Association on 30 October 1891, Knight & Co., 90 Fleet Street, London EC, 1891.

35  Ibid, 3, page 4.

36  Ibid, 3, page 4.

37  Ibid, 22, page 16.

38  Jose Harris, *William Beveridge: A Biography*, 2nd Edition, page 419 (see also Footnote 25 PRO, PIN 8/85 Report of the Official Committee on the Beveridge Report, early 1943), Oxford University Press, 1997.

39  Macnicol, op cit, pages 99–101.

40  Hardy, op cit, 22, page 16.

41  Thane, op cit, page 198.

42  Macnicol, op cit, pages 65–66.

43  Thane, op cit, page 198.

44  Ibid, page 198.

45  Ibid, page 198.

46  Macnicol, op cit, page 71.

47  Report of the Royal Commission on the Aged Poor 1895, Vol I, page iv.

48  Ibid, Vol I, page lxxxviii.

49  Ibid, Vol III, page 634, evidence no. 11706.

50  Ibid, Vol I, page lxxxviii.

51  Ibid, Vol I, page lxxxiii, para 1.

52  Ibid, Vol I, page lxxxiii, para 2.

53  Ibid, Vol I, page lxxxvi, para 23.

54  Ibid, Vol I, page lxxxvii, para 24.

55  Ibid, Vol I, pages lxxxix to xcii.

56  Ibid, Vol I, page xciii.

57  Ibid, Vol I, page xcviii.

58  Macnicol, op cit, page 78.

59  Charles Booth, *Pauperism, a picture; And the Endowment of Old Age, an Argument* 1892, page 168, quoted in Macnicol, op cit, page 78.

60  Macnicol, op cit, page 138.

61  Ibid, page 138.

62  Ibid, page 139.

63  Ibid, page 92.

64  Ibid, page 87.

65  Ibid, page 87.

66  Jose Harris, *Social Insurance and the Beveridge Plan*, pages 28–29 in Hugh Pemberton, Pat Thane, and Noel Whiteside *Britain's Pensions Crisis: History and Policy*, British Academy Occasional Paper 7, Oxford University Press 2006 (See also Macnicol, op cit, pages 169–171 and 203).

67  Thane, op cit, pages 205–206.

68  Macnicol, op cit, page 137.

69  Thane, op cit, page 206.

70  Ibid, pages 209–210.

71  Ibid, page 210.

72  Ibid, page 210 and Macnicol, op cit, page 146.

73  Ibid, pages 213–215 and B Seebohm Rowntree *Poverty: A study of Town Life*, Macmillan and Co. London, 1901, Centennial Edition, published by The Policy Press (Copyright the Joseph Rowntree Charitable Trust), Bristol, 2000.

74  Thane, op cit, pages 216–217.

## CHAPTER TWO
## Introduction of state old age pensions

1  Thane, op cit, page 220.

2  Ibid, page 220, and D Feldman cited therein.

3  Ibid, page 221.

4  Ibid, pages 221–222 and Harris, op cit, pages 168–175.

5  Thane, op cit, pages 223–224.

6  Ibid, page 223.

7  Bruce, op cit, page 179. (See also House of Lords, 20 July 1908, 192. Col. 1415)

8  Macnicol, op cit, page 156, and Sir Austen Chamberlain, *Politics From Inside: An Epistolary Chronicle 1906–1914* (1936), page 118 cited therein.

9  Macnicol, op cit, pages 160–163.

10  Thane, op cit, pages 231–232.

11  Bruce, op cit, pages 178–181.

12  Ibid, page 180.

13  Article *Old-Age Pensions The First Payments* in *The Times*, 31 December 1908.

14  Bruce, op cit, page 181.

15  Article *Old-Age Pensions The First Payments* in *The Times*, 31 December 1908.

16  Thane, op cit, pages 226–227.

17  Classic Encyclopedia website – http://www.1911encyclopedia.org/Old-Age_Pensions

18  G M Trevelyan, *A Shortened History of England*, page 529, Penguin Books, 1959.

19  Flora Thompson, *Lark Rise*, in *Lark Rise to Candleford*, pages 96–97, Penguin Books, 1973, (*Lark Rise* was first published by Oxford University Press 1939) referred to in Bruce, op cit, page 180.

20  Thane, op cit, page 227.

21  Ibid, page 232.

22  Ibid, page 232.

23  Bruce, op cit, pages 206–207.

24  Thane, op cit, page 233.

25  Thane, op cit, page 226.

26  Macnicol, op cit, page 168. (See also Thane, op cit, page 309, which mentions that during the war some old people transferred from pension to poor relief as the latter generally increased in line with inflation while the pension did not.)

27  Macnicol, op cit, page 168.

28  Macnicol, op cit, pages 168–169. Macnicol adds that, as a result of these additional allowances, the government, without admitting it, had raised the value of the pension by half.

## CHAPTER THREE
## Interwar years

1  Leslie Hannah *Inventing Retirement: The development of occupational pensions in Britain*, page 9, Cambridge University Press 1986 and *Report of the Commission on Superannuation in the Civil Service* Cmd 1744 (BPP, XXXIII 1903) cited in Footnote 41.

2  Thane, op cit, page 243.

3  Ibid, page 244.

4  Hannah, op cit, page 6.

5  Thane, op cit, pages 243–248.

6  Ibid, page 254 and Hannah, op cit, page 49.

7   Macnicol, op cit, page 169.

8   Thane, op cit, page 311. (See also *Hansard* (5th series) House of Commons, Vol. 110, col. 348)

9   Thane, op cit, page 311.

10  Macnicol, op cit, page 169.

11  Ibid, pages 171 and 177. (See also Thane, op cit, pages 318–319)

12  Thane, op cit, page 312, referring to the Appendix to the Report of the Departmental Committee on Old Age Pensions, including Minutes of Evidence, gn 8092, Cmd. 411, 1919.

13  Macnicol, op cit, page 169.

14  Thane, op cit, page 312. (Table 16.1 *Deaths of pensioners from starvation, 1909–1918*)

15  Macnicol, op cit, pages 171–172.

16  Ibid, pages 170–175.

17  Ibid, page 189.

18  Thane, op cit, pages 311–312.

19  Macnicol, op cit, pages 158–159 and Footnote 60.

20  Thane, op cit, page 315.

21  Macnicol, op cit, page 179.

22  Thane, op cit, page 317.

23  Macnicol, op cit, page 178.

24  Thane, op cit, page 317.

25  Macnicol, op cit, page 178.

26  Ibid, page 21.

27  Thane, op cit, page 318.

28  Thane, op cit, page 318 and Blaikie cited therein in Footnote 46.

29  Ibid, page 318.

30  Ibid, pages 318–319.

31  Ibid, pages 318–319.

32  Ibid, page 319.

33  Ibid, page 319.

34  Ibid, page 320 and Macnicol, op cit, page 192.

35  Ibid, page 320.

36  Ibid, page 322. (Thane and Macnicol both mention that the idea of a contributory supplement to the pension for the over seventies was rejected because it would have amounted to an admission that the pensions under the existing non-contributory scheme were inadequate. See also Macnicol, op cit, page 191.)

37  Harris, op cit, page 338.

38  Ibid, page 338.

39  Ibid, page 338, and P M Williams cited therein.

40  Ibid, page 338. (See also Thane, op cit, page 322)

41  Thane, op cit, pages 321–322.

42  Macnicol, op cit, page 181.

43  Thane, op cit, pages 333 & 336. (Thane points out that the birth rate had, in fact, been falling since the 1870s, but that fears of national economic decline hung over the population debate in the interwar years, giving it a different character from that of the pre-1914 period.)

44  Macnicol, op cit, page 181.

45  Ibid, pages 216–217 and 219. (Also W B Reddaway cited therein)

46  Ibid, page 193 and George Thorne cited therein.

47  Ibid, page 200.

48  Ibid, pages 202–203.

49  Ibid, page 205.

50  Ibid, page 209.

51  Ibid, page 222.

52  Hannah, op cit, page 29.

53  Macnicol, op cit, pages 215–216.

54  Ibid, page 182. (See also page 216)

55  Ibid, page 217 and Colin Clark cited therein.

56  Ibid, pages 213–214.

57  Ibid, page 214.

58  Ibid, page 214. (See also Report by Sir William Beveridge, op cit, page 211, Appendix B, para 8)

59  Thane, op cit, pages 326–327.

60  Ibid, pages 326–327.

61  Ibid, page 327.

62  Macnicol, op cit, page 208.

63  Bruce, op cit, page 251.

64  Sir Arnold Wilson and G S Mackay, *Old Age Pensions: An Historical and Critical Study*, page 176, Oxford, 1941, quoted in Thane, op cit, page 331.

65  Thane, op cit, page 331.

66  Report by Sir William Beveridge, op cit, pages 212–213, Appendix B, para 11.

67  Wilson and Mackay, op cit, page 184 quoted in Thane, op cit, page 331.

68  Thane, op cit, page 284 and F Le Gros Clark cited therein.

69  Ibid, page 284.

70  Ibid, pages 284–285.

71 Ibid, pages 284–285.

72 Parliamentary Committee on Pensions for Unmarried Women appointed on 13 April 1938. (See also Macnicol, op cit, pages 331–339)

73 *Report of the Committee on Pensions for Unmarried Women*, Cmd 5991, pages 33–36, London HMSO 1939, cited in Thane, op cit, pages 285–286.

74 Ibid, page 66, cited in Thane, op cit, page 286.

75 Macnicol, op cit, page 333. (See also Macnicol pages 325–341)

76 Thane, op cit, page 332.

77 Macnicol, op cit, page 340. (Macnicol mentions that about 310,000 women benefited from the reform. These comprised 140,000 previously uninsured wives of existing pensioners, 20,000 insured wives and 150,000 spinsters and other insured women. Thane (Thane, op cit, page 332) points out that the legislation increased women's national insurance contributions by 3d per week. She also expresses the view that, had it not been for the NSPA campaign, the reform would not have been introduced.)

78 Macnicol, op cit, page 342.

79 Ibid, pages 319–320.

80 Ibid, page 342.

## CHAPTER FOUR
# Beveridge Report and the National Insurance Scheme of 1948

1 Harris, op cit, pages 357–360.

2 Ibid, page 363. (See also Footnote 69)

3 Report by Sir William Beveridge, op cit, page 2.

4 Ibid, pages 19–20, para 40.

5 Ibid, page 20, para 40.

6 Ibid, page 2.

7 Ibid, page 20, para 40.

8 Harris, op cit, pages 413–433.

9 Hugh Pemberton, *Politics and Pensions in Post-war Britain* page 44 in Pemberton, Thane and Whiteside, *Britain's Pension Crisis: History and Policy*, Oxford University Press 2006.

10 Ibid, page 44.

11 Report by Sir William Beveridge, page 92, para 239, and page 122 para 307.

12 Howard Glennerster, *British Social Policy: 1945 to the Present*, Third Edition, page 32, Blackwell Publishing, Oxford 2007.

13 Sydney and Beatrice Webb, *Industrial Democracy (1897)* 2nd Edition, Longmans London 1920 and the *Last Hundred Years II*, page 546 (1929).

14 Glennerster, op cit, page 33.

15 Report by Sir William Beveridge, op cit pages 121–122.

16 Ibid, page 122, para 307.

17 B. Seebohm Rowntree: *'Poverty: A Study of Town Life*, Macmillan and Co. London 1901, Centennial Edition, The Policy Press, 2000.

18 Report by Sir William Beveridge, op cit, pages 77–90. (See also Thane, op cit, page 365, and Harris, op cit, page 387)

19 Thane, op cit, pages 365–366.

20 Glennerster, op cit, page 33.

21 Ibid, page 33.

22 Harris, op cit, page 382.

23 Ibid, page 382. (See also Footnote 49 PRO, CAB 87 / 79, *The Scale of Social Insurance Benefits and the Problem of Poverty*, by W H Beveridge, 16 Jan 1942)

24 Report by Sir William Beveridge, op cit, page 92, para 239.

25 Glennerster, op cit, pages 33–34.

26 Ibid, page 34. (See also Beveridge Papers VIII, 28 Rowntree to Beveridge, 1 July 1942 cited therein)

27 Harris, op cit, page 388.

28 Report by Sir William Beveridge, op cit, page 6, quoted in Thane, op cit, page 364.

29 Ibid, page 170, para 455, quoted in Thane, op cit, pages 364–365.

30 Glennerster, op cit, pages 31–32.

31 Harris, op cit, page 484.

32 Glennerster, op cit, page 31. (See also PRO CAB 87/76, SIC (41) cited therein)

33 Ibid, page 31 and footnote.

34 Jose Harris, *The Roots of Public Pensions Provision: Social Insurance and the Beveridge Plan* page 36, in Pemberton, Thane and Whiteside, *Britain's Pension Crisis: History and Policy*, Oxford University Press 2006.

35 Pat Thane, *The Scandal of Women's Pensions in Britain: How Did It Come About?*, pages 83–84, in Pemberton, Thane and Whiteside, *Britain's Pensions Crisis: History and Policy*, Oxford University Press 2006.

36  Jose Harris, *William Beveridge: A Biography*, 2nd Edition, page 391, Oxford University Press 1997.

37  Ibid, pages 391–392.

38  Ibid, pages 391–392.

39  Ibid, page 392. (See also Footnote 87, Kristy Parker, *Women MPs, Feminism and Domestic Policy in the Second World War* D Phil, diss, University of Oxford (1995) pages 126–160.

40  Thane in Pemberton et al, op cit, page 83.

41  Ibid, page 84.

42  Ibid, page 84, and Harris, op cit, page 392.

43  Ibid, page 84, and Harris, op cit, page 392.

44  Glennerster, op cit, page 35.

45  Ibid, page 35.

46  Harris, op cit, page 392.

47  Harris in Pemberton et al, op cit, page 31.

48  Ibid, page 34.

49  Report by Sir William Beveridge, op cit, Appendix A, Memorandum by the Government Actuary, *Finance of the Proposals of the report relating to Social Insurance and Security Benefits*, pages 173–210. (See also Bruce, op cit, page 306)

50  Harris in Pemberton et al, op cit, page 34. (See also Footnote 15, Memorandum by the Government Actuary, pages 180 and 210)

51  Ibid, page 34, and Footnote 15.

52  Ibid, page 35. (See also Footnote 18, Beveridge Papers IXA 37 (1), Keynes to Beveridge, 17 March 1942)

53  Report by Sir William Beveridge, op cit, para 233.

54  Bruce, op cit, page 308. (See also W. H. Beveridge, *Power and Influence*, pages 309 – 310)

55  Ibid, page 308.

56  Report by Sir William Beveridge, op cit, page 108.

57  Ibid, page 6, para 8.

58  Nicholas Timmins, *The Five Giants: A Biography of the Welfare States*, pages 23 – 25, Harper Collins, London 1995, Revised Edition 2001.

59  Ibid, page 25.

60  Ibid, page 43.

61  Ibid, page 44.

62  Glennerster, op cit, page 28.

63  Ibid, page 28.

64  Timmins, op cit, page 45.

65  Harris, op cit, page 419.

66  Ibid, page 419. (See also Footnote 25 PRO, PIN 8 / 85, Report of the Official Committee on the Beveridge Report, early 1943)

67  Timmins, op cit, page 46. (See also Angus Calder, *The People's War: Britain 1939–1945*, pages 531–532, Jonathan Cape, 1969, Pimlico Edition 1992)

68  Thane, op cit, page 369.

69  Timmins, op cit, page 46.

70  Thane, op cit, page 369.

71  Timmins, op cit, page 46. (See also Calder, op cit, page 532)

72  Harris, op cit, page 426, and Timmins, op cit, page 48.

73  Timmins, op cit, page 136.

74  Harris, op cit, page 433.

75  Ibid, page 433.

76  Macnicol, op cit, pages 394–395, and Footnote 28 (House of Commons Debates, 58 vol. CDIV, 2 Nov 944, cols 983–4).

77  Thane, op cit, page 36.

78  Ibid, page 369, Footnote 25 (Jones, *Conservative Party*, pages 68–69).

79  Timmins, op cit, page 33.

80  Ibid, page 33.

81  Calder, op cit, page 405. The Wartime Social Survey in a 1942 sample found that only one person in 7 (14%) was dissatisfied with rationing: 90% of housewives approved of it and 50% wanted it to continue after the war.

82  Harris, op cit, page 497. (See also Bruce, op cit, page 306. The words 'bread for everyone before cake for anyone' are taken from a speech by Beveridge on 10th March 1943, (*The Pillars of Security,* Beveridge's speeches, page 178), in which he described his proposals for the abolition of 'want' on the eve of a lecture tour in the USA.)

83  Harris, op cit, page 445.

84  Calder, op cit, page 530.

85  Harris, op cit, page 416.

86  Thane, op cit, page 369.

87  Kevin Jefferys, *The Attlee Governments, 1945 – 51*, page 15, Longman Group, 1992.

88  Ibid, pages 16–32. The free convertibility of pounds into dollars nearly caused financial ruination in August 1947 when large outflows of capital put sterling under intense pressure and convertibility had to be suspended.

89  Timmins, op cit, page 135.

[90] Hugh Pemberton, *Politics and Pensions in Post-war Britain*, pages 44–45. (See also Macnicol and Timmins cited in Footnote 22)

[91] Brian Abel-Smith, *The Beveridge Report: Its origins and outcomes*, York Papers, Vol. A, page 16, quoted in Timmins, op cit, page 136.

[92] Macnicol, op cit, page 397, and House of Commons Debates, 58 vol. CDXVIII, 6 Feb 1946, col 1742, cited in Footnote 37.

[93] Timmins, op cit, page 137. (See also Robert Pearce, *Attlee* pages 152–153, Longman 1997)

[94] Pemberton, in Pemberton et al, op cit, page 44.

[95] Timmins, op cit, pages 136–137.

[96] Macnicol, op cit, pages 385–386.

[97] Ibid, pages 390 and 405.

[98] Ibid, page 390.

[99] Ibid, page 398.

[100] Ibid, page 398.

[101] Ibid, page 367.

[102] Report by Sir William Beveridge, op cit, page 92, para 236.

[103] Bruce, op cit, page 324.

[104] Timmins, op cit, page 136.

[105] Bruce, op cit, pages 324–325.

[106] Incomes Data Services, *Pensions in Practice: The State System*, pages 10–11, para 1.24, IDS, London.

[107] Timmins, op cit, page 57.

[108] Ibid, page 57.

[109] Report by Sir William Beveridge, op cit, pages 110–111.

[110] Ibid, page 178, para 8.

[111] Ibid, page 206, para 82.

[112] Report of the Government Actuary on the Financial Provisions of the National Insurance Bill 1946 (January 1946), Cmd 6730, page 16.

[113] Pemberton in Pemberton et al, op cit, pages 44–45.

[114] Ibid, page 45.

[115] Ibid, page 45. (See also Footnote 24: The National Archive – Public Record Office T227 / 415, note by Miss Whalley under *NHS and National Insurance Contributions*, 1st May 1956)

[116] Ibid, page 45 and Footnote 25. (See also Rodney Lowe, *The Welfare State in Britain since 1945,* Third Edition, page 159 ('The insurance principle was therefore a convenient political fiction'), Palgrave Macmillan, 2005)

[117] Harris, op cit, page 468.

[118] Abel-Smith, op cit, quoted in Timmins, op cit, pages 136–137.

[119] Harris, op cit, page 468. (See also Bruce, op cit, pages 324–325, on this subject – 'the failure to relate other (Social Insurance) benefits to subsistence costs has kept the NAB (National Assistance Board) only too well-occupied'.)

[120] Harris, op cit, page 468.

[121] Report by Sir William Beveridge, op cit, pages 6–7, para 9.

[122] Harris, op cit, page 484.

[123] Report by Sir William Beveridge, op cit, page 108.

[124] Ibid, page 484.

[125] Ibid, page 452. Harris also attaches a footnote which briefly describes the origin and some of the history of the term 'welfare state' which was a translation of the German der Wohlfahrtsstaat which had been in use since the Bismarck reform of the late 19th century.

## CHAPTER FIVE
# Post-war Conservative social policy

[1] Tony Salter, *Pensions in the Welfare State*, pages 8–9, in *Benefits & Compensation International*, November 1977, London.

[2] Ibid, page 9. (See also M Pilch and V Wood, *Pension Scheme Practice* Hutchinson, London, 1967)

[3] Report of the Committee on the Taxation Treatment of Provisions for Retirement CMD 9063, 1954 (BPP, XIX, 1953–4) HMSO, London.

[4] Hannah, op cit, page 49.

[5] Report of the Committee on the Taxation Treatment of Provisions for Retirement, paras 160–161.

[6] Hannah, op cit, page 50.

[7] Salter, op cit, page 9.

[8] Glennerster, op cit, pages 72 – 73.

[9] Lowe, op cit, page 95.

[10] Glennerster, op cit, page 72. (See also Thane, op cit, page 371)

[11] Lowe, op cit, page 95.

[12] Ibid, page 95. Lowe points out that such a policy of selectivity, as Mcleod and Powell admitted, would involve an increase in means testing, which would be both electorally unpopular and administratively inefficient.

[13] Thane, op cit, page 371 and Jones, *Conservative Party*, op cit, page 219.

[14] Glennerster, op cit, page 73.

[15] Ibid, op cit, page 73 and Jones,
*Conservative Party*, op cit, page 79.

[16] Thane, op cit, pages 371 and 372. (See also
Glennerster, op cit, page 74: where the
Glennerster comments that the cost of welfare,
the way it was being financed, and the form it
was taking were all offensive to the economic
liberal view of the State's role that became
the basis of Conservative philosophy.)

[17] Thane, op cit, page 372.

[18] Ibid, page 372. (See also Jones, *Conservative
Party*, op cit, page 218–219)

[19] Glennerster, *Why so Different, Why so Bad
a Future*, page 68, in *Britain's Pensions
Crisis.: History and Policy*, Pemberton, Thane,
Whiteside, Oxford University Press 2006.

[20] Glennerster in Pemberton et al, op cit, page 68,
and Timmins, op cit, page 45. (Timmins refers
to Sir Thomas Phillips as an old adversary of
Beveridge having earlier in his career worked
for Beveridge at the Board of Trade.)

[21] Thane, op cit, page 372.

[22] Report of the Committee on the Economic
and Financial Problems of Provision for Old
Age (commonly referred to as the Report
of the Phillips Committee), page 56, para
212, Cmd 9333, HMSO, London, 1954,
quoted in Glennerster, op cit, page 90.

[23] Hannah, op cit, page 171, referred to in Footnote
31. (See also RCK Enso 1950, cited therein)

[24] Richard M Titmuss, *Pension Systems and
Population Change*, page 59, in *Essays on
the Welfare State* Third Edition 1976, George
Allen & Unwin, London. (See also Report
of the Phillips Committee, op cit.)

[25] Ibid, page 63.

[26] Thane, op cit, page 372.

[27] Report of the Phillips Committee,
op cit, page 51, para 193.

[28] Thane, op cit, page 372.

[29] Titmuss, op cit, pages 65–67, and
Thane, op cit, page 372.

[30] Alan Sked and Chris Cook, *Post-War Britain: A
Political History 1945–1992*, Fourth Edition,
pages 120–124, Penguin Books, 1993.

[31] Hannah, op cit, page 54.

[32] Lowe, op cit, pages 154 and 471, and Footnote
34 which states that the level of insurance
contributions had been based on an anticipated

rate of 8.5% unemployment, whereas the actual
rate was under 3%. The cost of unemployment
benefit in 1955, at 1948–9 prices, which had been
estimated by Beveridge at £123 million, was only
£11.3 million. (See also A W Dilnot, J Key, and C N
Morris, *The Reform of Social Security*, pages 14–15.)

[33] Lowe, op cit, page 154.

[34] Ibid, page 144–154.

[35] Timmins, op cit, page 193 and
Lowe, op cit, page 154.

[36] Timmins, op cit, page 193.

[37] Lowe, op cit, page 155 and page
471, and Footnote 35.

[38] Pemberton in Pemberton et al, op cit,
page 46, and H. Fawcett, *The Beveridge
Straight-jacket: Policy Formulation and the
Problem of Poverty in Old Age*, pages 20–42,
Contemporary British History, 10, 1 (1996).

[39] Ibid, page 46.

[40] Hannah, op cit, page 53, and Lowe, op cit, page 155.

[41] Hannah, op cit, page 53, and Lowe, op cit, page 155.

[42] Sked and Cook, op cit, pages 126–127.

[43] Ibid, pages 126–137.

[44] Titmuss, op cit, pages 68–73.

[45] Pemberton in Pemberton et al, pages 47 and 49.

[46] Richard M Titmuss, *The Social Division of Welfare*,
pages 34–55, in *Essays on the Welfare State*, Third
Edition, 1976, George Allen & Unwin, London.

[47] Ibid, page 40.

[48] Ibid, page 42.

[49] Ibid, page 44.

[50] Titmuss, *Pension Systems and Population Change*,
op cit, page 69. In the year to 31 March 1956,
the Exchequer payment totalled £100 million,
split £92 million to the National Insurance Fund
and £8 million to the Industrial Injuries Fund.
Titmuss estimated that the share of the Exchequer
supplement in respect of retirement pensions was
roughly half of that to the National Insurance
Fund; i.e. £45 million. Titmuss cites in his
footnote, *The Growth of Pension Rights and their
Impact on the National Economy*, a paper by F.W.
Bacon and others, published in the *Journal of the
Institute of Actuaries*, Vol. 50, Pt. 2, No. 355, 1954.
He also refers to an additional £34 million in
remitted tax on NI contributions which accentuates
the regressive nature of the contribution, quoting
as his source, *Hansard*, 13 December 1954, Vol.
535, col. 1441. The figure of £100 million in
respect of the cost to the Exchequer of private

pension schemes is taken from the Report of the Phillips Committee, op cit, page 62, para 230.

51  Titmuss *The Social Division of Welfare*, op cit, page 35.

52  Ibid, page 35. (See also I. Macleod and J E Powell, *The Social Services – Needs and Means*, Conservative Political Centre, London 1949.)

53  Richard M Titmuss, *Social Policy: an introduction*, pages 30–31, George Allen & Unwin, London, 1974.

54  Ibid, pages 30–31. (See also Titmuss, *The Social Division of Welfare*, op cit, page 35)

55  Glennerster, op cit, page 90.

56  Ibid, page 90

57  Pemberton in Pemberton et al, page 49.

58  Glennerster, op cit, page 90.

59  Thane, op cit, page 374.

60  Pemberton in Pemberton et al, op cit, page 49.

61  Timmins, op cit, page 195.

62  Pemberton in Pemberton et al, op cit, page 49. See also H. Fawcett, *The Beveridge Straight-jacket: Policy Formulation and the Problem of Poverty in Old Age*, Contemporary British History, 10, 1 (1996) 20–42 (25).

63  Lowe, op cit, page 155.

64  Glennerster, op cit, page 90.

65  Pemberton in Pemberton et al, op cit, page 49.

66  Ibid, pages 49 and 50 and Note 44 on page 50. (See also Timmins, op cit, page 195 and Ellis (Note 73) cited therein)

67  Hannah, op cit, pages 56 and 57. (See also Notes 41 and 42 on page 172)

68  Pemberton in Pemberton et al, op cit, page 50. (See also Note 45)

69  Ibid, page 50.

70  Ibid, page 50. (See also Note 46, *National Pension Scheme: note by the Minister of Labour*)

71  Ibid page 50.

72  Glennerster, op cit, page 90.

73  Glennerster, op cit, page 90.

74  Hannah, op cit, page 57.

75  Ibid page 57.

76  White Paper Provision for Old Age: *The future Development of the NI Scheme* Cmmd 538, HMSO London, 1958.

77  Timmins, op cit, page 196 & G D Gilling-Smith *The Complete Guide to Pensions and Superannuation*, pages 24–25, Penguin Books Ltd, Harmondsworth, 1967.

78  Timmins, op cit, page 196.

79  Ibid, page 192, and *Hansard*, 27 January 1959, col. 1013.

80  Sked and Cook, op cit, page 157.

81  Ibid, page 157.

82  Ibid, page 157.

83  Ibid, page 138.

84  Ibid, page 158.

85  G D Gilling-Smith, op cit, pages 24–25.

86  Ibid, pages 44–45

87  Ibid, page 275

88  Hannah, page 58, and Notes 45 and 46 on page 172. Note 45 states, inter alia, 'There were many guides to the contracting out decision at the time; for one of the sanest see R W Abbott FIA, *Growth of State Pensions and their Effect on Occupational Schemes*, published in *The Accountant*, 4 June 1960, 687–91.

89  Whiteside in Pemberton et al, op cit, page 133.

90  Hannah, op cit, page 53. (See also Note 29, page 171)

91  Ibid, page 53 and Note 29 on page 171.

92  Gilling-Smith, op cit, page 275.

93  Hannah, op cit, page 57.

## CHAPTER SIX
# Labour and National Superannuation

1  Glennerster, in Pemberton et al, op cit, page 68.

2  Ibid, page 68.

3  Titmuss, op cit, page 73.

4  Ibid, page 74.

5  Glennerster, in Pemberton et al, op cit, page 68.

6  Research Report No.58, *Social Security Programmes Throughout the World 1981*, pages 262–263, US Department of Health and Human Services, Social Security Administration.

7  Glennerster, in Pemberton et al, op cit, page 69.

8  Ibid, page 69.

9  Thane, op cit, page 373.

10  Titmuss, op cit, page 65 and Thane, op cit, page 373.

11  The Labour Party, *National Superannuation*, pages 8–9, London, 1957.

12 Hannah, op cit, page 55, and AT Haynes and RJ Kirton, *Income Tax in Relation to Social Security*, page 171, Note 35, published in the *Journal of the Institute of Actuaries*, LXXII, 1944–6.

13 Titmuss, op cit, page 69 and Thane, op cit, page 373.

14 Thane, op cit, page 373–4.

15 Ibid, page 374.

16 Ibid, page 374.

17 Hannah, op cit, page 55.

18 Thane, op cit, page 374

19 The Labour Party, *National Superannuation*, page 4, quoted in Thane, op cit, page 374.

20 Ibid, page 4.

21 Thane, op cit, page 374.

22 Ibid, page 374.

23 Ibid, page 375.

24 Hannah, page 56.

25 Ibid, page 56 and Glennerster, op cit, page 106.

26 Glennerster, op cit, page 106.

27 Glennerster, op cit, page 107.

28 Sked and Cook, op cit, page 186.

29 Ibid, page 187.

30 Ibid, pages 187–189.

31 Ibid, page 193.

32 Glennerster, op cit, page 107.

33 Sked and Cook, op cit, page 194.

34 Ibid, pages 198–199; Quotations from TR Fyvel and Nicholas Davenport.

35 Labour Party 1964 General Election Manifesto, quoted in Michael Hill, *The Welfare State in Britain: A Political History*, page 66, Edward Elgar Publishing Limited, Aldershot, England.

36 Hill, op cit, page 66.

37 Ibid, page 66.

38 Ibid, page 66.

39 Lowe, op cit, page 156.

40 Ibid, page 156.

41 Glennerster, op cit, page 109.

42 Timmins, op cit, page 225.

43 Glennerster, op cit, pages 109–110.

44 Ibid, page 108.

45 H Glennerster, *National Assistance: Service or Charity?*, page 33, London Fabian Society 1962, quoted in Glennerster, op cit, page 108.

46 Sked and Cook, op cit, page 202.

47 Ibid, page 203.

48 Ibid, page 209 and Glennerster, op cit, page 110.

49 Ibid, page 203.

50 Ibid, page 204

51 Lowe, op cit, page 156.

52 Glennerster, op cit, page 110 and Sked and Cook, op cit, page 203.

53 Sked and Cook, op cit, page 206.

54 RHS Crossman, *The Diaries of a Cabinet Minister, vol 1: Minister of Housing 1964–66*, Diary entry for 17 July, 1965, London: Hamish Hamilton, Jonathan Cape, quoted in Glennerster, op cit, page 110 and Thane, op cit, page 377.

55 Crossman, op cit, Diary entry for 17 July, 1965.

56 Ibid, Diary entry for 17 July, 1965.

57 Douglas Houghton, *Paying for Social Services*, Occasional Papers 16, page 12, Institute of Economic Affairs, 1967, quoted in Timmins, op cit, page 226.

58 Timmins, op. cit, page 226.

59 Report by Sir William Beveridge, op cit, page 145, para 385: 'The administration of the Plan for Social Security as a whole, including social insurance, national assistance, and voluntary insurance, will be undertaken by a Ministry of Social Security under a Cabinet Minister'.

60 Timmins, op. cit, page 226–7.

61 Crossman, op cit, Diary entry for 14 December, 1965 quoted in Timmins, op. cit, page 227.

62 Hill, op cit, pages 67–69.

63 Glennerster, op cit, page 110–111. (See also Hill, op cit, page 67 and Lowe, op cit, page 155)

64 Hill, op cit, pages 67–69.

65 Ruth Lister, *Social Security*, Table of Claimants receiving national assistance/supplementary benefit, 1948–74 (000s), Child Poverty Action Group poverty pamphlet No.22 1975, page 9, reproduced in Lowe, op cit, page 157.

66 Harold Wilson, *The Labour Government 1964–70*, page 282, Pelican, Penguin Books, Harmondsworth Middlesex 1971, quoted in Timmins, op. cit, page 227.

67 Sked and Cook, op cit, pages 214–215.

68 Ibid, page 216.

69 Ibid, page 217–220.

70 Ibid, page 218.

71 Ibid, page 221–222.

72 Thane, op cit, page 377.

[73] Sked and Cook, op cit, pages 223–224.

[74] Department for Work and Pensions (DWP), *The Abstract of Statistics for Benefits, National Insurance Contributions, and Indices of Prices and Earnings* 2007 Edition, Table 5.1: *Basic State Pension*, page 53, Information Directorate, DWP, Newcastle upon Tyne.

[75] Sked and Cook, op cit, pages 220–225.

[76] Ibid, pages 225–226.

[77] Glennerster, op cit, pages 107–108.

[78] Hill, op cit, page 68.

[79] Sked and Cook, op cit, pages 226–227.

[80] Ibid, op cit, pages 227–228.

[81] Timmins, op cit, page 264.

[82] Ibid, page 263.

[83] Ibid, page 265.

[84] Ibid, page 264.

[85] Crossman, op cit, Diary entry for 5 January, 1968, quoted in Timmins, op. cit, page 264.

[86] Keith Banting, *Poverty, Politics and Policy, Britain in the 1960s*, page 80, Macmillan, 1979, quoted in Timmins, op. cit, page 264.

[87] Timmins, op. cit, page 264–265.

[88] Ibid, page 265.

[89] Hannah, op cit, pages 58–59, and Footnote 47 on pages 172–173. The archives mentioned specifically the Life Offices' Association, the National Association of Pension Funds, the Trades Union Congress, the Labour Party and the Legal & General. Also quoted were National Association of Pension Funds (NAPF), *The Future Relationship of State and Occupational Pensions*, 1968 and the contribution of Stewart Lyon FIA to that discussion in the NAPF's Conference Report November 1968 pp 12 ff.; and Tony Lynes, *Labour's Pension Plan*, Fabian Tract 396, 1969.

[90] Glennerster, op cit, page 111.

[91] Hill, op cit, page 68.

[92] Glennerster, op cit, page 111.

[93] Crossman, op cit, vol 3, 1977, page 176, quoted in Hill, op cit, page 68.

[94] Hannah, op cit, page 60.

[95] Crossman, op cit, vol 3, 1977, page 176, quoted in Hill, op cit, page 68.

[96] Hannah, op cit, page 59.

[97] Ibid, page 59.

[98] Ibid, page 59.

[99] Ibid, page 59.

[100] Brian Ellis *Pensions in Britain* 1955–75, page 11, HMSO London 1989, quoted in Timmins, op cit, page 195.

[101] Hannah, op cit, page 59. 'By the early 1970s in Germany … the average married worker could expect to retire on 60% of net final earnings. Similar State provision was by then not unusual in other advanced Western nations … even in the traditionally laissez faire United States, the level was 56%.'

[102] Ibid, page 59.

[103] Ibid, page 59.

[104] Ibid, page 59.

[105] Hannah, op cit, page 60.

[106] Glennerster, op cit, page 111.

[107] Crossman, op cit, 1977, page 217, quoted in Glennerster, op cit, page 111–112.

[108] Hannah, op cit, page 59.

[109] Department of Health and Social Security, Explanatory Booklet, *The New Pensions Scheme, Latest Facts and Figures with examples*, page 6, HMSO, November 1969.

[110] White Paper, *National Superannuation and Social Insurance: Proposals for Earnings Related Social Security*, Cmnd 3883, DHSS, HMSO, 1969 and White Paper, *National Superannuation Terms for Partial Contracting-out of the National Superannuation Scheme*, CMND 4195, DHSS, HMSO, 1969.

[111] DHSS, *The New Pensions Scheme*, op cit. (See also *British Pension Plans – a case study* in Richard M Titmuss, *Social Policy: An Introduction*, pages 102–120, edited by Brian Abel-Smith and Kay Titmuss, George Allen & Unwin, London, 1974)

[112] Salter, op cit, pages 11–12.

[113] Ibid, page 16.

[114] Salter, op cit, pages 10–12 and White Paper, *National Superannuation Terms etc*, op cit.

[115] Sked and Cook, op cit, page 241.

[116] DWP, *The Abstract of Statistics for Benfits etc*, op cit, page 53.

[117] Sked and Cook, op cit, pages 242–243.

[118] Ibid, page 243.

[119] Salter, op cit, page 12 and Hannah, op cit, pages 50–51 and 117.

[120] Sked and Cook, op cit, page 243.

[121] Ibid, page 245, cited as being from the *Annual Register*.

[122] Ibid, page 246, quoting source, D Butler and A Sloman, *British Political Facts 1900–75*.

## CHAPTER SEVEN
## Conservative government 1970–74

[1] Timmins, op cit, pages 273–275.

[2] Anthony Barber, Speech to the House of Commons, *Hansard*, 27 October 1970, column 37, quoted in Timmins, op cit, page 280.

[3] Timmins, op cit, page 280.

[4] Ibid, page 281.

[5] Hill, op cit, page 92.

[6] Glennerster, op cit, page 113.

[7] Ibid, page 113.

[8] Ibid, page 112.

[9] Ibid, page 112.

[10] Ibid, page 112, and Hill, op cit, page 92.

[11] Conservative Party 1970 General Election Manifesto, quoted in Hill, op cit, page 92.

[12] Conservative Party 1970 General Election Manifesto, quoted in Hill, op cit, page 93.

[13] Hill, op cit, page 93.

[14] DHSS *Strategy for Pensions*, White Paper, CMD 4755, HMSO, 1971.

[15] *Social Security Act 1973: the reserve pension scheme*, Leaflet NP4 issued by the Department of Health and Social Security, August 1973, page 4: 'the amount of pension earned depends on the contributions paid and the employee's age at the time they were paid'.

[16] Sked and Cook, op cit, page 256.

[17] DWP, *The Abstract of Statistics for Benefits etc*, op cit, page 53.

[18] Sked and Cook, op cit, page 256.

[19] Hill, op cit, page 93.

[20] Report by Sir William Beveridge, op cit, page 107, *Taxation and Contributions*, para 272.

[21] Sir Keith Joseph, House of Commons Speech, 28 November 1972, *Hansard*, Col.243, quoted in Brian Ellis, *Pensions in Britain 1955–75*, page 42, London HMSO 1989, and in Hill, op cit, page 93.

[22] DHSS Leaflet NP4 (1973), op cit, page 2.

[23] Hill, op cit, page 94.

[24] DHSS Leaflet NP4 (1973), op cit, page 2.

[25] DHSS Leaflet NP4 (1973), op cit, page 2.

[26] *Hansard*, 9 May 1973.

[27] Hannah, op cit, page 60 and DHS Leaflet NP4 (1973), op cit, page 3.

[28] DHSS Leaflet NP4 (1973), op cit, page 3.

[29] Brian Ellis, *Pensions in Britain 1955–75*, page 41, London HMSO 1989, quoted in Hill, op cit, page 94.

[30] Titmuss, *Social Policy*, op cit, pages 115–120.

[31] *Social Security Statistics 1974* and *Social Security Statistics 1973*, Table 34.53, quoted in Ruth Lister, *Social Security: The Case for Reform*, Poverty Pamphlet No.22, Child Poverty Action Group, London 1975.

[32] Glennerster, op cit, page 112 and Hill, op cit, page 94.

[33] Fourth Survey of Occupational Pension Schemes by the Government Actuary.

[34] *Equal Opportunities for Men and Women* Department of Employment, September 1973.

[35] Ibid, para 2.

[36] Ruth Lister, *Social Security: The Case for Reform*, Poverty Pamphlet No. 22, Child Poverty Action Group, London, 1975.

[37] United Kingdom 1971 Census, *Population 1% sample* Tables, HMSO November 1973.

[38] Ibid.

[39] Hannah, op cit, page 60.

[40] Ibid, page 60.

[41] Hannah, op cit, page 60.

[42] Sked and Cook, op cit, page 256–7.

[43] Ibid, page 257.

[44] Ibid, page 257.

[45] Ibid, page 259.

[46] Ibid, page 259.

[47] Timmins, op cit, page 285.

[48] DWP, *The Abstract of Statistics for Benefits etc*, op cit, page 53.

[49] Sked and Cook, op cit, page 260.

[50] Ibid, page 262.

[51] Ibid, page 280

[52] Timmins, op cit, page 307

[53] Sked and Cook, op cit, page 280.

[54] DWP, *The Abstract of Statistics for Benefits etc*, op cit, page 53.

[55] Sked and Cook, op cit, page 281.

[56] Timmins, op cit, page 307.

57 White Paper, *Strategy for Pensions*, CMD 4755, DHSS, HMSO, 1971.

58 Timmins, op cit, page 286. See also Lowe, op cit, page 156.

59 Report by Sir William Beveridge, op cit, para 19(vi), page 10.

60 Lowe, op cit, page 156. (See also Hill, op cit, pages 96–97 and 99–100)

61 Lowe, op cit, page 158 and Note 37 on page 471. The expression *poverty trap* was coined by David Piachaud in an article in the *New Statesman* on 3 December 1971.

62 Hill, op cit, page 100.

63 Ibid, page 99.

64 Ibid, page 100.

65 Frank Field, *One Nation: The Conservatives' Record since June 1970*, Poverty Pamphlet 12, London, 1972, CPAG, quoted in Hill, op cit, page 97.

66 Lowe, op cit, page 158.

67 Sir Keith Joseph, Speech to the Conservative Party Conference October 1973, quoted in Timmins, op cit, page 287.

68 Ibid, page 287.

69 Hill, op cit, page 96.

70 Timmins, op cit, page 288.

71 Hill, op cit, page 96.

72 Lowe, op cit, page 158.

73 Hill, op cit, pages 88–90. Hill also quotes Alan Walker *Public Expenditure and Social Policy*, page 30, Heinemann 1989, who showed annual social expenditure growth rate of 6.8% for 1970–74 compared with 5.9% for 1964–70.

## CHAPTER EIGHT
## Labour governments 1974–79

1 Sked and Cook, op cit, page 283.

2 Ibid, pages 283–285.

3 Ibid, page 285.

4 Election Broadcast by Edward Heath, 12 February 1974 quoted in Sked and Cook, op cit, page 285.

5 Sked and Cook, op cit, page 285

6 Sked and Cook, op cit, page 285–286.

7 Labour Party Manifesto, General Election 28 February 1974, quoted in Timmins, op cit, page 314.

8 Timmins, op cit, page 314.

9 Sked and Cook, op cit, page 286,

10 Ibid, page 288, quoting source, D Butler and A Sloman, *British Political Facts 1900–75*. (See also Hill, op cit, page 106)

11 Hill, op cit, page 106.

12 Sked and Cook, op cit, pages 289–90.

13 Hill, op cit, page 106 and Sked and Cook, op cit, pages 293–94.

14 Sked and Cook, op cit, page 292.

15 Ibid, page 294.

16 Hill, op cit, page 108.

17 DWP, *The Abstract of Statistics for Benefits etc*, op cit, page 53.

18 Pat Thane, *Old Age in English History*, pages 377–8, Oxford University Press, 2000.

19 Timmins, op cit, page 342.

20 Ibid, page 342, and Thane op cit page 378.

21 Bryan Ellis, *Pensions in Britain 1955–1975*, page 46 para 161, HMSO London 1989.

22 Barbara Castle, House of Commons, 10 April 1974, reported in *Hansard*, Cols 463/464, quoted in Ellis, op cit, page 46.

23 Ellis, op cit, page 46.

24 Ibid, page 46.

25 Ibid, page 47.

26 Ibid, page 47.

27 Barbara Castle, House of Commons, 1 July 1974 reported in *Hansard*, Cols 111/112, quoted in Ellis, op cit, page 47.

28 Ibid, quoted in Ellis, op cit, pages 47–48.

29 Ellis, op cit, page 48.

30 Ibid, page 48 and Timmins, op cit, page 346.

31 Brian O'Malley, House of Commons, 1 July 1974 reported in *Hansard*, Col 158, quoted in Ellis, op cit, page 48.

32 Ellis, op cit, page 48.

33 Sked and Cook, op cit, pages 294–5.

34 Ibid, page 297.

35 Ibid, page 297.

36 Ibid, page 293.

37 Hill, op cit, page 106.

38 Sked and Cook, op cit, page 293.

39 Ibid, page 297 and Trevelyan, op cit, page 340–1.

40 White Paper, *Better Pensions*, page iii, Cmnd 5713, Department of Health and Social Security, HMSO 1974.

41 Ibid, page iii.

42 Ibid, page iii.

43 Ibid, page iii.

44 Ibid, page iii.

45 Ibid, page iii.

46 Ibid, para 6–7

47 Ibid, para 84

48 Ellis, op cit, page 52.

49 *Better Pensions*, op cit, paras 8 and 10 (iii).

50 Ibid, paras 8, 16 and 17.

51 Ibid, para 14.

52 Ibid, para 45 (iv).

53 Ibid, para 45 (v).

54 Ibid, para 45 (vi).

55 Ibid, para 45 (vi).

56 Ibid, para 45 (iii).

57 Ibid, paras 46–47.

58 Ibid, paras 30–32.

59 Ibid, para 54.

60 Ibid, para 55.

61 Ibid, para 56.

62 Ibid, para 56.

63 Ibid, para 53.

64 Ibid, para 52.

65 Ibid, para 57.

66 Ibid, para 58.

67 Ibid, para 58.

68 Ibid, para 59.

69 Ibid, para 59.

70 Ibid, para 62.

71 Ibid, paras 58 and 62.

72 Ellis, op cit, page 30.

73 Stewart Lyon, *Social Security and Occupational Pension Schemes*, para 9.2, Faculty of Actuaries, Edinburgh, November, 1967, quoted in Ellis, op cit, page 30.

74 Stewart Lyon, op cit, para 9.6 and Ellis, op cit, pages 31–32.

75 Ellis, op cit, page 31.

76 Ibid, page 31.

77 Ibid, page 31.

78 *Better Pensions*, op cit, para 65.

79 Ibid, para 11, Table 2 and para 14.

80 Ibid, paras 33–35.

81 Ibid, para 67 and Government Actuary's Memorandum, para 16.

82 Ibid, para 40.

83 Ibid, para 83.

84 Ibid, para 83.

85 Ibid, para 84.

86 Ibid, para 87.

87 Ibid, para 89.

88 Ibid, para 87.

89 Ellis, op cit, page 53.

90 Ibid, page 49.

91 Hannah, op cit, page 62, and Footnote 56 on page 173 for quotation from the Government Actuary's Survey of Occupational Pension Schemes, 1979; Sixth Survey, 1981, page 5: 'In 1979 only 1.3 million out of 11.6 million occupational pension scheme members were not contracted-out'.

92 Steven Nesbit, *British Pensions Policy Making in the 1980s: the rise and fall of a policy community*, page 20, Avebury, Aldershot, Hants 1995.

93 Hannah, op cit, page 62. (See also page 79. 'Funds being valued in the mid 1970s showed substantial deficits and, despite the contemporary profit squeeze, major employers usually made these up at their own expense to restore the funds' long-run finances'. Also Footnote 54 on page 178 cites Margaret Stone, *Pension Funds Feeling the Pinch*, printed in *The Times* on 14 March 1975, page 19.)

94 Ibid, page 61.

95 Ibid, page 61.

96 Nesbitt, op cit, page 20.

97 Ibid, page 20.

98 Hannah, op cit, page 61.

99 Sked and Cook, op cit, pages 297–299 quoting source, D Butler and A Sloman, *British Political Facts 1900–75*.

100 Hill, op cit, pages 106–107.

101 Ibid, page 107.

102 Sked and Cook, op cit, pages 299–300.

103 Sked and Cook, op cit, page 300.

104 Sked and Cook, op cit, page 300.

105 Ibid, page 306.

106 Ellis, op cit, page 53.

107 Ibid, page 53.

108 Ibid, page 53.

109 Barbara Castle, Speech in the House of Commons Debate on the Social Security Pensions Bill,

Second Reading, 18 March 1975, *Hansard*, Column 1489 quoted in Ellis, op cit, page 53.

[110] Ibid, Castle quoted by Ellis, page 53.

[111] Norman Fowler, Speech in the House of Commons Debate on the Social Security Pensions Bill, Second Reading, 18 March 1975, *Hansard*, Column 1513 quoted in Ellis, op cit, page 53.

[112] Ellis, op cit, page 53.

[113] Paul Dean, Speech in the House of Commons Debate on the Social Security Pensions Bill, Second Reading, 18 March 1975, *Hansard*, Column 1529 quoted in Ellis, op cit, page 53 and Timmins, op cit, page 341.

[114] Sir George Young, Speech in the House of Commons Debate on the Social Security Pensions Bill, Second Reading, 18 March 1975, *Hansard*, Column 1538 quoted in Ellis, op cit, page 54.

[115] Timmins, op cit, page 347.

[116] Kenneth Clarke, Standing Committee A, 8 April 1975, Column 3, quoted in Ellis, op cit, page 54.

[117] Ellis, op cit, page 54.

[118] David Penhaligon, Standing Committee A, 22 April 1975, Column 229/30, quoted in Ellis, op cit, pages 54–55.

[119] Ellis, op cit, page 55.

[120] Timmins, op cit, page 347.

[121] Ibid, page 347.

[122] Ibid, page 348.

[123] Lord Banks, Speech in the House of Lords Debate on the Social Security Pensions Bill, Second Reading, 24 June 1975, *Hansard*, Column 1363, quoted in Ellis, op cit, page 55.

[124] Lord Byers, Speech in the House of Lords Debate on the Social Security Pensions Bill, Second Reading, 24 June 1975, *Hansard*, Column 1342, quoted in Ellis, op cit, page 55.

[125] Ellis, op cit, pages 55–56.

[126] Hannah, op cit, page 61.

[127] Ibid, pages 61–62.

[128] Sked and Cook, op cit, page 308.

[129] Timmins, op cit, page 343. (See also Hilary Land, *The Child Benefit Fiasco*, in *The Year Book of Social Policy in Britain 1976*, Routledge & Kegan Paul, page 124 for reference to – Callaghan, it seems was regarded by Castle as 'a bit of a male chauvinist'. She was dismissed from the government before the amount of the new Child Benefit due to take effect in April 1977 had been agreed.)

[130] Ellis, op cit, page 57.

[131] Sked and Cook, op cit, page 314.

[132] DWP, *The Abstract of Statistics for Benefits etc*, op cit, page 53.

[133] Sked and Cook, op cit, pages 308–309.

[134] Ibid, pages 312–313.

[135] Ibid, page 315.

[136] DWP, *The Abstract of Statistics for Benefits etc*, op cit, page 53.

[137] Sked and Cook, op cit, pages 313–315.

[138] Ibid, page 315.

[139] DWP, *The Abstract of Statistics for Benefits etc*, op cit, page 53.

[140] Jack Jones, *Union Man*, page 332, William Collins Sons & Co, Glasgow 1986.

[141] Sked and Cook, op cit, page 321.

[142] DWP, *The Abstract of Statistics for Benefits etc*, op cit, page 53.

[143] Timmins, op cit, page 343. (Footnote 97: Conservative Research Dept Archive Bodleian Library CRD 4/7/14).

[144] Sked and Cook, op cit, page 321.

[145] Ibid, pages 321–323.

## CHAPTER NINE

# Thatcher's governments 1979–1990: New directions in pension policy

[1] Sked and Cook, op cit, page 323.

[2] Hill, op cit, page 123.

[3] Sked and Cook, op cit, page 322.

[4] Hill, op cit, page 123.

[5] Timmins, op cit, page 373.

[6] Sked and Cook, op cit, pages 323–324.

[7] Ibid, page 329.

[8] Friedrich von Hayek *Law, Legislation and Liberty*; vol. II: *The Mirage of Social Justice*, pages 68–69, Routledge & Kegan Paul, London, 1976.

[9] Sked and Cook, op cit, page 330.

[10] Ibid, page 329.

[11] Sir Ian Gilmour, *Inside Right: A Study of Conservatism*, page 118, Hutchinson, London, 1977.

[12] Sked and Cook, op cit, page 330. Mrs Thatcher 'entered office apparently committed to a set of beliefs and values which stressed the primacy of market forces, individualism and sound money. Other conservatives who

claimed the label 'Tory' … stressed the primacy of community over individuality'.

13   Sked and Cook, op cit, page 333.

14   Ibid, page 333.

15   Timmins, op cit, page 374.

16   Patrick Jenkin, House of Commons Statement, *Hansard*, 13 June 1979, column 439, quoted in Timmins, op cit, page 374.

17   Sked and Cook, op cit, page 334.

18   Steven Nesbitt, *British Pension Policy Making in the 1980s* pages 33–34, Avebury, Ashgate Publishing Ltd., Aldershot, Hants, 1995.

19   Ibid, page 34.

20   Andrew Gamble, *The Free Economy and the Strong State*, page 114, Macmillan London, 1988; quoted in Nesbitt, op cit, page 34.

21   DWP, *The Abstract of Statistics for Benefits etc*, op cit, page 53.

22   Ibid, pages 52–53.

23   Nesbitt, op cit, pages 35–36.

24   Timmins, op cit, page 374.

25   Nesbitt, op cit, page 36.

26   Lowe, op cit, page 324.

27   Ibid, page 324.

28   Sked and Cook, pages 335–336.

29   Ibid, pages 331–332.

30   DWP, *The Abstract of Statistics for Benefits etc*, op cit, page 53.

31   Nesbitt, op cit, page 36.

32   Ibid, op cit, page 36.

33   White Paper, *Growing Older*, page iii, Cmnd 8173, DHSS, London HMSO, 1981, quoted in Nesbitt, op cit, page 37.

34   Ibid, para 2.4, quoted in Nesbitt, page 37.

35   Ibid, paras 1.2 and 1.6, quoted in Nesbitt, page 37.

36   Nesbitt, op cit, pages 37–38.

37   Sked and Cook, page 336.

38   Peter Riddell, *The Thatcher Government*, Martin Robertson 1983, quoted in Sked and Cook, op cit, page 336.

39   Sked and Cook, op cit, page 336.

40   Timmins, op cit, page 386.

41   Sked and Cook, op cit, pages 335–336.

42   Lowe, op cit, page 325.

43   Timmins, op cit, pages 386–7.

43a   Sked and Cook, op cit, page 331

44   Timmins, op cit, page 387.

45   *Jack Jones, Union Man*, op cit, page 332. (See also page 143: Better treatment for the elderly was a crusade which had attracted my support from my early days on the docks.)

46   Ibid, page 337.

47   Ibid, pages 339–40.

48   Ibid, page 340.

49   Article in the *Daily Mail*, 2007.

50   DWP, *The Abstract of Statistics for Benefits etc*, op cit, page 53.

51   Lowe, op cit, pages 342–3.

52   Ibid, pages 342–3.

53   Timmins, op cit, pages 387–8.

54   Ibid, pages 388–90.

55   Ibid, pages 389–90, and Norman Fowler, *Ministers Decide*, page 186, Chapman, 1991, cited therein.

56   Timmins, op cit, page 390.

57   Nigel Lawson, *The View from Number Eleven*, op cit, page 303, quoted in Timmins, op cit, page 390.

58   Timmins, op cit, page 390.

59   *The Economist*, 18 September 1982, quoted in Nesbitt, op cit, page 43.

60   Fowler, op cit, page 186, quoted in Timmins, op cit, page 390.

61   Nesbitt, op cit, page 43.

62   Timmins, op cit, page 390.

63   Sked and Cook, op cit, pages 423.

64   Ibid, page 423. (See also pages 393–419 on the Falklands War)

65   DWP, *The Abstract of Statistics for Benefits etc*, op cit, page 53.

66   House of Commons, Third Report from the Social Services Committee, *Age of Retirement*, Volumes I and II, HM Stationery Office, London, 27 October 1982, quoted in Nesbitt, op cit, pages 40 and 46.

67   Nesbitt, op cit, page 40.

68   Ibid, page 40.

69   Social Services Committee, Report on the *Age of Retirement*, op cit, Volume II para 2.2, HMSO London, 1982.

70   Ibid, para 2.6.

71   Tony Salter, *Retirement age: Economic outcome or social choice*, page 258, Pensions, Vol.9.3 April 2004, Henry Stewart Publications, London.

[72] Ibid, page 258.

[73] Nesbit, op cit, page 46.

[74] Stewart Lyon, *The Outlook for Pensioning*, Presidential address to the Institute of Actuaries, 25 October 1982.

[75] Edward Johnston, *Pensions costs in the long term*, an article in *Pensions World*, October 1982, pages 569–571, quoted in Nesbitt, op cit, pages 45–46.

[76] Nesbit, op cit, pages 45–46.

[77] Ibid, page 44.

[78] Social Security Advisory Committee, Second Report, January 1983, HMSO, London.

[79] Nesbit, op cit, pages 47–48.

[80] Ibid, page 49.

[81] Ibid, page 49, and T Blackstone and W Plowden *Inside the Think Tank*, page 127, cited therein.

[82] Nigel Vinson and Philip Chappell, *Personal and Portable Pensions – For All*, Centre for Policy Studies, London, April 1983, cited in Nesbitt, pages 50–53.

[83] Nesbit, op cit, page 51, and Vinson and Chappell, page 13, cited therein.

[84] Ibid, page 51.

[85] Nigel Vinson, *Sharing the rice bowl – A citizen's pension*, page 7, Citizen's Income Bulletin, London, February 1998. 'Even in complex societies like our own, simple trible economics continues to apply – the economically able still have to grow rice for the economically disadvantaged'.

[86] Sked and Cook, op cit, page 435.

[87] Ibid, pages 435–436.

[88] Ibid, page 438.

[89] Ibid, pages 430–431.

[90] Ibid, page 431.

[91] Ibid, pages 432–433.

[92] Ibid, page 433.

[93] Timmins, op cit, quoted on page 393.

[94] Sked and Cook, op cit, pages 433 and 441.

[95] Ibid, page 434.

[96] Neil Kinnock, speech at Bridgend immediately before 1983 General Election, quoted in Timmins, op cit, page 393.

[97] Timmins, op cit, pages 393–394.

[98] Fowler, op cit, page 202, quoted in Timmins, op cit, page 394.

[99] Timmins, op cit, page 394.

[100] Sked and Cook, op cit, page 473.

[101] Ibid, page 472.

[102] Nesbitt, op cit, pages 57–58. (See also D.Rose, *Big Money turns the Key* Article in *The Guardian*, 11 January 1989, quoted in Nesbitt).

[103] Nesbitt, op cit, page 58.

[104] Ibid, page 58.

[105] Sked and Cook, op cit, page 472.

[106] Timmins, op cit, page 393.

[107] Sked and Cook, op cit, page 441.

[108] Ibid, page 473.

[109] DWP, *The Abstract of Statistics for Benefits etc*, op cit, page 53.

[110] DHSS, *Reply to the Third Report from the Social Services Committee, Session 1981–82, on The Age of Retirement*, para 11, Cmnd 9095, London HMSO, November1983; quoted in Nesbitt, op cit, page 63.

[111] Nesbitt, op cit, page 64.

[112] Timmins, op cit, page 395.

[113] Nesbitt, op cit, page 65.

[114] A Bevins, *Ministers criticise absent Thatcher over spending cuts* in *The Times*, 23 November 1983, quoted in Nesbitt, op cit, page 65.

[115] A Bevins, *Fowler challenges arguments for cuts* in *The Times*, 23 November 1983, quoted in Nesbitt, op cit, page 64.

[116] A Bevins, *Ministers criticise absent Thatcher over spending cuts* in *The Times*, 23 November 1983, quoted in Nesbitt, op cit, page 65.

[117] Nesbitt, op cit, pages 69–70.

[118] Ibid, pages 75–76.

[119] Ibid, page 76.

[120] Walter Goldsmith of the IoD, cited in *The Times*, 3 September 1983, quoted in Nesbitt, op cit, page 59.

[121] Timmins, op cit, pages 399–400.

[122] Ibid, page 400.

[123] Nesbitt, op cit, page 76.

[124] Ibid, page 76.

[125] Hugh Pemberton, *Politics and Pensions in Post-War Britain*, page 55, in *Britain's Pension Crisis: History and Policy*, edited by Pemberton, Thane and Whiteside, Oxford University Press, 2006.

[126] Nesbitt, op cit, page 77.

[127] Ibid, page 74–75. Nesbitt notes that the Government Actuary, Edward Johnston, was not a member of the Sub-Group implied that issues relating to the future of SERPS and its projected costs were not discussed in this form and this adds weight to the

assertion that the idea of personal pensions was not inextricably linked to the projected cost of SERPS.

[128] Nesbitt, op cit, pages 85–86.

[129] DHSS, *Personal Pensions: A Consultative Document*, HMSO, 16 July 1984, London, quoted in Nesbitt, op cit, pages 84–86.

[130] Ibid, page 67.

[131] Fowler, op cit, quoted in Nesbitt, op cit, pages 68–69.

[132] Nesbitt, op cit, page 86.

[133] Timmins, op cit, page 402.

[134] Hill, op cit, page 132.

[135] Glennerster, op cit, page 183.

[136] Ibid, page 183. (See also Department of Health and Social Security, *Population, Pension Costs and Pensioners Incomes: A Background Paper for the Inquiry into Provision for Retirement*, London, June 1984.)

[137] Ibid, page 402.

[138] Sked and Cook, op cit, page 474.

[139] Martin Holmes quoted in Sked and Cook, op cit, page 474.

[140] Sked and Cook, op cit, page 474.

[141] John Lloyd, *Understanding The Miners' Strike*, page 21, Fabian Tract 504, The Fabian Society, 11 Dartmouth Street, London SW1H 9BC.

[142] Sked and Cook, op cit, page 447.

[143] Ibid, pages 448–9.

[144] Ibid, pages 450–1.

[145] Ibid, page 451.

[146] Lloyd, op cit, page 40.

[147] Sked and Cook, op cit, page 474.

[148] DWP, *The Abstract of Statistics for Benefits etc*, op cit, page 53.

[149] Nesbitt, op cit, pages 81–82.

[150] Timmins, op cit, page 400.

[151] Ibid, page 400.

[152] Ibid, page 400.

[153] Ibid, page 400.

[154] Green Paper, *Reform of Social Security*, CMND 9517–9, DHSS, HMSO, London, 3 June, 1985, quoted in Nesbitt, op cit, page 88.

[155] Nesbitt, op cit, page 89.

[156] Ibid, page 89.

[157] Sked and Cook, op cit, pages 474–5.

[158] Ibid, page 475.

[159] Ibid, page 475.

[160] DWP, *The Abstract of Statistics for Benefits etc*, op cit, page 53.

[161] Sked and Cook, op cit, page 476. (In fact, the price of oil per barrel declined from about $30 in January to $10 in April, each dollar reduction in price representing roughly a £500 million loss in revenue to the Treasury.)

[162] Nesbitt, op cit, pages 89–90.

[163] White Paper, *Programme for Action*, Cmnd 9691, DHSS, HMSO, London, December 1985, quoted in Nesbitt pages 89–90.

[164] Ibid, Nesbitt, op cit, pages 89–90, and pages 125–127.

[165] Nesbitt, op cit, pages 94–95.

[166] Timmins, op cit, page 402.

[167] Ibid, page 402. (See also Hill, op cit, page 133)

[168] Hill, op cit, page 132.

[169] Glennerster, op cit, page 186.

[170] Ibid, page 187.

[171] Ibid, page 186.

[172] Timmins, op cit, page 401.

[173] Hill, op cit, page 133. (See also Glennerster, op cit, pages 185–86 and Timmins, op cit, pages 401–2)

[174] Timmins, op cit, page 401.

[175] Sked and Cook, op cit, page 516.

[176] Ibid, page 476.

[177] DWP, *The Abstract of Statistics for Benefits etc*, op cit, page 53.

[178] Ibid, page 52.

[179] Sked and Cook, op cit, pages 511–515.

[180] Ibid, page 518–519.

[181] Timmins, op cit, page 415.

[182] Sked and Cook, op cit, pages 519 and 526. (See also Timmins, op cit, page 447)

[183] Sked and Cook, op cit, page 519.

[184] Ibid, page 477.

[185] DWP, *The Abstract of Statistics for Benefits etc*, op cit, page 53.

[186] Timmins, op cit, page 400. (See also Nesbitt op cit, pages 93–4)

[187] Nesbitt op cit, pages 93–4.

[188] Timmins, op cit, page 400. (For 1990 figure quoted by National Audit Offices, see Nesbitt, op cit, page 96)

[189] Sked and Cook, op cit, page 530.

[190] Ibid, page 529. (See also Factset, Ecowin data)

[191] Ibid, page 529.

[192] Ibid, page 530.

[193] Ibid, page 477.

[194] Ibid, pages 530–531.

[195] TA Salter, *Pensions, Taxes and Welfare*, page 19, Basic Income Research Group (BIRG) Bulletin No.10 Autumn/Winter 1990, London.

[196] Ibid, page 19.

[197] National Association of Pension Funds (NAPF), *Truth Honour and Democracy*: The Finance Bill 1989, May 1989, 12/18 Grosvenor Gardens, London SW1W 0DH.

[198] Ibid.

[199] Ibid.

[200] Ibid. (Statement of a TUC spokesman quoted by the NAPF in the pamphlet).

[201] See Philip Chappell, *Back to Basics*, BIRG Bulletin No.7, Spring 1988, London.

[202] Pensions Management Institute's press release issued on 24 May 1989, as reported in PMI News Letter, June 1989, London.

[203] Sked and Cook, op cit, pages 532–3.

[204] Ibid, pages 527–8.

[205] Ibid, page 536.

[206] Ibid, page 537.

[207] Ibid, page 534.

[208] Timmins op cit, page 475.

[209] Ibid, page 476.

[210] Sked and Cook, op cit, pages 550–1.

[211] DWP, *The Abstract of Statistics, for benefits etc,* op cit, page 53.

[212] Lowe, op cit, page 343.

[213] Nesbitt, op cit, page 98.

[214] Ibid, page 98.

[215] Report by the Government Actuary Cmnd 2445, HMSO, London, 1994 quoted in Timmins, op cit, pages 400–1 and note 21 on page 639.

[216] DHSS, *Personal Pension Statistics 1992/3*, Revised Edition Government Statistical Service London 1994, shows that half a million employees had transferred benefits from their employer's occupational scheme after leaving service.

[217] Milton Friedman, *Capitalism and Freedom*, page 188, University Chicago Press, Chicago, 1970.

[218] Barbara Waine, *A Disaster Foretold? The Case of the Personal Pension*, pages 322–3, Social Policy & Administration Vol 29, No.4, December 1995 pages 317–334.

[219] Confederation of British Industry, *CBI Response to the Green Paper on Reform of Social Security*, page 2, London, 1985; quoted in Waine, op cit, page 323.

[220] Institute of Actuaries, *Reform of Social Security*, page 13, London, 195; quoted in Waine, op cit, page 323.

[221] Read Stenhouse *Reform of Social Security*, page 3, London September 1985; quoted in Waine, op cit, pagd 323.

[222] Nesbitt, op cit, page 127.

[223] Ibid, page 127.

[224] Financial Services Authority's press release dated 27 June 2002

[225] Leslie Hannah, *Occupational Pension Funds: Getting the Long-Run Answers Right*, Discussion Paper No.99, Centre for Economic Policy Research, London, April 1986.

[226] Ibid, Abstract

[227] Ibid, pagd 24. The 1% expense ratio for a State pension system applied even if the additional collection expenses falling on employers are included as well as the direct costs to the state.

[228] Ibid, pagd 25.

[229] Ibid, pagd 41.

[230] Ibid, Non-Technical Summary, page (iii).

[231] The First Report of the Pensions Commission, *Pensions: Challenges and Choices*, pages 214 and 251, The Stationery Office, 2004.

[232] Wain, op cit, page 332.

## CHAPTER TEN
# Major's governments 1990–1997

[1] Sked and Cook, op cit, pages 553–554.

[2] Timmins, op cit, page 477.

[3] Ibid, page 478.

[4] Lowe, op cit, page 327. The aim of the Citizen's Charter was to maintain a balance between consumers and producers not by open competition but by the agreement and monitoring of performance targets.

[5] Nicholas Ridley, *My Style of Government*, pages 78–81, Hutchinson 1991, quoted in Timmins, op cit, page 478.

[6] Timmins, op cit, page 476.

[7] Lowe, op cit, page 327.

8   Sked and Cook, op cit, page 555.

9   DWP, *The Abstract of Statistics for Benefits etc*, op cit, page 53.

10  *Hansard*, 16 May 1991, col.413 quoted in Timmins, op cit, page 479.

11  Sked and Cook, op cit, page 554. (See also Timmins, op cit, page 479).

12  Ibid, pages 556–556.

13  Timmins, op cit, page 479.

14  Sked and Cook, op cit, page 556.

15  DWP, *The Abstract of Statistics for Benefits etc*, op cit, page 53.

16  AMG Christopher, Foreword to *Thomas Stark A new A–Z of Income and Wealth*, page 4, (based on Income and Wealth in the 1980s'), Fabian Society, 1988 London.

17  Margaret Thatcher, *Let Our Children Grow Tall*, page 12, Selected Speeches, 1975–77, Centre for Policy Studies, 1982, quoted in Timmins, op cit, page 506.

18  *Hansard*, 17 May 1988 col 801, quoted in Timmins, op cit, page 507.

19  Timmins, op cit, page 507. The overall result was that by 1992 a quarter of the population had an income under half the average, against only 10 per cent in 1979.

20  Neil Kinnock, Interview, quoted in Timmins, op cit, page 489.

21  Timmins, op cit, page 487.

22  Ibid, page 489.

23  Ibid, page 489.

24  Sked and Cook, op cit, pages 581–2.

25  Timmins, op cit, page 489.

26  Sked and Cook, op cit pages 582–3.

27  Timmins, op cit, page 489.

28  Ibid, page 490.

29  D Kavanagh, *Thatcherism and British Politics*, second edition, Oxford, OUP 1990. quoted in Hill, op cit, page 156.

30  Hill, op cit, page 157. (Hill adds, however, that the main exposition of the universalist approach comes from academic supporters of the Labour Party rather than its political leaders. He cites Titmuss and Townsend as examples.)

31  Timmins, op cit, page 490.

32  Anthony Crosland, *Social Democracy in Europe*, page 2, Tract 438, Fabian Society, 11 Dartmouth Street, London SW1H 9BN.

33  Timmins, op cit, pages 446–7.

34  DWP, *The Abstract of Statistics for Benefits etc*, op cit, page 53.

35  Timmins, op cit, page 481.

36  Lowe, op cit, page 406.

37  Macnicol, op cit, page 402.

38  Ibid, page 403.

39  Ibid, page 403.

40  Harris, op cit, page 484.

41  Rodney Lowe, *The Welfare State in Britain Since 1945*; page 157, 1993 Edition, quoted in Macnicol, op cit, page 403.

42  Macnicol, op cit, page 406.

43  Peter Laslett, *In any Ageing World*, in the *New Society*, London, 27 October 1977.

44  Timmins, op cit, page 498.

45  Ibid, page 490.

46  Timmins, op cit, page 478.

47  Lowe, op cit, page 328.

48  Timmins, op cit, page 530.

49  Ibid, page 510.

50  *Hansard*, 8 February 1993, col.683, quoted in Timmins, op cit, page 491.

51  Timmins, op cit, page 501.

52  Ibid, page 510.

53  Ibid, page 510.

54  Ibid, page 510.

55  Ibid, page 509.

56  *The Times*, 2 December 1993, quoted in Timmins, op cit, page 510.

57  John Hills, *The future of welfare: A guide to the debate*, Joseph Rowntree Foundation, York, November 1993.

58  Ibid, page 7.

59  Ibid, page 4.

60  Ibid, pages 4–5.

61  Ibid, page 14.

62  Ibid, page 5.

63  Ibid, page 5.

64  Will Hutton, *Research defuses time-bomb view of Welfare State, The Guardian*, 9 November 1993.

65  Foreword to *The Growth of Social Security* Department of Social Security, HMSO, 1994 quoted in Timmins, op cit, page 509.

[66] DWP, *The Abstract of Statistics for Benefits etc*, op cit, page 53.

[67] John Hills, *The future of welfare*, op cit, pages 51–52.

[68] A Dilnot and P Johnson *What pension should the state provide?*, 1992, Institute of Fiscal Studies, 13(4) 1–20 quoted in Hills, op cit, page 54.

[69] Falkingham and P Johnson, *A Unified Funded Pension Scheme (UFPS) for Britain*, Welfare State Programme, Discussion WSP/90 STICERD, London School of Economics, 1993.

[70] J Falkingham and P Johnson, *Ageing and Economic Welfare* Sage Publications, London 1992.

[71] Tony Salter, *Being realistic about pensions reform*, page 10 Citizen's Income Bulletin 24 July 1997, Citizen's Income Research Group, London WC2A 2EX.

[72] Robert Merton, *The Role of Social Secretary as a Means of Efficient Risk Bearing in an Economy where Human Capital is not Tradeable*, University of Chicago Press, Chicago, 1983.

[73] Peter Townsend and Alan Walker, *The future of pensions; revitalizing national insurance*, Fabian Society Discussion Paper, no.22, Fabian Society, London SW1H 9BN, 1993.

[74] Frank Field and Matthew Owen, *Private Pensions for All: squaring the circle*, page 23, Fabian Society Discussion Paper, no.16, July 1993, Fabian Society, London SW1H 9BN.

[75] Ibid, pages 9 and 23.

[76] Ibid, pages 10–11.

[77] Frank Field, *Making Welfare Work: reconstructing welfare for the millennium*, Institute of Community Studies 1994, London SW1A 0AA.

[78] Commission on Wealth Creation and Social Cohesion, *Report on wealth creation and social cohesion in a free society*, London E14 3BJ, 1994.

[79] Bleddyn Davis, *Better Pensions for All*, Institute for Public Policy Research, London 1993.

[80] M Pirie, *The Radical Agenda*, Adam Smith Institute, London, 1993.

[81] *The Pensions Debate: A Report on Income and Pensions in Retirement*, Age Concern 1994, London SW16 4ER.

[82] Ibid, page 52.

[83] Ibid, page 52.

[84] Ibid, pages 50–51.

[85] Family Budget Unit, *Summary Budget Standards for Six Households*, University of York 1992.

[86] Age Concern *The Pensions Debate* op cit, pages 27–28.

[87] Ibid, page 53.

[88] Ibid, page 53.

[89] Timmins, op cit, page 532.

[90] John Smith, *New Paths to Victory* Labour Party leadership address, 30 April 1994, reported in *The Independent*, 1 May 1994, cited in Timmins, op cit, page 490.

[91] Timmins, op cit, page 490.

[92] Andrew Gamble *British Politics after Blair*, page 303, in *Developments in British Politics 8*, edited by Patrick Dunleary et al, Palgrave Macmillan, 2006.

[93] *Strategies for National Renewal*, The Report of the Commission on Social Justice, Vintage London 1994, (commonly referred to as the Borrie Report after its chairman, Sir Gordon Borrie).

[94] Timmins, op cit, pages 532–3.

[95] Field and Owen, *Private Pensions for All*, op cit, page 5.

[96] Ibid, page 11.

[97] Income Data Services Pensions Manual, page 10.5.1, London, 1996.

[98] Income Data Services Pensions Manual, op cit, pages 10.4.1 – 10.4.2.

[99] Income Data Services, *Pensions in Practice*, pages 4–5, London, 2004.

[100] Timmins, op cit, page 534.

[101] Tony Blair, Fabian Society Speech 5 July 1955. In *Young Country*, Fourth Estate, 1996, pages 7 and 15 quoted in Timmins, op cit, pages 533–534.

[102] The Labour Party, *Security in Retirement*, Millbank Tower, Millbank, London 1996.

[103] Barbara Castle, *Not to be uSERPSed*, paged 5–6, Fabian Review, Volume 108, No.5, 1996, Fabian Society, 11 Dartmouth Street, London SW1H 9BN.

[104] Ibid, pages 5–6.

[105] Ibid, pages 5–6.

[106] Barbara Castle and Peter Townsend, *We CAN afford the Welfare State*, published by *Security in Retirement for everyone*, 1996, Fabian Society, London SW1H 9BN.

[107] Ibid.

[108] Lowe, op cit, page 25.

[109] David Piachaud, *What's wrong with Fabianism*, Fabian Pamphlet, Fabian Society, London, quoted in Fabian Review, vol 105, no. 4.

[110] Timmins, op cit, pages 534 and 539.

111 Tony Blair, article in the *New Statesman*, 15 July 1994, quoted in Timmins, op cit, pages 539–540.

112 Timmins, op cit, page 533.

113 John Lloyd, *Now you see it, now you don't*, page 28, *New Statesman*, 12 July 1996.

114 Matthew Bishop, *Pocket Economist: The essentials of economics from A to Z*, page 220, The Economist Publications, Profile Books in association with The Economist Newspaper, London, 2000.

115 Lloyd, op cit, page 27.

116 Timmins, op cit, page 542.

117 Lloyd, op cit, page 28.

118 Timmins, op cit, pages 541–2 and Will Hutton, *The state we're in*, Jonathan Cape, London, 1995.

119 Lloyd, op cit, page 28.

120 Ibid, page 28.

121 Ibid, page 29.

122 Timmins, op cit, page 542.

123 Lloyd, op cit, page 29.

124 Lowe, op cit, page 423.

125 Crossland, op cit, page 2.

126 Timmins, op cit, page 552.

127 Department of Social Security, *Basic Pension Plus*, London, March 1997 reported in *The Financial Times*, and *The Independent* 6 March 1997.

128 Timmins, op cit, page 553.

129 DWP, *The Abstract of Statistics for Benefits etc*, op cit, page 53.

130 DSS, *Basic Pension Plus*, op cit.

131 Tony Salter, *Lilley's funded pensions still lay a burden on the future*, Letter in *The Independent*, 15 March 1997.

132 Ibid, *The Independent*, page 19.

133 Timmins, op cit, page 553.

134 Ibid, page 553.

## CHAPTER ELEVEN
## New Labour in government

1 Lowe, op cit, pages 384 and 402.

2 Ibid, page 376.

3 Ibid, page 402.

4 Ibid, page 32.

5 Anthony Giddens, *Beyond Left and Right: Future of Radical Politics*, Cambridge Polity, 1994. See also Andrew Gamble *British Politics after Blair*, op cit, page 300 and S Driver and L Martell, *Blair's Britain*, Cambridge Polity, 2002.

6 Lowe, op cit, page 32.

7 *The Independent*, 10 May 2005, page 2.

8 Ibid.

9 Ibid.

10 Timmins, op cit, page 558.

11 Ibid, page 560.

12 Ibid, pages 561–2.

13 Gordon Brown, HM Treasury, Budget Speech, July 1997.

14 Article by Margaret Doyle, *Anger at raid on pensions*, in *Daily Telegraph*, 3 July 1997.

15 Lowe, op cit, page 386.

16 Ibid, page 386.

17 Labour General Election Manifesto 1997, quoted in Timmins, op cit, page 564.

18 Roy Hattersley, *Why I'm no longer loyal to Labour*, in *The Guardian*, 26 July 1997, quoted in Timmins, op cit, page 565.

19 Timmins, op cit, page 565.

20 Peter Mandelson – speech on 14 August 1997 and *Labour's Next Steps: tackling social exclusion*, Fabian pamphlet 581, 1997, Fabian Society, London, SW1H 9BN, quoted in Timmins, op cit, pages 566–7.

21 Peter Mandelson, 14 August 1997, quoted in Timmins, op cit, page 559.

22 Lowe, op cit, page 378. See also Timmins, op cit, page 567.

23 Timmins, op cit, page 568.

24 Ibid, page 568.

25 Lowe, op cit, page 32.

26 Ibid, page 32 and Note 39 on page 459.

27 Timmins, op cit, page 569.

28 Lowe, op cit, pages 404–6.

29 National Pensioners Convention, *Pensions not Poor Relief: Submissions to the Government's Pension Review*, page 1, NPC, London, March 1998.

30 Ibid, page 39.

31 Ibid, page 40.

32 Department of Social Security, *A New Contract for Welfare*, Cm 3895, HMSO, London 1998.

33 Timmins, op cit, page 570.

34 Anthony Seldon, *Blair Unbound*, page 130, Simon & Schuster, London and New York, 2007.

35 Timmins, op cit, page 569.

[36] Ibid, page 569.

[37] Lowe, op cit, page 386.

[38] Timmins, op cit, page 573.

[39] Ibid, page 573.

[40] Ibid, page 573.

[41] Thane, op cit, page 179.

[42] Department of Social Security, *A New Contract for Welfare: Partnership in Pensions*, Cm 4179, December, 1998.

[43] Ibid, Chapter 4, para 1.

[44] Glennerster, op cit, page 257

[45] DSS *A New Contract for Welfare: Partnership in Pensions*, op cit, Summary.

[46] Report of the Commission on Social Justice, op cit.

[47] DSS, *A New Contract for Welfare: Partnership in Pensions*, op cit, Summary.

[48] Ibid, Chapter 5, para 8.

[49] Ibid, Chapter 5, para 8.

[50] Ibid, Summary.

[51] Ibid, Summary.

[52] Ibid, Summary.

[53] Glennerster, op cit, page 257.

[54] DSS, *A New Contract for Welfare: Partnership in Pensions*, op cit, Summary.

[55] Ibid Summary.

[56] PricewaterCoopers *Stakeholder Pensions*, TN44, October 2000.

[57] National Pensioners Convention, *A Partnership in Pensions – The Green Paper (Cm 4179)*, NPC, London, 13 January 1999.

[58] Ibid.

[59] Ibid.

[60] Timmins, op cit, page 589.

[61] Ibid, pages 589–590.

[62] Ibid, page 590.

[63] Lowe, op cit, page 406.

[64] Timmins, op cit, page 590.

[65] Ibid, page 570.

[66] Lowe, op cit, page 386, and Timmins, op cit, page 599.

[67] Timmins, op cit, page 570.

[68] Ibid.

[69] Ibid, page 600.

[70] DWP, *The Abstract of Statistics for Benefits etc*, op cit, page 53.

[71] Timmins, op cit, page 570.

[72] Ibid, page 570.

[73] Lowe, op cit, page 407 and Note 15, page 501.

[74] Ibid, page 408.

[75] Timmins, op cit, page 571.

[76] Ibid, page 571.

[77] Lowe, op cit, page 404.

[78] DWP, *The Abstract of Statistics for Benefits etc*, op cit, page 53.

[79] Timmins, op cit, page 600.

[80] Timmins, op cit, page 600.

[81] David Brindle, *Labour faces revolt over pension rise*, in *The Guardian*, 10 December 1999.

[82] Timmins, op cit, pages 600–601.

[83] Tony Blair, Labour Party Conference Speech, October 2000.

[84] Timmins, op cit, page 601.

[85] DWP, *The Pension Credit: A Consultation Paper*, Cm 4900, The Stationery Office, London, November 2000.

[86] Ibid, Introduction.

[87] NPC, *Pensions not Poor Relief*, op cit, page 1.

[88] DWP, *The Pension Credit: A Consultation Paper*, op cit, Chapter 2.

[89] Ibid.

[90] Timmins, op cit, page 601.

[91] DWP, *The Abstract of Statistics for Benefits etc*, op cit, page 53.

[92] *Pension Credit: A Consultation Paper*, op cit.

[93] NPC, *The Pension Credit: The National Pensioners Convention's consultation paper*, page 4, drafted by Tony Lynes, NPC London NW1 1HY 2001.

[94] Ibid, page 4.

[95] DWP, *The Pension Credit: A Consultation Paper*, op cit.

[96] Jeff Rooker, *Hansard*, 23 March 2000, quoted in NPC, *The Pension Credit: The National Pensioners Convention's consultation paper*, op cit, pages 8–9.

[97] P Toynbee and D Walker, *Did Things Get Better*, page 25, Harmondsworth, 2001 quoted in Lowe, op cit, page 409.

[98] *Pension Credit: A Consultation Paper*, op cit, Chapter 4, paras 9 and 10. Currently pensioners on the MIG are penalised for having built up savings or a second pension. So people who may have struggled during their working life to put a little aside see no benefit from this at all. And those

with incomes just above the MIG feel let down because they are often very little better off for having saved some of their hard earned money.

99    Martin Hewitt, *New Labour and the redefinition of social security*, in Powell (ed), *Evaluating New Labour's Welfare Reforms*, page 206, cited in Lowe, op cit, page 410.

100    NPC, *The Pension Credit: The National Pensioners Convention's consultation paper*, op cit, page 2.

101    Ibid, pages 5 and 13.

102    Ibid, pages 5 and 12.

103    Ibid, pages 6 and 12–14.

104    Ibid, pages 6–7 and 18–19.

105    Timmins, op cit, page 611.

106    Ibid, page 613.

107    Lowe, op cit, page 409.

108    Ibid, page 409 and table on page 407.

109    Timmins, op cit, page 613.

110    HM Treasury *2001 Pre-Budget Report*

111    Ibid.

112    Seldon, op cit, page 129.

113    Glennerster, op cit, page 247.

114    Timmins, op cit, page 611.

115    Lowe, op cit, page 432.

116    Timmins, op cit, page 611.

117    John Bartle and Samantha Laycock, *Elections and Voting*, page 9, in *Developments in British Politics*, edited by Dunleavy, Hefferman, Cowley and Hay, Palgrave Macmillan, 2006 and British Governments and Elections since 1945, http://www.psr.keele.ac.uk/area/uk/uktable.htm.

118    *The Independent*, 10 May 2005, page 2. See also *British Governments and Elections since 1945*, op cit.

119    Seldon, op cit, page 129.

120    Lowe, op cit, page 408.

121    Ibid, pages 407–408.

122    Ibid, pages 407–408.

123    Ibid, page 407, Table 15.1.

124    DWP *Households below average income 2001–02*, The Stationery Office, London.

125    Ibid.

126    Ruth Lister, *Poverty*, pages 41–42, Polity Press, Cambridge 2004.

127    Ibid, pages 41–42.

128    Jeff Rooker, *Hansard*, 30 November 2000, Col 852W, quoted in NPC, *The Pension Credit: The National Pensioners Convention's consultation paper*, op cit, page 11.

129    DWP, *Work and Pensions Statistics, 2002*, Table 1 (Income support and claimants by Statistical Group, May 1993 to May 2002) quoted in Age Concern *Older people in the United Kingdom: some basic facts, 2002*.

130    John Shuttleworth, *No Pay, No Gain*, an article in *Accountancy*, March 2002.

131    DWP *Pensioners' Incomes*, Series 2000–01, Section 9, Table 7 (Proportion of Pensioner units with more than 50% of income from state benefits 1994–05 to 2000–01) quoted in Age Concern *Older people in the United Kingdom, 2000*.

132    Timmins, op cit, page 573.

133    Lowe, op cit, page 409.

134    Ibid, page 409. See also Glennerster, op cit, pages 259–260.

135    Glennerster, op cit, pages 259–260.

136    Pensions Commission, *Pensions; Challenges and Choices,* The First Report of the Pensions Commission, page 85, The Stationary Office, London, 2004.

137    Glennerster, op cit, page 259.

138    Seldon, op cit, pages 129–130.

139    Ibid, page 130.

140    Ibid, page 130.

141    Green Paper, *Simplicity Security and Choice: Working and saving for retirement*, Cm 5677, The Stationery Office, London 2002.

142    Ibid, op cit.

143    Ibid, Chapter 6, paras 44–49.

144    Ibid.

145    Seldon, op cit, pages 130–131.

146    Glennerster, op cit, page 260.

147    Finance Act 2004.

148    Age Concern's response to the Green Paper, *Simplicity Security and Choice: Working and saving for retirement*, Age Concern, March 2003.

149    Ibid, Chapter 2, para 1.5, pages 8 and 9.

150    Ibid, Chapter 1, paras 7 and 8, page 5.

151    Ibid, page 3.

152    Ibid, Chapter 2, para 6.25, page 19.

153    Seldon, op cit, page 401.

[154] Pensions Commission: *Pensions, Challenges and Choices,* First Report, 2004, op cit.

[155] Glennerster, op cit, page 260.

[156] Pensions Commission, First Report, op cit, Executive Summary, page 2.

[157] Ibid, page X.

[158] Ibid, pages X and XI.

[159] Ibid, para 92.

[160] Ibid, pages X, XI and XIV

[161] Ibid, page XIII

[162] Seldon, op cit, pages 401–402.

[163] Patrick Dunleavy, Richard Hefferman, Philip Cowley and Colin Hay, *Britain beyond Blair - party politics and leadership succession*, page 15, in *Developments in British Politics*, edited by the authors, Palgrave Macmillan, 2006

[164] Bartle and Laycock, op cit, pages 78–79, and Electoral Reform Society, op cit.

[165] *UK National Strategy Report on Adequate and Sustainable Pensions* – An update report to the European Commission on the UK's progress since 2002 issued July 2005.

[166] Ibid, page 7.

[167] Bartle and Laycock, op cit, Table 5.4, page 84.

[168] Seldon, op cit, page 402.

[169] Ibid, page 402.

[170] Ibid, page 402.

[171] Ibid, pages 403–404.

[172] Pensions Commission *A New Pensions Settlement for the 21st Century*, The Second Report of the Pensions Commission, The Stationery Office, London, 2005.

[173] Ibid, Executive Summary, pages 4–6.

[174] Ibid, Executive Summary, page 6.

[175] William Beveridge *Insurance for All and Everything*, 1924, British Library of Political Science, Harris, op cit, page 338 and Report by Sir William Beveridge, op cit, page 108. Beveridge's proposal for a contributory flat rate national insurance pension was designed to reduce to a minimum the need for discretionary relief. Report by Sir William Beveridge, op cit, page 8, para 16 states that the proposal is to introduce for all citizens adequate pensions without means tests.

[176] Pensions Commission, Second Report, op cit, Executive Summary, pages 8–10.

[177] Ibid, Glennerster, op cit, page 261, and Pemberton, Thane and Whiteside, op cit, page 10.

[178] Ibid, Glennerster, op cit, page 261, and Paul Johnson *The Political Economy of Pension Reform in the UK*, page 180, in Pemberton, et al, op cit.

[179] Pensions Commission, Second Report, op cit, Executive Summary, pages 7 and 8, and Glennerster, op cit, page 261.

[180] Ibid.

[181] Seldon, op cit, pages 461–462.

[182] Ibid, page 462.

[183] Ibid, page 462.

[184] Pemberton, Thane and Whiteside, op cit, page 256.

[185] Thane, op cit, page 210.

[186] Pensions Commission *Implementing an integrated package of pension reforms*, The Final Report of the Pensions Commission, The Stationery Office, London, 2006.

[187] Ibid. See also Glennerster, op cit, page 262.

[188] Seldon, op cit, page 465 and NPC, Press Release to announce a 12 months campaign to mark 100 years of the state pension, 31 December 2007, London.

[189] White Paper, *Security in retirement: towards a new pensions system*, Cm 6841, DWP, The Stationery Office, May 2006 and Seldon, op cit, page 465.

[190] White Paper, *Security in retirement: towards a new pensions system*, op cit, page 17, para 37.

[191] Pemberton et al, op cit, page 256.

[192] Ibid, page 258.

[193] Ibid, page 258 and White Paper, *Security in retirement: towards a new pensions system*, op cit, Chapter 3, para 3.78.

[194] White Paper, *Security in retirement: towards a new pension system*, op cit, Chapter 3.

[195] Ibid.

[196] Ibid.

[197] Pemberton et al, op cit, page 260.

[198] NPC, press release, 18 October 2007.

[199] Jay Ginn, *Gender Inequalities: Sidelined in British Pension Policy*, pages 91–111, in Pemberton et al, op cit, page 106.

[200] Pensions Commission, First Report, Executive Summary, page XIV.

[201] Pensions Commission, Second Report, Executive Summary, para 7, page 22.

[202] Ginn, op cit, page 106.

[203] Debora Price, *Closing the Gender Gap in Retirement Income: What Difference Will Recent UK Pension Reforms Make?*, Journal of Social Policy, 36, 4, Cambridge University Press (2007).

204 Pemberton et al, op cit, pages 12–13 and 256–257.

205 Ibid, page 257.

206 Ibid, pages 257–259.

207 NPC, press release, *Pensioners betrayed by empty budget*, page 1, 31 March 2007.

208 Ibid, page 1.

209 DWP *Pension Credit Estimates of Take Up for 2005–2006*, London, 29 March 2007.

210 NPC, press release, *Pensions*, May 2001, page 1.

211 Early Day Motion 1987, *Pensioners' Charter of Rights*, put down in the House of Commons by Kelvin Hopkins on 24 July 2007.

212 NPC, press release, *Pensioners' Charter of Rights*, 24 July 2007.

213 NPC, press release, *State pension increase fuels older people's anger*, 18 October 2007.

214 Ibid.

215 Written parliamentary answer *Hansard* Column 466W by Mike O'Brien dated 9 October 2007.

216 Written parliamentary answer *Hansard* Column 280W by Dawn Primarolo dated 13 March 2007.

217 See Appendix 2.

218 Written parliamentary answer *Hansard* Column 467W by Mike O'Brien dated 9 October 2007.

219 Written parliamentary answer *Hansard* Column 482W by Dawn Primarolo dated 13 March 2007.

220 The announcement by Paymaster General Dawn Primarole and Pensions Reform Minister James Purnell – Joint press release of HM Revenue & Customs and the DWP dated 16 January 2007.

221 Report by the Government Actuary on the drafts of the Social Security Benefits Up-rating Order 2008 and the Social Security (Contributions) (Re-rating) Order 2008 (Cm 7312), January 2008, Appendix 9.

222 Jay Ginn's Essay published in 2006 and John Hills' article *Heading for Retirement? National Insurance, State Pensions and the Future of the Contributory Principle in the UK 2004*.

223 Written parliamentary answer *Hansard* Column 1857W by Mike O'Brien dated 21 April 2008.

224 Darling's budget speech, March 2008.

225 Article *Back to the Badlands* in *The Economist* of 14 August 2008.

226 Inflation Report August 2008 (Bank of England), August 2008.

227 Figures published by Department of Work and Pensions, 10 June 2008.

228 *Poverty, wealth and place in Britain 1968 to 2005* by D Dorling et al, (Joseph Rowntree Foundation) 2008.

229 Article in *The Times*, 31 July 2008.

230 NPC, press release, *Campaign marks 100 years of the state pension*, 31 December 2007.

## CHAPTER TWELVE
## Learning from the past

1 Figures published by Department of Work and Pensions, 10 June 2008.

2 Appendix 4, *Rate of basic state pension from 1909* table

3 Andrew Block, *Good Old Days*, article in *Pensions World*, April 2008.

4 Report of the Select Committee on the Aged Deserving Poor, 1899.

5 Alan Walker & Liam Foster, *Caught between Virtue and Ideological Necessity. A Century of Pension Policies in the UK*, Review of Political Economy, Volume 18, Number 3, 427–448, July 2006, page 429, quote from *Daily Chronicle* 24 December 1889

6 Report of the Select Committee on the Aged Deserving Poor, 1899 as quoted by Andrew Block, *Good Old Days*, article in *Pensions World*, April 2008

7 Richard Titmuss, *Pension Systems and Population Change*, page 74, in *Essays on the Welfare State*, 3rd edition 1976, George Allen & Unwin, London.

8 Alan Walker & Liam Foster, op cit, pages 432

9 Ibid, pages 433 and 437

10 Report, *2007 European Pensions Barometer*, published by Aon Consulting, 2007.

11 Report, *Pension Plan Design Survey 2008*, published by Watson Wyatt, 2008.

12 Alan Walker & Liam Foster, op cit, page 438.

13 Richard Titmuss, Eleanor Rathbone Memorial Lecture, *Social division of welfare*.

14 Report of the Royal Commission on the Aged Poor 1895, Vol III, page 634, evidence 11706.

15 DWP Quarterly Statistical study August 2008, published 13 August 2008.

16 Report, *Income related benefits estimates of take-up in 2006–07*, Department of Work and Pensions.

17 Report, *2007 European Pensions Barometer*, published by Aon Consulting, 2007.

18 Ibid, page 442.

[19] Appendix 4 *State Benefit Expenditure versus Gross Domestic Product* table and John Shuttleworth, *No Pay, No Gain*, an article in *Accountancy*, March 2002.

[20] Appendix 4, *Life Expectancy* table.

[21] Office of National Statistics, *UK Population estimates, 2007*, published 21 August 2008.

[22] Office of National Statistics website http://www.gad.gov.uk/Demography_Data/Population/2006/gb/wgb065y.xls

[23] Alan Walker & Liam Foster, op cit, pages 436–7.

[24] John Shuttleworth, *No pay, no gain*, an article in *Accountancy*, March 2002.

[25] Jay Ginn, *Gender Inequalities: Sidelined in British Pension Policy*, page 106 in Pemberton et al, op cit.

[26] Department of Social Security, *Equality in state pension ages*, HMSO, London, 1993.

[27] John Hills, *The Future of Welfare: A guide to the debate*, Social Policy Research Summary, Joseph Rowntree Foundation, York, 1993.

[28] A M Warnes, *The Demography of Ageing in the United Kingdom of Great Britain and Northern Ireland,* International Institute of Ageing, United Nations, Malta, 1993.

[29] Macnicol, op cit, page 403.

[30] Patrick Jenkin, House of Commons Statement, *Hansard*, 13 June 1979 Col. 439, quoted in Timmins, op cit, page 374.

[31] Department of Social Security, *A New Contract for Welfare Partnership in Pensions*, cm 4179, December 1991.

[32] Macnicol, op cit, page 403.

[33] Ibid, page 406.

[34] Ibid, page 406.

[35] Peter Laslett, *In any Ageing World*, in the *New Society*, London, 27 October 1977.

[36] John Hills, *Heading for Retirement? National Insurance, State Pensions, and the Future of the Contributory Principle in the UK*, International Social Policy, 33, 3, 347–71, Cambridge University Press, 2004, page 351.

[37] Ibid, pages 363–367.

[38] Ibid, page 365.

[39] Glennerster, op cit, page 257.

[40] *Security in Retirement*, The Labour Party, Millbank Tower, Millbank, London, 1996.

[41] Alan Walker & Liam Foster, op cit, page 439.

[42] Ibid, page 438.

[43] John Hills, op cit, pages 347–8.

# INDEX